Regions of Unlikeness

Regions
of

Unlikeness

Explaining
Contemporary
Poetry

Thomas Gardner

University of
Nebraska Press
Lincoln and
London

Publication of this book was assisted by a grant
from the Andrew W. Mellon Foundation.

Acknowledgments for the use of previously
published material appear on pages x–xii
Manufactured in the United States of America
⊗

Library of Congress Cataloging-in-Publication Data
Gardner, Thomas, 1952–
Regions of unlikeness : explaining contemporary
poetry / Thomas Gardner
    p.   cm.
Includes bibliographical references (p.   ) and index.
ISBN 0-8032-2176-2 (cl. : alk. paper)
1. American poetry—20th century—History and criticism.
2. Bishop, Elizabeth, 1911–1979—Criticism and
interpretation.   3. Palmer, Michael, 1943–   —Criticism
and interpretation.   4. Graham, Jorie, 1951–   —Criticism and
interpretation.   5. Ashbery, John—Criticism and interpretation.
6. Hass, Robert—Criticism and interpretation.
I. Title.
PS325.G37   1999
811'.5409—dc21   99–20935
CIP

For Laura

Contents

Acknowledgments

Jorie Graham, Robert Hass, and Michael Palmer were of very significant help to me in the early stages of my work on this book. The interviews that I conducted with each writer and our back-and-forth exchanges as we revised and extended those conversations gave me ears to hear what is at stake in contemporary writing. All the interviews were conducted in one or two sittings and then revised over the next several years. In editing the transcripts, I cut and rearranged some material in order to bring out the main lines of our conversations and then asked the poets to amplify or respond or consider again. Some years after the interviews were completed, I continue to draw from them, sometimes only slowly coming to understand what we were really talking about.

I am also pleased to acknowledge an NEH Summer Stipend that supported my work on the interviews. My title is drawn, with thanks, from Jorie Graham's 1991 *Region of Unlikeness*, itself drawn from Augustine's *Confessions*. In using the plainspoken term "explaining" in my subtitle, I have in mind Robert Hass's use of the term in "Not Going to New York: A Letter." "It is not poetry," he writes, "It only explains it—the way this early winter weather / makes life seem more commonplace and—at a certain angle / more intense."

Charles Altieri, Marjorie Perloff, and Helen Vendler are the major voices whose work this book is most in conversation with. I thank them for their writing and encouragement. Fred Carlisle, Marie Paretti, Esther Richey, and Robert Siegle—friends and colleagues at Virginia Tech—read or talked with me about early versions of much of this and helped me see what I was doing. William Dowling read a late draft and made a number of crucial and pointed suggestions for which I am indebted to him. I completed this book at the University of Helsinki where I served for a year as the Bicentennial Chair in American Studies. My thanks to the Fulbright Commission and to my hosts in Finland—Eino Lyytinen, Markku Henriksson, and Mikko Saikku—for the chance to write and speak about these issues in a strikingly beautiful setting.

My thanks as well to Virginia Tech for two periods of sabbatical leave during my work on this project.

Some portions of this book have been previously published, in most cases in different form. A longer version of the Ashbery chapter appeared in *Dictionary of Literary Biography*, volume 165: *American Poets since World War II*, edited by Joseph Conte (Copyright © 1996 Gale Research). "An Interview with Jorie Graham" originally appeared in *Denver Quarterly* vol. 26, no. 4 (spring 1992), edited by Donald Revell. Some portions of the introduction and the Bishop and Ashbery chapters are drawn from "Bishop and Ashbery: Two Ways Out of Stevens," which appeared in a special issue of *The Wallace Stevens Journal* vol. 19, no. 2, (fall 1995), edited by Jacqueline Vaught Brogan. Some material in the Graham chapter is drawn from "An Open, Habitable Space: Poetry 1991," *Contemporary Literature* vol. 33, no. 4 (Copyright © 1992; reprinted by permission of the University of Wisconsin Press). My thanks to all of the editors involved.

I am also grateful for permission to reprint the following material:

Excerpts from *The Complete Poems 1927–1979* by Elizabeth Bishop. Copyright © 1979, 1983 by Alice Methfessel. Reprinted by permission of Farrar, Straus & Giroux, Inc.

Excerpts from "Two Scenes" and "Some Trees," from *Some Trees* by John Ashbery (New Haven: Yale University Press, 1956). Copyright © by John Ashbery. Reprinted by permission of Georges Borchardt, Inc.

Excerpts from "Europe," "They Dream Only of America," and "The Skaters" from *The Tennis Court Oath* by John Ashbery. Copyright © 1962 by John Ashbery, Wesleyan University Press. Reprinted by permission of University Press of New England.

Excerpts from "Clepsydra" from *Rivers and Mountains* by John Ashbery (New York: Holt Rinehart & Winston, 1967). Copyright © 1962, 1963, 1964, 1966 by John Ashbery. Reprinted by permission of Georges Borchardt, Inc.

Excerpts from "Summer," "The Task," and "Soonest Mended" from *The Double Dream of Spring* by John Ashbery (New York: Dutton, 1970). Copyright © 1970, 1969, 1968, 1967, 1966 by John Ahsbery. Reprinted by permission of Georges Borchardt, Inc.

Excerpts from "The New Spirit," "The System," and "The Recital" from *Three Poems* by John Ashbery (New York: Viking, 1972). Copyright © 1970, 1971, 1972 by John Ashbery. Reprinted by permission of Georges Borchardt, Inc.

Excerpts from "Self-Portrait in a Convex Mirror" from *Self-Portrait in a*

Convex Mirror by John Ashbery. Copyright © 1974 by John Ashbery. Used by permission of Viking Penguin, a division of Penguin Putnam Inc.

Excerpts from "Unctuous Platitudes" from *Houseboat Days* by John Ashbery (New York: Viking, 1977). Copyright © 1975, 1976, 1977 by John Ashbery. Reprinted by permission of Georges Borchardt, Inc.

Excerpts from "Litany" from *As We Know* by John Ashbery. Copyright © 1979 by John Ashbery. Used by permission of Viking Penguin, a division of Penguin Putnam Inc.

Excerpts from "The Pursuit of Happiness," "Punishing the Myth," "Paradoxes and Oxymorons," and "The Vegetarians" from *Shadow Train* by John Ashbery (New York: Viking, 1981). Copyright © 1980, 1981 by John Ashbery. Reprinted by permission of Georges Borchardt, Inc.

Excerpts from *Flow Chart* by John Ashbery (New York: Knopf, 1991). Copyright © 1991 by John Ashbery. Reprinted by permission of Georges Borchardt, Inc.

Excerpts from *Hotel Lautréamont* by John Ashbery. Copyright © 1992 by John Ashbery. Reprinted by permission of Alfred A. Knopf Inc. and Carcanet Press Limited.

Excerpts from *Field Guide* by Robert Hass. Copyright © 1973 by Robert Hass. Reprinted by permission of Yale University Press.

Excerpts from "Meditation at Lagunitas," "Heroic Simile," "Transparent Garments," "Weed," "Winter Morning in Charlottesville," "Old Dominion," "Santa Lucia," "Not Going to New York: A Letter," and "Songs to Survive the Summer" from *Praise* by Robert Hass. Copyright © 1974, 1975, 1976, 1977, 1978, 1979 by Robert Hass. Reprinted by permission of The Ecco Press.

Excerpts from "Spring Drawing," "Vintage," "Museum," "Novella, "Tall Windows," "The Apple Trees at Olema," "Misery and Splendor," "Santa Barbara Road," and "Privilege of Being" from *Human Wishes* by Robert Hass. Copyright © 1989 by Robert Hass. Reprinted by permission of The Ecco Press.

Excerpts from "English: An Ode," "Faint Music," and "Regalia for a Black Hat Dancer" from *Sun Under Wood* by Robert Hass. Copyright © 1996 by Robert Hass. Reprinted by permission of The Ecco Press.

Excerpts from *Erosion* by Jorie Graham. Copyright © 1983 by Princeton University Press. Reprinted by permission of Princeton University Press.

Excerpts from "Self-Portrait as the Gesture Between Them," "On Difficulty," "Self-Portrait as Both Parties," "Orpheus and Eurydice," "Self-Portrait as Apollo and Daphne," "Eschatological Prayer," "Self-Portrait as Hurry and Delay," "Breakdancing," "Self-Portrait as Demeter and Persephone," and

"Imperialism" from *The End of Beauty* by Jorie Graham. Copyright © 1987 by Jorie Graham. Reprinted by permission of The Ecco Press.

Excerpts from "Fission," "From the New World," "Region of Unlikeness," "Picnic," and "History" from *Region of Unlikeness* by Jorie Graham. Copyright © 1991 by Jorie Graham. Reprinted by permission of The Ecco Press.

Excerpts from "Subjectivity," "Young Maples in the Wind," "Concerning the Right to Life," "Relativity: A Quartet," and "Manifest Destiny" from *Materialism* by Jorie Graham. Copyright © 1995 by Jorie Graham. Reprinted by permission of The Ecco Press.

Excerpts from "That Greater Than Which Nothing," "The Errancy," "The Scanning," "Le Manteau de Pascal," "Emergency," "The Guardian Angel of Not Feeling," "The Guardian Angel of Point-of-View," "The Guardian Angel of Self-Knowledge," "The Guardian Angel of the Private Life," "Manteau," and "The Guardian Angel of the Little Utopia" from *The Errancy* by Jorie Graham. Copyright © 1997 by Jorie Graham. Reprinted by permission of The Ecco Press.

Excerpts from *Notes for Echo Lake*, *First Figure*, and *Sun* by Michael Palmer reprinted by permission of the author. Copyright © 1981, 1984, 1988 by Michael Palmer.

Excerpts from *At Passages* by Michael Palmer. Copyright © 1995 by Michael Palmer. Reprinted by permission of New Directions Publishing Corporation.

Abbreviations

AG	Ashbery, *April Galleons*
AP	Palmer, *At Passages*
AS	Ashbery, *And the Stars Were Shining*
AWK	Ashbery, *As We Know*
B	Baudelaire, *Les Fleurs du mal*
C	Cavell, *Conditions Handsome and Unhandsome*
CP	Palmer, "Counter-Poetics and Current Practice"
CPO	Bishop, *The Complete Poems 1927–1979*
CPR	Bishop, *The Collected Prose*
CR	Cavell, *The Claim of Reason*
DD	Ashbery, *The Double Dream of Spring*
DK	Cavell, *Disowning Knowledge in Six Plays of Shakespeare*
E	Graham, *Erosion*
EB	Graham, *The End of Beauty*
EL	Palmer, *Notes for Echo Lake*
FC	Ashbery, *Flow Chart*
FF	Palmer, *First Figure*
FG	Hass, *Field Guide*
GO	Hass, "George Oppen: A Tribute"
H	Hölderlin, *Hymns and Fragments*
HD	Ashbery, *Houseboat Days*
HL	Ashbery, *Hotel Lautréamont*
HW	Hass, *Human Wishes*
I	Graham and Lehman, introduction to *The Best American Poetry 1990*
IQ	Cavell, *In Quest of the Ordinary*
J	Jackson, "The Imminence of a Revelation"
M	Graham, *Materialism*
MP	Palmer, "Michael Palmer: A Conversation"
MWH	Vendler, *The Music of What Happens*

MWM	Cavell, *Must We Mean What We Say?*
NYQ	Packard, *The Craft of Poetry*
OEW	Vendler, *On Extended Wings*
P	Hass, *Praise*
PI	Wittgenstein, *Philosophical Investigations*
RM	Ashbery, *Rivers and Mountains*
RU	Graham, *Region of Unlikeness*
S	Palmer, *Sun*
SAP	Stitt, "The Art of Poetry 33"
SCP	Stevens, *The Collected Poems*
SM	Benjamin, "On Some Motifs in Baudelaire"
SOT	Ashbery, *Some Trees*
SP	Ashbery, *Self-Portrait in a Convex Mirror*
ST	Ashbery, *Shadow Train*
SU	Hass, *Sun Under Wood*
SW	Cavell, *The Senses of Walden*
T	Cavell, *Themes Out of School*
TC	Hass, *Twentieth Century Pleasures*
TCO	Ashbery, *The Tennis Court Oath*
TE	Graham, *The Errancy*
TN	Cavell, *This New yet Unapproachable America*
TP	Ashbery, *Three Poems*
W	Ashbery, *A Wave*
Z	Zanzotto, *Selected Poetry*

Regions of Unlikeness

Introduction

What I investigate in this book is the way a number of our most important contemporary poets frame their work as taking place within, and being brought to life by, an acknowledgment of the limits of language. In the interview included here, for example, Jorie Graham remarks: "I find myself very drawn to situations in which the problems with reference are roiled up. I like to be kept on that hook. Because then when I go to write about anything—and after all, the poems are always 'about' something else—the issue of the medium they are enacted in is alive. . . . Under those conditions I feel I might get somewhere. Somewhere tenable. Somewhere trustworthy." Calling attention to themselves describing or remembering or speaking or writing, the poets I examine here also insist on bringing into play the limits of such acts. Sentences are sometimes not finished, descriptive patterns dissolve and reform, initial forays break off in a spray of ellipses, peculiar distortions are included—that such uses of language are the source of current poetry's difficulty as well as its claims to have brought to life something crucial about our human situation is the subject of this book.

Let me begin with an example. Robert Hass opens his 1989 collection *Human Wishes* with this acknowledgment of descriptive limits:

> A man thinks *lilacs against white houses*, having seen them in the
>   farm country south of Tacoma in April, and can't find his way to a
>   sentence, a brushstroke carrying the energy of *brush* and *stroke*
>
> —as if he were stranded on the aureole of the memory of a woman's
>   breast,
>
> and she, after the drive from the airport and a chat with her mother
>   and a shower, which is ritual cleansing and a passage through water
>   to mark transition,
>
> had walked up the mountain on a summer evening.

Away from, not toward.
("Spring Drawing," HW, 4)

Unable to "find his way to a sentence" that, in a live "stroke" of language's "brush," might offer up the remembered landscape whole and still radiant, the poet makes a move that seems to me characteristic of contemporary writing. Rather than attempt to push beyond this descriptive limit or settling for some sort of grief-soaked lamentation, he describes the stalled linguistic space itself. Not being able to complete a sentence feels "as if" one were left with only a memory while the person being brought to mind flew home, chatted, showered, and took an evening walk. Foregrounding the gap or interval on which a construction such as "as if" is based, opening it step by step in his description of the woman, the poet enters the space he had presumably been unable to bridge in his initial sentence about Tacoma farm country. It becomes clear as the poem continues on through a series of cascading "as if" statements that take him "away from not toward" a completed sentence, that what he is doing is meditating on various wishes or desires embedded in the language of description. Handling those desires, Hass concludes, attending to what is revealed when words stall and their drives become newly visible, may be a way of renewing language, inhabiting it without giving in to the always-frustrated wish to hold tight or know for sure:

> Only the force of the brushstroke keeps the lilacs from pathos—the
>   hes and shes of the comedy may or may not get together, but if they
>   are to get at all,
>
> then the interval created by *if*, to which mind and breath attend,
>   nervous as the grazing animals the first brushes painted,
>
> has become habitable space, lived in beyond wishing.
> (HW, 4)

While the method of being "kept on the hook" with regard to the limits of one's ability to describe or remember or complete a sentence varies from poet to poet, the drive to inhabit the issues made visible by that acknowledgment can be seen in the work of many of our most important contemporary writers. In what follows, I describe the careers of five representative writers; in each case I trace the rich and detailed history of the different ways each poet, through attending to language's limits, has attempted to bring words back to life. Poetry takes place within what Michael Oakeshott would call a larger intellectual conversation, and, in order to hear more fully what is at stake in the work of these poets, in this opening chapter I describe Stanley Cavell's remarkably similar engagement with the issues of skepticism and linguistic finitude. I also bring into the conversation the work of the modern poets who, for many contemporary writers, first suggested how poetry might inhabit these issues. And finally, later in the book, I present a set of interviews I have conducted with the three younger writers I focus on. In many ways, these interviews are the core of the book, demonstrating the intellectual reach of the charged struggles and mappings enacted in the poems. One might think of these conversations as collaborative performances—initial demonstrations of what is "alive" and "tenable" in poetry's roiling up of its linguistic patterns.

Why should attending to issues alive in the writing be part of poetry's getting somewhere? Why would anyone attempt to write from within "the interval created by *if*"? What would it mean to find within a stalled sentence "habitable space" somehow beyond or opposed to "wishing"? Hass's questions have also been central to the philosopher Stanley Cavell, and a brief account of his work should help us think about poetry's insistence on keeping alive the medium within which it acts.

Cavell's work focuses on the problem of skepticism. Raising "the question whether I know with certainty of the existence of the external world and of myself and others in it" (DK, 3), skepticism, for Cavell, voices "philosophy's discovery of the limitation of human knowledge . . . in its radical form" (IQ, 185). Cavell claims that the skeptic's refusal to settle for anything less than perfect knowledge of the world is in fact a "refusal to acknowledge his participation in finite human existence" (T, 60). We are time-bound, bodily creatures and the way we know and relate to ourselves and others is bound up in that. In its "drive to reach the unconditioned," skepticism, for Cavell, displays a "desire to refuse human limitation, the limitation of finitude" (DK, 17). This refusal is strikingly illustrated for Cavell in the world-dissolving drive of Shakespearean tragedy. In refusing to recognize "the (separate) existence of the world and of others in it" (DK, 13), Shakespeare's heroes offer a demonstration "of what drives skepticism—of what its emotion is, of what becomes of the world in its grip, its stranglehold, of what knowing has come to mean to us" (DK, 6). Hamlet's "refusal to admit himself to life" (DK, 13), Coriolanus's "enactment of disgust" (DK, 12), and Lear's "avoidance of Cordelia" (DK, 6) all illustrate, for Cavell, ways of turning away from a world that cannot be known with certainty.[1]

Skepticism, in such a light, is an "attempt to convert the human condition, the condition of humanity, into an intellectual difficulty, a riddle" (CR, 493). What Cavell is interested in is other responses to the truth about our finite condition that skepticism raises but turns away from in disgust. The "truth of skepticism" is "that the human creature's basis in the world as a whole, its relation to the world as such, is not that of knowing, anyway not what we think of as knowing" (CR, 241).[2] In the attention Wittgenstein, Emerson, and Thoreau give to ordinary or everyday language, Cavell finds one such response, a linguistic one, to human limitation.[3] Of Wittgenstein, he strikingly remarks: "He wishes an acknowledgment of human limitation which does not leave us chafed by our own skin, by a sense of powerlessness to penetrate beyond the human conditions of knowledge. The limitations of knowledge are no longer barriers to a more perfect apprehension, but conditions of knowledge" (MWM, 61). That desire to not imagine ourselves as chafed by the limits of the very skin within which we live, to not wish it otherwise, is exactly what Hass refers to when he speaks of making the intervals where language acknowledges its limits "habitable space, lived in beyond wishing."[4] Such poetry as Hass's, deliberately inhabiting language's finite conditions and bringing to life the various implications of not being able to grasp and know with certainty, is an attempt, then, to unfold the human situation. Language is a doorway, one way of accessing that set of issues.[5] Deliberately calling attention to itself speaking or remembering or praising, such poetry, to adapt Cavell's words, is an unfolding "of what Emerson calls 'human condition,' a further interpretation of finitude, a mode, as said, of inhabiting our investment in words, in the world" (C, 61).

I am suggesting, then, that when contemporary writers are "drawn to situations in which the problems with reference are roiled up," they are being drawn to situations in which the limits of knowledge, our finite skin, are in play and in which responses other than knowing (or turning in disgust from a failure to know) are possible. As Cavell puts it, "our capacity for disappointment by [words] is essential to the way we possess language" (IQ, 5). Continually bringing such a capacity for disappointment into play, keeping itself "on the hook," poetry that calls attention to its limits is attempting to explore our actual life "in words, in the world." In Graham's words quoted in chapter 6, "We want to be able to suffer the poem so that the actions that we take in the act of writing are true actions—in order to save ourselves."

One of my claims in this study is that this drive is remarkably wide ranging. It is visible in the work of a traditional poet such as Elizabeth Bishop who, to look at one example, keeps herself on the hook in "The Gentleman of Shalott" by imagining a figure who is afraid he has a looking glass where his spine should be (CPO, 9–10). He may be half person and half reflection; if so, there is no way of knowing "Which eye's his eye" and so on. Through this figure, Bishop imaginatively enters and is energized by human limits: "The uncertainty / he says he / finds exhilarating." That drive to enter an area where the limits of our human situation are fully engaged can also be seen in the work of an experimental poet such as Michael Palmer, who imagines his own version of Bishop's encounter with the question "which eye's his eye." In "Left Unfinished Sixteen Times," Palmer develops a related version of Bishop's exhilarated sense of "constant re-adjustment." Deliberately bringing our capacity for disappointment with the term *I* into play by imagining a situation where its definition is left unfinished over and over, Palmer also finds that linguistic uncertainty offers a chance to enlarge and inhabit our finite condition: "I is enclosed by the question where it's read as a letter. / . . . I refers to the pause or loss, the decision that a window will remain closed the better to watch. / I thought it would be nice to make some chemicals, to make some lexical adventures to enlarge the space, then reside forever in the silence of the letter" (FF, 45). There are, of course, important differences that become visible once this common ground is established, but the surprising resonance between these two quite different poets is an important and not often noted one.[6] Neither writer is chafed by his or her own skin. Both understand that in acknowledging pressures or questions about language, in entering its "pause or loss," our "investment in words, in the world" comes to life.

In his discussion of Wittgenstein and Thoreau, Cavell sketches two different ways of bringing language to life by keeping in play "our capacity for disappointment." Since these two approaches are present in many contemporary poems, sometimes separately, often in combination with each other, it might be useful to describe them in some detail. Cavell's ongoing reading of Wittgenstein is perhaps most accessibly found in "The Availability of Wittgenstein's Later Philosophy" in *Must We Mean What We Say?* (1969), in his book-length discussion of the philosopher *The Claim of Reason* (1979), and in "Declining Decline: Wittgenstein as a Philosopher of Culture" in *This New yet Unapproachable America* (1989). In his *Philosophical Investigations*, Wittgenstein enters into a "battle against the bewitchment of our intelligence by means of language" (PI, 47e, remark 109). As he describes the process: "When philosophers use a word—'knowledge,' 'being,' 'object,' 'I,' 'proposition,' 'name'—and try to grasp the *essence* of the thing, one must always ask oneself: is the word ever actually used in this way in the language-game which is its original home?—What *we* do is bring words back from their metaphysical to their everyday use" (PI, 48e, remark 116). According to Cavell, a metaphysical use of words is, for Wittgenstein, a "reject[ion] [of] the human. . . . He undertook, as I read him, to trace the mechanism of this rejection in the ways in which, in investigating ourselves, we are led to speak 'outside language games,' consider expressions apart from, and in opposition to, the natural forms of life which give those expressions the force they have" (CR, 207). Using words outside of the ordinary language games in which they are at home signals, for Cavell, "dissatisfaction with one's human powers of expression . . . a sense that words, to reveal the world, must carry more deeply than our agreements or attunements in criteria will negotiate" (IQ, 60). Like Shakespeare's tragic heroes, such a way of speaking expresses the "wish that underlies skepticism, a wish for the connection between my claims of knowledge and the objects upon which the claims are to fall to occur without my intervention, apart from my agreements" (CR, 351–52).

What is important for reading contemporary poetry is that Wittgenstein, in Cavell's reading, does not simply dismiss such "*ways* of arriving at the certainty of our lives, pictures of closeness and connection, that themselves deny the conditions of human closeness" (TN, 45). Instead, he allows that desire for certainty to play within his own words because of what is revealed in what it disappointedly turns from: "our shared home of language" (IQ, 186); "this haphazard, unsponsored state" (CR, 439). In keeping that desire to know with certainty alive, indeed by suggesting that it is a desire he can reliably locate within himself, Wittgenstein also keeps alive the truth of human limits. Through such a process, "one's humanity, or finitude, is . . . accepted, suffered" (TN, 39), the world is "regained as gone" (IQ, 172), and we are "return[ed] . . . to the everyday" (TN, 66). For Cavell, then, the *Investigations* "finds its victory exactly in never claiming a final philosophical victory over (the temptation to) skepticism, which would mean a victory over the human" (TN, 38). As we will see, the shape of that confrontation, "endless specific succumbings to the conditions of skepticism and endless specific recoveries from it, endless as a circle, as a serpent swallowing itself" (DK, 30), is a strikingly precise description of one way poetry brings into play, and inhabits, our life in language.[7]

If Wittgenstein offers a model for how poetry's finite space might be continually discovered, Thoreau, in Cavell's reading, helps us to see how poetry operates there. Cavell sees *Walden* as a "book about its own writing and reading" (SW, xiii), its hero a writer "discovering what writing is" (SW, 5). Thoreau writes that "Not till we are lost . . . do we begin to find ourselves, and realize where we are and the infinite extent of our relations" (SW, 50), and Cavell understands Thoreau's building at a distance from civilization as an attempt to inhabit a space where, for example, such notions as language's transparency or immediate connection to the world are "lost." In such a space, Thoreau is able to "assume the conditions of language as such; re-experience, as it were, the fact that there is such a thing as language at all and assume responsibility for it—find a way to acknowledge it" (sw, 33). For Cavell, what Thoreau is "building is writing . . . [his] writing is, as it realizes itself daily under [his] hands, sentence by shunning sentence, the accomplishment of inhabitation" (sw, 134). Cavell's Thoreau is engaged in "endless computations of . . . words" (sw, 63), attempting to enter our condition through investigatory "puns and paradoxes, . . . fracturing of idiom and twisting of quotation, . . . drones of fact and flights of impersonation" (sw, 16). Measuring what is visible in that space where "we are lost" is in fact part of his daily life, as seen by the way Thoreau continually tracks back and forth between writing and other human activities visible there. Cavell writes: "Each calling—what the writer means (and what anyone means, more or less) by a 'field' of action or labor—is isomorphic with every other. This is why building a house and hoeing and writing and reading (and we could add, walking and preparing food and receiving visitors and giving charity and hammering a nail and surveying the ice) are allegories and measures of one another. . . . What matters is that he show in the way he writes his faithfulness to the specific conditions and acts of writing as such" (sw, 61–62).

Both Wittgenstein and Thoreau, in this view, bring to charged life our use of "words, in the world"—Wittgenstein by struggling with the desire to find words to be otherwise than human, Thoreau by measuring our use of words against the activities it touches on or shares space with. Cavell writes that "Thoreau is doing with our ordinary assertions what Wittgenstein does with our more patently philosophical assertions—bringing them back to a context in which they are alive" (sw, 92). Much contemporary poetry, in its "constant re-adjustment" and "lexical adventures," is doing the same thing.[8]

In fact, poetry would seem to be the ideal way to investigate such a response to limits. Cavell, who has done much to link poetry and philosophy on this issue, suggests as much, noting that just as Heidegger was indebted to Hölderlin "not alone for lessons of thought but [also] for lessons in reading" (sw, 134) so Emerson and Thoreau, in "their interest in their own writing [were] their own Hölderlins." That is, as they foregrounded their own writing, as they read and struggled with the implications of their own unfolding work, Emerson and Thoreau were working as poets. It would seem appropriate, then, to add to the conversation around the issues raised by Hass's desire to make the interval opened by *if* habitable, the voices of poets—I have in mind those of Pound, H. D., Stevens, Frost, and Eliot—for it is clear that contemporary writers have heard in the powerful voices of modern poetry a call, similar to Cavell's, to inhabit the live space of their own finite linguistic acts.

The interviews included here give a rich sense of the various voices the three younger poets build on or contest, and among those voices consistently in play are those of the modernists. Hass, for example, in our interview, points to what is still live in modernism's legacy by calling attention to the way, "in insisting on brokenness rather than wholeness, that the relation between words and things is not a given," modern poetry found its way to "a more powerful, less facile, more expressive language [able] to get at the uniqueness of the inner experience of a person." Michael Palmer locates himself within a particular understanding of "the anxiety of signification that comes along with modernism and, also, with contemporary linguistics and philosophy. The sense of doubt about the relationship between . . . the acoustical image and the concept, which is one way of looking abstractly at the sign" (CP, 11). Graham speaks of wishing to return to the vital, wide-ranging questions opened by modernism's entry into the finitude of speaking or writing: "I feel like I'm writing as part of a group of poets—historically—who are potentially looking at the end of the medium itself as a vital part of their culture—unless they do something to help it to reconnect itself to mystery and power. However great their enterprise, we have been handed by the generation *after* the modernists . . . an almost untenably narrow notion of what that in-between space is capable of" (see chapter 6; emphasis mine).[9]

To sketch a representative version of modernism's acknowledgment and entrance into language's limits, let me turn to Wallace Stevens's "The Auroras of Autumn"—a meditation on the ways we inhabit the spaces between language's claims to master or hold, the spaces where language reveals its brokenness and live sense of limits.[10] As Helen Vendler has noted in *The Music of What Happens*, Stevens's is a poetry of "enacted mental process." (MWH, 79). In his most famous formulation, it is "the mind in the act of finding / What will suffice," the poet "A metaphysician in the dark, twanging/ . . . [the] wiry string" of language (SCP, 239, 240). Twanging, it might be said—thinking by handling material textures—marks Stevens's investigation as a poetic one. The world he lives in is a world that, because its "squirming facts exceed the squamous mind" (SCP, 215), seems to have "expelled us and our images" (SCP, 381). But rather than bring the mind to a halt, that acknowledgment proves generative in Stevens, and language springs to full and charged life out of our not being able to grasp and know and make a home: "From this the poem springs: that we live in a place / That is not our own and, much more, not ourselves / And hard it is in spite of blazoned days" (scp, 383). "The Auroras of Autumn" is Stevens's most powerful investigation of the "skeptical music" (scp, 122) of that place—the poet, as Charles Altieri puts it, "fully inhabiting the forms of desire that most articulately give voice to the world."[11]

As Vendler notes in *On Extended Wings*, the poem begins "in the lyric present" (oew, 246), something unmasterable and overwhelming putting pressure on the speaker of the poem: the northern lights which, as a serpent coiling and uncoiling, its flashing skin continually sloughed off and abandoned, seem to insist on the observer's finiteness:

> This is where the serpent lives. This is his nest,
> These fields, these hills, these tinted distances,
> And the pines above and along and beside the sea.
>
> This is form gulping after formlessness,
> Skin flashing to wished-for disappearances
> And the serpent body flashing without the skin.
> (scp, 411)

The serpent's domain is dominated by the brute fact of the world's constant motion, form momentarily gathering into a distinguishable pattern and then immediately gulping toward its own dissolution. Much as in Dickinson, these snaking lights both make visible the landscape's "distances" and proclaim its unmasterable separateness. Though the shifting lights may embody some sort of unseen principle of coherence—think of that as the serpent "in another nest," mastering from above "the maze / Of body and air and forms and images"—its "poison," or the knowledge it leads us to as we wrestle with "forms and images" here below in the "moving grass," is that we become, as observers, progressively "less . . . sure" of such a "possession of happiness." As Stevens writes: "This is his poison: that we should disbelieve / Even that" (scp, 411).

What is most striking in this poem is the way Stevens, in the three cantos that follow, allows the auroras to play against, or put pressure on, his own work as a poet. This is quite deliberate, and is much like Cavell's insistence that "our capacity for disappointment by [words] is essential to the way we possess language." Three times the phrase "Farewell to an idea" and its accompanying elliptical pause acknowledge what happens to the poet's language when confronted with a world that reveals its ideas of mastery to be fragile, wind-swept things. Stevens dramatizes being forced to say farewell, under pressure, to such things as language's purpose and transparency, its abilities to mark and measure. Vendler describes the tone of these sections as one of "anticipatory mourning" (OEW, 252); Harold Bloom speaks of them as "chilled synecdoches of waning power . . . a lament . . . for the driving away of tropes and colors by the glare of the auroras";[12] B. J. Leggett speaks of the way, in these sections, "the ordering power of the individual imagination is shrunken in the face of an external power."[13] These descriptions are accurate, but what they leave out, and what contemporary poetry's interest in this space of farewell perhaps has taught us to anticipate, is that these unburdening gestures also look forward to some sort of compensatory gain in the new linguistic space opened up.[14]

Briefly, the second canto turns from the auroras to a deserted cabin on the beach in order to think about inhabiting or acknowledging the limitations involved in our attempts to mark or make visible our existence. Stevens works this out by means of the cabin's whiteness. Its color seems established "by a custom or according to / An ancestral theme." "[A] little dried," the white flowers against its wall seem "a kind of mark / Reminding, trying to remind, of a white / That was different, something else, last year / Or before, not the white of an aging afternoon" (SCP, 412). The cabin's whiteness, then, seems a deliberate exercise in making and marking: "Here, being visible is being white, / Is being of the solid of white, the accomplishment / Of an extremist in an exercise . . ." But the cabin, we are reminded, is deserted. We hear this in the ellipsis above where Stevens seems to give up his claim as soon as he makes it, in his acknowledgment that the whiteness might be only the result of the "infinite course" of erosion, and in the double-clutched phrasing of "reminding [or] *trying* to remind." And just at this point, the poem opens up, for giving up that white cabin, saying farewell to the ability to mark or make permanently visible, leaves the poet "turn[ing] blankly on the sand," turning to acknowledge what can't be confined:

> And the whiteness grows less vivid on the wall.
> The man who is walking turns blankly on the sand.
> He observes how the north is always enlarging the change,
>
> With its frigid brilliances, its blue-red sweeps
> And gusts of great enkindlings, its polar green,
> The color of ice and fire and solitude.
> (SCP, 412–13)

In similar terms, the third canto develops an allegory of a mother and children, together at evening, in order to explore what it feels like to say "good-night," under the pressure of the aurora, to "The mother's face, / The purpose of the poem." As Vendler remarks, this canto "depends on the continuing antithesis of the beauty and the dissolution of the mother" (OEW, 256). Another house is involved. As with the white cabin, Stevens registers both the lovely dream of an achieved purpose—"It is the mother they possess, / Who gives transparence to their present peace," "They are at ease in a shelter of the mind" (SCP, 413)—and, as he continually touches and pulls back from that dream, the painful alertness of its loss. Every luxurious reenactment of the dream is framed with a reminder of its loss. The house where the children possess the mother is, for example, also the house of "evening, half dissolved." The speaker knows that "Only the half they can never possess remains"; its starry sky will stand though "The house will crumble and the books will burn." That double movement, desiring and then saying farewell to the idea of an achieved, transparent purpose, brings the poem to a striking moment. A number of writers have noted that as the mother falls asleep, as the warm interior light gives way, the dissolving shelter is relit, recording on the outside of its windows the streaming auroras and the annihilating power they speak for.[15] We might think of this as Hass's "habitable space, lived in beyond wishing." The house is a powerful picture of language, its dream of transparency dissolved and an ability to register rediscovered:

> Upstairs
> The windows will be lighted, not the rooms.
>
> A wind will spread its windy grandeurs round
> And knock like a rifle-butt against the door.
> The wind will command them with invincible sound.
> (SCP, 413–14)

In the figure of the father who sits still and yet roams discerningly through his senses, canto 4 speaks for and then lets dissolve yet another form of mastery. Call it the active intellect, insisting in its forward movement that "The cancellings, / The negations are never final," saying "no to no and yes to yes." To acknowledge a limit to this power, then, would be to say "yes / To no; and in saying yes he says farewell" (SCP, 414). Stevens allegorizes intellect as a "master seated by the fire / And yet in space," describing him both "sit[ting] in quiet and green-a-day" and "measur[ing] the velocities of change" or tracing great arcs of discovery and differentiation "In flights of eye and ear." The intellect's world is always on the edge of drama, or made meaning. It is always sorting through things that attend it until it hears

The supernatural preludes of its own,
At the moment when the angelic eye defines
Its actors approaching, in company, in their masks

And yet, writes Stevens, eyes on an even grander play of intelligence, what is that father and his teased-out dramas compared to the tearing wind and the restless lights on fire in the sky: "Look at this present throne. What company, / In masks, can choir *it* with the naked wind?" (my emphasis). Three times, then, the poem tracks the way the power of the auroras both reduces the claims of language and opens up, in that collapse, a new space of response.

Cantos 5 and 6 reflectively explore that space by imagining a sort of drama—cabin, mother, father—that might go on there. What's to be seen?

The mother invites humanity to her house
And table. The father fetches tellers of tales
And musicians who mute much, muse much, on the tales.
(SCP, 415)

What we have, however, despite the father's drive to fetch "pageants out of air" and to produce "slavered and panting halves / Of breath, obedient to his trumpet's touch" is not a festival but a "loud, disordered mooch." There is no world-encompassing drama that the poet nudges into visibility; in fact, "There is no play. / Or, the persons act one merely by being here." What that failure does, however, as we have seen before with the lights of the auroras flaring on the windows of the deserted house, is yield an openness to forces beyond the poet's management. There *is* a theater, one visible now in the collapse of ours:

It is a theatre floating through the clouds,
Itself a cloud, although of misted rock
And mountains running like water, wave on wave,

Through waves of light. It is of cloud transformed
To cloud transformed again, idly, the way
A season changes color to no end,

Except the lavishing of itself in change.
(SCP, 416)

How does one play a part in that theater, when all one can do is merely be there? Well, Stevens argues, you record how it feels to continually slide through "forms and images" without confidently anticipating "possession of happiness," acknowledging that "the denouement has to be postponed." You record, on your own nerve endings, the conditions of being in language or in a body:

> This is nothing until in a single man contained,
> Nothing until this named thing nameless is
> And is destroyed. He opens the door of his house
>
> On flames. The scholar of one candle sees
> An Arctic effulgence flaring on the frame
> Of everything he is. And he feels afraid.
> (SCP, 416–17)

This is what Stevens and the other moderns pass on as a challenge to contemporary writers: the notion that in this space where language threatens to give way and leave the world "nameless" and "destroyed" as far as human usefulness is concerned, human limits might be measured on the skin of a single observer—a measurement making visible a world free to flare and run, lighting windows from the outside and floating as theater through the clouds.

What Stevens and Cavell demonstrate is that an acknowledgment of limits opens up a space where the finite "drama that we live" (SCP, 419) in language can be enacted. I have been calling that a charged or live use of language, alert to the tensions and possibilities that a more straightforward speaking disregards.[16] What contemporary poetry brings to these investigations is an approach that is both more personal and more broad-ranging. On the one hand, the writer becomes more vulnerable and the struggle he or she undergoes more live, as we realize that Stevens's "single man," his ability to name and contain destroyed by the flames, is in fact the man or woman writing or describing or remembering—caught up in an encounter with language. In contemporary writing, one often encounters not a white cabin under the unmasterable, form-erasing auroras, but someone speaking or remembering or praising, acutely aware that these are finite activities, riddled with the temptation to claim certainty. Succumbing to and recovering from that temptation, contemporary writing often says farewell to simple description and then, eyes open, goes on to describe anyway. On the other hand, the reflective work of measuring and allegorizing our life in language as it becomes visible in that fragile, finite space is more far-reaching; it is conducted not simply by making parables about language's innocence or chilly isolation as Stevens does in the final cantos of "The Auroras of Autumn" but by measuring the reach of the sentence against the ravages of colonialism or holding up the play of voices within the phrase against the scatterings of schizophrenia. These poets speak to both modernism's discovery of the renewed life let loose by the coming undone of language and "philosophy's discovery of the limitations of human knowledge" by showing just how charged and fluent and far-reaching in its implications such an "investment in words, in the world" might be. Hass comments in the interview included here: "Is the problem played out? Hardly. It's hard to deny that poetry stands in the middle of a wasteland still, a wreckage of all previous metaphysics that made us feel at home in the world or promised us a home elsewhere." For contemporary poets, the drive to renew language, to open a space where it can once again be live and intimate and responsive, is pressing and acute; for many writers it is a drama that can be teased out of the everyday business of handling ourselves where language knots and swirls. For such writers, as I have said, poetry is the act of inhabiting language's finite conditions, bringing language to life by living out the various and wide-ranging implications of our not being able to grasp and know with certainty.[17]

As an initial illustration of contemporary poetry's manner of "inhabiting our investment in words, in the world," let me sketch representative readings of poems by the five writers I focus on. I begin with Elizabeth Bishop's "Brazil, January 1, 1502" (CPO, 91–92), a striking example of how, through a struggle with language, succumbing to and recovering from the drive to fix and be certain, in Cavell's words, "one's humanity, or finitude, is . . . accepted, suffered." The second in a series of poems in Bishop's *Questions of Travel* (1965) about encountering, and eventually establishing a home in, Brazil, it begins by linking her response to the Brazilian interior with that of Portuguese explorers 450 years earlier. Both had been all but overwhelmed:

> Januaries, Nature greets our eyes
> exactly as she must have greeted theirs:
> every square inch filling in with foliage—
> big leaves, little leaves, and giant leaves,
> blue, blue-green, and olive,
> with occasional lighter veins and edges,
> or a satin underleaf turned over

What is interesting here is the way the "every square inch" cliché, employed to talk about the overpowering landscape, also points us to the poet, if not at her desk, certainly alert to the language she's using to try to describe this scene.

Bishop plays out the desire for order implicit in our use of such language by transforming the scene in front of her into a tapestry—deftly calling attention to her need to fit it into a frame. As she catalogs the scene, now reduced to her cliché's filled-in square inches, she works it out as an orderly variation of sizes and colors, noticing, for example, a "satin underleaf" and ferns "in silver-gray relief," then completing the arrangement by describing the entire scene as "solid but airy; fresh as if just finished / and taken off the frame." In Richard Poirier's terms, she tropes or puns on that cliché by literalizing it. She goes further, however, not simply skeptically identifying and (one would think) abandoning the cliché, but listening to and playing out the descriptive limits and powers it speaks for. Cavell would describe this as an initial "succumbing to the conditions of skepticism." Accordingly, the second stanza of the poem runs with the idea of making Brazil into an anxious tapestry. The sky becomes "a simple web, / backing for [the] feathery detail" of such worked representations as "brief arcs" readable as palms, "big symbolic birds" posed in profile, and, "in the foreground," an arrangement of lizards and rocks that seems to offer a point (and title) to what is being represented: "Still in the foreground there is Sin: / five sooty dragons near some massy rocks." Her crucial move is realizing that, in uneasiness, we need to know (or "mark," Stevens would say), and then playing out the limitations of knowing by giving into that desire—here, the quick way her eye solves the scenery by reading male lizards clustered around "the smaller, female one . . . / her wicked tail straight up and over, / red as a red-hot wire" as an illustration of sexual sin, the familiar story of temptation in a garden complete all the way down to moss taking the form of "threaten[ing]" though "lovely[,] hell-green flames."

What Bishop has done here is identify and acknowledge (by playing out) our desire to know and be certain, to find ourselves within a familiar story. But, we discover, as soon as she offers this attempt at knowing, she feels it dissolve and is left instead with the heart-sickening sense of having handled and acknowledged, in that drive to simplify, more than she had realized:

Just so the Christians, hard as nails,
tiny as nails, and glinting,
in creaking armor, came and found it all,
not unfamiliar:
no lovers' walks, no bowers,
no cherries to be picked, no lute music,
but corresponding, nevertheless,
to an old dream of wealth and luxury

already out of style when they left home—
wealth, plus a brand-new pleasure.

Trusting that the "not unfamiliar" scene corresponded to "an old dream" that had at its root "a brand-new pleasure," the explorers gave themselves permission to act on what their interpretive tapestries had offered them—a world ready for the taking, the inhabitants seen both as spoil and as players in an ancient sexual drama. Heartsick, her "Just so" playing out the connections between her own descriptive simplifications and the raping of Brazil, Bishop suffers the truth of skepticism; she sees and takes responsibility for what an anxious avoidance of finitude had come to. In Cavell's terms, she "measures" her descriptive activity against a 450-year-old terror and is broken by it. "Farewell to an idea . . . ," she might have said. Her words shattered, the world comes back again, flowing away from her:

they ripped away into the hanging fabric,
each out to catch an Indian for himself—
those maddening little women who kept calling,
calling to each other (or had the birds waked up?)
and retreating, always retreating, behind it.

In the interval opened up by her initial cliché, Bishop sees her linguistic gesture and its implications. She sees herself "in words, in the world," that gesture opening on an historical situation which she also must assume responsibility for.

John Ashbery, whom I move to next, is perhaps the purest example we have of a writer who engages these issues reflectively, setting up writing situations that establish, often in the form of landscapes, various features of language that he can then travel through and map.[18] As we will see, he has made a career out of dreaming up generative ways of establishing writing scenes in which to "re-experience, as it were, the fact that there is such a thing as language at all and assume responsibility for it" (SW, 33). The devices he has employed run from the use of cut out phrases to the piling up of words that have "taken on that look of worn familiarity, like pebbles polished over and over again by the sea" (TP, 117), from the construction of juxtaposed columns commenting on each other (*"Two . . . / Go[ing] on at once without special permission,"* AWK, 16) to the book-length reliance on a relentless form so "perfect in its outrageous / Regularity" (ST, 1) that every turn of phrase seems commentary on that expression of language's otherness. "Clepsydra," to take as an example an early poem from *Rivers and Mountains* (1966), defines Ashbery's reflective territory as the fact that there is a "dividing force / Between our slightest steps and the notes taken on them" (RM, 32).[19] The poem opens a space for that condition to be acknowledged and investigated by performing a characteristically simple linguistic distortion: the poem catches up to Ashbery's thought process after it has already started and begins there, the poem having gone a good way down a certain track before the poet begins writing. The effect of this is to force our eyes to pay attention to the writing itself rather than the now all-but-inaccessible subject it is discussing. Later in the poem Ashbery speaks of the effect of such a beginning as forcing the words so close to our eyes that they are no longer legible:

> there was no statement
> At the beginning. There was only a breathless waste,
> A dumb cry shaping everything in projected
> After-effects orphaned by playing the part intended for them,
> Though one must not forget that the nature of this
> Emptiness, these previsions,
> Was that it could only happen here, on this page held
> Too close to be legible, sprouting erasures, except that they
> Ended everything in the transparent sphere of what was
> Intended only a moment ago, spiraling further out, its
> Gesture finally dissolving in the weather.
> (RM, 29)

Much as in our daily speech, the poem's "orphaned" words are made participants in a great unscripted play by being separated from an originating "statement." Tracing them back leads only to something "dumb" or "breathless" or empty, not to something "transparent" resting on something "intended." We are invited to watch words in that space play some other "part" and then, like Stevens's transparent mother or his cabin's solid white, "dissolv[e] in the weather." By holding his words so close to his eyes that he loses track of their intention, Ashbery creates a reflective space where language, in all its finite richness, can be seen.

If we look at the poem's opening lines, we do in fact find it beginning after the beginning:

> Hasn't the sky? Returned from moving the other
> Authority recently dropped, wrested as much of

That severe sunshine as you need now on the way
You go.
(RM, 27)

Such an opening says farewell to certain expectations. Though later we realize that the "you" of the poem is probably Ashbery's writing self,[20] and that a distinction between the sky (as invisible whole) and the air (a temporary statement of the sky—hazy, steamy, windy) is probably being made, we begin with all of that withheld. Perhaps it is morning and Ashbery's speaker is wondering if the sky, in replacing one authority (the moon?) with another (sunshine), has not, at some symbolic level, declared all form—including the "you" belatedly if gracefully uttering itself down its form-making ways— temporary. Other lines suggest as much:

> Each moment
> Of utterance is the true one; likewise none are true,
> Only is the bounding from air to air, a serpentine
> Gesture which hides the truth behind a congruent
> Message, the way air hides the sky, is, in fact,
> Tearing it limb from limb this very moment: but
> The sky has pleaded already and this is about
> As graceful a kind of non-absence as either
> Has a right to expect
> (RM, 27)

But the point is that Ashbery begins not with this explanation but in the act of bounding itself—tearing something silent limb from limb. Beginning with the connection between prevision and eventual statement dissolved allows him to silently put language's limits into play: "This means never getting any closer to the basic / Principle operating behind it than to the distracted / Entity of a mirage" (RM, 27). What "Clepsydra" does, then, is monitor itself in this space where the poet encounters what he calls the "almost / Exaggerated strictness of the condition" (RM, 30) of our being in language. Looking at what has just been said—"both mirage and the little / That was present, the miserable totality / Mustered at any given moment"—and treating those words as something "to be constantly coming back from— / . . . continu[ing] the dialogue into / Those mysterious and near regions that are / Precisely the time of its being furthered" (RM, 28), Ashbery builds his poem by handling and interrogating ("coming back from") those phrases he has just uttered. Much as Stevens reflects through analogy or juxtaposed phrases, but in characteristically large sweeps of utterance, Ashbery joins with or inhabits what is revealed in the blind self-display of our words:

> the condition
> Of those moments of timeless elasticity and blindness
> Was being joined secretly so
> That their paths would cross again and be separated
> Only to join again in a final assumption rising like a shout
> And be endless in the discovery of the declamatory
> Nature of the distance traveled.
> (RM, 29)

Playing out those orphaned parts, then, makes clear—in linguistic or "declamatory" terms—the distance we constantly travel from prevision to utterance.

The dialogue seems to be about the value of poetry—that is, being conscious about your language, about its rich but empty distance from the events it speaks for:

> a half-triumph, an imaginary feeling
> Which still protected its events and pauses, the way
> A telescope protects its view of distant mountains
> And all they include, the coming and going,
> Moving correctly up to other levels, preparing to spend the night
> There where the tiny figures halt as darkness comes on,
> Beside some loud torrent in an empty yet personal
> Landscape
> (RM, 29)

Such reflection protects and offers, in a full if miniaturized drama, language in all its comings and goings. It keeps those turns and tendencies visible—doesn't try to solve or dismiss them. As Ashbery puts the idea in *Three Poems*: "How harmless and even helpful the painted wooden components of the Juggernaut look scattered around the yard, patiently waiting to be reassembled!" (TP, 20). What that protection provides is an arena or stage to work out and take responsibility for the many-sided give-and-take going on between steps and words: "hadn't the point / Of all this new construction been to provide / A protected medium for the exchanges each felt of such vital / Concern" (RM, 31). The result is:

> a kind of sweet acknowledgment of how
> The past is yours, to keep invisible if you wish

But also to make absurd elaborations with
And in this way prolong your dance of non-discovery
In brittle, useless architecture that is nevertheless
The map of your desires, irreproachable, beyond
Madness and the toe of approaching night, if only
You desire to arrange it this way.
(RM, 31)

Such a poetry acknowledges and works out the limits of our desire to know, but in a protected place where we can really see it since it has been pulled out of discovery's straightforward drive, at least for a moment. It displays the drama we, as finite creatures, participate in.

In the second half of this book, I examine the careers of three younger writers who combine, in various ways, the two different manners of bringing to life the finite possibilities of "our investment in words, in the world" (C, 61) I have been examining. Like Bishop and Wittgenstein, they often enter areas where language's limits are in play through suffering the collapse of the desire to know with certainty. And like Ashbery and Thoreau, they have discovered various methods of reflectively exploring that area. Hass's "Meditation at Lagunitas" from *Praise* (1979, pp. 4–5) is a good example of how individually distinctive each poet's combination of suffering and exploring limits turns out to be. Hass began the poem, he remarked in a 1981 interview, in response to a friend's description of what we now call, simply, theory.[21] We can hear, as the poem begins, how the poet wants to sound assured in his clipped, dismissive handling of his friend's skeptical abstractions but is in fact susceptible to them, comfortable only in those specifics where he can rest, momentarily, in the sound of his own voice:

All the new thinking is about loss.
In this it resembles all the old thinking.
The idea, for example, that each particular erases
the luminous clarity of a general idea. That the clown-
faced woodpecker probing the dead sculpted trunk
of that black birch is, by his presence,
some tragic falling off from a first world
of undivided light. Or the other notion that,
because there is in this world no one thing
to which the bramble of *blackberry* corresponds,
a word is elegy to what it signifies.

From the Greeks to Derrida, two different notions are pulled together in a single sense of loss. As Alan Shapiro puts it in commenting on these much-remarked lines, in the fall from "general idea" or "undivided" "first world" to a clown-faced "particular," and then in the second slip from that particular to the words that only testify to its absence, we are drenched in an elegiac sense of "double erasure."[22] The uneasiness in Hass's voice, however, is not with these skeptical facts themselves; it is an uneasiness, rather, with a certain way of talking:

> We talked about it late last night and in the voice
> of my friend, there was a thin wire of grief, a tone
> almost querulous. After a while I understood that,
> talking this way, everything dissolves: *justice*,
> *pine, hair, woman, you*, and *I*.

Hass understands, along with Cavell, that there is something both disquieting and "essential to the way we possess language" in such grief at its nonguaranteed concepts. It is an easy, familiar grief, a too-simple response to finitude that Hass explores by entering into it, trying it out for himself. What drives such a way of speaking? Does he have an Othello in himself? "After a while," he notes, "I understood." He realizes, thinking through his own experience, that such grief is generated by the dynamics of desire itself. Looking back, in his present-tense meditation, on the discussion last night, he notes how easy it had been to enter into that way of speaking and its world-erasing dynamics:

> There was a woman
> I made love to and I remembered how, holding
> her small shoulders in my hands sometimes,
> I felt a violent wonder at her presence
> like a thirst for salt, for my childhood river
> with its island willows, silly music from the pleasure boat,
> muddy places where we caught the little orange-silver fish
> called *pumpkinseed*. It hardly had to do with her.
> Longing, we say, because desire is full
> of endless distances. I must have been the same to her.

Hass does not deny the path desire takes. As his friend had suggested, the violence of "wonder" had dissolved her physical "presence," leaving it behind as a "tragic falling off from a first world"—a world, in all its maternal fluidity, over there, its music sung across an unbridgeable distance. She was so lost that the embrace, as skepticism tells us, "hardly had to do with her."

What is crucial, though, is the next phrase, apparently a throwaway, where Hass pauses over the way we speak about such experiences: "Longing, we say, because desire is full / of endless distances." The word we use about such situations, *longing*, has built within it a picture of the object of desire as over there, at a *long*, impossible distance. Such a way of speaking understands desire as inevitably driven and subverted by distance, the world always, eventually, to be left for dead. But if that is only a way of speaking, the poet realizes as he looks back on last night, there must be other ways of handling finitude that do not give away the world. He remembers again, *in the present*:

> But I remember so much, the way her hands dismantled bread,
> the thing her father said that hurt her, what
> she dreamed. There are moments when the body is as numinous
> as words, days that are the good flesh continuing.
> Such tenderness, those afternoons and evenings,
> saying *blackberry, blackberry, blackberry*.

Stepping back from that late-night way of talking or, in Cavell's terms, recovering from, after succumbing to, "the conditions of skepticism," he names a stubborn series of particulars that do not give way before its claims: not a lost paradise but the way her hands moved, things her father said, what she dreamed. That he was able to notice these things without staking a claim of possession must mean, he continues, that there is another way of responding to the world: what he describes as using words "tenderly." (Other Hass poems use the terms "casually" or "intimately" here.) Just as the separateness of another person, part of any intimate encounter, could open your eyes to *her* hands or dreams rather than call into play the groaning machinery of longing, so a "tender" use of words, recognizing that the "brambles of *blackberry*" correspond to no one thing, might hold them lightly, letting them touch the world without having to consider mastering it. "Words come to us from a distance," writes Cavell: "Meaning them is accepting that fact of their distance." "Tenderness," then, would be a use of language that brings together an acknowledgment of finitude—one that calls the temporary world of flesh "good"—with the poet's sense, discovered as he writes, that there is something "numinous" or fully alive in what doesn't hold forever.

An early poem by Jorie Graham, "Two Paintings by Gustav Klimt" from *Erosion* (1983, pp. 61–63), quite powerfully demonstrates how different in texture, from poet to poet, is the realm where, as Graham puts it, she "experience[s] the limits of the imagination . . . feel[ing] (in the act of writing the poem) what it is that escapes me, what judges me, keeping me true."[23]

The poem begins with the poet examining a late-nineteenth-century painting by Klimt of a beech forest. As Graham describes it, what attracts her to the painting is the way, light "glitter[ing] / on the trees / row after perfect row," it answers our demand for beauty, showing what can be made of the world's differently angled and valued surfaces: "the sum / of these delays / is the beautiful, the human / beautiful, / body of flaws.[24] This opening response—in which the poet, arranging words, finds herself gazing at another beautiful arrangement—raises the issue of "the conditions of language as such" that the poem will go on to explore. And much like Bishop playing out her tapestry or Hass mimicking his friend's tone of voice, Graham must unfold her instinctive assent to the painting in order to acknowledge, for herself, its attraction. The painting's beauty seems related to its solidity, its sense of certainty and clear definition. "The dead," she proposes, feeling her way through the idea, "would give anything" to be returned from openness to this grounded world where "flaws" are predictably handled:

> The dead
>   in their sheer
> open parenthesis, what they
>   wouldn't give
>
> for something to lean on
>   that won't
> give way. I think I
>   would weep
> for the moral nature
>   of this world,
>
> for right and wrong like pools
>   of shadow
> and light you can step in
>   and out of

If *I* were dead, she remarks, I would weep in longing for a world as solid as "this yellow beech forest, / this *buchen-wald*." With the uttering of that dark term, the name of the Nazi death camp, the poem falters, almost stutters—the word itself, and then the painting, and then Graham's instinctive assent to (her succumbing to) its claims all stained by the twentieth-century import of the term. Graham begins to take responsibility for the loved, now-broken words she holds in her hand by ever-so-slightly referring us back to her previous references in the poem to injustice and the anonymous dead and imagining herself, post-Holocaust, walking such a beech-forest:

> one autumn afternoon, late
>   in the twentieth
> century, in hollow light,
>   in gaseous light. . . .

As in the manner of both Bishop and Stevens, the stuttered ellipsis signals a collapse in her initial leaning on certainty. It opens a space for the poet to trace out, and suffer through, the sources of that quick assent to the promises of the beautiful. Though the scene is a poet gazing at a painting, she is also, in Gerald Bruns's words about Heidegger, at "a loss for words," exposed to their "mystery, . . . density, . . . danger."[25]

She enters that space by remembering another painting by Klimt—an incomplete study of a woman's body "found in his studio" after his sudden death. Her body, in the painting, is:

> open at its point of
>   entry,
> rendered in graphic,
>   pornographic,
>
> detail—something like
>   a scream
> between her legs. Slowly,
>   feathery,
> he had begun to paint
>   a delicate
>
> garment (his trademark)
>   over this mouth
> of her body.

That the painting was discovered in an unfinished state exposes both the violation knowingly engaged in by the painter—the scream is an inadvertent acknowledgment—and its connection with his "delicate" beautiful surfaces. With this garment, we find ourselves in territory very close to Bishop's link between the eye's tapestry and colonialism. Held up to our consideration by the two accidents (*Buchenwald* passed from one century to the next, the unfinished painting), both Klimt's "garment" and the first painting's "blue air . . . yellow trees" with its notion of "right and wrong like pools / of shadow

/ and light" are eroded by the screams they seem based on. A never-ending series of questions appears in the space of the once beautiful and solid.

But the poem goes even farther, I think, for the poet has also found herself, in her own attraction to beauty and solidity, brought up short. What she has seen—what she has suffered the display and unraveling of—is the way our human drive for a firm surface, a coherent story line, and a recasting of flaws as beauty is potentially complicit with such horrors. Think of that fabric partly painted in—what does it reveal, or "measure," about the drive to know and define and gaze in wonder?

> The fabric
>
> defines the surface,
> > the story,
> so we are drawn to it,
> > its blues
> and yellows glittering
> > like a stand
>
> of beech trees late
> > one afternoon
> in Germany, in fall.
> > It is called
> Buchenwald, it is
> > 1890. In
>
> the finished painting
> > the argument
> has something to do
> > with pleasure.

In the silence at the end of this poem, I would suggest, the same "argument" goes on—this poem, like Wittgenstein's wrestling with his own voice, being crucially not finished, the attraction to and the eroding of confidence in the pleasures this poem takes in beauty and stability being never settled. That struggle has brought her to a place where she sees, as if it were a landscape reflectively to be explored, the full emotional and social import of describing or ordering or establishing a boundary—sees it by living through its collapse.

The first of Michael Palmer's twelve-part sequence "Notes for Echo Lake," in his book of the same title (1982), offers a final example of both dramatically and reflectively inhabiting our finite linguistic conditions (EL, 3–6). This is a difficult poem, and not all of it will become clear until it is read within the context of the entire book in which it appears. I will unfold that context in chapter 7, but a rough pass through the poem now will offer one last demonstration of how an acknowledgment of language's limits becomes a first step in its renewal. This first section of the poem is composed of thirty-three groups of sentences, lined out as prose. What initiated the poem, Palmer remarks in our interview (see chapter 8), was a request by Charles Bernstein to "tell us a little something about yourself" for Bernstein's magazine, *L=A=N=G=U=A=G=E*. Palmer took that as a chance to "sort through and to see how, in an utterly counter-Wordsworthian way perhaps, one might inscribe past experience and even past epiphanies, so to speak." Bernstein asked Palmer to perform the basic ("Wordsworthian") lyric task of describing or creating a self, which Palmer attempted while also responding to the truth that skepticism about such notions as the self had presented him with. And he did so deliberately, wondering if, by reflectively "sort[ing] through" and attending to the now-acknowledged-as-fragile space of inscribing one's past, a new mode of expression might be generated. What becomes visible and usable, he asks, when one is "at a loss for words" (EL, 11)? In what sort of words, to borrow from Cavell, is the self "regained as gone"?

"Notes for Echo Lake 1" begins in this way:

He says this red as dust, eyes a literal self among selves and picks the coffee up.

Memory is kind, a kindness, a kind of unlistening, a grey wall even toward which you move.

It was the woman beside him who remarked that he never looked anyone in the eye. (This by water's edge.)

This by water's edge.

And all of the song 'divided into silences', or 'quartered in three silences'.

Dear Charles, I began again and again to work, always with no confidence as Melville might explain. Might complain.

A message possibly intercepted, possibly never written. A letter she had sent him.

But what had his phrase been exactly, "Welcome to the Valley of Tears," or maybe "Valley of Sorrows." At least one did feel welcome, wherever it was.

A kind of straight grey wall beside which they walk, she the older by a dozen years, he carefully unlistening.

What can we do with this? The first thing to notice is that Palmer acknowledges the difficulty of giving an account of himself; instead of producing the straightforward bit of self-reflection demanded, he finds himself, like, say Gertrude Stein or Willem de Kooning, beginning "again and again . . . with no confidence."[26] Working in such a way forces him to operate without certainty, entering a realm where, as Thoreau puts it, acknowledging that "we are lost" allows us to "begin to find ourselves, and realize where we are and the infinite extent of our relations" (SW, 50). Each of these thirty-three prose stabs, in returning to and writing out of an experience of not-knowing or of not being certain, helps unfold that finite condition, showing what is generated "If one lives in it" (EL, 4). Though the past, in such an approach, is dismembered rather than remembered—"By stages you dismember the story" (EL, 68), Palmer writes later in the poem—inhabiting such an uncertain space becomes rich and charged. We will see something similar in each of the poets I examine here. Refusing to allow an already understood narrative to move the work forward on its own, the poet dwells within a sense of heightened attention to his own words; he makes "our investment in words, in the world" visible by beginning again and again.[27]

We can go on, noting that what Palmer does in these opening lines is link notes on his present linguistic situation with notes on other, apparently quite distant situations, allowing one set to draw the other out and begin forming, together, a new figure—not the requested self-portrait but the reflective thinking (the "sort[ing] through") generated by the request. Elements of Palmer's background, then, are pulled into the poem, but in a way that insists on their ties to the unfolding poem, not to what actually happened. "Each calling," as Cavell puts it, "is isomorphic with every other . . . allegories and measures of one another. . . . What matters is that he show in the way he writes his faithfulness to the specific conditions and acts of writing as such" (SW, 61–62). Crucial events appear and reappear, but often in quite different forms as the unfolding figure of the poem makes new demands on them and seeks to use them in new areas of exploration. Palmer puts it this way a few lines later: "Beginning and ending. As a work begins and ends itself or begins and rebegins or starts and stops. Ideas as elements of the working not as propositions of a work, even in a propositional art. (Someone said someone thought.)" That is, ideas and events, what someone might have said or thought, are first of all, in this charged area, "elements of the working." They are important as elements in the poet's reflective unfolding of the uncertain landscape he has entered. We must read, then, in much the same way— tracking the results of our act of attention, being willing to continually descend into and acknowledge our uncertainty, since a confirming, all-now-revealed pattern is likely never to be supplied, either by poet or by reader.

But there is much that we *can* do here. For example, the uncertainty in the act of writing gets picked up in a charged, unsettled interchange between a man and a woman that is repeated throughout the entire sequence. One imagines this as an element of what Palmer might have used to describe himself, now present as a half-erased fragment speaking more forcefully to the uncertain writing situation than to any picture of the self. Part of what is dramatized in the poem is the poet's struggle to see clearly the implications of the couple's interchange. How does it go? The man says something out of embarrassment ("red as dust"), perhaps responding to the charge that "he never looked anyone in the eye." One can imagine that he responded, red-faced, to that charge of self-absorption by looking at her ("eyes a literal self among selves"), picking up a cup, and perhaps by muttering "Welcome to the Valley of Tears"—words, like the actions, that are distancing and self-protective. If one is willing to speculate a bit, in a direction increasingly confirmed as the poem moves on, we might note that she plays Echo to his Narcissus, attempting, "by water's edge," to call his attention to and jolt him out of what seems a world-denying self-absorption. In a way, as in Ovid, she's propositioning him, saying "look me in the eye" or "listen to me." She unsettles him and forces him to try to decide what is going on. My point here is that the uncertainty held in common between the under-skeptical-pressure writing situation and the red-faced encounter prompts Palmer to draw the two figures toward each other, making a third figure. The act of remembering, trying to eye and find the "literal self" that Charles Bernstein had asked for, is compared to "a kind of unlistening, a grey wall even," but that is also the same wall where the "carefully unlistening" younger man walks alongside the older woman. Reading the figures together as they interact in the writing situation, we might say that in the act of making our selves coherent and consecutive, we, like Narcissus or the young man, fail to listen. In attempting to eye a simple "literal self," we establish a wall or a barrier between our current selves and our pasts. Like Bishop's uneasiness about the way we map new territories or Graham's shocked questions about our attraction to beauty, this becomes the acknowledgment of language's finitude the poem enters and explores. The young man and the poet, each red-faced and uncertain, are accused (perhaps accuse themselves) of "unlistening" and thus are forced, in an acknowledgment of limits, to listen, to look "again and again" into the *I*; perhaps, in so doing, they will be able to renew language.

One finds these ideas confirmed as Palmer continues his first set of notes, folding into the growing figure a set of remarks on language that are woven together with another fragment of a memory. Here, too, the issue of uncertainty—being brought up short at the accusation of not listening—is crucial. I am doing a bit of selection here in order to bring this strand of thought out more clearly:

> Breaking like glass Tom had said and the woman from the island. Regaining consciousness he saw first stars then a face leaning over him and heard the concerned voice, "Hey baby you almost got *too* high."
>
> Was was and is. In the story the subject disappears.
>
> They had agreed the sign was particular precisely because arbitrary and that it included the potential for (carried the sign of) its own dissolution, and that there was a micro-syntax below the order of the sentence and even of the word, and that in the story the subject disappears it never disappears. 1963: only one of the two had the gift of memory.
>
> . . . .
>
> If one lives in it. 'Local' and 'specific' and so on finally seeming less interesting than the 'particular' whatever that may locate.
>
> "What I really want to show here is that it is not at all clear *a priori* which are the simple colour concepts."
>
> Sign that empties itself at each instance of meaning, and how else to reinvent attention.
>
> Sign that empties . . . That is *he* would ask *her*. He would be the asker and she unlistening, nameless mountains in the background partly hidden by cloud.
>
> . . . .
>
> As I began again and again, and each beginning identical with the next, meaning each one accurate, each a projection, each a head bending over the motionless form.
>
> And he sees himself now as the one motionless on the ground, now as the one bending over. Lying in an alley between a house and a fence (space barely wide enough for a body), opening his eyes he saw stars and heard white noise followed in time by a face and a single voice.

The memory, losing consciousness ("Breaking like glass") and then coming to an awareness of a face leaning over and a single voice, becomes, as these lines progress and reflect on themselves, a version of Palmer's work in the poem: each note, each tentative beginning out of uncertainty, is a "projection . . . a head bending over the motionless form" and a discovery of voice. Each new attempt at developing the poem, perhaps even switching the roles of he and she, uses language in a way "that empties itself at each instance of meaning"—the poet continuing, "how else to reinvent attention." That is, the act of paying renewed attention that the woman demanded of the young man and that Charles Bernstein requested is accomplished through an emptying of confidence—a breaking or dissolving of "consciousness": "Lying in an alley between a house and a fence . . . opening his eyes." In linguistic terms, now also folded into this experience of uncertainty, it is an act of attention made possible by acknowledging that the sign "included the potential for (carried the sign of) its own dissolution." That dissolution (of the sign, the *I*, consciousness, memory), "If one lives in it," bending over and beginning again and again where "the subject disappears," opens up a series of connections "below the order of the sentence and even of the word." And as we have seen even in these first lines, the subject "never disappears"; it reappears as an act of attention.

Thus, the difference between "Was was and is," which the poet is wrestling with in telling his story, or Wittgenstein's insistence, quoted here, that "simple colour concepts" disappear upon close examination, become not crippling limitations but means of emptying one's confident deployment of such tools as memory or the *I* in order to "reinvent attention" to what had been silenced by those confident signs.[28] In fact, Wittgenstein's remark that in his *Philosophical Investigations* he was offering not a coherent road guide but an account of "travel[ing] over a wide field of thought criss-cross in every direction" seems very much to describe the sort of nonconfident, renewed attention Palmer achieves here.[29] We could say that in "liv[ing] in" language's limits—that is, in reflectively drawing out the implications of having no confidence as a language user—Palmer has attentively opened a door. As the last lines of "Notes for Echo Lake 1" suggest, the poet-as-Narcissus has seen the simple notion of language mirroring the self shatter and has fallen (and been welcomed) into a different notion of language: "She stands before the mirror touches the floor. Language reaches for the talk as someone falls. A dead language opens and opens one door." Returning to the couple and the half-understood proposition, one could think of that as entering a risky, nonguaranteed ground: "There is a grey wall past which we walk arm in arm, fools if we do greater fools if we don't." In this reflective space, "arm in arm" with the uncertainties of inhabiting language, Palmer and the other poets whose careers I now go on to examine risk foolishness and find life.

1. Elizabeth Bishop's Fine, Torn Fish-Nets

Elizabeth Bishop's work is my first example of a poetry that is interested in, and increasingly takes place within, spaces where we live out what Stanley Cavell calls "the truth of skepticism" (CR, 241)—the fact that our placement in the world, our condition, is not guaranteed by knowing and is not marked by certainty. Her poems look closely at or acknowledge the limits of our drives to grasp or know or make a home; and they discover that such drives, once forced to operate without guarantees of mastery, are quite powerfully charged and frail and alive.[1] Our actions (and their implications and the cloud of questions that surround them) open up and become newly visible. As Bishop's poem "Over 2,000 Illustrations and a Complete Concordance" (CPO, 57–59) puts it in an often-repeated figure: descriptive lines, under the pressure of the demand to know with certainty, break down and are seen as too coarse. They lose hold of the world; the lines move apart, and a space opens up between where, authority and certainty dispersed, our now-seen-as-finite human drives to create order ignite in a rainbow of questions and fragile distinctions. In Cavell's language, through a process of "endless specific succumbings . . . and endless specific recoveries," "one's humanity, or finitude, is . . . accepted, suffered" (DK, 30; TN, 39). The image in "Over 2,000 Illustrations" is an engraving in a family Bible:

> The eye drops, weighted, through the lines
> the burin made, the lines that move apart
> like ripples above sand,
> dispersing storms, God's spreading fingerprint,
> and painfully, finally, that ignite
> in watery prismatic white-and-blue.

Her poems, to put it simply, investigate what is ignited in this space where the fragility of our gestures comes painfully alive. Her strongest poems are like "Jerónimo's House" in her first book—structures of "perishable / clapboards" or "chewed-up paper / glued with spit," which, when looked at closely enough, are seen as splintered by "writing-paper / lines of light" swirling and torn with life.

She spent an entire career thinking about how best to frame and dramatize this investigation, and in this chapter I would like to try to describe the steps she went through in this process. Her distinction as a poet—and, I am convinced, the reason for her enormous influence on younger writers—is that she demonstrates, in a completely persuasive way, that making a home within the charged uneasiness of language ("the word") measures and is measured by the equally charged and uneasy uses we put it to "in the world": remembering, describing, traveling, loving. Questions raised by language's starts and stops are as incandescent as (are in fact the same as) questions raised by the breaking down of the self or the home or the everyday. Though Bishop makes the connection between these activities seem inevitable, it took some very careful work.

Let me begin with three early parables from her first book, *North & South* (1946), which quite clearly lay out the crucial features of this territory.[2] "The Unbeliever" (CPO, 22) borrows an image from John Bunyan—"He sleeps on the top of a mast"—to picture a skeptical refusal to be taken in by a too-simple belief in human constructs. Unlike a cloud that, peering at his own reflection, pronounces itself "founded on marble pillars" and "secure in introspection," and unlike a gull that, upon a similar downward glance, sees itself gracing the top of a marble monument, the unbeliever refuses such blinded claims. Instead:

> he sleeps on the top of his mast
> with his eyes closed tight.
> The gull inquired into his dream
> which was, "I must not fall.
> The spangled sea below wants me to fall.
> It is hard as diamonds; it wants to destroy us all."

He is right, of course; there is nothing secure about being perched above a sea that could easily destroy him, but his response, "eyes fast closed," is clearly inadequate. How might he move forward? "The Gentleman of Shalott" (CPO, 9–10) begins to answer by playing off of Tennyson's meditation on the charged distance between reflection and the world (or reflection and the spangled sea) by creating a character who, convinced he is "half looking-glass" with "a mirrored reflection / somewhere along the line / of what we call the spine," finds himself thrust into the middle of a series of questions. "Which eye's his eye?" he is forced to ask, thrown out of his normal ease with his body and apparently single self into a space where he's "in doubt" and where there's "little margin for error." As I noted in the introduction, he enters that charged space between and, knowing that a sudden slip of the glass would put him "in a fix— / only one leg, etc.," he senses a sort of responsive aliveness in the constant self-monitoring he has to perform in order to walk or run or even clasp hands: "The uncertainty / he says he / finds exhilarating. He loves / that sense of constant re-adjustment." Aware of the mirrored limits he works within, working within a system without believing in it, Bishop's gentleman suggests a way for the unbeliever to open his eyes.[3]

"The Man-Moth" (CPO, 14–15) goes one step further and describes how it is that one's confidence in the eyes or hands or other apparently straightforward machinery of our lives slips in the first place. Its central figure is derived from a newspaper misprint. Part human, part moth drawn to the light, thinking "the moon is a small hole at the top of the sky, / proving the sky quite useless for protection," he climbs toward a confrontation with the fragility of our condition. Although he fails, he is left, when he returns to his home down below, "facing the wrong way" when attempting to use or inhabit the machinery most of us take for granted:

> he returns
> to the pale subways of cement he calls his home. He flits,
> he flutters, and cannot get aboard the silent trains
> fast enough to suit him. The doors close swiftly.
> The Man-Moth always seats himself facing the wrong way
> and the train starts at once at its full, terrible speed,
> without a shift in gears or a gradation of any sort.
> He cannot tell the rate at which he travels backwards.

Most Bishop poems take place in the uneasy awareness described here. A hole in the sky having proven home or family or self "quite useless for protection," her poems explore how it feels, in response to that failure, to be seated backwards on such subways as description or reflection or memory. Deprived of the comforting belief that movement is securely governed by "gears" or "gradation," they open themselves to its "full, terrible" implications, "constant[ly] re-adjust[ing]" in a world where one cannot, with certainty, "tell the rate at which he travels." Such an experience of fragility, the poem continues, leaves the skeptic dangerously out of control—"recurrent dreams / . . . underlie / his rushing brain," and, as in "The Unbeliever," suicide beckons— but the experience also has the potential to produce a new sort of speech. Call it a tear:

from the lids
one tear, his only possession, like the bee's sting, slips.
Slyly he palms it, and if you're not paying attention
he'll swallow it. However, if you watch, he'll hand it over,
cool as from underground springs and pure enough to drink.

Bishop's poetry traces the way she gradually learned to watch for and share the prismatic, teary rainbows produced by an awareness of the fragility of our nets and structures and means of ordering. It shows the way she learned to open her eyes, move off of her mast, and inhabit the space of finitude, inhabit the truth of skepticism.

How to inhabit those conditions is the issue raised by most of the poems in *North & South*. The poems in the first half of the book begin an answer by pointing toward objects or situations in the world that seem actively to acknowledge and struggle with the limits of their claims. Though this is never explicitly stated, they provide Bishop with models by which she might measure her own voice. Let me look at four. The glassed-over map that Bishop examines in the book's opening poem seems to deliberately look at and call attention to its own activity. Or more precisely, Bishop reads the map in this way, as if it were signaling its struggle with these issues. "The Map" (CPO, 3) frames representation as a sort of tension between the active, agitated land and the quiet sea. Bishop's eye is first drawn to the space where the land and the sea meet. There, a certain ambiguity in the map's shading—"Shadows, or are they shallows, at its edges"—leads her into a series of questions about representation. You could say that the distinction between land and sea is blurred or is seen as too coarse. When it is examined, it opens up a series of unsettled issues. If the shading represents shallows, perhaps we are seeing ledges off the coast where "weeds hang to the simple blue from green." Or perhaps the land is leaning down "to lift the sea from under, / drawing it unperturbed around itself." Though the discussion moves on, the notion that the sea is being represented as "simple" or "unperturbed" echoes throughout the poem. The watery shadow around Newfoundland, for example, "lies flat and still." Under glass, the ocean seems enclosed in a greenhouse, its bays coddled "as if they were expected to blossom." In fact, the water has a smooth, attractive finish we feel compelled to touch: "These peninsulas take the water between thumb and finger / like women feeling for the smoothness of yard-goods." At the same time, even as the map calls attention to the waves' quiet "conformation" to its investigatory expectations, it also seems to think hard about the amount of effort necessary to maintain that illusion of mastery.

"Mapped waters are more quiet than the land is," she remarks, linking the land's leaning and tugging to the way "Norway's hare runs south in agitation," various "profiles investigate the sea," and, most strikingly, to the way the mapmaker signals his own flustered boundary-breaking:

> The names of seashore towns run out to sea,
> the names of cities cross the neighboring mountains
> —the printer here experiencing the same excitement
> as when emotion too far exceeds its cause.

The map, that is, seems to deliberately acknowledge and display the impossibility of accomplishing what it claims to be about—mastering and quieting, making "flat and still" a world that is moving and various. Apparently backwards to the act of representing, it seems to come alive in the dilemma, raising a shower of questions.[4] Its colors are "delicate" rather than coarse because they are unsettled, torn, and enlivened by a series of questions.

"Large Bad Picture" and "Cirque d'Hiver" work in much the same way; they are objects that, as Bishop plays them out, seem to sit backwards to their conventions and model a possible poetry. "Large Bad Picture" (CPO, 11–12), with its suspended ships and awkward technique—too-high cliffs, "perfect waves," "burnt match-stick" spars, and birds "hanging in *n*'s in banks"—seems to call attention both to its drive to comprehend and master and to its failure to complete that exchange:

> In the pink light
> the small red sun goes rolling, rolling,
> round and round and round at the same height
> in perpetual sunset, comprehensive, consoling,
>
> while the ships consider it.
> Apparently they have reached their destination.
> It would be hard to say what brought them there,
> commerce or contemplation.

Commerce, let us suppose, is what subways or an artist's facility with paint make possible; it gets us from one point to another, hands something over. Contemplation happens when commerce breaks down or takes a holiday and no goal is reached. This painting—the awkwardness of its technique playing against its stalled ships to suggest that the limits of painting are what is being "consider[ed]" here—seems to propose that the failure of commerce allows you to see or contemplate other live issues. Not entirely convincingly, Bishop gestures toward the liveness of this tangle of questions by describing birds "crying, crying, / the only sound there is / except for occasional sighing / as a large aquatic animal breathes." Bishop reads the mechanical toy in "Cirque d'Hiver" (CPO, 31) in much the same way. Composed of a "circus horse with *real* white hair" and a dancer on his back turning under a "spray of *artificial* roses," the object here again dramatizes a confrontation with its limits. The toy wants to look real but acknowledges its artificiality. That problem, in fact, seems to animate the horse—as it did the land in "The Map" or the stalled ships in "Large Bad Picture." The horse "has a formal, melancholy soul," one both made and alive. It feels the dancer's toes "dangl[ing] *toward* his back" but seems not to sense the pole piercing his body and reappearing "as a big tin key." The horse brings representation to life because it raises such issues "rather desperately." The poet stares at him because, in his declaration of limits—"we stare and say, 'Well, we have come this far' "—he is "the more intelligent by far." He brings to life the full, terrible weight of finitude.

So does "The Monument" (CPO, 23–25), when we learn how to look at it. In fact, learning to look at the issues it raises, learning to hear and respond to the acknowledgment of limits embodied in its creation, is its plot. Its two voices play out for us the implications of its acknowledgment of its status, claiming eventually that all art (all fully conscious behavior) begins with an entrance into such an awareness of limits:

> It is the beginning of a painting,
> a piece of sculpture, or poem, or monument,
> and all of wood. Watch it closely.

In the next stage of Bishop's growth as a writer she will be able to watch those conditions at play in her own actions; here, she is still explicating the gestures of someone else. The monument Bishop describes, as Bonnie Costello has shown, is patterned after a Max Ernst frottage—a paper on wood rubbing in which patterns in the wood's grain are made visible on paper.[5] In this case, selective rubbing (shading, we might say, recalling "The Map") seems to have produced a set of wooden boxes, each turned at an angle from the one below, topped with something like a wooden fleur-de-lys with slanting poles. This structure so dominates the rubbing that we cannot get beyond it: "there is no 'far away,' / and we are far away within the view." Just as the map's shadows or the circus horse's hair raise and open issues that seemingly dominate each object's commentary, so we quickly find ourselves "far away within" the monument's issues. Think of the lines of an engraving giving way

and an observer's eyes being drawn deep within the space between. The rest
of the rubbing is a blank background that our eyes read as sky against sea:

> A sea of narrow, horizontal boards
> lies out behind our lonely monument,
> its long grains alternating right and left
> like floor-boards—spotted, swarming-still,
> and motionless. A sky runs parallel,
> and it is palings, coarser than the sea's:
> splintery sunlight and long-fibred clouds.

As one voice tries, fairly straightforwardly, to get another to see a pattern in
the rubbing—an "artist-prince / might have wanted to build a monument /
to mark a tomb or boundary"—another voice, eyes on the issues the piece
raises, skeptically resists:

> the sky looks wooden, grained with cloud.
> It's like a stage-set; it is all so flat!
> Those clouds are full of glistening splinters!
> . . . .
> A temple of crates in cramped and crated scenery,
> what can it prove?
> I am tired of breathing this *eroded* air,
> this dryness in which the monument is cracking. (emphasis mine)

Together, playing off each other, the voices bring the poem to a position where,
like the bad painting or self-critical map, the monument's apparent claims
to mean or dominate are "eroded," and it seems instead to be raising and
responding to what the poem calls "the conditions of its existence." It hovers
between "commerce or contemplation." Its foregrounded acknowledgment
of its own texture calls attention to the fact that "It is an artifact / of wood"
and therefore a deliberately chosen, vulnerable, counter statement to the
continuous world in which "the light goes around it / like a prowling animal,
/ or the rain falls on it, or the wind blows into it":

> Wood holds together better
> than sea or cloud or sand could by itself,
> much better than real sea or sand or cloud.
> It *chose* that way to grow and not to move. (emphasis mine)

The monument is a commentary on human choice. The choice to mean or
"commemorate" is made within limits, and certain claims are off limits. Which

is to say, "there is no 'far away.'" There is neither an assured connection to a far away grounding for this odd scene nor is there a convincing means of dismissing it (it's nothing—the bones are far away). There is only a chance to move "far away within" the monument's playing out its role as shelter—that is, a form by which we inhabit our condition:

> The bones of the artist-prince may be inside
> or far away on even drier soil.
> But roughly but adequately it can shelter
> what is within (which after all
> cannot have been intended to be seen).

That there is no way of knowing opens the lines and gives us a space in which to move and think and suffer. Declaring off limits the claim that what is inside can be made visible opens up a different and more finite game: the play between roughness and adequacy which directs all of our human concerns. Enter into *that* play, suggests the monument. As John Ashbery will write, years later: "it is a metaphor / Made to include us" (SP, 76).

Another set of poems in this first book describes the mental experience of entering into such an acknowledgment of limits. But, stopping just short of actively entering the area herself, Bishop offers allegories or dream representations of that state. She describes, rather than enacts, the mental events we have seen her discovering in maps and paintings and circus toys. Let me look at this set of poems briefly. "From the Country to the City" (CPO, 13) uses the act of driving toward a city to picture an intense mental state. The road the poet travels on seems like the tights of a harlequin, while the neon-lit city can be seen as his "scribbled over" trunk, shining brain, and "shadowy, tall dunce-cap." Startled at sunlight flashing on telephone wires far distant from the city, the writer realizes that the "glittering," reflective arrangements of that brain are not easily confinable: their threatening, dunce-cap vibrations are drawn "for miles . . . out countrywards." A related picture of reflective disturbance can be found in Bishop's dream poem "The Weed" (CPO, 20–21). There, a dead body's cold heart, holding to a "final thought / . . . drawn immense and clear," is split apart by a weed pushing up through it. As a result—"a flood of water" breaking into two streams from the split-open thought, each stream composed "of racing images / . . . scenes that it had once reflected"— the heart's fixed, final thought is shattered into a fluid, contradictory flood of racing emotions. Similarly, in "Sleeping Standing Up" (CPO, 30), the idea that the world turns as we sleep suggests not only that a bureau could be thought of as lying "on the wall" but also that the controlled, orderly, "recumbent" thoughts of day "rise as the others fall, / stand up and make a forest of thick-set trees." "The armored cars of dreams," she suggests, playing out the idea, are designed for the "dangerous" work of moving through such "thick-set" thoughts. And yet what actually happens when we venture into such woods, attempting like Hansel and Gretel to follow a trail of "crumbs or pebbles" home, is that all trails disappear or dissolve in the moss:

> sometimes we went too fast
> and ground them underneath. How stupidly we steered
>   until the night was past
> and never found out where the cottage was.

In all three of these poems, then, Bishop describes the limits of reflection or analysis. Though the images are different—incessant, never-quiet vibrations; racing, non–still images; or a trackless maze—each poem imagines what happens when we are forced backward to our normal expectations about thinking. What does it feel like to live with doubts about commerce, or our ability to conceptually navigate and hold fast? these poems ask. Their answers, through an indirect screen, are ones we are now becoming used to: one feels frightened, alive, exposed, desperate.

The other question that drives these poems is where best to experience such moments of productive suspension? Where might we play out, and not just point out, the brain's alive wandering? Where does our desire to mark and know get eroded into a sense of desperate alertness? The two prose fables Bishop wrote at about this time attempt to answer. To put it simply, they suggest that the finite places a poet might come fully to inhabit are linguistic ones. "The Sea & Its Shore" (1937) describes a situation in which it is possible to live "the most literary life possible" (CPR, 172). In its invented world, a Bishop namesake, Edwin Boomer, is given the job of keeping a stretch of shoreline free of paper.[6] He is surrounded by words. The air is full of blowing paper; the sand is covered with inscriptions; at times, "the whole world . . . seem[ed] printed" (CPR, 178). Yet, because all of these words are destined to be burned or scuffed out, language here has had its authority erased or altered—just like the map's or the monument's or the dunce-cap neon's claims to represent. In such a place, Boomer sits backward to the normal functioning of language. Where birds flying by seem "inspired by a brain, by long tradition, by a desire that could often be understood to reach some place or obtain some thing," papers loose in the same wind "had no discernible goal, no brain, no feeling of race or group. They soared up, fell down, could not decide, hesitated, subsided, flew straight to their doom in the sea, or turned over in mid-air to collapse on the sand without another motion. If any manner was their favorite, it seemed to be an oblique one, slipping sidewise" (CPR, 174). That is, these goalless, nondirectional papers perform the same hesitant, collapsing, self-reversing maneuvers we've seen illustrated in many of *North & South*'s figures and situations. Like "The Map," they describe reflective dilemmas. But Bishop describes more than watching in these fables, for here, in his tiny hut or "shelter for thinking in," her character Boomer enters into unsponsored flight himself, teasing scraps saved for a few days into various wandering, fantastic sequences. Though he cannot understand or convincingly order all of the scraps, he feels, in the "intensity of his concentration" (CPR, 172), as if he is able "to use his natural faculties more freely" and as if he is "unnaturally wide awake" (CPR, 176, 178). He is like one of those ships "consider[ing]" a perpetual sunset, though his alertness is more convincingly rendered. Boomer enters into the fragility of words, knowing that everything here must in time be burned: "twisting into shapes that sometimes resembled beautiful wrought-iron work, but afterwards . . . dropped apart at a breath" (CPR, 179).

"In Prison" imagines a similar sort of world in which, as Bishop's narrator puts it, being shut off from society with no "inner conviction of . . . eventual relief" (CPR, 184) leads her to "fully . . . realize" her faculties. Here again, "limitations and possibilities" (CPR, 185) or "necessity" and "freedom" (CPR, 191) are combined, alertness actively opening up within a limited space. The very fact that the prisoner's words will have no effect on the world means that she sits backward to their usual drives, a position that frees her to experience what is fresh or alive in their use.[7] For example, she imagines reading in prison "one very dull book . . . on a subject completely foreign to me" whose "terms and purpose" of necessity remain stubbornly opaque. As she imagines it, such a nontransparent text would produce a "sensation of wave-like freshness" by affording her, in "the pleasure, perverse, I suppose, of interpreting it not at all according to its intent," a kind a freely wandering speech in which her choices, like the monument's, would be visible and her own. Constantly readjusting those words—"From my detached, rock-like book I shall be able to draw vast generalizations, abstractions of the grandest, most illuminating sort, like allegories or poems, . . . posing fragments of it against the surroundings and conversations of my prison"—she would be forced into alertness (CPR, 187–88). Similarly, the writing she imagines scribbling on the walls of her cell—commentaries on or adaptations of "the inscriptions already there"—would also be freed by virtue of its anonymous, ungrounded context to demonstrate and experience the true conditions of human speech: "brief, suggestive, anguished, but full of the lights of revelation" (CPR, 188–89). In such situations as these fables sketch, words, rather than a toy horse's "real hair," foreground the "conditions of [our] existence" (CPO, 24).

These fables point to situations in which language might work like a map or a monument to acknowledge and investigate its fragility and corresponding alertness. They know what that alertness would look like, but they do not know where—in what circumstances—such a charged use of language might reasonably occur. Let's say I was in prison, these stories propose; let's say I drank while clearing the beach of trash. Where, in language, do we actively live out the truth of skepticism? In many ways that question drives Bishop's career as a writer. Her first answer, as everyone concerned with her work has noted, is "within the act of description."[8] Description, once one turns backward to it, opens and becomes a place for thinking in, its lines having moved apart. But Bishop's movement to this position was not immediate; it developed slowly. In *North & South*, "Roosters" and "The Fish" are the two most powerful enactments of descriptive tensions, but two other poems, "Love Lies Sleeping" and "Florida," show how she edged up on such poems and are worth some thought. They are interesting because they show her wrestling with how to best frame an acknowledgment of language's fragility or finitude.

"Love Lies Sleeping" (CPO, 16–17) traces the multiple, frail wanderings of the poet's eye and ear making sense of morning in the city. Bishop frames this description with opening and closing addresses that are designed to make clear how frail and tentative such a waking vision actually is. Such a frame is like the map's self-commentary or the frottage's wood grain or the circus horse's desperate eye. It reminds us of how insecure vision is—that it might be lost, in a blink of the eye. It voices the skeptical truth of description, but from outside the process itself. The poem's opening address, for example, asks "earliest morning" to "draw us into daylight" and to "clear away what presses on the brain"—chiefly the "pinks and yellows, letters and twitching signs" of a hangover swelling "between the eyes." The threat sketched here, that since the brain might not fight free of such distorted shapes, its reflective glass might slip at any time, puts all the description that follows in a charged state of potential "re-adjustment." That skeptical threat is renewed by the poem's closing plea to the "queer cupids" of cascading alarms to go easy on the lovers whose hearts are daily sent out for "scourging" and growth, since some, defeated, will never rise again into vision. On any given morning, one might become the figure for whom, head fallen over the edge of the bed, vision is

"inverted and distorted. No. I mean / distorted and revealed, / if he sees at all."
Both addresses—to morning and to the alarms—acknowledge the potentially
disabling, potentially revelatory pressures that vision and description work
under, but they do so at a slight remove from the process itself. It is no surprise
that under these potentially distorting pressures, vision within the poem's
frame constantly shifts scale. Outside her window, the poet sees "an immense
city" that seems "to waver" in "a weak white sky" like a trembling "chemical
'garden' in a jar"; smoke clouds become "ball[s] / of blossom" that bloom and
explode and move off, replaced by a water wagon whose "hissing, snowy fan"
dries to "the pattern / of the cool watermelon."[9] If we read this as we read
Bishop's "The Map," what seems to be at issue is the way description seeks to
domesticate (garden, blossoms, watermelon) something quite resistant, even
violent and threatening; we can almost see her, constantly shifting scale, trying
and failing to bring the city under control. But her energy as a writer seems
devoted to the frame that raises these issues rather than to the descriptive
details alert within such tensions.

The long, powerful first stanza of "Florida" (CPO, 32–33) contains the
same sort of constantly readjusted details. It repeatedly shifts both scale and
pattern, as in its opening lines:

> The state with the prettiest name,
> the state that floats in brackish water,
> held together by mangrove roots
> that bear while living oysters in clusters,
> and when dead strew white swamps with skeletons,
> dotted as if bombarded, with green hummocks
> like ancient cannon-balls sprouting grass.

Clearly, the speaker—shifting from the entire floating state to individual
oysters and hummocks, from pretty to brackish, from living to dead and
back around again—is backward to the confident claims of description. No
pattern is guaranteed; she is skeptical that any single pattern will hold for
long. Instead, she suggests that something live and delicate comes in the
intersection of several fragile patterns—as in the "gray rag" of the beach,
bearing rain-freshened shells: "with these the monotonous, endless, sagging
coast-line / is delicately ornamented." What is interesting, however, is the way
Bishop finds it necessary to pull away from these powerfully contradictory
patterns in order to bring out (or explain) the power of these descriptive
tensions. Rather than moving "far away within" these tensions, she pulls back

in order to insist on the fine, finite delicacy of multiple, contradictory patterns. Her example is buzzards over a burned-over swamp, apparently negative creatures drifting through a world of beautiful, finely seen textures:

> Thirty or more buzzards are drifting down, down, down,
> over something they have spotted in the swamp,
> in circles like stirred-up flakes of sediment
> sinking through water.
> Smoke from woods-fires filters fine blue solvents.
> On stumps and trees the charring is like black velvet.

Contrast that, she suggests, with the coarse-meshed world that moonlight brings. Insisting on simple, fixed patterns, Florida in the moonlight is a dead, dull postcard:

> Cold white, not bright, the moonlight is coarse-meshed,
> and the careless, corrupt state is all black specks
> too far apart, and ugly whites; the poorest
> post-card of itself.

The problem Bishop struggles with in this poem is how to make representation itself (making a postcard out of the world) into an issue. Pulling back from her unsettled portrait of Florida in order to point out to us its fine-because-broken-and-multiple mesh, she describes rather than enacts the descriptive issues she finds herself enmeshed in. Description clearly puts one between the claims of commerce and contemplation, but how does one best move around in and explore that place?

"Roosters" and "The Fish" seem a step forward because they are able to dramatize the same acknowledgment of limits and the same claim of freshness within the descriptive act itself. "Roosters" (CPO, 35–39) begins at four in the morning, "in the gun-metal blue dark"—the "first crow of the first cock" waking two people and then setting off replies and echoes "all over town." Bishop's initial description makes army officers out of the birds and the coarse mesh of their "uncontrolled, traditional cries." She follows a single pattern: a "senseless order" floats from deep in their medal-hung chests, "marking out maps" and claiming territory by "active / displacement[s] in perspective." Bishop's dismissive description, it seems safe to say, responds to that assault on her boundaries by forcefully counterattacking:

> what right have you to give
> commands and tell us how to live,

cry "Here!" and "Here!"
and wake us here where are
unwanted love, conceit and war?

The suggestion here is that the roosters' cries have brought her back to a
world where love is not returned, where partners are perhaps blinded by
territory-claiming "conceit," and where war is going on at various levels.[10] To
the agent of that sudden reminder, she screams back: "This is where I live!"
This is *my* territory. If so, it would follow, then, that at some level the midair
battle between inflamed roosters that she goes on to imagine—one still flying,
one fallen, both bloodied—is as much an extrapolation and dismissal of her
own feelings of wounded aggression, as expressed in her initial description,
as it is a critique of the roosters' senseless, insistent means of ordering.

If so, the second, alternate description she offers of the roosters—their cry
marked Peter's betrayal of Christ as both a denial (an example of "unwanted
love") and an opportunity to be forgiven and to grow—seems a reexamination
of the first. She dramatizes herself realizing its limits; she readjusts, in the
act of describing. Rooster crying, she imagines Peter "wait[ing]" and "heart-
sick" as his denial is marked, but sees that such a fall could also be one of
"inescapable hope, the pivot." Rather than stepping back, as she describes,
she uses the material she handles (the roosters' cries) to look at description
itself. This seems to me a crucial turn in her poetry; it is much like a map
using shadows or a monument using wood to talk about representation. Just
as Peter, in the high priest's courtyard, fell, "beneath the flares, / among the
'servants and officers,' " so Bishop acknowledges her fall into the company of
her own officers, her roosters compared to soldiers. Sensing her involvement
in their maintaining of senseless orders, she too stands with Peter, "two fingers
raised / to surprised lips, both as if dazed," attention directed toward the
rooster. And in that charged, backward pause she extrapolates again, to a day
when Peter and others had been forgiven, when it becomes clear that, for
all of them—lovers, soldiers, disciples—" 'Deny deny deny' / is not all the
roosters cry."

This pivot between descriptive takes puts her in a live, because now no
longer clearly plotted, place. "How could the night have come to grief," she
wonders, loosened from that seemingly predetermined plot to one without
such insistencies. The sun's first blush of order lights from underneath not
the fixed "senseless" mesh of territory fought for by lovers and roosters but
the "lines of pink cloud in the sky" that look like "wandering lines in marble."
In such a world, distinctions break down; we are like Peter inhabiting a space

between descriptive labels, "following 'to see the end,' / faithful as enemy, or friend." The poem wanders freely through the implications of shattered, shattering denials.

"The Fish" (CPO, 42–44) is similar. Again, the poet's own situation generates her first descriptive response. Disappointed that the "tremendous" fish she had caught simply "hung a grunting weight," her eye makes something worn and domestic, knowable if uninviting, out of her capture. He is "battered" and "homely"; his skin hangs in stained, worn strips "like ancient wallpaper." It is as if successfully claiming to domesticate or master the fish leaves it limp. Responding to skeptical pressures, the poem makes its first readjustment when, by means of the entrance inside offered by the gills—"the frightening gills, / fresh and crisp with blood, / that can cut so badly"—Bishop begins describing in a new sort of way. Like the map's shadows, the gills offer her eye an in-between area where patterns seem more up-for-grabs. Her descriptions, in this live space—"coarse white flesh / packed in like feathers," "the dramatic reds and blacks / of his shiny entrails"—become textured, bright, shiny with excitement. This is not unlike the fluid descriptive play of "Florida" or "Love Lies Sleeping." The crucial move of the poem comes next, however, when the expected course of its descriptive pattern—from outer to inner to the romantic breaking down of the distance between observer and object—is played out but fails. That is, the net the poet is using at the moment is revealed as too coarse, too easily established, and it tears. The poet looks into the fish's eyes, expecting, to follow that plot, a sort of bonding. But she finds something not only "far larger than mine / but shallower, and yellowed, / the irises backed and packed / with tarnished tinfoil." The fish shatters her descriptive expectations, its opaque eyes responding only "like the tipping / of an object toward the light." In that descriptive pause, in that acknowledgment of finitude, the poet is forced to look again without the security of plot. She sees both the tentativeness of her own descriptive efforts and, in their torn spaces, the fish in its own terms. She sees finely now—from its lip, "A green line, frayed at the end / where he broke it, two heavier lines, / and a fine black thread / still crimped from the strain and snap / when it broke and he got away"—at least in part because her seeing acknowledges her imprecise mediation between worlds. "His lower lip," she writes, "if you could call it a lip." "Medals," "beard of wisdom," "aching jaw," she writes, in just the same nonguaranteed way.[11] The "victory" that fills up the "little rented boat" at the conclusion of the poem, then, is her coming to see in such an ungrounded way—a victory whose liveness is echoed by an oil slick spreading a "rainbow" over the boat's "rusted," "cracked" and "rented" surfaces. The victory, it seems, is in struggling to look after the fish's eyes have turned opaque—looking while confessing you cannot master, looking becoming a form of "let[ting] the fish go." Bruns would describe this as the "letting go" of language. That victory—the rainbow here like the man-moth's tear—comes as live issues are opened and played out, the act of description itself becoming a net that tears.

What I have been suggesting, then, is that the strongest descriptive poems in *North & South* both signal and enact descriptive limits. They open up space within their dissolving lines where Bishop's charged, wandering awareness of her own mind's activities becomes as important as the roosters or fish she describes. The descriptive poems in her second book, *A Cold Spring* (1955), roughly the first half of that book, continue this investigation. They describe Bishop's actions in the space where her nets dissolve, attempting to characterize and name her mind's now-exposed work in that space. Like the map thinking with color or the frottage thinking with its wood grain, they use the materials handled in the descriptive act itself to take us "far away within" its implications. Let me survey those investigations. "A Cold Spring" (CPO, 55–56) describes the coming of spring on her friend Jane Dewey's farm—describes to Dewey something she already knows, but offers it back to her in the form of a tribute—that is, a nonpossessive knowing, or handling. As we have come to expect, the poem finds the space of tribute within a stutter or hesitancy in an expected pattern:

> A cold spring:
> The violet was flawed on the lawn.
> For two weeks or more the trees hesitated.

That hesitation puts her backward to spring. It no longer says itself directly; instead, it seems composed of signs that can be read only tentatively. Nothing is a sure shot. There are no guarantees—not the leaves "carefully indicating their characteristics," nor the mis-signaling "wretched flag" of a cow's afterbirth, nor the dogwood petals "burned, *apparently*, by a cigarette-butt." To read or describe spring, once the eye slows and notices the season's machinery, is to be put into a charged, unsure place where, for example, one sees redbud not as a small tree but as a blur. Describing it pulls the poet into a space between movement and color: it is "motionless, but almost more / like movement than any placeable color." Improvising a kind of celebratory party in that difficult, insecure place, Bishop makes the pause come alive. Deer "practised leaping," new leaves "swung" through an oak, a "complementary cardinal / cracked a whip," she writes to Dewey. Spring becomes a version of Fitzgerald's *Gatsby*: frogs provide part of the orchestra—"slack strings plucked by heavy thumbs"; moths become "Chinese fans" flattened against a door, under a light; fireflies—in the same motion seen in "Florida"—become "bubbles in champagne," rising "up, then down, then up again." Such descriptive displays, we understand, such "glowing tributes," enter and offer homage to a world they can't master. They measure or allegorize description as a sort of improvised, high-wire performance.

"The Bight" (CPO, 60–61) is similar. It describes our work in this area as an "untidy activity . . . / awful but cheerful." Describing a scene that, she remarks in a letter to the poet Robert Lowell, resembles her desk, Bishop finds her mental activity mimed back to her by the area she describes.[12] The poem brings representation forward as an issue by beginning with the observation that, at low tide, the water in the bight is "sheer." It seems a thin skin, almost transparent. That gets countered, or a readjustment is forced, when Bishop notes the dryness of the tide-exposed boats and pilings and ribs of marl: they are dry, she speculates, because the water, which her descriptive eye had intended to take in, seems to be sucking all life into itself, "Absorbing, rather than being absorbed." One thinks here of "The Map" foregrounding its own struggles to simplify and make things conform. Bishop responds by turning the water into "the color of the gas flame" but then notes, inadequately, that "if one were Baudelaire / one could probably hear it turning to marimba music." She is not; such mastery of correspondences is not to be had here. Instead, as with the party outside Jane Dewey's farm, she is drawn into a world bustling with failed or inadequate attempts to master the "sheer . . . water." A dredge plays "perfectly off-beat claves"; pelicans "crash / into this peculiar gas unnecessarily hard"; sponge boats look like "frowsy . . . retrievers"; other boats are "stove in, / . . . like torn-open, unanswered letters." She joins in, her descriptions simply adding to this litter of "old correspondences"; authority erased, she becomes part of the live, if "untidy activity . . . / awful but cheerful."

Three other descriptive poems in this book quite deliberately place their explorations of the issue of representation in a space where the coarse nets of simple correspondence have given away. "Over 2,000 Illustrations and a Complete Concordance" (CPO, 57–59) acknowledges the limits of such nets in its first stanza by staring at a series of engravings in a family Bible and commenting on the misfit between such representations and a just-completed set of travels. Turning to those engravings for something to lean on—"Thus should have been our travels: / serious, engravable"—she finds instead that, under the pressure of questions about accuracy (hesitancy, "A Cold Spring" put it), the engravings start to look like her self-reflexive map or circus horse, calling attention to their struggling, insistent attempts to "diagram" a world that remains "foreign" and "far gone in history or theology." As Bishop puts it, such engravings, arranged in her book in various ways, some shaped in "grim lunette[s]," some "caught in the toils of an initial letter, / when dwelt upon, they all resolve themselves." They separate themselves from their surroundings, she means; they resolve by becoming distinguishable and recognizable. But Bishop takes the word another way as well; when looked at carefully, when their struggle to hold is lived close to, dwelt with and inhabited, the engravings give way, and we move far away within the implications of their views:

> when dwelt upon, they all resolve themselves.
> The eye drops, weighted, through the lines
> the burin made, the lines that move apart

Resolve in the sense of separate, pull apart. Using such a net, one whose lines move apart, (as all lines do, even the serious ones), "ignites" the act of description and leaves her, in the poem's second stanza, to recount her previous travels through a world in which "Everything [was] only connected by 'and' and 'and,'" no pattern holding. Such a world, as the unbeliever, eyes closed on his mast, feared, not only mixes "a golden length of evening" and "rotting hulks" but also offers things empty and unmasterable, almost intolerably other:

>   somewhere near there
> I saw what frightened me most of all:
> A holy grave, not looking particularly holy,
> one of a group under a keyhole-arched stone baldaquin
> open to every wind from the pink desert.
> An open, gritty, marble trough, carved solid
> with exhortation, yellowed
> as scattered cattle-teeth;
> half-filled with dust

No wonder her eyes tear-up "painfully" as the coarse nets of the serious engravings are torn apart. This poem discovers not the awful clutter of a writer's littered desk or the half-looped celebratory shouts of a party in this space where commerce gives way; rather, it discovers Eliot's waste land—holiness and the solidity of language reduced to a fearful handful of dust. That, too, is part of what becomes visible in the finite space made visible by skeptical uncertainty.

The third stanza uses that family Bible, in a sort of nostalgic exercise, to bring out the generative pain of this world in which lines move apart. She opens the Bible again and notes that its "gilt rubs off the edges / of the pages and pollinates the fingertips." "Pollinates" is this poem's "live" word for the space where the book's engravings open up, but this pollination is in some sense produced by guilt. The pun seems intended—the guilt, for example, of *not* having lost one's infant sight (one's naive trust in straightforward organization) by encountering something like this powerful nativity scene:

> —the dark ajar, the rocks breaking with light,
> an undisturbed, unbreathing flame,
> colorless, sparkless, freely fed on straw,
> and, lulled within, a family with pets

Instead, she has painfully lost her infant sight by something closer to erosion and the sheer wearing away of pattern. That pollinating, if painful, guilt becomes clear to her, the issues distinguishable, in the poem's acknowledgment of limits.

When nets break, one painfully encounters a multiple world, one in which activities are pollinated and brought to life by an awareness of distance from it. "At the Fishhouses" (CPO, 64–66) goes even further with this exploration. Like "Over 2,000 Illustrations," its first long stanza carefully establishes and then erodes the poet's descriptive net. Its opening scene quite literally acknowledges the limits we have been discussing:

> Although it is a cold evening,
> down by one of the fishhouses
> an old man sits netting,
> his net, in the gloaming almost invisible,
> a dark purple-brown,
> and his shuttle worn and polished.
> The air smells so strongly of codfish
> it makes one's nose run and one's eyes water.

The old man, the net he works on, and his worn shuttle seem versions of each other; all share the similar fate of giving way under the cold and dark and the strong smell of codfish. Bishop's work is so much of a piece that we shouldn't hesitate to connect the watery eyes here to the "watery, prismatic" response to a similar situation in the previous poem. Once again, the poet seems to pull back from this skeptical tug by lighting on something stronger, more permanent, all abrupt and dramatically angled: "The five fishhouses have steeply peaked roofs / and narrow, cleated gangplanks slant up / to storerooms in the gables / for the wheelbarrows to be pushed up and down on." The fishhouses, as the previous poem put it, seem "serious, engravable." But then a subtle thing happens. The poet swings her eye and notices that "the heavy surface of the sea"—opaque and silver—seems to be swelling "as if considering spilling over." She realizes as well that the shore is scattered with tools—benches, lobster pots, masts—which, also silver but "of an apparent translucence," seem to have been dissolved by that heavy, silver sea. In response, she silently revises her own description; that is, she lets her net, her descriptive pattern, dissolve, the fishhouses becoming, on second thought, readjusted to "small old buildings with an emerald moss / growing on their shoreward walls."[13] The rest of the first stanza's catalog, then—fish tubs and wheelbarrows dominated by herring scales, a wooden capstan bleached and cracked and stained, the old man and his knife "almost worn away"—echoes the fragility of her descriptive tools. Like the map, the scene described everywhere comments on the finite act she's engaged in.

Just as the man-moth moves toward "what he fears most," so her eye, in that ungrounded space, edges toward the sea, quite deliberately allowing it to splinter into rainbows the issues involved in seeing and making patterns. In a motion we have seen before, the eye seems to move fluidly and fearfully at once, up and down, up and down the gradations that she now knows will not really manage the passage for her:

> Down at the water's edge, at the place
> where they haul up the boats, up the long ramp
> descending into the water, thin silver
> tree trunks are laid horizontally
> across the gray stones, down and down
> at intervals of four or five feet.

Think of this as sitting backward on a subway, well aware of its "full, terrible speed." And how is that world described, the poet's nervous flickering eyes spreading the steps below her, like the lines of an engraving or the descriptive takes of the first stanza, into grand open spaces? What issues are raised here?

> Cold dark deep and absolutely clear,
> element bearable to no mortal,
> to fish and to seals . . . One seal particularly
> I have seen here evening after evening.
> He was curious about me. He was interested in music;
> like me a believer in total immersion,
> so I used to sing him Baptist hymns.

> I also sang "A Mighty Fortress is Our God."
> He stood up in the water and regarded me
> steadily, moving his head a little.

We can think of this ellipsis as the place where the net tears and she enters a live space. It is as if the lovely, high language she yearns to use ("cold dark deep") dissolves when she follows its claims all the way down to the dream of "total immersion." And in the space of that break, in the space of the ellipsis, she touches not the sea but the issue of description as an approach to something other. The joke here—like the tributes and painful confessions we've already examined—acknowledges and handles the truth made visible by the failure of her first descriptive attempts. She believes, as someone staring in a fish's eyes believes, "in total immersion." Singing a Baptist hymn to an oblivious fellow believer is a way to signal and look at that belief while acknowledging its impossibility. The giddy joke brings her condition alive, insisting on singing and having a sort of communion in that space.

The serious, quite famous end of the poem sees something more. Such acts—torn description, awful jokes—are the only way we have to approach that icily free realm that "we imagine knowledge to be: / dark, salt, clear, moving, utterly free." Such torn acts, visible in these poems from *A Cold Spring*, are in fact what we can only call, in contrast, "*our* knowledge." Knowledge, like the impossibly cold sea, is "drawn from the cold hard mouth / of the world, derived from the rocky breasts / forever, flowing and drawn," but when patterned, as it must be, by such finite organizing concepts as the "historical," it is also "flowing, and flown." It moves through our nets, reduces them to finite jokes, and then is flown—lost. The uneasy descriptive gaps of these poems, spaces where broken nets touch the flowing world, become stages where the tension between the terms flowing and flown comes most painfully (and cheerfully) alive. That is what knowing is: that tension, that liveness, letting the fish go as the fingerprint spreads.

"Cape Breton" (CPO, 67–68) takes this investigation of the torn, line-spreading net of description one step further. Once again, the world seen becomes full of commentary on the task of entering and ordering. As we have come to expect, the poem's first stanza presents, in a charged form, the issue of lines or edges. Birds on the islands of Ciboux and Hertford, off Cape Breton, stand "in solemn, uneven lines along the cliff's brown grass-frayed edge." But, the first stanza insists, such lines are precarious or temporary: sheep stampede over that edge; the woven lines of the sea they fall into disappear "under the mist"; the lined-out "pulse" of a motor breaks through and then is "incorporate[d]" into the same dissolving mist. Moving to the mainland in the second stanza, moving further within the tension between lines and fog, one discovers "the same mist . . . / . . . ghosts of glaciers" drifting between folds of mountain risers and leaving those "saw-tooth edge[s]" adrift in a sort of dismembering of perspective. We see both the clear claims of perspective and, as in the competing cries of the roosters we looked at earlier, its collapse; they are "alike, but certain as a stereoscopic view." One thinks of the trees "Too much alike to mark or name a place by / So as to say for certain I was here / Or somewhere else" in Frost's investigation of a similarly unstable state in "The Wood-Pile." The third stanza takes us even deeper within the view. Now, the edge becomes a road "along the brink of the coast" that, because it is Sunday, "appears to have been abandoned." Dissolving, it gives up any chance of making or netting meaning:

> Whatever the landscape had of meaning appears to have been
> abandoned,
> unless the road is holding it back, in the interior,
> where we cannot see.

What goes on in this space of acknowledgment where lines give way and meaning has been abandoned? All of these descriptive poems in *A Cold Spring* ask that question. This poem, reaching back to "Florida" and the prose fables, characterizes our finite work there (our songs) as fine because torn, free because limited, and shared:

> these regions now have little to say for themselves
> except in thousands of light song-sparrow songs floating upward
> freely, dispassionately, through the mist, and meshing
> in brown-wet, fine, torn fish-nets.

The songs pass through the corrosive, dissolving mist, lose their authority, but mesh with other torn voices.[14] In many ways, that image describes the way Bishop has found herself, in singing her failures to master, becoming one with the inhabitants of a bight or the heralds of spring who are proclaiming the same sense of limits. As if in response to this thought, Bishop closes the poem by illustrating, in a simple move, a human being entering that open, apparently abandoned world. It's very deftly done and takes our eye and hers along with him. A bus comes along that Sunday road; a man with a baby gets off, climbs over a stile and goes "down through a small steep meadow, / which establishes its poverty in a snowfall of daisies, / to his invisible house beside the water." That is, taking our eye along with him, he moves down through a

non-cultivated, non-meaning-making meadow to a place "invisible" to us—
a place where "meaning appears to have been abandoned, / . . . where we
cannot see." He slips in easily, inviting us to follow.

Bishop's second book further investigates how living out the truth of skep-
ticism makes visible our condition by noting that relationships also frame the
same problem. As Cavell puts it, our relationships are "isomorphic" with other
ways we inhabit this charged space and thus speak to or "measure" (continually
deepen the question of) our "faithfulness to the specific conditions and acts
of writing as such" (sw, 62). We can move a bit more quickly now, since
the strategies are familiar although the material has been expanded. Space
between lovers is much like that between a person and the object or field
or open area he or she attempts to describe. When bonds turn frail and are
no longer guaranteed, a pause or distance (here, between two people) opens
and our desire to know and solve becomes desperately clear. The heart wants
to know for sure. How does that uncertain space where it acknowledges its
limits feel? What in our condition becomes live and visible there? "Faustina,
or Rock Roses" (cpo, 72–74) describes this nongrounded space as one of
"helplessly proliferative" questions. A visitor comes to see a bedridden older
woman who is being tended by another woman, and the visitor begins asking
herself what she is staring at in that relationship displayed before her. Is the
older woman being granted a sort of deep "freedom," a "dream of protection
and rest"? Or is she caught in an abusive, "unimaginable nightmare"? The
visitor finds herself, as did Bishop's describers, with "no way of telling. / The
eyes say only either." Like the "split apart" thought of "The Weed" or the far-
distant mental disturbances of "From the Country to the City," the either/or
question raised here forks and flickers:

> a snake-tongue flickering;
> blurs further, blunts, softens,
> separates, falls, our problems
> becoming helplessly
>   proliferative.

Although it is investigated no further, later echoes of this language suggest
that the unsettling question might become something like the bunch of roses
that the visitor hands over at the end of the poem, "wonder[ing] oh, whence
come / all the petals." That is, there is a suggestion that this disturbing question
might lead to the softening, separating, "falling petals" that appear here. Might
something flower in this skeptical space? the poem almost asks, then stops
short.

"Four Poems" (CPO, 76–79) tries to answer the question, giving, in fact, in its four love poems, four different descriptions of what flowers in this space. "Conversation" describes being held where there is no way of telling as inhabiting a space where a heart in "tumult" cannot tell the difference between its questions and answers. A clear question and a convincing answer become, in this space where there is no knowing, too blunt or coarse an expectation. Frantic to think something through, the heart has been pulled into a realm where "there is no sense"; everything is uttered and abandoned, proposed and erased, in "the same tone of voice." What do we see in this space between? Perhaps nothing more than the desperate desire to separate and solve and distinguish. The next poem, in fact, describes "the puzzle of their prison" being "solved . . . with an unexpected kiss." Questions vanishing feels, as the title puts it, like a sudden "Rain Towards Morning"—the rain simultaneously a great, broken-up cage of falling wire and "a million birds" racing free. "While Someone Telephones" describes "the heart's release" from not knowing in a more tentative way. Suspended in what the poem calls "*nothing*," or what we have been calling the hole in a net—the "wasted minutes" of someone's "barbaric condescension" in which words are once again "accretions to no purpose"—the figure in the poem finds herself staring out a window into the dark woods and waiting: "maybe even now these minutes' host / emerges, some relaxed uncondescending stranger, / the heart's release." The last poem in the sequence, "O Breath," describes that space of waiting and wanting and nothingness as an "equivocal"—it could be either solved or left open—space. In this poem asthma, difficulty in breathing, seems to be at issue, marked by the gaps in many of the lines. The speaker, who by her gasping lines seems to be struggling with her breath coming to her all in a tumult, comments that the person she is addressing is so "restrained" that she "cannot fathom even a ripple" "with what clamor" the other is internally dealing with things:

Beneath that loved   and celebrated breast,
silent, bored really   blindly veined,
grieves, maybe   lives and lets
live, passes   bets,
something moving   but invisibly

How does it feel, desperate either to be sure or to be released from a commitment, when the other does not respond and there is no way of knowing? The other three poems suggest that our desire to know becomes agonizingly clear there. This poem goes further and suggests that though the lover's spirit (or breath) is restrained, it is "bound to be there." If we acknowledge that we are always in a skeptical space where the other cannot be known directly, if the puzzle can't be solved once and for all, or if the two cannot know for sure, perhaps "we must own equivalents for" that solution. That is, perhaps a relationship is an indirect "bargain[ing] with," a getting "beneath / within if never with," which is as live as any non-equivocal release of the heart. Such a world, in Cavell's terms, is "regained as gone" (IQ, 172). Relationships show us our nature as bargainers, yearners, negotiators; they show us how desperately and inventively we are driven to people and bargain with the invisible. We have strewn petals, made bargains and sketched equivalents, without ever having a guaranteed grasp of what must stay "invisible." Love poems bring us again to a place where meaning is abandoned, replaced by the torn nets of bargains. Echoing the description of birdsong in "Cape Breton," these four poems together suggest that such finitude is what we have in common.

Two other love poems here, if one pairs them, make a shape in that backwards space. "Argument" (CPO, 81) voices the skeptical claim, describing yet another unresolved, blurry space. Separated from someone by both "Days and Distance," Bishop's speaker finds that this separation does not resolve her feelings. Where she had tried to separate herself from her lover in order to see and solve the question of what if anything existed between them, time and distance have not made anything clearer. The two categories simply "argue argue argue with me / endlessly / neither proving you less wanted nor less dear." Distance becomes the sandy coastline seen from a plane between their two cities, "stretching indistinguishably / all the way, / all the way to where my reasons end?" The way to the end of her reasons for loving or for separating cannot yet be made out—we are still in that open spot. Similarly, their days apart look like "those cluttered instruments, / one to a fact, / canceling each other's experience" on the plane's instrument panel. These days apart, like the crying roosters, do not come clear; they pile up, canceling each other on "some hideous calendar" issued simultaneously by both "Never & Forever, Inc." In such a space, the poem can end only with a plea—that those quarreling "voices / . . . can and shall be vanquished" and resolved and the distance settled, "gone / . . . for good." We feel quite forcefully the finite condition under which that desire is voiced.

"The Shampoo" (CPO, 84), quite wonderfully, though with a different lover, sketches what a gesture toward knowing would look like in that uncertain, dimensionless space. It takes place in a world where, once again, finitude is figured as an ongoing disruptive fact—in this case, a set of ringed, surrounding shocks one cannot pull out of and settle things apart from. We live in a world of "still explosions" in which "the lichens grow / by spreading, gray, concentric shocks" and eventually, though in some unimaginably distant future, "arrang[e] / to meet the rings around the moon." In such a space, the speaker's lover has, perhaps equivocally, solved the puzzle; she has done something "precipitate and pragmatical" that has suddenly shown the dissolving pattern of time to be, at least temporarily, "amenable." Whatever has happened, whatever declaration has been made, stars go shooting and the distant moon becomes as near as a "battered and shiny" basin. We see how the finite fragile act looks as it takes shape within those open, empty circles. Like the comparison to the moon, the gesture between lovers is suddenly and deeply visible in its battered frailness.

Travel, going to Brazil, offered Bishop yet another "isomorphic" realm to suffer these issues and measure that space where our finitude becomes visible.[15] The arrangement of the Brazil poems in her third book, *Questions of Travel* (1965), quite deliberately lays these issues out. "Arrival at Santos" (CPO, 89–90) makes it clear that the poet approaches this new area with:

> immodest demands for a different world,
> and a better life, and complete comprehension
> of both at last, and immediately,
> after eighteen days of suspension.

That "suspension" is, of course, being at sea, but much more than that, it is being in a pause, an unresolvable state where, as we have seen, one's need to mark and know has become visible—"full of the lights of revelation" (CPR, 189). That explains her tongue-in-cheek account of desiring to completely and immediately comprehend both world and life. Let's say that she moves out of that suspension and encounters the world with the authority of those "immodest demands" undermined. Reading with eyes open, we note that the gingerly way she "climb[s] down the ladder backward / . . . descending into the midst of twenty-six freighters" brings both the backward ride of the "Man-Moth" and the descent into the corrosive mist of "Cape Breton" back into play. Passing through this realm before "driving to the interior" means passing through and acknowledging the limits of her tools—in this case, soap or stamps are the examples, her tools "wasting away like the former, slipping the way the latter / do"—before actually beginning to use them in this new country. It means acknowledging that the pause has both made our desire to comprehend visible and thrown it off center.

Three of these Brazil poems actively explore what happens when such eroded tools are used while another set of poems finds figures who are models or examples of such eroded performances. Travel continually puts the poet in a state where her linguistic moves are, along with other aspects of our finite condition, visible and under pressure. We have already looked at the way "Brazil, January 1, 1502" measures her instinctive turn toward the comforts of correspondence against Brazil's centuries-old violation as it was colonized. Our desire to know becomes one of the anguished revelations she had previously imagined handling in prison or on the paper-strewn shore. "The Armadillo" (CPO, 103–4) is similar. It presents another fog-corroded tool that Bishop uses, lets crumble, and then uses against itself to feel out what is exposed about our human condition. Its first five stanzas display a kind of distanced confidence as they describe "the frail, illegal" Saint John's Day fire-balloons. The balloons are predictable; "this is the time of year" they appear. The farther off they get, the more lovely they seem—"flush[ing] and fill[ing] with light / . . . like hearts," looking like stars or planets as they drift or seem to steer. Wise to the instability of such a safe perspective, Bishop readjusts, asking what can be seen when, "in the downdraft from a peak," that distance is taken away. Focusing even more particularly on "Last night [when] another big one fell / . . . behind the house," she describes the still-foreign scene in a second way:

> The flames ran down. We saw the pair
>
> of owls who nest there flying up
> and up, their whirling black-and-white
> stained bright pink underneath, until
> they shrieked up out of sight.
>
> The ancient owls' nest must have burned.

This is a quite peculiar way of seeing. Though the distance has been partially broken down, and there is some empathy in her response to the homeless, shrieking owls, we also notice a kind of head-cocked detachment. She still operates from within a stable, though coarse, distinction. She stands here, the owls are over there. Her eye notices a visual rhyming of the balloon's frail beauty in the way the "black-and-white" of the owls is "stained bright pink" by the fire's reflected light. There is a kind of doubleness here, like the uneasy mixing of freshness and death in "Florida", which is, in this case, played out much more deliberately. We see it repeated, two more times: an armadillo moves "hastily, all alone / . . . head down, tail down" away from the fire, that gust of empathy laced with a cool-eyed appreciation of its "glistening," "rose-flecked" armor as the fire light dances on its surface. A baby rabbit jumps out with both "fixed, ignited eyes" and characteristics safely handled from farther off: the oddness of its short ears, the ironic way its color and texture—"a handful of intangible ash"—rhymes with such a situation. What is going on here, I think, is that she is studying her traveler's representational net, the postcard she has made of Brazil. All of that begins to give way as Bishop starts to sense that the distinction between herself and the animals and between beauty and terror had been too simple, too coarse. That distinction blurs and she finds herself lost and undefended within a space that has suddenly opened up:

> *Too pretty, dreamlike mimicry!*
> *O falling fire and piercing cry*
> *and panic, and a weak mailed fist*
> *clenched ignorant against the sky!*

That is, the prettiness of the scene, its mimicking of a dream, had fooled her. Giving way, it leaves her too a victim of disaster from nowhere, surrounded by cries and panic. It leaves her, in fact, her tiny fist clenched, in a state of ignorance and not knowing. It is a state where she and the animals are linked in their defenselessness, indicated by the sentence's suggestion that her clenched fist is covered with the armadillo's now-seen-as-ineffectual armor. That this is *her* fist metaphorically covered with inadequate "mail," linking her with the displaced creatures, and not simply the armadillo looking like a clueless (ignorant) fist is supported by the observation that often in Bishop such a dissolving of lines opens not only terror and exhilaration and giddiness but also the possibility of joining with "thousands of . . . songs floating upward."

"Questions of Travel" (CPO, 93–95) gives this idea the grandest spin. It begins with an exhausted traveler lamenting the fraying of her descriptive, ordering nets:

> There are too many waterfalls here; the crowded streams
> hurry too rapidly down to the sea,
> and the pressure of so many clouds on the mountaintops
> makes them spill over the sides in soft slow-motion,
> turning to waterfalls under our very eyes.

The off-handed comparison of waterfalls to spilling tears "under our very eyes" helps locate us again in that blurry, potentially ignitable space between lines.

That exhaustion, as we might expect, opens up, within its acknowledgment of limits, a space of questioning. She roams around there. "Should we have stayed at home and thought of here?" Is it "childishness," she asks, traveling in order "to stare at some inexplicable old stonework, / inexplicable and impenetrable, / at any view, / instantly seen and always, always delightful?" Those initial questions, eventually dismissing as a joke the drive to master and toss into her suitcase "one more folded sunset, still quite warm," have, like the map's shading and other features, acknowledged the tension between the traveler's experience of the world's impenetrability and her drive to have it, "instantly." That acknowledged tension opens a space in the poem's third stanza where, mastery put aside, that inexplicable world remains. Now, the questions handled in that open space become not "should we have stayed at home" but wouldn't it "have been a pity / not to have seen" such Florida-like places where overlapping, nonmatched planes coexist: clogs of disparate pitch, a bamboo bird cage in the form of a baroque church over a broken gas pump, and so on. In such a space one is forced (and able) to ponder:

> blurr'dly and inconclusively,
> on what connection can exist for centuries
> between the crudest wooden footwear
> and, careful and finicky,
> the whittled fantasies of wooden cages.

Bishop brings us around, at the end of the third stanza's list of opportunities for blurred ponderings it would have been a pity to have missed, to the unraveling moment that actually initiated this poem's investigations. It would have been a pity, she writes:

> never to have had to listen to rain
> so much like politicians' speeches:
> two hours of unrelenting oratory
> and then a sudden golden silence
> in which the traveler takes a notebook, writes:

> *"Is it lack of imagination that makes us come*
> *to imagined places, not just stay at home?*
> *Or could Pascal have been not entirely right*
> *about just sitting quietly in one's room?*

> *Continent, city, country, society:*
> *the choice is never wide and never free.*

And here, or there . . . No. Should we have stayed at home,
wherever that may be?"

The italicized lines here, opening out of the collapse of the relentless oratory, are in miniature the dance performed by the poem. The first set of skeptical questions performed in the "golden silence"—*"Should we have stayed at home?"*—was not full enough because the questions had been resting on the stable plank of "choice." They had assumed home versus away was a stable distinction with the issue being choosing between them. When that distinction becomes too crude—*"And here, or there . . . No."*—and dissolves, home itself as a category blurs: *"wherever that may be?"* As this poem has demonstrated, traveling becomes, then, a live exercise in locating ourselves, watching ourselves make distinctions, in homelessness—in a blurred, open-ended place. Traveling, like writing or describing or waiting for a lover, means looking and then looking again at the questions raised there—"watch[ing] [them] . . . closely" (CPO, 25).

The other Brazil poems in this volume describe figures—often seen through the mist—who inhabit this uncertain territory in exemplary ways. They provide models for the kind of exploratory thinking Bishop finds herself drawn toward. They function like Jerónimo's house did, earlier, or like "The Map" did before that. Although they are not strong enactments of these issues, they are—in the way their characters acknowledge limits and move freely around within them—valuable guides to the issues being on "foreign" soil brought out into the open for Bishop. Let me give a few examples. "Squatter's Children" (CPO, 95) describes a boy and a girl, at some distance, playing outside their home as storm clouds pile up. Children with no rights (their parents are squatters), clinging doggedly to a house which is no more than a "little, soluble, / unwarrantable ark" battered by the oncoming rain's meaningless "echolalia," they seem to be released by the failure of their parents' structure to participate, and circulate within, a larger one. Within this charged hole, "their laughter spreads / effulgence in the thunderheads, / weak flashes of inquiry / direct as is the puppy's bark." Their apparently giddy "flashes of inquiry," magnified in the lightning, act out the equally non-guaranteed questions Bishop, as traveler, pursues. *In my father's house are many mansions*, Bishop's speaker seems to remember, describing the inquiries growing out of their acknowledgment of limit as a means of inhabiting a different sort of house—a larger and unfixed emptiness, free from the law's restrictions:

wet and beguiled, you stand among
the mansions you may choose
out of a bigger house than yours,
whose lawfulness endures.

The same family seems to be described in "Manuelzinho" (CPO, 96–99), a poem in the voice of Lota de Macedo Soares about a squatter who, "a helpless, foolish man," "improvident as the dawn," supposedly helps with the gardens. What he does in actuality is inhabit that uneasy space between things. "Twined in wisps of fog," his family stares "off into fog and space"; "coming down at night, / in silence" they move freely through a dissolved openness like creatures for whom such a space seems natural:

Between us float a few
big, soft, pale-blue
sluggish fireflies,
the jellyfish of the air . . .

"The Riverman" (CPO, 105–9), on his way to become "a serious *sacaca*" or witch doctor, inhabits the same territory. Following the dolphin through "the river mist" to an inward opening in the Amazon's flow, Bishop's *sacaca*-in-training goes on moonlit nights to a place where both language and the world's elemental secrets seem dissolved together in a "deep, enchanted silt" above which the river makes the sound of "fast, high whispering / like a hundred people at once." Watching Bishop's witch doctor breathe and swerve and move, we find ourselves again in Cape Breton's torn-birdsong interior. Balthazar, named after one of the three magi, as he moves through "the thin gray mist" of Cabo Frio (Bishop's seacoast getaway) on the Feast of the Epiphany, inhabits the same free area in "Twelfth Morning" (CPO, 110–11). Living in a "foundered house," surrounded by fences of "pure rust," where on a foggy morning "perspective [is] dozing" and much "remains in doubt," Balthazar sings and slides through a world which seems to have him as "its highlight." And finally, Bishop and Lota themselves, during the rainy season, seem, in a poem of that name, to also inhabit such a dwelling "in the high fog," "in a private cloud" (101–2). In such a season, the house—"open house / to the white dew / and the milk-white sunrise"—is a haven for the "small shadowy life" of "silver fish, mouse, / bookworms, / big moths . . . / . . . the mildew's / ignorant map; / [things] darkened and tarnished / by the warm touch / of the warm breath." Bishop's reminder to herself that she is only a temporary tenant of such a place of non-knowing—with a change in seasons, the "forgiving air / and the high fog [will be] gone"—helps us realize that she needs to continually work her way back to these dissolved areas where the squatters and the birds live.

The "Elsewhere" poems in *Questions of Travel* begin Bishop's final exploration of the fragility visible in free, ungrounded spaces. These, I think, are her most wide-reaching poems; they suggest that our limits become visible not only in attempting to describe something overwhelming or in trying to solve a relationship or in staying afloat in something foreign, but that they can also be acknowledged in the most daily events and assumptions of our lives—all of which are woven through with finitude.[16] The poems in this volume are fairly tentative in their approach to this area but prepare the way for *Geography III*. What is perhaps not immediately obvious is that the story "In the Village," which Bishop placed before these poems in *Questions of Travel*, sets the stage for all of this work. There, Bishop, in recounting her mother's breakdown during her last stay at home, quietly lays claim to being herself a Manuelzinho or Jerónimo; she shows that she, too, in her daily life, is an unhoused squatter, living in a foundering house or soluble ark. The story claims that "the echo of a scream" hangs over her "Nova Scotian village." Though vanished, it is "alive forever. Its pitch would be the pitch of my village. Flick the lightning rod on top of the church steeple with your fingernail and you will hear it." (CPR, 251). That scream, of course, is her mother's mad scream, which, like the man-moth's hole proving the sky useless for protection, has opened up a gap in daily patterns and changed everything.[17] The entire village, all of its rituals and sounds and smells, seems eaten away by its mist; the scream is the village's deep down pitch—its source of instability, but also of its uneasy life. It is a sign of finitude, woven through everything.

The story does two important things with the mother's scream. First, it links it with a chain of similarly inflected events and items—"mortal" things (CPR, 274) the narrator calls them. Included here, along with her mother's "morning" clothes and broken china, her grandmother's empty front bedroom and tears in the potato mash, is language itself. The scream seems to have loosened the colored metallic crystals on her mother's old postcards: "Some cards, instead of lines around the buildings, have words written in their skies with the same stuff, crumbling, dazzling and crumbling, raining down a little on little people who sometimes stand about below: pictures of Pentecost?" (CPR, 255). The scream's loosening effects are also felt in household voices, desperate to find a solution to the open-ended situation it has produced: "But now I am caught in a skein of voices, my aunts' and my grandmother's, saying the same things over and over, sometimes loudly, sometimes in whispers. . . .

I am struggling to free myself" (CPR, 270). Though the scream changes all it touches, its effect is probably most clear on language, as in the narrator's weekly trial of bearing to the post office a package with "the address of the sanatorium . . . in my grandmother's handwriting, in purple indelible pencil, on smoothed-out wrapping paper. It will never come off" (CPR, 272).

The other thing the story does is play out—here, in the domestic and familiar—how one moves through such a now-seen-as-finite world, under a dazzling rain of language. The child is forced to desperately study her way of making sense or living out her finitude. She does two things. First, as she moves through her now scream-pitched village—delivering messages, running errands, walking the cow to its rented pasture—her eyes are kept on the details of those processes that temporarily offer distraction and safety, but soon give way to "an immense, sibilant, glistening loneliness" (CPR, 265).[18] This is the blurred, live wandering we have seen before as one authoritative stance or another was eroded. She is alive in a domestic, but now nonguaranteed space. Second, as she wanders, she yearns for another sort of home—a religious yearning for something free of the mortal and the finite. She hears it promised in "the pure note: pure and angelic" (CPR, 253) of the blacksmith's clanging hammer that, momentarily, seems to lift her away from the tension of watching her mother unravel and is picked up again when she visits the blacksmith's in the middle of the crisis—a place where horses and men are "perfectly at home . . . very much at home" (CPR, 257). But, as the last lines of the story make clear, such relief is only there to be sought and yearned for. As in "Over 2,000 Illustrations," its ever-withheld alternative voice makes mortality more painful and more alive. Its "beautiful pure sound," which "turns everything else to silence" and takes us completely out of frail human speech, never comes completely:

> It sounds like a bell buoy out at sea.
> It is the elements speaking: earth, air, fire, water.
> All those other things—clothes, crumbling postcards, broken china; things damaged and lost, sickened or destroyed; even the frail, almost lost scream—are they too frail for us to hear their voices long, too mortal?
> Nate!
> Oh, beautiful sound, strike again! (CPR, 274)

Essentially, what Bishop does in the domestic poems that follow is attempt to hear and move around inside those frail, dazzling, and crumbling voices. They are voices she hears about her and ways of voicing the world she discovers within herself; eyes always on the alert, ears on the alert, she both waits for them to collapse and yearns for another sort of sound entirely. The childhood poems in the "Elsewhere" section of *Questions of Travel* all work in this way—each sets up a frame or net or structure and then allows the child's eye to show it begin to unravel or dissolve. "Manners" (CPO, 121–22) is the simplest. It admiringly lays out the rules of the road followed by the poet's grandfather from his wagon seat—always speak to everyone you meet, always offer everyone a ride—then notices how frail such gestures look in a world in which, say, the automobile is also present: "When automobiles went by, / the dust hid the people's faces, / but we shouted 'Good day! Good day! / Fine day!' at the top of our voices."

Words also unravel in Bishop's justly-famous "Sestina" (123–24). There, a child watches her grandmother trying to busy herself in order to hide her tears, and finds her eyes obsessively drawn to the almanac, returned to us by the sestina's structure in each stanza. The almanac's hold on things dissolves and is reconstituted, step by step. It is a frail, torn fish-net. It is first the source of jokes that the grandmother reads out loud "to hide her tears," then the predictor of dark inevitabilities "only known to a grandmother," then a frail, "half open," page-riffled loosening of secrets which "fall down like tears" and plant themselves in the child's knowing drawings, her own equally finite attempts to hide and displace and control pain.

The same passed-on dissolving of order occurs in "First Death in Nova Scotia" (CPO, 125–26). There, the child's eye keeps trying to find a comforting equivalent to explain her dead cousin laid out in the parlor. Of course, no equivalent holds, and they loosen and intersect terribly. Her eye seems to race around the room looking for something not fragile. Is the child like the stuffed loon on a table near the coffin? That line seems to hold. "His breast was deep and white, / cold and caressable; / his eyes were red glass, / much to be desired." No, the child's eyes are different—they are shut; worse, the loon's red eyes seem to fix greedily on the "little frosted cake" of the coffin, as if the crumbling equivalent had left in its wake something much worse. Perhaps the child is like a doll. But if so, he is a white unpainted one, brushed with red, but not like the red-brushed Maple Leaf which for a Canadian lasts "Forever." And he is certainly not "the smallest page" being sent off to the court of the English royalty displayed on the wall above him. "How could Arthur go," she asks, "with his eyes shut up so tight / and the roads deep in snow?" In her childlike voice, she moves around a space opening up within this frayed red and white net that is as seriously unbounded as any we have seen.[19]

These ordinary domestic situations in which structures have been rendered fragile and give way offer a transition to the poems of *Geography III* (1976), most of which understand the everyday itself to be the finite space we are forced to wander, torn and alert. What issues get handled here, in Wittgenstein's "haphazard, unsponsored" everyday (CR, 439)? "In the Waiting Room" (CPO, 159–61) remembers the way an almost-seven-year-old's experience of reading and studying an issue of *National Geographic* in a dentist's waiting room broke her free from the structures that once held her afloat and pulled her into a dissolved space. What the child finds in the magazine's photographs is something like that skein of tangled voices that would not allow her to progress or like those eyes that said "only either" (CPO, 74) and offered propositions that could not be sensibly distinguished. She discovers a set of images that are both foreign and yet, when "carefully studied," seem so deeply interwoven with each other that they create a chain that seems to include her as well. A volcano "spilling over / in rivulets of fire," explorers in laced boots, a man "slung on a pole," "babies with pointed heads / wound round and round with string," and women with necks wound with wire all seem images of the same winding, and pull her—"too shy to stop"—far away within the view. The coarse distinction of self and other gives way. Though she attempts to reestablish the net by pulling back to the magazine's frame—"the yellow margins, the date"—she has clearly slipped to that familiar place of open fragility. And how does she wander there? Her aunt's cry from within the office guides her, for in the child's nonordered state, that cry seems to her "my voice, in my mouth. / Without thinking at all / I was my foolish aunt, / I—we— were falling, falling, / our eyes glued to the cover." That is, she falls through the net, to a place where thought-out, apparently knowable distinctions between people have dissolved. That unmasterable gust of connection with her aunt, proposing possible linkages in all sorts of new directions, shows her that the self itself is as fragile, scream-ridden, and dissolving a structure as was a tourist's defenses or Jerónimo's house. And *that* means that, at some level, living within such a fragile structure entails living within something awful and cheerful, something always suspended between. In the cracks of the self, others flow in:

I felt: you are an *I*,
you are an *Elizabeth*,
you are one of *them*.
Why should you be one, too?
I scarcely dared to look

to see what it was I was.
I gave a sidelong glance

The astonishing thing in this poem is to find this dissolve—"nothing / stranger could ever happen"—so close to home. You do not need to be in prison to wander in this free anguished way; just bearing a name, that map, testifies to your implication in this dilemma. One's self is a torn, finite net. Being an *I* is like being on the abandoned road of Cape Breton, knowing that beyond its edges, within its unmarked interiors, unlikely as it seems, are many voices one is enmeshed with.

"Crusoe in England" (CPO, 162–66) proposes that we think of home as another fragile stay against confusion. In retrospect, as Crusoe looking back at his old island, Bishop finally describes herself as a Manuelzinho. The "Brazil" she looks at was a home—however fragile—and not just an unsettling foreignness. But the same issues were alive. Looking back, Crusoe sees that his fragile, temporary home, like all of Bishop's other finite structures, "reeked of meaning" and "lived." That island home is, in many ways, a summary of all of Bishop's wandering entrances into tears in the net. Crusoe was active there with what Bishop calls his "home-made" "island industries." In a space where he "didn't know enough," where his memory was "full of blanks," he was forced to be active, "registering" the world around him. He counted "small volcanoes" amid a confusion of sizes; he built a sort of minimalist poetry by combining the limited features of that world (one variety each of tree snail, tree, berry, and so on) and playing their combinations as if on a "home-made flute" with "the weirdest scale on earth"; he entered "the questioning shrieks [and] equivocal replies / over a ground of hissing rain" of the island's conversations; he played with names; he stumbled into dreams of unmarked "infinities" opening before him; and he made a temporary relationship with Friday. What Crusoe realizes, returned to the coarse mesh of England and seeing many of his tools now only as souvenirs, is that what was live about them was their fragility—their active fragility that, like description, came alive when used:

The knife there on the shelf—
it reeked of meaning, like a crucifix.
It lived. How many years did I
beg it, implore it, not to break?
I knew each nick and scratch by heart,
the bluish blade, the broken tip,

the lines of wood-grain on the handle . . .
Now it won't look at me at all.

"The Moose" (CPO, 169–73) gradually gains a look through our finitude
at two impossible-to-master things: "life . . . / . . . (also death)" and the "im-
penetrable wood" of nature. And it does so through the most casual of
dissolvings—the rocking rhythms of a nighttime bus trip gradually pulling
away all structures and leaving only "a dreamy divagation" that goes on and on.
In this last book, we dream our way through the same blurry, alert, potentially
acute areas Bishop has always explored—but now they are broad areas: the
self, home, nature, the finite rhythms of life. What is wonderful in "The
Moose" is how casual the whole thing is. The poem's first long sentence pulls
her away from home and the unfamiliar. She is transported from "narrow
provinces" where all is predictable; even extraordinary sights like a river
"enter[ing] or retreat[ing] / in a wall of brown foam" or the sun setting before
a "red sea" or across "burning rivulets" depend on the predictability of "the
bay coming in, / the bay not at home." "Home," in fact, pulses through these
opening stanzas like a quieting metronome. Away from home, the bus trip
quietly erases the ability to see as, evening coming on, "the light / grows richer;
[and] the fog, / shifting, salty, thin, / comes closing in." This produces in the
traveler a kind of half-sight, half-blurred-dream exploration, as if she can see
"crystals [of fog] / form and slide and settle" not on the bus windows but on the
hens' feathers outside. In that dissolved place, then, we ask, as always, what
can we see and notice and hear? Two things. First, the poem acknowledges
and enters the finite rhythms of our lives. Bishop's narrator gets to that by
dreamily drifting in the dark bus into a place of not-knowing. "[A] gentle,
auditory, / slow hallucination" leads her into a conversation in the back of the
bus. The voices are old enough, torn enough, that they are like birdsongs;
they talk as if on porches in Eternity with all of life visible and "things cleared
up finally." And what is mentioned and cleared up, it seems by the knowing
rhythms and the "sharp, indrawn breath[s], / half groan, half acceptance," is
"deaths, deaths and sicknesses," the inexorable erosion of our lives. And yet,
in this wandering place outside the rational, the poet hears those tearing facts
being greeted with a rhythmic " 'Yes . . .' that peculiar / affirmative. 'Yes . . .'
/ . . . We know *it* (also death)." Life is known in this let-loose-to-wander space.

And then second, matching the "peaceful" acceptance of the unmasterable
rhythms of life, a moose comes "out of / the impenetrable wood" and stops the
dreamy bus, "stands there, looms, rather." She simply towers, sniffs, allows
herself to be seen, offering not complete immersion in the impenetrable but

a pleasure nonetheless—one "flowing and flown." Without a home, without an explanatory sentence to rely on, the speaker discovers the world itself to be "homely as a house":

> Taking her time,
> she looks the bus over,
> grand, otherworldly.
> Why, why do we feel
> (we all feel) this sweet
> sensation of joy?

So, though it won't last, and the net heals up again, a peaceful gaze at a world not knowable or masterable seems also an option for Bishop's wanderer.

"Poem" (CPO, 176–77) does the same thing with the broad concept of memory.[20] Just as we have seen what comes alive in looking or loving or traveling or having a self, this poem dramatizes how our finite condition comes alive in the act of remembering. It's another exploratory drama, opening up from within the act of remembering. The poem initially raises the issue of finitude by looking at another painting by her great uncle that, "About the size of an old-style dollar bill," seems deliberately to raise the issue of value and then to signal its failures within that system. The poet confirms that lead: the painting has "never earned any money," is at best "a minor family relic"; it is "useless and free." So, once again, a claim to properly represent or master or order has been dissolved. But, as always, that leaves an opening to wander through and explore. What's to be seen there, in this failed representation?

> It must be Nova Scotia; only there
> does one see gabled wooden houses
> painted that awful shade of brown.
> The other houses, the bits that show, are white.
> Elm trees, low hills, a thin church steeple
> —that gray-blue wisp—or is it? In the foreground
> a water meadow with some tiny cows,
> two brushstrokes each, but confidently cows;
> two minuscule white geese in the blue water,
> back-to-back, feeding, and a slanting stick.
> Up closer, a wild iris, white and yellow,
> fresh-squiggled from the tube.
> The air is fresh and cold; cold early spring
> clear as gray glass; a half inch of blue sky

below the steel-gray storm clouds.
(They were the artist's specialty.)
A specklike bird is flying to the left.
Or is it a flyspeck looking like a bird?

What Bishop sees is a kind of drama going on. A series of torn gestures has been recorded. As she reads shades and wisps, brushstrokes and squiggles, a half inch of blue and steel-gray clouds, she pieces together a plausible interpretation: Nova Scotia; cows, geese, and iris in a "water meadow"; cold early spring. And, accentuating the tentativeness of the act, some parts of the gesture seem obviously inadequate. Is that a steeple? Is that a bird?

As we have perhaps become adept at noticing, handling finite paint in this way causes representation (once its authority has eroded) to come even more fully alive. In this nonauthorized space, Bishop's speaker realizes that she knows—or thinks she knows—the place being represented and brings the issue of representation to intense yet inviting life:

Heavens, I recognize the place, I know it!
It's behind—I can almost remember the farmer's name.
His barn backed on that meadow. There it is,
titanium white, one dab. The hint of steeple,
filaments of brush-hairs, barely there,
must be the Presbyterian church.
Would that be Miss Gillespie's house?
Those particular geese and cows
are naturally before my time.

Like Robinson Crusoe on the island, memory here becomes a sort of home-made, tentative, filled-with-blanks affair. The one who remembers is pulled into the issues of representation—of naming and remembering—just like she had been pulled into the issue of creating a self or confronting life's rhythms on the bus. Working with dabs of paint and brush-hair hints, and with equally sketchy traces of her own memory—"I can almost remember," "Would that be?" "those particular geese and cows" I can't be expected to remember—she shifts between paint and world and memory. It's carefully done, this drama. Memory allows her to identify that white "dab" as a particular barn rather than (as before) the "bit that shows" of some house, and then, as if moving through the painted world, to find a particular church (no guesses now) and perhaps a particular house. Think of the issues alive here, the questions raised. The painting feels like life, but it's actually paint, isn't it? It feels like life, but by life we must mean memory, itself incomplete, time-bound, compressed. This place has a name, but what are names and how much do they hold? What comes alive is the whole complicated set of issues raised in remembering (or having a self and so on).

What has happened is that the coincidence of sharing an experience has opened up, in a powerful way, the "which is which" issues involved in looking at and shaping the world:

> Our visions coincided—"visions" is
> too serious a word—our looks, two looks:
> art "copying from life" and life itself,
> life and the memory of it so compressed
> they've turned into each other. Which is which?

Which is life and which my reduction—my copy, my memory—of it? "Which eye's his eye?" This is not an impossible question to answer, but it takes continuous work because, as this poem has shown, the two are always turning into each other and the question has to be answered again and again. It is not enough, this poem suggests, to rest with the first stanza and say we have only the copy—that skeptical response leaves our human condition dead. Nor is it enough to say that language or paint gives us life there in front of us. We are in between, Bishop suggests, in a place where one has to pay attention even to flyspecks. Art's compression of life, memory's compression of life, our inevitable reduction of experience to "little paintings"—these situations, if we look deeply, bring us to these uncertain places where we are most human because most aware of our finite condition. Bishop's poetry is all about measuring our activities in those finite places, and it is about quietly insisting that in suffering those activities, in dramatizing the issues raised there, we coincide with others—we meet them, bird songs out of the mist, across the space of our finitude.

Life is an endless handling of these questions, an endless acting on their implications. What comes alive in Bishop is the dilemma of being human, of being involved in a place where no single answer is "useful" or guaranteed. Call it, to look back and revise the poem's first lament, the space where one is both "useless and free":

> Life and the memory of it cramped,
> dim, on a piece of Bristol board,

dim, but how live, how touching in detail
—the little we get for free,
the little of our earthly trust. Not much.

The "little we get for free" is the small, finite space "of our abidance." It is where, in the face of knowledge that this scene will soon be "dismantled," we struggle with our limits, all the questions it raises coming at us alive and shivering. As the poets who work with Bishop's framing of these issues testify, we abide in that struggle and those questions.

2. John Ashbery's New Voice

In a 1961 piece for *ArtNews* on the murmuring intimacy of Henri Michaux's work, John Ashbery singled out this statement of Michaux's aims: "Instead of one vision which excludes others, I would have liked to draw the moments that, placed side by side, go to make up a life. To expose the interior phrase for people to see, the phrase that has no words, a rope which uncoils sinuously, and intimately accompanies everything that impinges from the outside or the inside. I wanted to draw the consciousness of existence and the flow of time. As you would take your pulse."[1] One of the many remarkable things about this passage, reprinted in Ashbery's collected art criticism *Reported Sightings* (1989), is the hold it must have had on his imagination. Years later, the desire to make the many sides of consciousness visible—what Michaux calls here the wordless "interior phrase" playing responsively against what "impinges from the outside or the inside"—still drives his work. In a bold sort of literalism, most Ashbery poems, in the name of reflecting what he calls in an interview "the whole mind," focus on writing, since that is what he is engaged in as he tries to draw consciousness into visibility.[2] Though other concerns move in and out of his mind, it is the attempt to reflect (and reflect on) "the maximum of my experience when I'm writing" that drives most of the colliding analogies and comparisons of his poems (NYQ, 128). Ashbery argues in an interview that, far from pulling him away from his experience, "The interests of realism in poetry are actually enhanced in the long run by a close involvement with language; thought created by language and creating it are the nucleus of the poem" (J, 71). That involvement, inevitably bringing him to grips with the limits and frailties of words, often leads him into what he calls a pause or a halt in language's straightforward drive to master or order the world—a pause, however, that itself generates a new series of concerns or reflections.[3] Most Ashbery poems both enact, and reflect on, the free unfolding there of Michaux's many-sided phrase. As he comments in a number of interviews, in that pause, "concentrating attentively in order to pick up whatever is in the air . . . the disparate circumstances that as I say are with us at every moment," "somehow elucidat[ing] a lot of almost invisible currents and knocking them into some sort of shape," he finds himself able to "reproduce the polyphony that goes on inside me, which I don't think is radically different from that of other people" (NYQ, 113, 119, 121; SAP, 50). In the end, he comments, "a person is somehow given an embodiment out of those proliferating reflections that are occurring in a generalized mind which eventually run together into the image of a specific person, 'he' or 'me,' who was not there when the poem began" (NYQ, 131–32).[4]

Ashbery's books offer an almost bewildering array of different ways of reflectively involving himself with language. We have looked at Stanley Cavell's argument that in fully inhabiting our linguistic condition we are in fact reminding ourselves of our human finitude: "Words come to us from a distance; they were there before we were born; we are born into them. Meaning them is accepting that fact of their condition" (SW, 64). He claims, using Thoreau's *Walden* as an example, that such an acknowledgment brings us "back to a context in which [words] are alive" (SW, 92) because of their finitude— their distance or strangeness. Cavell finds in *Walden's* "endless computations of words," its "puns and paradoxes, its fracturing of idiom and twisting of quotation, its drones of fact and flights of impersonation" (SW, 63, 16), a forceful illustration of how that acknowledgment can generate a wide-awake response to one's experience. Ashbery's work is the strongest contemporary example we have of such an endless computation of language's condition—a deceptively casual pulse-taking that finds, in "inhabiting our investment in words, in the world" (C, 61), the opportunity, in Thoreau's terms, to "begin to find ourselves, and realize where we are and the infinite extent of our relations" (SW, 50).[5] If, as I have suggested, Elizabeth Bishop's work is deeply important to younger writers because of the way she implicates more and more of the world in the "fine, torn fish-nets" of her struggles with language, Ashbery's work is equally important for the cascade of other finite "systems" his poems measure themselves against as they reflectively enter these same linguistic issues. His work has become a sourcebook for poets conducting similar investigations, and in what follows, I will try to describe the different features and implications of his various ways of framing and generating such reflections. Ashbery calls this, in one poem, "Bringing a system of them [words, ways of organizing the world] into play" (ST, 3), and adds, in another, "By so many systems / As we are involved in, by just so many / Are we set free on an ocean of language" (W, 71). That demonstration of freedom, finally, is his legacy to contemporary poets.[6]

Ashbery's first book, *Some Trees* (1956), is composed of a series of often oblique sketches of expression's problematic nature. Its parrots and painters, young men and novices raise problems and then usually wander off the page. The book's first poem, for example, presents, as its title puts it, "Two Scenes" (SOT, 21)—one in which the poet asserts that visible action might articulate an unspoken relationship ("We see us as we truly behave"); and one in which the complexity of reading such an articulation is acknowledged: "In the evening / Everything has a schedule, if you can find out what it is." These early poems tend to end with such problematic acknowledgments. "In the flickering evening the martins grow denser," one poem puts it. "Rivers of wings surround us and vast tribulation" (SOT, 34). Though the poems seem convinced that, as "The Picture of Little J. A. in a Prospect of Flowers" has it, "only in the light of lost words / Can we imagine our rewards" (SOT, 41), most do not go far with such an imagining.

Two frequently reprinted poems from this first book do, however, offer some sense of how Ashbery's reflections will develop. The title poem suggestively links one of the book's problematic scenes with the poem being written before us. It begins by finding a note of assurance about the possibilities of speech in the way winter trees confidently sketch their alphabets against the sky: "each / Joining a neighbor, as though speech / Were a still performance" (SOT, 62). Emboldened by that promise and far enough from the world's threatening insistencies to feel safe, the poet turns toward a lover and speaks:

> you and I
> Are suddenly what the trees try
>
> To tell us we are:
> That their merely being there
> Means something; that soon
> We may touch, love, explain.

Even before that speech is quite articulated, however, before the couple, like the winter trees, actually touches and loves and explains, that still performance gives way and grows multiple and complicated:

> And glad not to have invented
> Such comeliness, we are surrounded:
> A silence already filled with noises,
> A canvas on which emerges
>
> A chorus of smiles, a winter morning.

Like the unreadable "schedule" replacing true behavior, this emerging canvas of the day is not what the trees promised. And yet, "Some Trees" suggests by its tone that there *is* some sort of touching and explaining being accomplished in that non-still chorus of morning noises. Further, it declares the poem itself—"these accents" in the last line responding to "these . . . amazing" trees in the first—to be an example of the wandering, claiming slyly that though its words seem like self-defense, perhaps they are, in their apparent reticence, in their limits, freely moving words of love: "Placed in a puzzling light, and moving, / Our days put on such reticence / These accents seem their own defense."[7]

"The Instruction Manual" (SOT, 26–30) is a first demonstration of what will become an often-repeated move in Ashbery—entering into the moving puzzlement of words in order to tease out life and freedom. It begins with a speaker bored with his job of "writ[ing] the instruction manual on the uses of a new metal." He almost immediately wanders away from that comically straightforward use of language by leaning out his window, looking down at the street, and dreaming of Guadalajara. In this bored pause, he plays out a visit never actually made. As his daydreaming reflections continue, he works out, in "lost words" doing no work, what he calls "the whole network" of the city's colors and neighborhoods and various lovers. What he discovers, in that mapless wandering, language let loose to play, is room to breathe—"a last breeze." He exults: "How limited, but how complete withal, has been our experience of Guadalajara!" One of the important moves Ashbery's poems will make, as they develop, is learning how to combine these two poems—how to marry an exuberant playing out of limits with an acknowledgment of the finite conditions of his own, never-still, written "accents."

But first, Ashbery made a step back toward greater reticence, his accents becoming even more puzzling. He wrote most of the poems in his second collection, *The Tennis Court Oath* (1962), in France, more aware of an acute sense of distance than of his role in the developing New York School of poetry he had become associated with. Although the same desire to find a breathing space within an acknowledgment of distance and finitude is present, this volume insists that the reader deal first (and I suppose primarily) with what it calls the "wreckage" of language. "They Dream Only of America" (TCO, 13) is a clear example. Here are its first three stanzas—apparently an oblique collection of non sequiturs, a heap of fragments:

> They dream only of America
> To be lost among the thirteen million pillars of grass:
> "This honey is delicious

Though it burns the throat."

And hiding from darkness in barns
They can be grownups now
And the murderer's ash tray is more easily—
The lake a lilac cube.

He holds a key in his right hand.
"Please," he asked willingly.
He is thirty years old.
That was before

The wreckage sorts a bit if you take the tense shifts as reliable. Provisionally, you can see here an event in the past being described. We seem to see a first encounter with a lover: " 'Please,' he asked" and "that was before." The fourth stanza fills in a bit more—"When his headache grew worse we / Stopped at a wire filling station"—while the fifth stanza pulls these glimpses together: "He went slowly into the bedroom." The present tense comments describe a mature stage in that relationship: "grownups now." At this stage what is delicious also "burns the throat," and "hiding" is involved. Most strikingly, it is a stage where that initial affair has become a complicated unraveling of signs and gestures—expressed either in the language of pulp fiction ("the murderer's ash tray") or domestic detail ("He holds a key.") As the fifth stanza has it, the desire to "touch, love, explain" has now come to be seen as a wearingly linguistic adventure:

Now he cared only about signs.
Was the cigar a sign?
And what about the key?

The dark sixth stanza—a speaker with a broken leg, back beside the bed, "waiting" in horror for "liberation"—helps us understand why the poem begins by looking forward, in the future, to traveling to "America" and being lost in what might be called a new, expansive way of speaking. The "many uttering tongues" celebrated in Whitman's leaves become here "thirteen million pillars of grass," freely broadcast across a landscape where, as the fourth stanza puts it, "We could drive for hundreds of miles / At night through dandelions." The poem, then, becomes readable as a tentative imagining of freedom in response to a relationship's constricting code, but the larger point still stands.[8] Ashbery attempts to find breathing room within these reflections on how we "touch, love, explain," but, with the rewards of that free space not easily imaginable, the wreckage of "lost words" dominates the poem's self-presentation. This is a reticent, defensive poem that suggests it might be more if we listen.

So, too, is the notorious collage "Europe"—a poem in 111 sections, many of its details cut out of a 1917 British detective novel entitled *Beryl of the Biplane* and seemingly exploded across the page. The first section, for example, reads:

> To employ her
> construction ball
> Morning fed on the
> light blue wood
> of the mouth
>   cannot understand
> feels deeply)
> (TCO, 64)

As John Shoptaw has pointed out, the World War I story of Beryl and Ronald Pryor and their plane "The Hornet," with its emphasis on codes and disguises and secret agents, has obvious connections to the "paranoid" political atmosphere of the 1950s, and Ashbery might usefully be read here as picking through the wreckage of that decade.[9] But one might also note that the fragments of the story of Beryl's experimental flying machine also allow us to think about Ashbery's reflections on the conditions—let's say the limits, here displayed as wreckage—of language. What "rewards" can be imagined in light of our acknowledgment of the "lostness" of our words? What "America" does wrecked "Europe" dream of? How might that wreckage be reassembled?

It is possible to identify two chains of language that speak to just these issues. First, one can find throughout the poem references to wreckage linked with the failure to understand—wreckage being connected to signs becoming unreadable or unusable, the work on the instruction manual being halted. The section I have just quoted, for example, juxtaposes a "construction ball" tearing down abandoned structures to a situation like this splintered poem where the gap between what the writer "feels deeply" and what he can express "of the mouth" is filled with tumbling words we "cannot understand." Sections 13 and 14 link "human waste" to that empty period of waiting "until the truth can be explained." Section 10 describes someone who had "mistaken his book for garbage" while 34 links a similar failure to "understand their terror" to "waste . . . offal." Most directly, the close of the poem, collaging together a few fragments of a plane wreck in *Beryl* caused by "steel bolts / having been replaced / by a painting of / one of wood!," comments on the result of that misrepresentation in this stark phrase: "I don't understand wreckage" (TCO, 83). At the same time, one can also take note of a second chain of fragments that begins to suggest a way to respond to that wreckage, or begins to find within the acknowledged failure to understand life and movement. Significantly, what emerges is deeply disguised and reticent—a plane, equipped with a "silencer" rising above the waste and disappearing from view—much like the ending of "Some Trees." Section 8 begins with "slight engine trouble" but eventually declares that "All was now ready for the continuance of the journey" while section 14 leaps from standing "Before the waste" to something that "went up." Successful runs of the disguised, silenced machine, reading much like a reorienting of language, occur in sections 37—the machine "described a half-circle, and, though / still rising rapidly, . . . head[ed] eastward in / the direction of the sea"—and 48, 66, and 68. The last three are all variations of the same observation: "She followed a straight line leading / due north through Suffolk and Norfolk." The poem's last section completes this chain by describing "a beam of intense, white light" that, mimicking the silenced plane's movements, sweeps the sky with its coded, unreadable reflections. The poem, I take it, holds on to the thought that movement and freedom are potential within the acknowledgment of wreckage, but can as yet only imagine, in that reassembled plane, the obvious feature of reticence.

Ashbery's third volume, *Rivers and Mountains* (1966), published after his return to the United States, is a turning point, for here he works out first versions of many of his mature approaches to these issues. We have already looked at the way in "Clepsydra" (RM, 27–33) the "serpentine" "dance of non-discovery"—the poet reflecting on the act of thinking he engages in as he writes, but the "page held / Too close to be legible"—"examine[s] the distance" involved in writing and unfolds its seemingly limitless, loopy potential. And we have thought about the way the poem's *I* speaks to its *you*—the intimate tone of this address seemingly generated by the speaker holding a specific lover in mind, but the *you* itself being something closer to consciousness made visible. Reflecting on *you*, the *I* both speaks about the features and conditions of language and opens a space to love freely. Cavell would say one situation measures the other. The other major poem in *Rivers and Mountains* is the long poem "The Skaters" (RM, 34–63). It is another reflective entry into what it calls the labyrinth, "that mazy business / About writing" (RM, 47), but in feel it is so much closer to the exuberant investigation of Guadalajara in *Some Trees* than it is to the intimate self-monitoring of "Clepsydra" that one can almost overlook the fact that it is another investigation of language's distance from what it would speak for: "it is you I am parodying, / Your invisible denials" (RM, 42).[10]

Deliberately echoing the connection between "these trees" and "these accents" in "Some Trees," Ashbery begins the poem by remarking of a bright mass of turning skaters in February that, "These decibels / Are a kind of flagellation, an entity of sound / Into which being enters, and is apart" (RM, 34). This comparison between the way the bright shouts of the skaters focus the day's energy and hold it out for display and the way the sounded syllables of our language perform the same bright trick continually surfaces and holds the poem together. He writes, for example, that when we move into language, what happens is that "this normal, shapeless entity" of consciousness is "Forgotten as the words fly briskly across, each time / Bringing down meaning as snow from a low sky, or rabbits flushed from a wood" (RM, 35–36). The most striking part of the comparison is the realization that the brisk mass of flying skaters, that beautiful, dissolving movement into language, continually spins off a series of individual performers: "skaters [who] elaborate their distances, / Taking a separate line to its end. Returning to the mass, they join each other / Blotted in an incredible mess of dark colors, and again reappearing to take the theme / Some little distance" (RM, 37). Such formal elaborations of being's visible "apart[ness]" are one way the mass "turns to look at itself" (RM, 38). The parallel holds, for the parodies of linguistic performance— "knowing where men *are* coming from . . . hold[ing] the candle up to the album" (RM, 41)—that make up the concluding sections of the poem can be seen as elaborating language's distance from what it would speak for, playing out that denial (those "orphaned after-effects") with great high spirits.[11]

The strongest poems in *The Double Dream of Spring* (1970) return to the way "Clepsydra" addresses and reflects on *you*—what I have been calling consciousness-made-visible. Many of these poems adopt, in that reflective space, the sort of intimate, murmuring lover's tone that we first saw in "Some Trees." "I've been thinking about you / . . . Reflecting among arabesques of speech that arise," Ashbery whispers in "The Hod Carrier" (DD, 57). "You," he promises in "Spring Day," "Gracious and growing thing, with those leaves like stars, / We shall soon give all our attention to you" (DD, 15). This tone both acknowledges a sense of separation from the world's way of speaking and turns aside to enter into that difference: "life is divided up / Between you and me, and among all the others out there" (DD, 20). Like the bored pause in "The Instruction Manual" or the in-process beginning of "Clepsydra," this tone leaves the poet with what the first poem calls a "Task" (DD, 13). In "a predicated romance," where the lover will eventually "return unfruitful,"

Ashbery claims to find a value in reflection's "linear acting into that time"—what I have been calling a reflective playing out of the conditions the lovers share. Said simply, in that tone I have been referring to: "if these are regrets they stir only lightly / The children playing after supper, / Promise of the pillow and so much in the night to come. / I plan to stay here a little while." What is most important about this volume, I think, is the way Ashbery begins to describe what is gained in such reflective elaborations. What does it mean to be able to breathe free in an imagined Guadalajara or America?

"Soonest Mended" (DD, 17–19) describes *you* and *I* as "Barely tolerated, living on the margin / In our technological society," "merely spectators" rather than "players." Why? Because the two, refusing to claim a unity between consciousness and its verbal display, are in a relationship one could describe as "fence-sitting / Raised to the level of an esthetic ideal" or "cowering / . . . in the early lessons, since the promise of learning / Is a delusion . . . / . . . thinking not to grow up." What is gained by "this . . . action, this not being sure, this careless / Preparing, sowing the seeds crooked in the furrow" is an ability to step away from language's blinding, inherited drive to master and complete: "To step free at last, minuscule on the gigantic plateau— / This was our ambition: to be small and clear and free." That gigantic plateau, I take it, is what is not languageable—consciousness, the world outside of us, an other. One is free from having to hold and own it precisely because one has been forced into the same situation with respect to words. Ashbery, that is to say, is involving himself with: "The being of our sentences, in the climate that fostered them, / Not ours to own, like a book, but to be with, and sometimes / To be without, alone and desperate."

Ashbery's book-length prose meditation, *Three Poems* (1972), works out many of the ideas I have been developing at great length. It is the poem in which many of Ashbery's readers first began to get a handle on his issues and his typical ways of conducting his linguistic investigations. Certainly, I have had its manner of acknowledging language's conditions and reflectively dramatizing those issues in mind as I have sketched in the preceding readings. Like "Clepsydra" or much of the work in *The Double Dream of Spring*, the poem is another address to *you*, now clearly defined as that portion of consciousness made visible. One example of *you*, of course, is the poem taking shape before us: "I thought that if I could put it all down, that would be one way. And next the thought came to me that to leave all out would be another, and truer, way. . . . But, forget as we will, something soon comes to stand in their place. Not the truth, perhaps, but—yourself" (TP, 3). The fact that the *you* that takes form is never "true" provides the grounds for the initial opening up in "The New Spirit" of a pause or gap in language's straightforward flow. It acknowledges skepticism's truth about human limits. With that pause acknowledged, *you* becomes a "System"—as the second poem's title has it— that can be entered and played out and freely reassembled. If the first poem points to the limits of "these accents," the second poem is a wandering visit through its vast network. That is to say, it convincingly combines "Some Trees" and "The Instruction Manual." The third poem performs a brief "Recital" of these names—a closing that Ashbery will employ in many different ways in subsequent books. And further, like the cut out phrases in "Europe," the poem deliberately adopts a language that, in its worn familiarity and lack of drive, serves as a constant reminder of language's limits and, paradoxically, provides an area within which one can be, as if on a gigantic plateau, "small and clear and free."[12] That worn language, like Thoreau's distance from civilization, provides the reflective ground within which Ashbery works.

"The New Spirit" is clear from its first sentences that *you* will never be an adequate representation of consciousness. This acknowledgment of language's finitude is imagined as breaking open or revealing its true nature as a tomb or as the guardian of an empty center. What the first poem wants to do is establish the conditions whereby the implications of that finitude can be displayed: "We have broken through into the meaning of the tomb. But the act is still proposed, before us, // it needs pronouncing. To formulate oneself around this hollow, empty sphere . . . To be your breath as it is taken in and shoved out. Then, quietly, it would be as objects placed along the top of a wall: a battery jar, a rusted pulley, shapeless wooden boxes, an open can of axle grease, two lengths of pipe. . . . We see this moment from outside as within" (TP, 5). We can think of these objects as the "orphaned . . . after-effects" of expression or "circulating" bits of language, freed by that acknowledgment and "carted off" to the backyard. Ashbery writes: "you will have to take apart the notion of you so as to reconstruct it from an intimate knowledge of its inner workings. How harmless and even helpful the painted wooden components of the Juggernaut look scattered around the yard, waiting to be reassembled" (TP, 19–20). Deliberately adopting a language he describes as having "taken on that look of worn familiarity, like pebbles polished over and over again by the sea" (TP, 117), and producing, in its use, "a vast wetness as of sea and air combined, a single smooth, anonymous matrix without surface or depth" (TP, 118), Ashbery creates an exaggerated display of consciousness tracked, as it must be, "from outside" (TP, 5). He calls it the establishment of an "outer rhythm," an accessing of language's finite, nonideal conditions: "you must grow up, the outer rhythm more and more accelerate, past the ideal rhythm of the spheres that seemed to dictate you, that seemed the establishment of your seed and the conditions of its growing, upward, someday into leaves and fruition and final sap" (TP, 6). What that tracking of consciousness will produce, the poem hopes, is not just a version of the poet's speaking self but a re-seeing of language as "a medium through which we address one another, the independent life we were hoping to create. . . . A permanent medium in which we are lost, since becoming robs it of its potential" (TP, 13). Staying lost with language, then, becomes a demonstration of a place of potential—call it a "safe vacuum" where one can becomes "small and clear and free":

> Is it correct for me to use you to demonstrate all this? Perhaps what I am saying is that it is I the subject, recoiling from you at an ever-increasing speed just so as to be able to say I exist in that safe vacuum I had managed to define from my friends' disinterested turning away. As if I were only a flower after all and not the map of the country in which it grows. There is more to be said about this, I guess, but it does not seem to alter anything that I am the spectator, you what is apprehended. (TP, 15)

In "The System," Ashbery begins his work as reflective spectator, working within the "open field of narrative possibilities" (TP, 41) that language has now become. I think it is one of the most important poems he has written. Ashbery begins with an almost ritual acknowledgment of limits, in a sense bringing all of "The New Spirit" back into play at the start of this poem. Poetry, he notes, is in the business of describing how "being" "logically unshuffl[es] into . . . morning," a process that involves "mastering the many pauses and the abrupt, sharp accretions of regular being in the clotted sphere of today's activities" (TP, 53–54). Though a difficult task, it is one a poet is expected to accomplish. Call it making a habitation for the soul: "All the facts are here and it remains only to use them in the right combinations, but that building will be the size of today, the rooms habitable and leading into one another in a lasting sequence, eternal and of the greatest timeliness" (TP, 54) However, this poet has come to glory in the fact that such a habitation (the previous poem had called it "the completed Tower of Babel"—TP, 50) is beyond him; there are always "dry churrings of no timbre, hysterical staccato passages that one cannot master or turn away from" (TP, 54). Such a realization means that alongside "the classic truths of daily life" (TP, 55)—the expectation that everyone "really knew what it [truth] *was* [and] life uncurled around it . . . as though innumerable transparent tissues hovered around these two entities and joined them in some way," the truth expressing itself in "sentences [that] . . . were dry and clear, as though made of wood"—alongside those confident sentences, there must exist "a residue, a kind of fiction" which could be made out exploring those non-masterable sensations and the sentences they generate and start up (TP, 55). One could call this an "other tradition," formed out of reflecting on the conditions of language in a space where it doesn't move confidently forward: "other, unrelated happenings that form a kind of sequence of fantastic reflections as they succeed each other at a pace and according to an inner necessity of their own . . . The living aspect of these obscure phenomena has never to my knowledge been examined from a point of view like the painter's: in the round" (TP, 56).

"The System" both unfolds its own sequence of fantastic reflections and meditates on what is "living" or breathing about them. In a sense, it is a response to concerns left hanging in "Some Trees" and "Europe." What could such a poetry be other than self-defense? What is living about it? How could an elaboration of distance offer a place to breathe? In this poem, those fantastic reflections are generated by the disorienting experience of falling in love: "The switches had been tripped, as it were; the entire world or one's limited but accurate idea of it was bathed in a glowing love" (TP, 56). Such an experience produces a "roiling [of] the clear waters of the reflective intellect" with "the bases for true reflective thinking . . . annihilated" and an opportunity presented for following out "idle and frivolous trains of thought leading who knows where" (TP, 57). These trains of thought are the objects on the wall or the bits of circulating information spoken about earlier, what Ashbery describes here as a "cosmic welter of attractions . . . coming to stand for the real thing, which has to be colorless and featureless if it is to be the true reflection of the primeval energy from which it issued forth" (TP, 58). What becomes crucial now is Ashbery's discussion of their value.

At the very least, "mov[ing] around in our little ventilated situation, how roomy it seems!" (TP, 88), the poet has gained a deep awareness of, or sympathy with, our ways of speaking:

> And it is no longer a nameless thing, but something colorful and full of interest, a chronicle play of our lives, with the last act still in the dim future, so that we can't tell yet whether it is a comedy or a tragedy, all we know is that it is crammed with action and the substance of life. Surely all of this living that has gone on that is ours is good in some way, though we cannot tell why: we know only that our sympathy has deepened, quickened by the onrushing spectacle, to the point where we are like spectators swarming up onto the stage to be absorbed into

the play, though always aware that this is an impossibility, and that the actors continue to recite their lines as if we weren't there. (TP, 93–94)

Most importantly, he can be said to have developed a new voice, one that sees that the limits of words are the ground for an intimate, awestruck relation to what words would grasp—an other, the world, one's self:

> The person sitting opposite you who asked you a question is still waiting for the answer; he has not yet found your hesitation unusual, but it is up to you to grasp it with both hands, wrenching it from the web of connectives to rub off the grime that has obscured its brilliance so as to restore it to him, that pause which is the answer you have both been expecting. . . . It needs a new voice to tell it, otherwise it will seem just another awkward pause in a conversation largely made up of similar ones, and will never be able to realize its potential as a catalyst. (TP, 97)

The "new voice" of these reflections is the very thing all Ashbery poems seem to be searching for. Think of this, finally, as a reply to "Some Trees." The ground for touching, loving, and explaining turns out to be an acknowledgment that words shift and grow in puzzling, noncontainable ways; the "pause" becomes "the shortest distance between your aims and those of the beloved, the only human ground that can nurture your hopes and fears into the tree of life" (TP, 98).

The short final section of this poem, as its title indicates, recites what the poem has come to see and points the reader back to the poem's style as itself an acting out of these issues. It begins with a summary acknowledgment of limit. The reason *you* and *I* separate or are unable to order accurately what a new emotion sets in motion is that "not one-tenth or even one one-hundredth of the ravishing possibilities the birds sing about at dawn could ever be realized in the course of a single day" (TP, 107). This means, inevitably, that "we cannot interpret everything, we must be selective, and so the tale we are telling begins little by little to leave reality behind. It is no longer so much our description of the way things happen to us as our private song, sung in the wilderness" (TP, 109). Ritually pointing to this territory, he recites over and over: "Any reckoning of the sum total of the things we are is of course doomed to failure from the start, that is if it intends to present a true, wholly objective picture" (TP, 113). But he has also shown that such an acknowledgment opens up a new relation to "the insistent now that baffles and surrounds you in its loose-knit embrace that always seems to be falling away and yet remains behind, stubbornly drawing you, the unwilling spectator who had thought to stop only just for a moment, into the sphere of its solemn and suddenly utterly vast activities, on a new scale as it were, that you have neither the time nor the wish to unravel" (TP, 115). And it does so by means of its reflective, dramatized sentences that, like Thoreau's "endless computations of words," in their acknowledgment of limits and finitude, have acted out for their readers the generativity of language's limits: "conjugating in this way the distance and emptiness, transforming the scarcely noticeable bleakness into something both intimate and noble" (TP, 118).

The title poem from *Self-Portrait in a Convex Mirror* (1975) consolidates these gains, dramatizing these issues in a more accessible manner that must account for the poem's immense popularity—the book swept the Pulitzer Prize, National Book Award, and National Book Critics Circle Award. In making Parmigianino's riddling mirror painting (1524; Vienna, Kunsthistorisches Museum) the *you* addressed in the poem and the system entered, Ashbery essentially recapitulates the strategies of his work to date in more familiar form. Allowing the painter's reproduction of the distorted face and large, foregrounded hand reflected in his convex mirror to function as a more directly approached version of the same *you* addressed and described in such poems as "Clepsydra" or "The New Spirit," Ashbery offers the reader something that seems at first closer to art criticism than to his more typical (and Stevensian) "mind in the act of finding." As well, in allowing the painting's distortions of hand, head, and background to bring to a halt the poem's attempt at the straightforward business of "Lifting the pencil to [his own] self-portrait" SP, 71), Ashbery recapitulates the way *Three Poems* and all its earlier variants found themselves forced by their own worn language to stop and grasp the pause in both hands, searching for a new voice to open and tell it.

The poem is broken into five sections, the first one serving, in a manner now familiar, to acknowledge (by describing) the distortions of form or focused consciousness. As I have worked out in detail in another context, Parmigianino's deliberately produced reflection seems to the poet to offer a series of comments about the limits of form.[13] Working out the implications of the foregrounded hand "protect[ing] / What it advertises," the "sequestered" face peering out from deep within the ball, and the room's background reduced to a few beams and flashes of window surrounding the presentation in a "coral ring" (SP, 68), Ashbery, in his own words, "reads" in the painting the "conditions" of its self-presentation (SP, 69). What are the limits within which "the soul establishes itself," he asks the painting, drawing particular attention to what the portrait "says" about the necessary distortions of medium—"its dimension, / What carries it" (SP, 68, 69). The painter's face being so far removed from the apparent surface of the globe seems an argument about the "distance" of a made thing from what it represents. The "soul," according to this reading, is, in this form, "a captive, treated humanely" (SP, 68). Its unmarked fluidity reduced so dramatically, it is in many ways "not a soul" at all: it "has to stay where it is, / Even though restless" (SP, 69). The foregrounded hand of art seems both to cause the distortion and to be straining, impossibly, to break "out of the globe" and do away with its material means of becoming visible. And the reduction of the background to surface seems to assert the medium's partiality in a particularly striking way:

> The surface is what's there
> And nothing can exist except what's there.
> There are no recesses in the room, only alcoves,
> And the window doesn't matter much, or that
> Sliver of window or mirror on the right
> (SP, 70)

All in all, the painting, in its "serene" presentation of such conditions of form as these in a "gesture which is neither embrace not warning / But which holds something of both" (SP, 70), seems a rich complex of remarks about language and writing and art.

As we have seen before, Ashbery, in staring at what could be his own reflection, must, in order to live into (or reflect on) those conditions, open up what he calls "the straight way out, / The distance between us" (SP, 71). He does so by emphasizing such things as the difference between his irregular, multiple-voiced sense of himself—"How many people came and stayed a certain time, / Uttered light or dark speech that became part of you"—and the control exerted by the painting's "curved hand" over such "irregular," "windblown" influences (SP, 71). He pulls back just as forcefully from the painting's background and its dizzying insistence on reducing multiplicity to a single gesture:

> desks, papers, books,
> Photographs of friends, the window and the trees
> Merging in one neutral band that surrounds
> Me on all sides, everywhere I look.
> And I cannot explain the action of leveling,
> Why it should all boil down to one
> Uniform substance, a magma of interiors.
> (SP, 71)

Three Poems, we remember, proposed that such an opened space paradoxically might provide "the shortest distance between your aims and those of the beloved, the only human ground" of live, intimate contact. What remains is for this poem to act out, speculate on, the life of the "distorted" language in this space.

The next three sections spin out a series of reflections. What is the relation between form and the uncharted vacuum of a "dream which includes them all" which they draw from and necessarily distort? Through form, "Something like living occurs, a movement / Out of the dream into its codification" (SP, 73). And why is seeing yourself in the otherness of form, being conscious of it, important? Why slow the process down (distort it) so it can be examined? Because, to put it simply, this is how we live, in and out of poems. The painting, the poem's examined *you*, has become a metaphor or a way to make visible the larger process of moving through life and time:

> Since it is a metaphor
> Made to include us, we are part of it and
> Can live in it as in fact we have done,
> Only leaving our minds bare for questioning
> We now see will not take place at random
> But in an orderly way that means to menace
> Nobody—the normal way things are done,
> Like the concentric growing up of days
> Around a life
> (SP, 76)

The last section of the poem, as is customary, becomes a recital. The poet pulls back from the mirror, insisting that "you can't live there" (SP, 79), yet working through a number of descriptions of the value of its "demonstration." Most powerfully, the painting—or poetry, or consciousness of mental activity—is valuable because we are able to feel our way into this most fundamental and generative of human activities:

> Is there anything
> To be serious about beyond this otherness
> That gets included in the most ordinary
> Forms of daily activity, changing everything
> Slightly and profoundly, and tearing the matter
> Of creation, any creation, not just artistic creation

Out of our hands, to install it on some monstrous, near
Peak, too close to ignore, too far
For one to intervene. This otherness, this
"Not-being-us" is all there is to look at
In the mirror, though no one can say
How it came to be this way.
(SP, 80–81)

That is, poetry (all of Ashbery's poetry) makes visible the otherness or distance from us of all our attempts at order. It reveals them to be finite, as distorted as a convex mirror. And it allows us to handle a sense of distance that is—as the live, tentative ground of all human activity—the only thing worth being serious about. Poetry changes our instrumental approach to language.

The careful discussion of method in *Three Poems* and "Self-Portrait" seems to have made it possible for Ashbery, in the work that followed, to quickly allude to those issues and bring that notion of the generative pause in language much more quickly into play. In *Houseboat Days* (1977), for example, simply calling attention to the lyric—its compression and comparisons, its turn toward meaning—is enough to foreground the distorted hand of art. Almost every poem in this collection contributes to a discussion of poetics—"What Is Poetry," one title asks—as if the *I* of the poem looks across at the *you* of the lyrics it is accumulating and then reflects on that distance. Much of this discussion is quite straightforward, as if in an interview or discussion with students.[14] What prompts the peculiar slide into private song of a typical Ashbery lyric, poised and listening to itself? "Sometimes a word will start it, like / Hands and feet, sun and gloves. The way / Is fraught with danger, you say, and I / Notice the word 'fraught' as you are telling / Me about huge secret valleys" (HD, 4). Why this attraction to mouthing what the title of one poem calls "Unctuous Platitudes" (HD, 12)?

I like the really wonderful way you express things
So that it might be said, that of all the ways in which to

Emphasize a posture or a particular mental climate
Like this gray-violet one with a thin white irregular line

Descending the two vertical sides, these are those which
Can also unsay an infinite number of pauses

In the ceramic day.

Isn't there something dangerously self-absorbed about all this insistent "un-saying" of one's own "ceramic" intentions? What about the real world outside of language?

> It is argued that these structures address themselves
> To exclusively aesthetic concerns, like windmills
> On a vast plain. To which it is answered
> That there are no other questions than these,
> Half squashed in mud, emerging out of the moment
> We all live, learning to like it.
> (HD, 48)

As Cavell might say, the question of poetry is really a version of all questions about our finite condition. The lyric itself, we might say, is a generative pause, a coming undone of language. To understand that "songs decorate our notion of the world / And mark its limits, like a frieze of soap-bubbles" (HD, 18) is to become aware of the "tentative ground" (HD, 22) of all our dealings with the world.

It becomes clear that one of the things Ashbery prides himself on is the inventiveness with which he sets up his explorations of the conditions of language—arrangements designed to "restore the pause" and surprise him into "tell[ing] it with a new voice." "Litany," a sixty-page poem from *As We Know* (1979), is his most striking improvisation. Written by dividing notebook pages into columns in order to keep two separate meditations afloat, the piece was published as a poem in two columns—one roman, one italic—conducting what Ashbery calls "simultaneous but independent monologues."[15] Although such a form leaves many choices up to the reader and appears to render a complete account of the poem all but impossible, it seems to me that some of our previous observations about Ashbery's ways of dramatizing these issues yield interesting fruit if applied here. I would argue, in fact, that the two voices, both of them the poet's, pursue two different aspects of the problem. What I will call voice A (in roman, on the left side of the page) calls attention to, over and over, the limits of writing and form. It is the voice of acknowledgment, calling attention to the placement of our structures "on death's dark river" (AWK, 46). We have seen that voice of acknowledgment in the first sections of "Self-Portrait" and *Three Poems*, the discussions of wreckage in "Europe," and the turn towards puzzlement and movement in "Some Trees"—to mention just a few examples. The poem's second, italic, voice—call it B—describes the landscape opened up in the pause or gap in language, showing the new sort of alertness possible in that breakdown. We saw that voice describing Guadalajara, or offering linguistic versions of skaters' displays, or playing out the implications of Parmigianino's "metaphor made to include us," or "spectating" in *Three Poems*. It is the "new voice," telling the pause. Together, they form a litany, not so much responding to each other point by point as an acknowledgment in one voice leading to an opening explored by the other voice leading to a renewed acknowledgment, and so on.

What is inventive in this poem is the presentation of these two concerns simultaneously, with each voice standing at a distance from the other—dramatized by the white space between them—and thus appearing to borrow from, support, contradict, and ignore the other voice. That presentation, like the worn clichés of *Three Poems* or the deliberately foregrounded distortion of Parmigianino's self-portrait or the display of the lyric's characteristics in *Houseboat Days*, acts out formally what the poem is about. It provides the "system" engaged with.[16] Both voices seem to talk constantly about the fact of their simultaneous existence—the easily grasped idea that we all have many potential trains of thought in our heads—often by taking note of the white space between them. Their simultaneity puts both reader and writer in a state of heightened uneasiness, never sure if what is seen can stand up to the implied criticism of the other voice, quite sure that this is no "still performance." As John Keeling argues, such reading and writing, with some things always unsettled and not taken in, provides what Ashbery calls an exercise in "*not knowing*" (AWK, 58).[17] But it is a not knowing native to the conditions of our language, the uneasy "human ground" where our work takes place. Let me, then, without a clear warrant, uneasily propose one way of reading this poem. I will first work out the separate tracks each voice goes down, repeated, I would assert, in each of the poem's three sections, then I will offer a few examples of how the simultaneous writing and presentation of these voices both unsettles and demonstrates those very ideas.

The first section of "Litany," at sixteen pages, is short enough to show this pattern clearly. In column A, the poet describes himself as someone, busy about his "accounts," who likes still performances—things "Kept in one place" (AWK, 3). That, he assures us, is why he is engaging in raising the flowers of this poem: "They do not stand for flowers or / Anything pretty they are / Code names for the silence" (AWK, 4). Encoding his silent experience, however, bringing it to visibility and voice, immediately brings him face to face with the limits of his tools. Think of this realization as noticing "dust blow[ing] through / A diagram of a room":

The dust blows in.
The disturbance is
Nonverbal communication:
Meaningless syllables that
Have a music of their own,
The music of sex, or any
Nameless event, something
That can only be taken as
Itself.
(AWK, 4)

This means, as we have seen for example in the wreckage of "Europe," that if not all of the "event" can be known, then language becomes a "great implosion" testifying to how much of the event it is silent about: "it persists / In dumbness which isn't even / A negative articulation—persists / And collapses into itself" (AWK, 5). At best, then, the articulation of a life articulates language's struggle with itself: "The motion by which a life / May be known and recognized, / [Is] a shipwreck seen from the shore, / A puzzling column of figures" (AWK, 6). Striking analogies for that puzzling wreckage mount, each new linguistic turn itself an example of the impossibility of fully pronouncing the poem's center-of-the-page blank. Language offers: a "rush of disguises / For the elegant truth" (AWK, 6); "a talking picture of you" reduced by a ticking clock to "mummified writing / . . . That never completes its curve / Or the thought of what / It was going to say" (AWK, 8); "A sheaf of selected odes / Bundled on the waters" (AWK, 11); the "zillionth" sampling of the past here, at the "fixed wall of water / That indicates where the present leaves off / And the past begins" (AWK, 12). It produces, to put it bluntly, a feeling of life being "woven on death's loom" (AWK, 15).

Ashbery's second voice eyes that same space, but describes that *"hole"* as a *"cloud / . . . haze that casts / The milk of enchantment / Over the whole town,"* revealing what *"Could be happening / Behind tall hedges / Of dark, lissome knowledge"* (AWK, 3). And what is there when knowledge has been stopped? One would have to describe it as the stuff of language, what other poems have called "ways of speaking," displayed before us: *"Around us are signposts / Pointing to the past, / The old-fashioned, pointed / Wooden kind. And nothing directs / To the present"* (AWK, 3). But ways of speaking displayed and made available—in familiar phrasing, *"A new alertness changes / Into the look of things / Placed on the railing / Of this terrace"* (AWK, 5). The terrace this time is the center gap, acknowledged by A; the "things" are what other poems have called the linguistic "workings" of *you* scattered around the backyard, disassembled and known intimately. Think of the backyard of this poem, to mention just one of its striking analogies, as a place in language where, like the academy, our ways of speaking of the world are held in solution:

> *Certainly the academy has performed*
> *A useful function. Where else could*
> *Tiny flecks of plaster float almost*
> *Forever in innocuous sundown almost*
> *Fashionable as the dark probes again.*
> (AWK, 14–15)

The most interesting thing that happens to these two voices in the first section of "Litany" is that as they begin to wind down—"You knew / You were coming to the end by the way the other / Would be beginning again, so that nobody / Was ever lonesome" (AWK, 15)—they begin to take explicit note of what the distortion of the two voices together has produced. Voice A speaks of the way the constant pressure of alternate ways of voicing produces "only picture-making" and no "dramatic conclusion," but comments on the fragile intimacy, aware of the live edges between things, that has been experienced as a result:

> Under
> The intimate light of the lantern
> One really felt rather than saw
> The thin, terrifying edges between things
> And their terrible cold breath.
> And no one longed for the great generalities
> These seemed to preclude.
> (AWK, 16)

Voice B, a little softer, insists that the sentences' collapse, the breaking off of generalities, and the wandering without authority, have produced in this section another version of "the shortest distance between your aims and those of the beloved, the only human ground" (TP, 98):

> *Two could*
> *Go on at once without special permission*
> *And the dreams were responsible to no base*
> *Of authority but could wander on for*
> *Short distances into the amazing nearness*

That the world seemed to be.
(AWK, 16)

The world is near because of language's acknowledged finitude; "small and clear and free" (DD, 17), words leave the edges between things.

The second section is quite long—forty pages. Let me oversimplify and just trace out a thread or two, to demonstrate the play of voices. Voice A is concerned this time with the way the attempt to unfold the complexities of the moment inevitably leads away from singleness to an ever-expanding network. As in "Some Trees," the poem acknowledges the powers of that almost-monstrous expansion:

> There comes a time when the moment
> Is full of, knows only itself.
> . . . .
> Then there are two moments,
> How can I explain?
> It was as though this thing—
> More creature than person—
> Lumbered at me out of the storm,
> Brandishing a half-demolished beach umbrella,
> So that there might be merely this thing
> And me to tell about it.
> (AWK, 18–19)

As always, a series of analogies follows. The loss of the moment is like never being able to catch up with oneself: "All that fall I wanted to be with you, / Tried to catch up to you in the streets / Of that time" (AWK, 19). It is a pursuit conducted with a certain stylistic charm:

>   Poetry
> Has already happened. And the agony
> Of looking steadily at something isn't
> Really there at all, it's something you
> Once read about; its narrative thrust
> Carries it far beyond what it thought it was
> All het up about; its charm, no longer
> A diversionary tactic, is something like
> Grace, in the long run, which is what poetry is.
> (AWK, 37–38)

Most forcefully, that loss is a performed failure of the word, an exfoliation of terms and analogies out of a central crater or tomb:

> It all boils down to
> Nothing, one supposes. There is a central crater
> Which is the word, and around it
> All the things that have names, a commotion
> Of thrushes pretending to have hatched
> Out of the great egg that still hasn't been laid.
> These one gets to know, and by then
> They have formed tightly compartmented, almost feudal
> Societies claiming kinship with the word.
> (AWK, 55)

Across the gap, accompanying this acknowledgment, is the second voice, pointing to what is possible in language, now that the sentence's claims are derailed and *"the code is ventilated"* (AWK, 44). We are, this voice insists, able now *"to get inside the frame"* (AWK, 28) or move freely *"inside its space"* (AWK, 30), having grown *"aware through the layers of numbing comfort, / the eiderdown of materialism and space, how much meaning / Was there languishing at the roots, and how / To take some of it home before it melts"* (AWK, 29). An extended analogy linking an acknowledgment of language's gaps—its inability to ever complete its notation of a series of moments—and the life-giving ventilation of the code we all live within can usefully summarize many of the concerns of this section. Ashbery writes, recalling a scene from *Three Poems*:

> *The shops here don't sell anything*
> *One would want to buy.*
> *It's even hard to tell exactly what*
> *They're selling—in one, you might*
> *Find a pile of ventilators next*
> *To a lot of cuckoo-clock parts,*
> *Plus used government documents and stacks*
> *Of cans of brine shrimp*
> . . . .
>   *You*
> *Pick up certain things here, where*
> *You need them, and*
> *Do without the others for a moment,*

> *Essential though they may be.*
> *Every collection is notable for its gaps*
> *As for what's there. The wisest among us*
> *Collect gaps, knowing it's the only way*
> *To realize a more complete collection.*
> (AWK, 18–19)

Putting one use of language aside (let's call it buying) and taking on another (call it gap collecting, of which Ashbery is a master) enables all sorts of things to happen. *"We can breathe!"* we hear a few pages later. But perhaps most important is that, in such collections, we establish a new, intimate ground where, always realizing the incompleteness of each current effort, we keep looking forward to new voices and expansions. Such an unfolding of our life in language is, Ashbery would claim, a display of the human condition—the range of his voice nothing less than an ambitious claim for his art:

> *But exactly whom are you aware of*
> *Who can describe the exact feel*
> *And slant of a field in such a way as to*
> *Make you wish you were in it, or better yet*
> *To make you realize that you actually are in it*
> *For better or worse, with no*
> *Conceivable way of getting out?*
> *That is what*
> *Great poets of the past have done, and a few*
> *Great critics as well. But today*
> *Nobody cares or stands for anything.*
> (AWK, 33)

The last section of "Litany" is another recital. It is only ten pages long, with both voices attempting to lay claim to having most forcefully demonstrated the implications of the poem's form—that is, in a phrase they both repeat, that poetry "starts out / With some notion and switches to both" (AWK, 63). Perhaps the best way to note the successful way they seem to chatter at, disarm, and build from each other is simply to notice that B begins, from the first page of this section, by missing the other voice. *"I want him here,"* it states, noting the need for that other voice in order to prompt reflection on the powers of "not knowing":

> *The sunset is no reflection*
> *Of its not knowing—even its knowing*

Can be known but is not
A reflection
(AWK, 58)

As the voice across the gap begins to speak, reflecting and bending B's investigatory claims, B takes note: *"But the sunset sees its reflection, and /* *In the curve / Is cured. People, not all, come back / To us in pairs or threes"* (AWK, 59). That intimate exchange concludes, in the poem's last lines, with A speaking by itself of that chiming play:

> It would probably be best though
> To hang on to these words if only
> For the rhyme. Little enough,
> But later on, at the summit, it won't
> Matter so much that they fled like arrows
> From the taut sting of restrained
> Consciousness, only that they mattered.
> For the present, our not-knowing
> Delights them.
> (AWK, 68)

The poem returns to words, demonstrating an attitude we might take toward them that delights and frees both them and us—an attitude that acknowledges what Bishop calls "the little that we get for free" and the limits of replacing consciousness with matter, but understands now that "it won't / matter so much."

Shadow Train (1981) conjugates the distance in yet another way. It is a collection of fifty poems, each in an identical sixteen-line, four-stanza form. The opening poem, "The Pursuit of Happiness" (ST, 1), quite explicitly contrasts the method of dramatizing the conditions of language employed in "Litany" with the formal problem or system played out in these poems.[18] "It came about that there was no way of passing / Between the twin partitions that presented / A unified facade" Ashbery writes, leaving unstated the fact that it was precisely the failure to pass through such divisions of the voice that ventilated the code and provided that poem an opportunity to open up the "exact feel and slant of [the] field" that he insists we must find ourselves in. What drives *these* poems, Ashbery suggests, is the idea of regularity— poem after four-stanza poem reminding us by their tidy boxes of language's fierce drive to order and regularize. Like Parmigianino's mirror, the "incisive shadow" of form, "too perfect in its outrageous / Regularity," becomes the acknowledgment that drives the poems. The poems, if you will, link together as a single meditation—a shadow train—on the conditions of language that their own form visibly foregrounds. Their form is the tomb or gap or lyric foreshortening they attempt to pronounce. Their overregularity forces us to pause in our unblinking approach to language as if it were a simple, transparent tool.

The poems describe themselves, out of Stevens, as dramatizations of language. References to drama or the stage occur in at least half of the poems. The second and third poems are quite explicit about the book's approach. Watching itself at work, "Punishing the Myth" (ST, 2) suggests that the demands of form quickly foreground the distance between language and what it would grasp:

> At first it came easily, with the knowledge of the shadow line
> Picking its way through various landscapes before coming
> To stand far from you, to bless you incidentally
> In sorting out what was best for it, and most suitable

Form's way of knowing, its sorting through various physical and mental landscapes, can be thought of as a shadow across the hills. As with Dickinson's "certain Slant of light," it leaves the world far from us, and yet, *Shadow Train* will argue, "bless[es] you incidentally." How? By staging for us (and making accessible) the ground of our knowing—our separateness: "So we wiggled in our separate positions / And stayed in them for a time. After something has passed // You begin to see yourself as you would look to yourself on a stage." "Paradoxes and Oxymorons" (ST, 3) goes on, even more explicitly, to identify itself as "concerned with language on a very plain level." "Look at it talking to you," the poet insists and tugs us to see the way these meditations dramatize systems of words:

> Bringing a system of them into play. Play?
> Well, actually, yes, but I consider play to be
>
> A deeper outside thing, a dreamed role-pattern,
> As in the division of grace these long August days
> Without proof. Open-ended. And before you know
> It gets lost in the steam and chatter of typewriters.
>
> It has been played once more.

Here is a summary of Ashbery's career. Words in formal systems, outside us and not the same as us, can be played out—their roles or patterns stepped through in exaggerated, visible ways. Quickly lost and abandoned, these played-out systems demonstrate their ungrounded status. There is no "proof" for their claims, no ground for the way they divide up the world daily given to us, and there is an "open-ended" variety of ways in which they can be used and responded to. But they show us ourselves, small, clear, and free.

The book's final poem functions, as we have seen before, as a ritual summary of how we are to take and use these little dramas. If form reminds us of a shadowy train or a series of "long tables leading down to the sun, / A great gesture building" (ST, 50), then what these poems do with each verbal gesture, its authority deflated by its convex-mirror-like exaggeration, is "accept it so as to play with it / And translate when its attention is deflated for the one second / Of eternity." What these poems insist on, as always, is that what is translated and dramatized for us is something we already know, a condition that we are casually aware of as we employ form in our daily encounters—a pause, a passing shadow, that we simply adjust to, and are spurred on by:

> Extreme patience and persistence are required,

> Yet everybody succeeds at this before being handed
> The surprise box lunch of the rest of his life. But what is
> Truly startling is that it all happens modestly in the vein of
> True living.

It is that "one second / Of eternity," there in all of our sentences, that Ashbery, by whatever means possible, continually seeks to dramatize, for as "attention is deflated" and as the gap is acknowledged, a new sort of linguistic breathing occurs: "Not until someone falls, or hesitates, does the renewal occur, // And then it's only for a second, like a breath of air / On a hot, muggy afternoon with no air conditioning" (ST, 21).

The six-hundred-line title poem from *A Wave* (1984) offers yet another way to dramatize these issues. Instead of a series of illustrations or dramas, Ashbery chooses one. His thinking seems to be that the act of focusing on one of a myriad of ideas is enough of a foregrounded distortion, like sixteen lines or a convex mirror, to put his language on a near peak where its sense of "Not-being-us" might be seen and speculatively entered. It is an elegant proposal:

> One idea is enough to organize a life and project it
> Into unusual but viable forms, but many ideas merely
> Lead one thither into a morass of their own good intentions.

> Think how many the average person has during the course of a day, or
>   night,
> So that they become a luminous backdrop to ever-repeated
> Gestures, having no life of their own, but only echoing
> The suspicions of their possessor. It's fun to scratch around
> And maybe come up with something. But for the tender blur
> Of the setting to mean something, words must be ejected bodily,
> A certain crispness be avoided in favor of a density
> Of strutted opinion doomed to wilt in oblivion
> (w, 69)

That single idea, that fixed account of consciousness as it "Focuses itself, . . . the backward part of a life that is / Partially coming into view" (w, 70), offers a way of breaking free of the blur of already-established, glanced-over thought patterns that we naturally sink toward, but it is a break doomed in advance to "wilt" as its distance from our multiple world becomes clear: "It passes through you, emerges on the other side / And is now a distant city, with all / The possibilities shrouded in a narrative moratorium" (w, 68). It is that distance that the poem conjugates.

Unlike some Ashbery poems, this one, though it feints otherwise—"the topic / Of today's lecture doesn't exist yet" (w, 74)—is quite free in informing us about the identity of that idea, brought forward and then lost in "that dream of rubble that was the city of our starting out" (w, 74). It is the idea, in a word, of love—thought about, one supposes, under the shadow of a serious spinal infection that, in 1982, threatened the poet. He describes himself as "putting together notes related to the question of love / For the many, for two people at once, and for myself / In a time of need unlike those that have arisen so far" (w, 73), insisting that his handling of such materials is really intended to demonstrate the course of a single idea and to move about within the space opened up by the inevitably broken-off authority of that system. He speculatively enters the ground established by:

> the trials and dangerous situations that any love,
> However well-meaning, has to use as terms in the argument
> That is the reflexive play of our living and being lost
> And then changed again, a harmless fantasy that must grow
> Progressively serious, and soon state its case succinctly
> And dangerously
> (w, 73)

What he proposes, then, is to keep his eye on this idea as its wave crashes into thought and (like "being" in "The Skaters") passes on through, opening up a sense of non-congruent distance:

> And as the luckless describe love in glowing terms to strangers
> In taverns, and the seemingly blessed may be unaware of having lost it,
> So always there is a small remnant
> Whose lives are congruent with their souls
> And who ever afterward know no mystery in it,
> The cimmerian moment in which all lives, all destinies
> And incomplete destinies were swamped
> As though by a giant wave that picks itself up
> Out of a calm sea and retreats again into nowhere
> Once its damage is done.
> (w, 81)

Ashbery watches that wave, watches himself think in it, and speculatively plays out what he notices about his own system of thinking, proposing to make visible, by means of that "harmless fantasy," the grounds "of our living."

His comments are much more directly focused on such observations than we have seen before. "I hadn't expected a glance to be that direct, coming from a sculpture / Of moments, thoughts added on" (w, 71), he notes after delivering the powerfully expressed statement about being "set free on an ocean of language" that I quoted at the beginning of this essay. It is as though his thought (which we never entirely see) is going on across a gap—as if one of the simultaneous columns of "Litany" is invisibly there, chattering away, and we hear only the second voice describing it:

> Moving on we approached the top
> Of the thing, only it was dark and no one could see,
> Only somebody said it was a miracle we had gotten past the
> Previous phase, now faced with each other's conflicting
> Wishes and the hope for a certain peace, so this would be
> Our box and we would stay in it for as long
> As we found it comfortable, for the broken desires
> Inside were as nothing to the steady shelving terrain outside
> (w, 73–4)

Halfway through this poem of one idea, he declares himself ready to meet it:

the poem, growing up through the floor,
Standing tall in tubers, invading and smashing the ritual
Parlor, demands to be met on its own terms now,
Now that the preliminary negotiations are at last over.
(W, 79)

Ten pages later, as he winds toward a conclusion, he looks at his thoughts about the "invisible current" of that idea and notes, as if looking into the parts yard of *Three Poems* or the network of Guadalajara:

I feel at peace with the parts of myself
That questioned this other, easygoing side, chafed it
To a knotted rope of guesswork looming out of storms
And darkness and proceeding on its way into nowhere
Barely muttering. Always, a few errands
Summon us periodically from the room of our forethought
And that is a good thing. And such attentiveness
Besides!
(W, 88–89)

A MacArthur Award in 1985 allowed Ashbery to resign from a position as art critic at *Newsweek* that he had held since the early 1980s. Perhaps as a result, the individual lyrics of *April Galleons* (1987) all have to do with the outside world—the weather, the seasons, the rush of detail outside the "window" of one's consciousness all functioning as the language or "system" by which one articulates oneself. That constant circling around to "the moist, imprecise sky" (AG, 9) or the "rush / Of season into season" (AG, 55) or "the combination of fog and wind" (AG, 87) is enough to foreground the issue of articulation—the weather raising the problem of language's finitude as surely as a constant discussion of the lyric or a book-length struggle with the confines of form. Not unexpectedly, the landscape outside is so various and unmasterable that in entering it armed with words one enters an experience of limits: "its pictures / Teasing our notion of fragility with their monumental permanence" (AG, 59).

In reading the poems as a sequence, we can see certain repeated features of the experience of "listen[ing] to see what words materialize / On the windowpane this time" (AG, 27) or "look[ing] out of the window / Past his or her own reflection, to the bright, patterned, / Timeless unofficial truth hanging around out there" (AG, 53) that have been there throughout Ashbery's career. First, "say[ing] it like that . . . / Dream[ing] it like that over landscapes

spotted with cream" (AG, 6) inevitably prompts "the feeling that something /
Enormous, like a huge canvas, is happening . . . / . . . without one single scrap
of information being vouchsafed" (AG, 7). That experience of not knowing
leaves you, tools in trouble, in a "large, square, open landscape" where objects
are alive in their individual peculiarity:

> Our fathers, who had so many categories
> For so few things, could have supplied a term
> Like a special brush for bathing, and in due course this
> Particularity would have faded into the sum of the light,
> An entity no more. But we perceive it as another kind of thing,
> From another order
> (AG, 20)

But also, as is especially clear in Ashbery's later books, that experience of
being brought face to face with our distance from storm or sky, our lack of
"assimilation" (AG, 93) continually places us in a position from which words
start up again:

> those who lived in a landscape without fully understanding it, may,
> By their ignorance and needing help blossom again in the same season
> into a new
> Angle or knot, without feeling unwanted again.
> (AG, 28)

This blossoming, in which one is "always . . . quite conscious of the edges
of things" (AG, 33), their separate existence, is for me the key experience
of Ashbery's poetry. It is as if, out of silence and one's imposed muteness,
the largeness surrounding us shatters the monolith of language into a rich
shimmer of displayed parts, each now freed to go its own way:

> I have my notebook ready.
> And the richly falling light will transform us
> Then, into mute and privileged spectators.
> I never do know how to end any season,
> Do you? And it never matters; between the catch
> And the fall, a new series has been propounded
> With brio and elan.
> (AG, 68–69)

Flow Chart (1991), a poem written over the course of six months, in
six sections, each composed of almost daily, one-to-four page uncoilings of

thought, is Ashbery's boldest attempt to record "consciousness of existence."[19] His invitation to *you* this time seems marked by something close to sheer nerve and desperation:

> Which reminds me:
> when are we going to get together? I mean really—not just for a
> drink and smoke, but *really*
> invade each other's privacy in a significant way that will make sense
> and later amends to both of us for having done so, for I am
> short of the mark despite my bluster and my swaggering,
> have no real home and no one to inhabit it except you
> whom I am in danger of losing permanently as a bluefish slips off
> the deck of a ship, as a tuna flounders, but say, you know all that.
> (FC, 27)

Once again we have a poem that takes our realization that much of what passes for the union of speech and wordlessness is in fact "bluster and . . . swaggering," takes our awareness that the "interior phrase" has "no real home," and finds in that a generative problem to be struggled with. As we have come to expect, *Flow Chart* engages the medium of representation in order to demonstrate a new way to "make sense," promising, if we hold ourselves in that area, "amends for having done so." What is new, I think, is that this poem offers Ashbery's most sustained demonstration of *how* one might find in language's pause a blossoming of new relations.

The poem's first section is quite clear about these issues. If not a real home, what might the *I* expect of its uneasy appeal to the wordless *you*?

> it seems we must
> stay in an uneasy relationship, not quite fitting
> together, not precisely friends or lovers though certainly not enemies, if
> the buoyancy of the spongy terrain on which we exist is to be experienced
> as an ichor, not a commentary on all that is missing from the reflection
> in the mirror. *Did I say that? Can this be me?* Otherwise the treaty will
> seem premature, the peace unearned, and one might as well slink back
> into the solitude of the kennel, for the blunder to be read as anything
> but willful, self-indulgent.
> (FC, 10)

Ashbery proposes here that keeping the uneasiness of his relationship with the *you* constantly before his eyes—the raised eyebrow at what has just passed for expression ("*Can this be me?*")—renders the terrain of language both spongy and buoyant. Emerson, who in "The Poet" looked forward to a writer who would be able to step back from and "articulate" the tropes we inhabit, described the "strange and beautiful" results of such a project as an "immortal ichor."[20] Though Ashbery's tongue is firmly in his cheek when he picks up the word, he means it as well, for in handling language, in uneasily working its terrain,—Frost's frozen swamp in "The Wood-Pile" where no labor of the mind holds for long—he intends to release and "chart" language's "flow." The trick is to keep the terrain uneasy, the too-easy retreat into seeing language as "a commentary on all that is missing from the reflection / in the mirror" as much a threat to that flow as a too easy embrace.

The way *Flow Chart* acknowledges and enters language's conditions (this uneasy relationship) is through allowing its sentences to drift. The poem's great length seems to encourage this. That, I take it, is the distinction that the book's first page makes between "those who . . . / . . . know enough not to look up / from the page they are reading, the plaited lines that extend / like a bronze chain into eternity" and someone else who acknowledges, *"It seems I was reading something; /* I have forgotten the sense of it or what the small / role of the central poem made me want to feel. No matter" (FC, 3). Letting language go its own way, Ashbery describes himself in that not-knowing as watching or listening as his sentences "untie / gently, like a knotted shoelace, and then little expressions of relief occur in the whorls" (FC, 37). In those pockets of relief, "the subject / going off on its own again" (FC, 20), language is reestablished as an area where we can "pause and inspect / the still-fertile ground of our once-valid compact / with the ordinary and the true" (FC, 9).

Such is the position we find ourselves in as the poem begins—within expression, aware of its eventual collapse, but still free to question and handle it, still free to breathe:

> Still in the published city but not yet
> overtaken by a new form of despair, I ask
> the diagram: is it the foretaste of pain
> it might easily be? Or an emptiness
> so sudden it leaves the girders
> whanging in the absence of wind,
> the sky milk-blue and astringent?
> (FC, 3)

These questions, alive in those whorls where language has been freed of the responsibility of proceeding toward an end, produce exploratory runs of speech whose authority has been "delegated" and dispersed into a myriad of such investigations:

> Oh I'm so sorry, golly, how
> nothing ever really comes to fruition. But by the same token I am
>   relieved of manifold responsibilities,
> am allowed to delegate authority, and before I know it, my mood
> has changed, like a torn circus poster that becomes pristine again in
>   reverse cinematography,
> and these moments of course matter, and fall by the wayside in a
>   positive sense.
> (FC, 39)

These quotations have all been drawn from the poem's first section. It seems to me that one might legitimately argue that the other sections of the poem, much like Ashbery's collections of lyrics working over a single problem or shape, simply rework those concerns, on one "channel" or "frequency" and then another. To go on and argue, as I would, that these repeated concerns are raised in order to keep the relationship between *I* and *you* uneasy, the terrain they share "spongy" and "fertile," is to see that it is not the problem that is of real interest in the poem but the varied responses to it.

As in many Ashbery poems, the last two sections of *Flow Chart* are extended summaries—evaluations in which the poet looks back over his words and listens as they fall silent. "So that's it, really," he writes, "The proper walk must be aborted / and tangled hope restored to its rightful place in the hierarchy of dutiful devotions" (FC, 168). That restoration, that tangled letting be of language, offers not a real home for what is interior, but a rich record of awareness:

> your house or my house,
> this time?
>   I really think it's my turn,
> but the variations don't let you proceed along one footpath normally;
>   there are
> too many ways to go. I guess that's what I meant. Why I was worried,
> all along, I mean, though I knew it was superfluous and that you'd love
>   me for it
> or for anything else as long as I could sort out the strands that brought
>   us together
> and dye them for identification purposes further on, but you

don't have to remain that generalized.
(FC, 167–68)

All of that tangle is loose and at play here. The *I* invites *you* to its house,
conscious that there is no direct way there. The richness of that tangled
space between—let's call it language—is a source of worry (will we get lost?),
and yet it is "what I meant." Worry and what it shows about language—
that relationship alive and no longer "generalized"—is what is meant. This
is language not as a poet "normally" moves through it, generating a few
strands of complication to be dyed and separated by the figure in charge, but
language allowed to itself be "normal" (FC, 168). And that, I take it, can only
be generated and made visible by the sort of "tangled hope" that drives this
poem—at the same time "wanting to know" and accepting "colorful inroads":

> If you can think constructively, cogently,
> on a spring morning like this and really want to know the result in
>   advance, and can
> accept the inroads colorful difficulties can sometimes make as well as
>   all the
> fortunate happening, the unexpected pleasures and all that
> (FC, 168)

Both desires engaged, hope tangles, language spreads, and effort is recorded.
Something "exterior" forms and slides and twists into visibility. That is the rule
followed here, one that renders the medium charged and almost erotically
alive:

> And though the armature
> that supports all these varied and indeed desperate initiatives has
>   begun
> to exhibit signs of metal fatigue it is nonetheless sound and beautiful
>   in its capacity to perform
> functions and imagine new ones when appropriate, the best model
>   anyone has thought up
> so far, like a poplar that bends and bends and is always capable of
>   straightening itself
> after the wind has gone; in short it is my home, and you are welcome
>   in it
> for as long as you wish to stay and abide by the rules. Still,
> the doubling impulse that draws me toward it like some insane sexual
>   attraction can

not be realized here.
(FC, 199–200)

Hotel Lautréamont (1992) continues *Flow Chart*'s exploration of the meta-phor of the unending wandering journey but, in the manner of *April Galleons*'s play with the metaphor of weather, works that notion out in a series of single lyrics, almost all of which frame themselves as discussions of movement. One learns, after multiple readings, to listen for the verbs related to movement: *stay, advance, stop, wait, get off, move on, emerge, stumble, trot, wander, travel, walk, ride, march, run, crawl, waltz, plod, backtrack, drift, leave, hover, jiggle, bushwhack, slither, chase, bumble, approach, limp, turn, tour,* and so on, this but a partial listing. One might call this book an examination of "Great travel writing" (HL, 135)—the repeated words, like the convex mirror, foregrounding certain aspects of the writing process, bringing "a system" of concerns into play. I would identify this as Ashbery's greatest gift as a writer—the way he illustrates (makes visible and thus playable) our life in language. What does our entry into language look like in terms of movement?

One of us stays behind.
One of us advances on the bridge
as on a carpet. Life—it's marvelous—
follows and falls behind.
(HL, 3)

As *you* advances, its initial attempts at describing our shared life driven by the demands of description off on its own way, *I* "stays behind." Life, not seized because of that separation, remains ungrasped and—this is crucial—"marvelous." It is marvelous in the not-knowing. Because there is no end, no "knowing where to stop an adventure" (HL, 3), one is ushered once again into an open space where new possibilities can be teased out or unraveled:

this space
between me and what I had to say
is inspiring. There's a freshness
to the air; the crowds on Fifth Avenue
are pertinent, and the days up ahead,
still formless, unseen.
(HL, 103)

As with many of his recent books, the inventive ways Ashbery allegorizes and describes the pause where the space between me and my speech opens up are especially notable. Cavell calls these "allegories and measures of one another," demonstrations of "his faithfulness to the specific conditions and acts of writing as such" (SW, 62). One might read such allegories as the parts of language's conditions scattered around the backyard, waiting to be reassembled, or as new possibilities of utterance suddenly coming within range. "I frequently get off before the stop that is mine / not out of modesty but a failure to keep the lines of communication / open within myself" (HL, 10), one poem puts it, linking the limits of its language to not reaching a destination. "I am in this street because I was / going someplace, and now, not to be there is here" (HL, 29), he writes in another poem, eyes on his never-completed chronicle. "There's the well where the message fell apart" (HL, 73) comments a voice at the beginning of another poem. "My train is being flagged down" (HL, 128); "in the autumn the roads freeze over" (HL, 141); "An old jalopy with wobbly wheels was seen to limp / into an abandoned filling station" (HL, 142)—part of the oddness of these poems is that we need to see these wonderfully distorted but lovely images of "going nowhere" (HL, 113) or "hav[ing] no place to go" (HL, 51) as generated by the very lack of forward movement that they describe. Think of this as simultaneously describing and generating experience—making writing experience. Writing thus becomes the place where new parts of the picture unravel and are experienced. Ashbery refigures writing as "the courage to know nothing and simultaneously / be attentive" (HL, 39); as knowing "It is from the multiplication / of similar wacko configurations that theses do arise" (HL, 40); as giving up the drive "to contrast the ending / with the articulations that have gone before" and seeing in the space of those lost words "a single and sparing sharpness / that is an education in itself" (HL, 51); or as responding to "the cleft that produced nothing and knowledge, / the freedom to wait" (HL, 94).

And the Stars Were Shining (1994) completes a sort of trilogy with *Hotel Lautréamont* and *April Galleons*. Also composed primarily of short lyrics, it presents itself as joining what the first and last poems call "the celebration" (AS, 3, 85)—a celebration, I take it, of the conditions that call Ashbery's poems into being and the freedom of expression he discovers in them. Much of what goes on in each poem seems readable as a metaphorical equivalent to such an examination. "My own shoes have scarred the walk I've taken" (AS, 3), Ashbery writes (sounding like both Pound and Lowell) in the first poem. "I look ever closer / into the mirror, into the poured grain of its surface, until another I / seems to have turned brusquely to face me, ready / to reply at last to those questions put long ago" (AS, 69), another poem asserts, eyes on the grain of language as it has over the years reflectively distorted him. As always, the tone varies—here, from the matter-of-fact ("Rummaging through some old poems / for ideas"—AS, 85) to the lyric: "O sweetest song, / color of berries, that I lied for and extended / improbably a little distance from the given grave" (AS, 96). The poems as a whole compose a many-voiced meditation on the multiple inherited "grains" of language's reflective surface. Both the texture of the poems and numerous explicit statements claim that entrance into language breaks an unspoken wholeness into turning, contradictory pieces. Words "divide the answer among them" (AS, 80), the title poem asserts. Words are notable for "their unique / indifference to each other . . . / . . . and their tendency to fall apart" (AS, 8). We are far from the days of logical connections:

> If only we weren't old-fashioned, and could swallow
> one word like a pill, and it would branch out thoughtfully
> to all the other words, like the sun following behind the cloud shadow
> on a hummock, and our basket would be full,
> too ripe for the undoing, yet too spare for sleep,
> and the temperature would be exactly right.
> (AS, 47)

In moving into words, we move into a territory where the soul is never quite found: "the soul isn't engaged in trade. / It's woven of sleep and the weather /of sleep" (AS, 64).

The litany goes on. How can such an account of trade encroaching on sacrament, as Dickinson puts it, be seen as a celebration? Part of the answer is provided by the metaphorical furniture of these poems, a majority of which turn out to take place at or near, at the least glancingly referring to, the city or the sea. "You / will have to come up with something, / be it a terraced gambit above the sea / or gossip overheard in the marketplace" (AS, 41), he writes to himself concerning the materials available for his metaphorical self-examination. Those two settings are deliberately chosen, for they forcefully dramatize the multiple, noncoherent elements or pieces from which a person's experience is constructed: people on the street, fragments of overheard conversations (many of the poems have inset, discordant quotations), grains of sand, wave washing wave. Such details provide material and turns for the poems' picturing of our trade in words. Gradually, what the constant references to things rich and multiple show is that art is composed out of what the first poem calls "a common light [that] bathes us, / a common fiction [that] reverberates as we pass"—a storehouse of fragments, worn and anonymous. Call it "All the vulgarity / of time, from the Stone Age / to our present" but also "a life / to the life that is given you" (AS, 3).

One can think of Ashbery, then, as looking over his work by engaging in "trade." He "celebrates" what his work has shown him about the freedom of words by, like Whitman, embracing the city and its voices rushing by. He measures those words out by making metaphors, for "comparison shopping is what this place's / all about" (AS, 51). One can begin to list some of the most striking of the comparisons—all that follow here being accounts of what happens when we enter into words, "dream[s] turned inside out, exploded / into pieces of meaning" (AS, 23):

a slow train from Podunk, the ironed faces
of the passengers at each window expressing something precise
but nothing in particular.
(AS, 13)

So, lost with the unclaimed lottery junk,
uninventoried, you are an heir to anything.
(AS, 17)

Shards, smiling beaches,
abandon us somehow even as we converse with them.
(AS, 23)

        Count the pigeons, the people,
townspeople, running fast in all directions.
(AS, 50)

How funny your name would be
if you could follow it back to where
the first person thought of saying it,
. . . .
        It would
be like following a river to its source,
which would be impossible.
(AS, 65)

But finally, one is left with the unmistakable sense that it is the invigorating push and pull of the crowd of words and formulations that matters most and is being celebrated. The title poem is clearest about this. It argues that in finding a voice for the limits of articulation, we enter, sensing the smallness of our efforts, a grand free territory:

It was a day, after all. One of those things like a length of sleep
like a woman's stocking, that you lay flat
and it becomes a unit of your life—and this is where it
gets complicated—of so many others' lives as well
that there is no point in trying to make out, even less read,
the superimposed scripts in which the changes of the decades
were rung, endlessly
. . . .
                    in an instant we realize we are free
to go and return indefinitely.
(AS, 76–77)

3. Robert Hass and the Line's Tension

In a brief essay on George Oppen published in 1985, Robert Hass praises the older poet for the force of his example "at the level of composition, at the level of how you function when you're writing" (GO, 38). Oppen's poems, like those of the writers I explore in this book, call attention to how the poet handles himself in the writing situation. As Hass puts it, in Oppen's work, "you can actually watch, as the words are laid down on the page, the process from which the perception of the thing gets born into its numinous quality as a word, an abstraction out of the thing" (GO, 39). Understanding that the movement from thing to word is neither simple nor guaranteed, understanding that it is his own to make, Oppen takes responsibility for the use of each phrase, uttering and examining them one by one. Hass writes: "what's extraordinary about George Oppen's poetry is, moment after moment in his work, line by line, syllable by syllable, you have a sense of an enormous ethical pressure brought to bear on the act of perception" (GO, 40). That pressure, in Oppen's words, forces him "to notice," "not rushing over the subject matter in order to make a comment upon it" (GO, 38). And what results, as Hass puts it, is a poetry that can be described as "the activity of consciousness itself," clearing a "place of pure attention" (GO, 41).

Oppen's poetry matters to Hass because it seems a response to limits not at the foreground of current debates:

> in my generation of writers at least, the issue of the noun has become very difficult. The work of the language poets, particularly some of the essays of Ron Silliman, has suggested a profound distrust of the mimetic idea that there is a connection between word and thing; they have suggested, in fact, that the connection between word and thing has become a sort of conspiracy among the writer, the reader, and the merchant to convince themselves that the objects of desire are real. And that the light given off by them is not a property of the mind but a property of their obtainability and that the practice of mimetic art at all

is to repeat the lie of capitalist economics. Which is a profound charge, and a very similar charge is made by Robert Pinsky in his *Situation of Poetry* which argues that the passion of modernist poetry has turned out to be the passion of romantic poetry, to possess the particular by using words which are always general, so that language is trying intensely to do what language doesn't do, and that modernism has failed as a project in the way that romanticism failed as a project by necessarily producing a body of poetry whose subject is passionate disappointment. (GO, 39)

Distrust or disappointment: if two responses to questions about the connection between word and thing that Hass sketches above are "a self-referential and hermetic poetry on one side, and on the other [a] passionate quest which strains toward and against dissolution" (GO, 41), Oppen's poems, which "are remarkably free of both these passions," offer a response to limitation that neither turns away from the world nor, failing to possess it, drenches it in an awareness of loss. As Cavell found in Wittgenstein, Oppen's painstaking reflections on his language as he uses it offer "an acknowledgment of human limitation which does not leave us chafed by our own skin, by a sense of powerlessness to penetrate beyond the human conditions of knowledge" (MWM, 61).

Though the essay is just a sketch, it locates in Oppen's example two major concerns in Hass's own poetry: the obligation to put reflective pressure on language as one writes and the sense that under such pressure language might come alive as a "place of pure attention." Hass's poetry is an attempt to explore how one idea follows from the other. In fact, if we read through Hass's essays on poets and poetry collected in *Twentieth Century Pleasures* (1984) we find the possibility of such a generative response to the limits of language constantly raised. For example, in Robert Creeley's "loathing for eloquence" (TC, 159)—his realization that, in the face of what we know about how the built-in assumptions of language "speak us" whenever we use it, anyone "who believes that consciousness is sufficient and in control" is in fact wildly "out of control" (TC, 157)—Hass finds a powerful response to limit. By taking "the ordinary, threadbare phrases and sentences by which we locate ourselves and . . . put[ting] them under the immense pressure of the rhythms of poetry" (TC, 160), making "the impulses of his own speech the object of scrutiny," Creeley makes "a brilliant and unnerving music" out of attending to "the tension between speaking and being spoken through language" (157). In Creeley, language becomes charged through a kind of lacerating "Puritan self-examination." Avoiding not only an impossible to sustain illusion of control but also much of "the spiritual loneliness of the twentieth century," which has assumed that language's "freight of loss and guilt and symbolic power" inevitably leaves the world "inaccessible" (TC, 152, 153) and dead, Creeley creates what Hass calls an "erotics of language: the stunned, lovely, slow insistence on accuracy that the mind is, in language" (TC, 156).

We see a similar acknowledgment of pressure in Czesław Miłosz, as Hass renders *his* work. Hass finds in Miłosz a set of "powerful and conflicting" (TC, 196) responses to limitation—to our knowledge that the things of the earth we love inevitably pass away. On the one hand, Hass identifies in Miłosz a Gnostic tendency that, understanding "time and matter [as] a prison" (TC, 210), leads one to "the impulse to reject nature, the matter-universe, entirely since time and change have nothing but death and loss to offer to the human soul" (TC, 184). But that impulse is countered by "a large part of Miłosz's nature [that] would have made a very good materialist poet, . . . praising socks, cats and lemons, dying and being born" (TC, 194). For Hass, Miłosz becomes a great poet by, in his own words, "making the contradiction [in his responses] as acute as possible" (TC, 201). The sequences written late in Miłosz's career allow these contradictory impulses full play. They take as their task the call "to suffer time, to contemplate being, and to live in the hope of the redemption of the world" (TC, 212). Through an "incessant questioning of where to stand, how to see, what to say," the poems clear a space where, as Cavell puts it about Wittgenstein, "one's humanity, or finitude, is . . . accepted, suffered" (TN, 39). What results is "a kind of ontological vertigo, a deep feeling of dread and wonder at being alive" (TC, 208).

Creeley and Miłosz prompt Hass to think about poetry as a charged taking-on of responsibility for the tensions or contradictions within one's own use of language. Other essays in the collection discuss the sort of attention that such a torn acknowledgment of different responses to limitation generates. His chapter on Rainer Maria Rilke is a powerful example. Limitation for Rilke is "a tormented sense of our human incompleteness" (TC, 243); it is a sense of poverty generated by moments of "vivid experience" (TC, 229) that open up the possibility of "a more vivid and permanent world" (TC, 244) and then, in passing, leave this one dead and ashen. As Hass reads him, Rilke first defined and then relinquished a poetics in which "our inner emptiness . . . generat[es] that need for things which mutilates the world and turns it into badly handled objects" (TC, 249), a need that "turns every experience into desolation, because beauty is not what we want at those moments, death is what we want, an end to limit, an end to time" (TC, 257). In the *Duino Elegies* and *The Sonnets to Orpheus*, Rilke eventually came to see a way to make a world-attentive poetry out of "estrangement as it returns to the world, moving among things, touching them with the knowledge of death which they acquire when they acquire their names in human language" (TC, 261). Such work, responding to longing's despairing acknowledgment of human finitude by returning to the world, has come to understand that "the pure activity of being consciously alive is sufficient to itself" (TC, 262). In relinquishing the desire for permanence, such work emerges "praising" (TC, 257).

In Hass's essay on the Japanese poets Issa, Buson, and Bashō, we see a similar sort of attentive consciousness described—one no longer trying to overleap limitation but dwelling within it. The key seems to be the way these poets use images, acknowledging that each image is partial—"no one of them feels like the whole truth and they do not last" (TC, 303)—and finding in that partiality a forced opportunity for "quiet attention" (TC, 273). Understanding the image in such a way produces, at its best, a poetry that "does not record sickness, yearning, unsatisfied hunger. Nor is it exactly objective or detached. It sits just in between" (TC, 278). Such poems "marry the world, but they do not claim to possess it, and in this they have the power and the limitations of intimate knowledge" (TC, 305). They are examples of "that clear, deep act of acceptance and relinquishment which human beings are capable of" (TC, 305).

Hass's work attempts to locate itself here. His poems are acutely aware of what he calls the "swift, opposing currents" (SU, 57) of our differing responses to limitation. In taking responsibility for those responses playing through his own acts of writing and engagement with the world, Hass hopes both to relinquish those drives that "turn every experience into desolation" and to establish in their place something charged and attentive.[1] As we will see, his four books are marked by a quiet but continuous re-seeing of how that reflective taking-on of responsibility occurs.

Most of this reflection is already in motion in his first book, *Field Guide* (1973). Its first section, fifteen poems grouped under the heading "The Coast," powerfully illustrates this. The coast is that of northern California: "this fragile coast" (FG, 43) of fogs and great dry beauty, scarred by the human hunger to order and use it—"the old fury of land grants, maps, / and deeds of trust" (26). Like Cavell's Thoreau, Hass foregrounds his estrangement from this world and then explores the forms by which he might attempt, through that estrangement, to reconnect himself to it. Crucially, he comes to see that he also plays a part in the story of that "old fury." Such an acknowledgment charges *Field Guide*'s central forms of attention: naming, describing, establishing a household.

"On the Coast near Sausalito" (FG, 3–4), the book's first poem, makes much of this clear. If, as the poem acknowledges, one cannot "say much for the sea" and its "antediluvian depths," one can perhaps approach the "slimed rocks" of a coastline at low tide with the expectation of being able to involve oneself with its teeming complications. "Here," writes Hass, in a line we can take as referring to this and every other in-between area in his work, "filthy life begins." What he does is fish for cabezone, fishing described in such a way that a poetics gets quickly sketched:

> Fish-
> ing, as Melville said,
> "to purge the spleen,"
> to put to task my clumsy hands
> my hands that bruise by
> not touching

By involving himself in the actual textures of this task, the poet wants to free himself from an attitude toward the world that has two faces. One is "not touching," the other the pouring out of one's spleen—what many of these poems call the possessive rage of "violence" or "malice." Both are responses to limit that leave the world dead. Not touching bruises by turning away from what cannot be mastered; the spleen strangles what cannot be held. The hands-on act of fishing, on the other hand, leads to a recognition of otherness: "Catching one, the fierce quiver of surprise / and the line's tension / are a recognition. / . . . Creature and creature, / we stared down centuries." Bishop's "The Fish" is not far behind this, but what is important for our purposes is that the "sudden feel of life" generated by this experience comes from an awareness of tension in the line. The spleen's anger at not being able to master or possess is replaced by a responsiveness generated by the play of tension. That we are also to hear in this first poem a reference to the poetic line is suggested by the linguistic turn that follows from this recognition— the poet turning from one sort of speech ("The danger is / to moralize / that strangeness") to a recipe, another sort: "fry the pale, almost bluish flesh / in olive oil with a sprig / of fresh rosemary."

That responding to "the line's tension" is a language issue and not simply fishing advice is further insisted upon by the book's second poem, "Fall" (FG, 5). There, the task to which his hands are put—identifying edible mushrooms out of a field guide—is both more literally linguistic and more spectacularly tense. To be aware of the line's tension, this poem suggests, is to acknowledge that the distance between word and thing is constantly unsettled, a sense of linguistic finitude foregrounded here as the threat of death: "Amateurs . . . / . . . half expecting to be / killed by a mistake." And what is gained by an amateur's awareness of the slippery, nontransparency of language, its lack of guarantees? Once again, unlike friends who "only ate the ones / that we most *certainly* survived" (emphasis mine), Hass records, in that death-touched drift between names and things, an attentive feel for life:

> Death shook us more than once
> those days and floating back
> it felt like life. Earth-wet, slithery,
> we drifted toward the names of things.

Many of the poems in this first section work out an amateur's live feel for the tension between words and things or between observer and the coast by countering a hard or world-dissolving professionalism with something looser, often, as above, referred to as "drifting." Hass repeats the move so often that we would do well to identify it as one of his favored forms of reflection. In Cavell's terms, many of these poems first give voice to a frustrated drive for certainty, then turn from it and attempt to enter the condition of uncertainty that drive has located. They unfold an amateur's use of language by pushing off against a professional's. Cavell speaks of this in Wittgenstein as "endless specific succumbings to the conditions of skepticism and endless specific recoveries from it" (DK, 30). Bishop describes it as being caught between different responses to "The Monument." Both uses of language respond to limits, but what one would overcome the other enters. For example, in one poem, Hass's speaker fights free of the "blind" "dull[ness]" induced in him by a friend's work—poems in which "pain" is asked to produce "the totem griefs / we hope will give us / power to look at trees, / at stones"—by countering that drive for "power" with a simple acknowledgment of distance:

> What can I say, my friend?
> There are tricks of animal grace,
> poems in the mind
>
> we survive on. It isn't much.
> You are 4,000 miles away &
> this world did not invite us.
> ("Letter to a Poet," 12–13)

A similar move occurs in "Spring" (FG, 16), where a "bearded bird-like man" in a bookstore, hearing a remark in passing, pushes between the poet and his wife, "cleared / his cultural throat, and / told us both interminably / who Ugo Betti was." In contrast to his "imperial" language about the Italian dramatist, the poet and his wife, later that night, explore a different sort of speech, one richly and variously alive within Wittgenstein's sense of limits:

> You chanted, "Ugo Betti has no bones,"
> and when I said, "The limits of my language
> are the limits of my world," you laughed.
> We spoke all night in tongues,
> in fingertips, in teeth.

Or, to give a third example, the poet wakes to early heat and, watching shadows move, charts his day: his wife and children will be off to the beach ("a faint salt sheen / across your belly"); he will stay home, reading "that hard man Thomas Hobbes / on the causes of the English civil wars. / There are no women in his world, / Hobbes, brothers fighting brothers / over goods." And once again, countering that hard, world-dissolving way of speaking allows the poet to posit a different, more fragile yet more responsive, sort of speech:

>   Traveling
> in Europe Hobbes was haunted by motion.
> Sailing or riding, he was suddenly aware
> that all things move.
>   We will lie down,
> finally, in our heaviness
>   and touch and drift toward morning.
> (FG, 28–29)

What the haunted Hobbes would regulate, the poet would enter. These poems attempt to make a home in a world that moves or drifts from its names and does not invite us; what is at issue is the tension, or the difference in response, between noticing the sheen of salt on someone's belly and attempting to establish "the causes of the English civil wars."

A more complicated variation on this pattern occurs when Hass discovers that initial language of mastery within himself and pushes off from, attempts to purge, his own hunger for order. "San Pedro Road" (FG, 20), for example, contrasts a tense-handed attempt to fish a salt creek—"in the ferocious pointless heat I dream, / half in anger, of the great white bass, / the curious striper, bright-eyed, rising to the bait"—with an acceptance of limits: "finally dumb animal I understand, kick off boots, pants, socks, / and swim, / . . . done with casting, reeling in slowly, casting . . . ." "Song" (FG, 21) shifts from a defeated claim of possession—a man "yelling, 'Hey, I'm home!' / to an empty house"—to a haiku-like attentive entering of that empty space:

> On the oak table
> filets of sole
> stewing in the juice of tangerines
> slices of green pepper
> on a bone-white dish.

"Black Mountain, Los Altos" (FG, 6), perhaps most powerfully of the poems working in this manner, discovers that malice alive inside the speaker and simply halts, in an uncomfortable act of recognition. On a midmorning walk in the coastal hills, discovering "bleached bones / weirdly grey in the runoff / between ridges," the poet counters that uneasiness by listing and describing. Five deer, three species of trees: "I feel / furry as sage," he remarks, apparently having made a sure connection. Then it begins to give way. Near here, "padres / taught the sorrowful mysteries / with a whip"; over there in the fog, they manufacture napalm for the unending war in Vietnam. He discovers himself responding to that now-troubled landscape with an equally-troubled self-righteousness, ready to kill what he cannot fix, himself embodying the line's tension:

> I think of the village
> of Bien Hoa, the early spring
> death in the buckeyes
> and up the long valley
> my eyes flash, another
> knife, clean as malice.

All of these poems lead up to a sequence entitled "Palo Alto: The Marshes" (FG, 24–27), one of the two important poems in this section. Dedicated to Mariana Richardson (1830–91), whose "father owned the land / where I grew up," and who, like the poet, "dreamed along the beaches of this coast" until it was snatched from her by John Frémont and Kit Carson, the poem explores the connections between her response to the loss of the land and that of the poet. The connections are complicated and unsettling. Not only do the two share a habit of attention different from that of the soldiers and thieves—she too "had watched the hills seep blue with lupine after rain, / seen the young peppers, heavy and intent, / first rosy drupes and then the acrid fruit"—but they also share, in their rage against "the goddamned Anglo-Yankee yoke," a disturbing turn of mind. As Hass moves through this estranged, snatched-away place, thinking to make himself at home there by naming and describing, he discovers in Mariana troubling "measures and allegories" of his own effort. Unfolding those, pushing off one way and then another, he plays out "the line's tension." Looking at John Ashbery, we described this as a reflective exploration of limit's landscape.

The poem's eleven sections are assembled around a single morning walk:

Walking, I recite the hard
explosive names of birds:
egret, killdeer, bittern, tern.
Dull in the wind and early morning light,
the striped shadows of the cattails
twitch like nerves.

Why that "explosive" naming? What is its connection to the roar of "Kit Carson's antique .45" still echoing there? In a space where names are not transparent, such questions need to be addressed. If these marshes are composed of "mud, roots, old cartridges, and blood," then there are things that must be remembered: the blood of Mariana's lover, killed in the Bear Flag War, still "runs darkly to the old ooze"; "the long silence" of "the other California / and its bitter absent ghosts"—those tribes routed by Carson, the black smoke of whose burned villages still "smear[s] the sky above the pines"—needs to be spoken for. The explosive naming that the poet engages in, then, seems at first a righteous, properly bitter, response to loss:

Black as her hair
the unreflecting venom of those eyes
is an aftermath I know, like these brackish
russet pools a strange life feeds in[.]

Naming and describing fight against loss. On "pale yellow mornings / when the mist burns slowly into day," trying to get the names of your world right somehow "stings / like autumn, clarifies / like pain." It fights against Carson's thick, world-dissolving smoke that still seems to hover there:

Here everything seems clear,
firmly etched against the pale
smoky sky: sedge, flag, owl's clover,
rotting wharves. A tanker lugs silver
bomb-shaped napalm tins toward

port at Redwood City. Again,
my eye performs
the lobotomy of description.
Again, almost with yearning,
I see the malice of her ancient eyes.

And yet, he sees, what also unfolds is his own complicity, as a language user and shaper, in acts of malice and venom. Lobotomizing what he describes, he finds himself reflected in both Mariana's blank rage and in the noncomprehension of California's murderers and takers. As with Creeley making "the impulses of his own speech the object of scrutiny," Hass discovers a "strange life" indeed "feed[ing] in" the tensions in his own acts of description. A host of such responses is loose in this place; playing out the tension, Hass creates a dark sort of map, live because estranged—a map etched everywhere by its distance from the world:

Bird cries and the unembittered sun,
wings and white bodies of the birds,
it is morning. Citizens are rising
to murder in their moral dreams.

"Maps" (FG, 7–10), the other powerful poem in this section, not only contrasts two sorts of speech in order to unfold the tension in our use of words but also offers a many-voiced catalog of such torn expressions. This is a form Hass will return to in each of his next three books. Its seventeen quick takes sketch various maps—names of such things as food, towns, vegetation— that the speaker, at some distance now from his native coast, would use to reconnect himself to that world. "Of all the laws / that bind us to the past," he writes, "the names of things are / stubbornest." One can work back through the rich sounds of "Mendocino Sausalito San Rafael" or "the fruity warmth of zinfandel" or "the mottled amanita / delicate phallic toxic" to a world that seems almost there. As Hass puts it, almost chewing through "clams, abalones, cockles, chitons, crabs," such names propose a world seemingly "felt along the flesh." But such rich, stubborn words are anything but transparent. In their very thickness, they have distance built into them—distance and a still-alive, darkening tension that Hass, as an amateur, sees and plays out. Think, for example, of three "staples of the China trade: / sea otter, sandalwood, and bêche-de-mer." What gets mapped when, hungering for a lost world, one tries to use such names to bring it back? "Bêche-de-mer" is the sea cucumber, used by the Chinese in making soup; its thick name holds some of the history of trade and exploitation that brought a labor force to California to build its railroads. In handling that word, in hungering for it and trading with it, Hass acknowledges an involvement in that history:

> Plucked from algae sea spray
> cold sun and a low rank tide
>   sea cucumbers
> lolling in the crevices of rock
> they traded men enough
> to carve old Crocker's railway out of rock
> to eat these slugs
> bêche-de-mer

Or think of "the pointillist look of laurels / their dappled pale green body stirs / down valley in the morning wind." Hass plays out the erotic charge of that stirring body, remembering Ovid's Daphne, who was turned into a laurel tree to escape the pursuing Apollo's desire: "Daphne was supple / my wife is tan, blue-rippled / pale in the dark hollows." The name laurel, then, through Daphne and his wife as a version of Daphne, seems almost to marry him—a favorite phrase—to the landscape he desires:

> Late summer—
> red berries darken the hawthorns
> curls of yellow in the laurels
>
> your body and the undulant
> sharp edges of the hills

And yet, the confession recorded in the laurel's map also remains—that the eye thinking it "owns what is familiar" is also the greedy god's—taking and pursuing and claiming rights. The word, like "the bleak intricate erosion of these cliffs," bears the history of its use; hungering with it, trying to make an imaginative purchase on this coast, the poet finds himself, here and throughout these poems, involved in a dense, live, never-transparent network of responses. At the same time, this very tension, insisting that the world cannot be straightforwardly possessed, forces him to attend to the world on its own terms: "that clear, deep act of acceptance and relinquishment which human beings are capable of."

The concluding section of *Field Guide* opens up another arena within which to dramatize dwelling within estrangement in the image of a house—a house, significantly for this California poet, located in Buffalo. If a house, as

Hass puts it in an essay on Wendell Berry written about the same time as these poems, is "a form of consciousness in the world," then a description of its form as "wakeful, temporary, desiring" or "frail, delicate, and fully alive" suggests that we should read these poems as participating in the same intellectual exploration as the West Coast naming poems.[2] Like those names through which one approaches the California coast, this frail house opens a space where one can acknowledge and unfold a live response to the truth that skepticism locates. "Letter" (FG, 65–66), written to his absent wife—the family has apparently gone back to California—carefully links naming and dwelling in a house. Attempting to describe for his wife a tanager he had just seen "below the pond" and "a new blue flower," he writes:

> But I had the odd
> feeling, walking to the house
> to write this down, that I had left
> the birds and flowers in the field,
> rooted or feeding. They are not in my
> head, are not now on this page.
> It was very strange to me, but I think
> their loss was your absence.

That is, the truth that birds and flowers are not captured in the act of writing ("are not now on this page") can be figured as the empty house and his wife's "absence." That figure gives him a way of playing out a version of language's limits. If the poet had "believed so long / in the magic of names and poems. / I hadn't thought them bodiless / at all," he now is forced to visualize the tension within the notion of words as embodiments of the world. For starters, if, as he says to his wife, " you are the body / of my world . . . / . . . you're the names of things," then the simple fact that she can leave and that body dissolve attaches all sorts of finite conditions—needing to be explored—to that act of embodiment.

And that is exactly what the poems in this section do—thinking about houses, marriage, and names simultaneously, using one to measure the other two. Houses, in Buffalo, seem like weighty, decaying prisons. One poem remarks: "They peel like lizards / in the dying avenues of elm." But there is more to it than that. "House" (FG, 54–55) adds the crucial idea that just as words carry histories that must be entered and played out, so do the "premises" one inhabits or carries about. The poem begins with an almost sentimental celebration of stability, the poet standing at a window on an April morning, breakfast underway, and music filtering in from another room:

I am conscious of being
    myself the inhabitant
of certain premises:
    coffee & bacon & Handel
& upstairs asleep my wife.

But "Very suddenly / old dusks break over me, / the thick shagged heads / of fig trees near the fence / & not wanting to go in / . . . & all that terror / in the house," and he realizes that some of the premises he inhabits in his house and marriage are inherited from childhood terrors—his parents' problems that made life in that West Coast house unstable and terrifying. Just as naming involves you in the voices of others, inhabiting a house means sharing its premises or being torn between them. That tension is part of what has to be handled.

The most successful playing out of these linguistic / domestic tensions comes in a sequence entitled "In Weather" (FG, 59–64). It works much like "Palo Alto: The Marshes," the writer identifying within himself a certain refusal of limits and then pushing off of that response and back to the world. The poem begins with the poet's complaint that he is being held in time or "in weather"; he feels himself in a sort of prison of finitude. Buried in the "pearly repetitions" of a Buffalo winter, "grieved and dull," he "hunger[s]" for a visionary alternative, a movement outside these deadening cycles. But that hunger leads only to a dark tangle, as in this image of trees at dusk: "the bare structure / of their hunger for light / reach[ing] to where darkness / joined them. The dark / and the limbs tangled / luxuriant as hair." Home, with its steady domestic fires and "uxorious amber repetitions" seems an alternative, but a lesser one that he feels sentenced to. In fact, as the second section suggests, home seems dominated by the steady downbeat of decay—epitomized by the family's garbage, scattered nightly by creatures "alert / to the smells of warm decay." A deep sense of disgust with time and limit, with "the refuse of my life / . . . and the sense of waste / in the dreary gathering of it," grips the poem's opening sections, broken only by the impossible lures of life "across great distances"—for example, strewn and rotting lobster shells offering up, as if from the Pacific, "a faint rank fragrance of sea."

The third and fourth sections of the poem explore two dangerous responses to the dreary confines of limit. We have seen them before in Cavell's discussion of skepticism and in *Field Guide*'s opening images of "spleen" and "not touching." In the third section, the poet begins with his sense of feeling lost and smothered and plays it out, wishing for a "more complete" ignorance—

say, sleep or death, being buried alive in time's weary confines. His image for this state is a striking one, called up by that previous reminder of the ocean: a tiny male sea worm living within an "inch-thick" female one, dependent on the plankton she churns through. "My mind became the male," he writes, "drowsing in that inland sea / who lives in darkness, / drops seed twice in twenty years, / and dies." Section four's counter to his weary imprisonment is an equally disturbing one: a visionary grasping, like that of the nighttime trees, for a certainty outside of the finite confines of wife and home, an attempt to become "homeless / and perfected in the empty dark. / . . . a thrust of infinite desire / beyond the tame musk / of companionable holes." What the speaker sees in this section, allowing himself to be carried along by the "cruel music" of a friend's dismissal of the poverty of "mere enactment" or embodiment, is that such a refusal of anything less than perfection, as Cavell would say, plays out a sense of disgust with the "nerved, irreducible" world. Such a "thrust," Hass realizes, like Othello's world-dissolving jealousy, is a way of "hack[ing] / the body till the source was gone." It is of a piece with the pornographic "contempt" of "cutting her apart, / bloody and exultant / in the bad lighting and scratchy track / of butcher shops / in short experimental films."

What this play between sleep and hacking apart does, I would suggest, is force Hass to acknowledge that, mapped within his own attitudes (as within laurel or bêche-de-mer or the explosiveness of description) are responses to finitude that would leave the world dull or kill it. But, as Cavell suggests, such an acknowledgment also allows him, almost in exhaustion, to ask if other responses to the finite premises of domesticity also exist. As we will see in each of Hass's books, they exist swirled together. Section 5 offers a quick sketch: the poet wakens to a moment of joy one night in March; hearing through the "hard frost" on his windows the "soft confusion" of owls mating, he repeats their "almost human wail" while he lies in bed next to his sleeping, stirring wife. And what sound does he make, in imitation? "*Twoo, twoo*": twoness, as in two bodies, separate but confusedly coming together. Neither dismissal nor entrapped dullness, this suggests a sort of intimacy. As the final section of the poem understands, that poised wakefulness is no more than an "alertness"; linked to an awareness of a human world that is potentially "vacant," "cerebral," "attenuated," or "redundant," it is an alertness or attentiveness produced by the poet's awareness of just how limited is his grasp of things:

I know that I know myself
no more than a seed

curled in the dark of a winged pod
knows flourishing.

Although *Field Guide* is quite direct in pointing out parallels between tensions in various uses of language and those discovered wandering a child-hood coast or turning in on oneself within a snow-locked house, it keeps those investigations, for the most part, separate. One has to read with a metaphorical cast of mind to see what is really at stake in the conversation. A further indication of this separation is that the second section of the book, which seems much less fully worked out, is comprised of language-centered poems: translations, an odd series on pornography, a set of appreciations and critiques of other writers. But the poems are set apart from the rest of the book. One crucial part of Hass's development as a writer will be bringing these metaphorically equivalent discussions together. His second volume, *Praise* (1979), goes some distance down that way by, not unexpectedly, reversing the direction of *Field Guide*. Now language becomes the primary area of investigation. *Praise* looks at how our culture speaks and asks whether the different responses to limits recorded there—the line's tension—might not yield a live attentiveness. As in *Field Guide*, this reflection often proceeds by first identifying and then turning away from what it calls an easy or habitual sort of speech—the world-dissolving refusal of limits exemplified by Kit Carson or the winter-weary husband being replaced here by similar responses discovered in the way our culture speaks. As with *Field Guide*, the linguistic and the social or domestic situations dramatized in *Praise* point toward and metaphorically measure each other, though the reader often has to draw these conversations out. "Heroic Simile" (P, 2–3), the book's opening poem, offers a simple version of live speech within limits. It parallels, in many ways, the opening poem of *Field Guide*, replacing fishing on an uneasy coast with watching a movie as the source of the tension to be attended to and temporarily inhabited. The poem begins by acknowledging the distance between representation and the actual world:

When the swordsman fell in Kurosawa's *Seven Samurai*
in the gray rain,
in Cinemascope and the Tokugawa dynasty,
he fell straight as a pine, he fell
as Ajax fell in Homer
in chanted dactyls and the tree was so huge
the woodsman returned for two days

to that lucky place before he was done with the sawing
and on the third day he brought his uncle.

There is nothing simply transparent here. Just as our use of bêche-de-mer is thickened by an awareness of its history, so our response to the falling swordsman has been shaped by what we know of a director's vision within an oeuvre, by a number of intersecting movie and narrative genres we may or may not be conscious of, by film's particular technical resources, and the movie's physical and historical referents. The poet, of course, is aware of all this. By referring to Homer, yet another cultural voice that has contributed to the making of this hero, he signals the fact that he is entering into this play of tensions—that he is neither turning away nor hacking it apart in skeptical disappointment. We can say even more: Hass employs, out of Homer, a way of speaking that dwells within just such an awareness of limit or nontransparency. Think of the way Homer's similes deliberately halt the narrative drive of his poem and encourage in that pause a sort of open-eyed encounter with the distance between home and away or war and peace. The simile's thickness, freed momentarily from the need to make a point or complete a tale, opens up the distance between, say, a narrated battle and the reader, reminding us of domestic rhythms different from warfare and thus offering an acute taste of life. In the *Iliad*, for example, Menelaos and Helenos let fly at each other with a javelin and an arrow, respectively. Homer writes:

The son of Priam hit him then on the chest with an arrow
in the hollow of the corselet, but the arrow sprang far back.
As along a great threshing floor from the broad blade
of a shovel the black-skinned beans and the chickpeas bounce high
under the whistling blast and the sweep of the winnowing fan, so
back from the corselet of glorious Menelaos the bitter
arrow rebounded far away, being driven hard back.[3]

Hass's simile, which he plays out for three more stanzas, is a similar opening up of distance, a rich foregrounding of limits. As Hass puts it, backing out of his playful dramatizing of the woodsman's great windfall by withholding the "pack animal / or primitive wagon" needed to bring all of the wood to market:

there's nothing I can do.
The path from here to that village
is not translated. A hero, dying,
gives off stillness to the air.
A man and a woman walk from the movies

to the house in the silence of separate fidelities.

There are limits to imagination.

But within that limited space opened by the acknowledgment that there is no direct path from word to thing, or from bird to page, or from home to away—that we always work through layers of mediation—within that space there are rich, playful ways of speaking that attend to and make something of that stillness.⁴ And, to again take another step, that way of speaking—that reflective unfolding of limits—speaks to and helps us visualize other rich experiences of limit: the "house" being returned to here, which takes us back to *Field Guide*; and the separate yet intimate couple, sharing a charged admission of limit, whom we will focus on in detail in *Human Wishes*.

Praise is in two parts. The poems in the first section, much as the professional/amateur poems of *Field Guide*, tend to unfold live ways of speaking by pushing off of or responding to inherited, less alert ways of imagining. In Cavell's terms, they unfold what skepticism has made visible in denial. The sequence "Songs to Survive the Summer," which makes up the second section, is a variation on its predecessor "Maps"—another catalog of ways of mapping or singing one's finitude. What is new, or more visibly developed, in this volume, aside from the focus on language, is an emphasis on what Cavell would call the ordinary—the sense, out of Wittgenstein's "return to ordinary or everyday language," "that our natural relation to the world's existence is . . . closer, or more intimate, than the ideas of believing or knowing are made to convey. . . . This sense of, let me say, my natural relation to existence is what Thoreau means by our being *next* to the laws of nature, by our *neighboring* the world, by our being *beside* ourselves" (T, 192, 193). For Cavell, the ordinary acknowledges rather than seeks to overcome separation or finiteness. Hass's work in this volume is the best illustration of those ideas I know of.

We have already looked at the way Hass's "Meditation at Lagunitas" worked its way back to a "tender" way of speaking by responding to the finitude or sense of distance that a "querulous" way of speaking ("in the voice / of my friend, there was a thin wire of grief") had acknowledged in a disappointed turn of the head. What is interesting about the poems in the remainder of the first section of *Praise* is the number of different ways this reflective self-scrutiny gets played out and the number of different cultural voices that are taken on and resisted. I'll give a few examples. Some of the poems quite directly meditate on language itself. "Transparent Garments" (P, 15–16), for example, thinks about the way we react to the fact that words are not transparent and wonders if there is not a response to that idea that is "neither easy nor difficult," one which does not make the approach to the world a contest:

> Because it is neither easy nor difficult,
> because the outer dark is not passport
> nor is the inner dark, the horror
> held in memory as talisman. Not to go in
> stupidly holding out dark as some
> wrong promise of fidelity, but to go in
> as one can, empty or worshipping.

Ultimately, what Hass works off of is the notion—common to both our poetry and our talk shows—that some failure or horror, some inner or outer "dark," can function as a simple "passport" to an accurate vision of the world. Holding out before you the collapse of a "promise of fidelity"—whether it be the expectation that words can marry the world, or that a house or marriage or treasured landscape will stand forever, or that a lover or parent will behave as promised—holding its collapse out before you as if it, in itself, guarantees authenticity is to give up the live intricacies of thinking and describing for something easy. (That this is one of Hass's consistent temptations, wounded as he was by a difficult childhood, can be heard behind the too-harsh dismissal of "stupidly" "talking this way.") What other way might there be, he asks? Take the word "White, as a proposition":

> Not leprous
> by easy association nor painfully radiant.
> Or maybe that, yes, maybe painfully.
> To go into that. As: I am walking in the city
> and there is the whiteness of the houses,
> little cubes of it bleaching in the sunlight,
> luminous with attritions of light, the failure
> of matter in the steadiness of light,
> a purification, not burning away,
> nothing so violent, something clearer
> that stings and stings and is then
> past pain or this slow levitation of joy.

Here is the pattern we saw in "Meditation at Lagunitas." Hass refuses the "easy association[s]" of white with loss, that too-easy use of words treating them as transparent, then discovers in that traditional association a trace of the word's still-live involvement with the world's painful passage through time—San Francisco's white houses "luminous" in the way the light steadily and unblinkingly records the steady pulse of their material "failure." The word, that is, touches on the to-be-lost world we all live in, but "clearly," freed for a moment from the grand human plots of pain or joy to record what seems a lesser thing. Such an attentiveness, "neither easy nor difficult," might allow one to move, by way of language, to a place where the world is handled tenderly:

> And to emerge, where the juniper
> is simply juniper and there is the smell
> of new shingle, a power saw outside
> and inside a woman in the bath,
> a scent of lemon and a drift of song,
> a heartfelt imitation of Bessie Smith.
> The given, as in given up
> or given out, as in testimony.

The last two lines save the poem from sentimentality. The poet imagines approaching the "given," "giv[ing] up" the notion that words are a simple passport while yet insisting that, in the way words are commonly used, something is "given out" as testimony.

"Weed" (P, 33), a poem even more directly concerned with handling words, follows much the same pattern. Thinking about "horse-parsnips" seen along the roadside, Hass contrasts the acknowledgment of limits involved in that use of language—"Horse is Lorca's word, fierce as wind, / . . . and parsnip is hopeless, / second cousin to the rhubarb / . . . Marrying the words / to the coarse white umbels sprouting / on the first of May is history / but conveys nothing"—with the story of desire suggested in another sort of naming:

> it is not the veined
>   body of Queen Anne's lace
> I found, bored, in a spring classroom
>   from which I walked hands tingling
> for the breasts that are meadows in New Jersey
>   in 1933; it is thicker, shaggier, and the name
> is absurd.

In contrast to the sort of naming employed by William Carlos Williams in his poem "Queen Anne's Lace" and deliciously encountered by Hass as a boy— "Each flower is a hand's span / of her whiteness. Wherever / his hand has lain there is / a tiny purple blemish"—this marrying of words and landscape "conveys nothing."⁵ And for Hass, properly so. Where Williams tracks the desire to lay a hand on "her whiteness" all the way to the inevitable loss of what desire longs for—"the whole field is a / white desire, empty, a single stem, / a cluster, flower by flower, / a pious wish to whiteness gone over— / or nothing"—Hass thinks he hears in the refusal of the term *horse-parsnips* to assert a claim of mastery a "durable / unimaginative [taking of] pleasure" in a world free of the blemish of a man's "tingling" hands. Such a word offers testimony.

Another set of poems, a cluster of responses to the Charlottesville area, moves from thinking about single words (*white, horse-parsnips*) to thinking more generally about attitudes toward words. "Winter Morning in Charlottesville" (P, 28) finds in the morning's "Lead skies / and gothic traceries of poplar" a version of the fifteenth-century Florentine reformer Girolamo Savonarola's ascetic "rage against the carnal word." But that is to treat the world's temporary rhythms as empty and death-directed, and the word that would traffic with them as flawed and limited and "carnal." On a day of such clean refusals, one sees the attraction of Savonarola's skeptical dismissal, and yet one sees also—the poet seems to discover it in his use of "carnal"—that what is natural and bodily and finite is quite far reaching in its testimony. Noticing dogwoods edging toward bloom, a white-crowned sparrow in the grass, and thinking about this area as home to Jefferson's Declaration of Independence, Hass reminds himself of the connections between the way words create and give birth and the way the world itself does. Though separate from a world that will inevitably shift and change, words are yet, in their carnality, married to that world they exist alongside of. That is too much to give up to the mind of winter:

> By a natural
> selection, the word
> originates its species,
>   the blood flowers,
> republics scrawl their hurried declarations
> & small birds scavenge
>   in the chaste late winter grass.

In "Old Dominion" (P, 29), apparently set at the University of Virginia, Hass plays off of the state's nickname, beginning the poem with another expression of uneasiness about the "dominion" of an "old" and too easily inherited way of thinking and speaking about the world:

The shadows of late afternoon and the odors
of honeysuckle are a congruent sadness.
Everything is easy but wrong. I am walking
across thick lawns under maples in borrowed tennis whites.

That easy sadness, Hass reflects, working the idea out by means of a picture he remembers of a long-faced Randall Jarrell in an analogous position, flows seductively from a use of words in which life stands over there, outside of words, a cast of the eyes as deeply written into our language as distance is in *longing*:

It puzzled me that in his art, like Chekhov's,
everyone was lost, that the main chance was never seized
because it is only there as a thing to be dreamed of
or because someone somewhere had set the old words
to the old tune: we live by habit and it doesn't hurt.

In both this and the third Charlottesville poem, on taking a tour of Jefferson's "Monticello" (P, 30–31) and becoming uneasy with another version of desire fencing itself off from the world—"one wing for Governor Randolph when he comes, / the other wing for love, / private places / in the public weal / that ache against the teeth like ice"—the poet ends by taking flight rather than working out more "natural" or ordinary uses of words. "I begin making resolutions," he writes: "to take risks, not to stay / in the south, to somehow do honor to Randall Jarrell." And yet, in opening these old tunes up from within, he adds to his survey of how we speak in the uneasy spaces of finitude.

"Santa Lucia" (P, 21–24), a dramatic monologue in the voice of a woman who feels herself hemmed in by "Male fear, male eyes and art," pushes away from the attempt to avoid finitude in yet another way. As the woman who narrates the poem describes the pressure of those male eyes, she speaks for the bodily limits desire seeks to overcome. Her pursuer makes clear, in his gifts, the connection between art and desire. The speaker remarks on the "glut & desperation" of his tokens, the way they mount up as if desperately trying to bridge or transcend a gap, refusing to acknowledge distance or separation:

Art & love: he camps outside my door,
innocent, carnivorous. As if desire
were actually a flute, as if the little song
transcend, transcend could get you anywhere.
He brings me wine; he believes in the arts
and uses them for beauty.

Complicating the situation, she realizes that she has inherited from her culture this way of seeing. She has been handed "the eyes I use to see myself / in love"—eyes that understand a woman as something to struggle for and possess:

> I see my body.
> Walking in the galleries at the Louvre,
> I was, each moment, naked & possessed.
> Tourists gorged on goosenecked Florentine girls
> by Pollaiuolo. He sees me like a painter.
> I hear his words for me: white, gold.

Fighting free, then, giving up those male eyes, is no simple thing. That is why the title, though it refers to the Santa Lucia Mountains near Big Sur where she walks and muses, also points us to the virgin saint who tore out her eyes rather than give up her purity: "Santa Lucia: eyes jellied on a plate." To give up those eyes is to pull away from what Hass calls the whole "riddle of desire," the question, as he puts it in an essay, of "whether one possesses being in desire or the cessation of desire" (TC, 207). What if "possession" was no longer the question?

> It's not the riddle
> of desire that interests me; it is the riddle
> of good hands, chervil in a windowbox,
> the white pages of a book, someone says
> I'm tired, someone turning on the light.
> . . . .
> What I want happens
> not when the deer freezes in the shade
> and looks at you and you hold very still
> and meet her gaze but in the moment after
> when she flicks her ears & starts to feed again.

That moment leaves her free from the gaze, not owned, but sharing the same finite space as her observer or companion and acknowledging distance as part of the equation.

The most accomplished of the poems in the first section, "Not Going to New York: A Letter" (P, 43–46), plays out the entire process at greater length. The poet's apology for not flying from California to New York connects New York with the dismissive response to finitude that these poems consistently turn away from, and it offers, as a counter-example, the sort of response that its own form—casual, durable, "a letter of apology, unrhymed"—embodies. The letter, making grand, casually connected loops, is like the name *horse-parsnips* or the bramble of the word *blackberry*; in "giv[ing] up" a claim to master and hold tight, it "give[s] out . . . testimony" (P, 16). Cavell would call it an ordinary form. As Hass puts it, after skidding through a series of associations that the thought of New York calls up, such a form of writing is not what we have been taught to think of as art:

> This has nothing to do with the odd terror in my memory.
> It only explains it—the way this early winter weather
> makes life seem more commonplace and—at a certain angle—
> more intense. It is not poetry where decay and a created
> radiance lie hidden inside words the way that memory
> folds them into living.

Like a thick, shaggy word that "conveys nothing," a letter is a more limited form, lying beside, not making a terrible radiance out of, the presence of decay in memory's folds. The way its acknowledgment of limits makes something both commonplace and attentive out of estrangement, Hass remarks, might be compared to what happens in translation. Think of Boris Pasternak working on Shakespeare. As "Meditation at Lagunitas" would have it, the act from one point of view is an impossible one, rotten with loss. And yet, think what does not dissolve. Call it attention itself, not the lost thing or world or person, but the form of noticing itself, the translator's tenderness arising in an acknowledgment of distance:

> He would have noticed the articles as a native speaker wouldn't:
> *a* bird, *the* haunch; and understood a little what persists
> when, eyes half-closed, lattice-shadow on his face,
> he murmured the phrase in the dark vowels of his mother tongue.

What the letter plays out, then, is two different responses to the problem of finitude—two "swift, opposing currents" (SU, 57) the poet lies down in, or two contradictory "premises" he inhabits. They can be sketched as follows. The poet connects his decision not to fly east to a memory of Buffalo winters and February thaws that "hardened the heart / against the wish for spring":

> The windows faced east and a furred snow reassumed the pines
> but arrived only mottled in the fields so that its flesh
> was my grandmother's in the kitchen of the house
> on Jackson Street, and she was crying. I was a good boy.

She held me so tight when she said that, smelling like sleep
rotting if sleep rots, that I always knew how death would come
to get me and the soft folds of her quivery white neck
were what I saw

New York is associated with the rotting smell of death not only through the
way its muddy, snow-mottled fields resembled his grandmother's neck but
also because flying east involves heading across the Sierras and, at certain
seasons, being startled by the same pattern: "sometimes on an airplane I look
down / to snow covering the arroyos on the east side of the Sierra / and it's
grandmother's flesh and I look away." Further, by means of its connection to
this grandmother, New York is associated with a response to the muddy, dying
world the poet developed as a child:

In the house
on Jackson Street, I am the figure against the wall
in Bonnard's *The Breakfast Room*. The light is terrible. It is
wishes that are fat dogs, already sated, snuffling
at the heart in dreams. The table linen is so crisp
it puts an end to fantasies of rectitude, clean hands, high art
and the blue beside the white in the striping is the color
of the river Loire when you read about it in old books
and dreamed of provincial breakfasts, the sun the color
of bread crust and the fruit icy cold and there was no
terrified figure dwarf-like and correct, disappearing
off the edge of Bonnard's *The Breakfast Room*. It was not
grandmother weeping in the breakfast room

That is, he responded to that rotting smell by wishing for a world so high
and clean and correct and icy cold that he—"terrified . . . dwarf-like"—would
disappear. We might call that poetry or the old dominion or the old thinking.
Unlike such approaches in which distance is a threat that can only be met by
dissolving the world and breaking free of time, Hass lives now in something
like the translator's world, dwelling within estrangement's casual breaking up
of order. That is what staying in California, writing a letter and not a poem,
means:

Summer dries us out with golden light, so winter
is a kind of spring here—wet trees, a reptile odor
in the earth, mild greening—and the seasonal myths
lie across one another in the quick darkening of days.

Kristin and Luke are bent to a puzzle, some allegory
of the quattrocento cut in a thousand small uneven pieces
which, on the floor, they recompose with rapt,
leisurely attention.

The point of Hass's work, I'm suggesting, is not correctness: it is not the thousand-piece puzzle put together or the seasonal myths restored or the deer freezing in the shade; it is the rapt attention that the smallness of certain gestures makes possible.

The final poem in the book, the twenty-page "Songs to Survive the Summer" (P, 48–68), offers an extensively developed example of the attentive use of language generated by an unfolding of the line's tension. Like "Maps," it gives little attention to the language of control that most Hass poems push off of. Instead, much like an Ashbery poem in this regard, it simply goes about the business of describing and enacting a different use of words. Its situation, like the lost coast of "Maps," is inescapably finite: the poem is addressed to the poet's daughter, distraught over the death of a friend's mother. Her loss combines with the July heat—"stunned days, / faceless, droning"—and the writer's uneasiness with the direction of his work—"time islanded / in poems of dwindled time"—to produce the skeptical temptation at the heart of most Hass poems:

mist rising from soaked lawns,
gone world, everything
rises and dissolves in air,

whatever it is would
clear the air
dissolves in air and the knot

of days unties
invisibly like a shoelace.

Countering this temptation, responding to the condition it identifies and disappointedly turns away from, he offers his daughter a series of stories (what we have called maps or houses or names). Such songs or stories, he comments several times, "Saved no one." And yet, he proposes, essentially rephrasing Frost on the "small man-made figure[s] of order and concentration" we juxtapose against "black and utter chaos," such "curiously shaped" things are "the frailest stay[s] against / our fears." Why? Because like a wooden nickel he was given as a child that "married / in my mind with summer," such shaped things respond to death or limits. They describe death, or finitude, back to us not simply as a dissolving force but as a part of what we touch or attend to or make use of in the world. Death's presence, limit's presence, lusters our ordinary responses to the world—shows them to us as momentary, but also live or radiant:

> It is every
> thing touched casually,
> lovers, the images
>
> of saviors, books, the coin
> I carried in my pocket
> till it shone, it is
>
> all things lustered
> by the steady thoughtlessness
> of human use.

Here we are very close to a merging of Frost and Wittgenstein: those frail stays becoming common testaments of human use, luminous maps for dwelling in finitude.

If we think about the various "wooden nickels" that Hass offers his daughter, we begin to see some patterns. Wallace Stevens, whose line from "Sunday Morning," "Death is the mother of beauty" taught Hass to attend to the world, made the ordinary act of "walking equably to work" a form by which to shape and wander through "the war between desire / and dailiness"—the gap between the vibrant-winged world we sense from time to time and the daily one that tears it from us. "Chekhov's / tenderness" shows us not only a world in which "the night eats me" but one in which we prize such lustered shapings as "a new recipe for onion soup" that concludes: "Surround yourself with friends. / Huddle in a warm place. / Ladle. Eat." Similarly, "Wilhelm Steller, form's / hero," a naturalist on Vitus Bering's 1741 expedition who was sent ashore to gather the materials for "a healing broth" to save the disoriented captain and his crew from scurvy, noticed a jay reminiscent of a painting of a Carolina jay he had seen in Europe,[6] and made a shape, a connection:

> America, we're saved.
> No one believed him or,
> sick for home, he didn't care
>
> what wilderness
> it was. They set sail
> west. Bering died.

Like Stevens, Steller was "form's hero" not because he ended the war between desire and dailiness or, in his case, made a convincing case that Bering had successfully crossed from Siberia to Alaska. Rather, quite literally, he was form's hero because he made an attentive shape in that wandering space between—as the name we still used testifies: "*Steller's jay*, by which / I found Alaska. / He wrote it in his book." He focused it, touched it, began its lustering. All of these forms the poet offers his daughter are similarly human-sized acts of attention; they all fail, but like the haiku, also celebrated in this poem, they bring forward the fact that it's "*a strange thing! / To be alive / beneath plum blossoms.*"

Hass's *Human Wishes* (1989) strikes me as a successful combination of his first two books. If *Field Guide* turned first to such situations as marrying oneself to a place or living within the confines of a house and then measured those explorations of estrangement or distance against the act of writing, and if *Praise* reversed that pattern by concentrating first on ways of speaking before moving to metaphorically equivalent situations, *Human Wishes* attempts to give equal attention to both. It explores what Hass now calls an "interval"—the opening made visible by the failure of the drive to discern meaning and make sense (previously called the line's tension or the brambles of *blackberry* or *horse-parsnips*) where our finite position in the world can be slowed and attended to. Discovering, like Bishop, that the same interval or gap appears between a word and a thing as between one lover and another, Hass makes a fluid intellectual drama out of paying attention to the "lustered" frailness of our forms of attention in that space. Words, making love, chatting with friends—like Whitman before him, in this volume Hass begins to find his defining issues raised in every situation the world places in his path. One exploration, as Cavell puts it, "is isomorphic with every other . . . allegories and measures of one another" (SW, 62). In fanning out in such a way, the entire book becomes a powerful working out of the catalog-poetics of "Maps" or "Songs to Survive the Summer."

The first section of *Human Wishes* is the one most explicitly about the act of writing. Its six poems all move through an ungoverned space, using disconnected, prose-shaped lines to slow down and explore such issues as rendering a scene or simulating a natural process. Think of the way description was studied in "Palo Alto: The Marshes" or dwelling in a home was explored in "In Weather," but replace the dove-tailed connections between sections of these poems with a series of cuts and reversals. That is how reflection works in these poems—a graph rather than a story. We saw in the introduction how "Spring Drawing" (HW, 3–4), in its freewheeling reflection on "common nouns" and "complicated forms," discovers "as if" to be a form of attention "lustered by the steady thoughtlessness / of human use" (P, 68): an "interval . . . to which mind and breath attend, . . . / . . . habitable space lived in beyond wishing."[7] The other poems in this section acknowledge and open up similar spaces within a writer's ambitions. What can be noticed, they ask, if we start from the acknowledgment that the world "moves its own way," gathering and dispersing, leaving its "theme[s]" "unstated" (HW, 7)? Or if we acknowledge that the fact that "things change" leaves attempts at "narration" clutching at air and somehow beside the point (HW, 10)? What do we see about language when we acknowledge that "Poetry proposes no solutions" to the problem of injustice or that it has no direct response to "the innocence of all the suffering on earth" (HW, 11, 13)? Within each of these disruptive questions a place of radiant attention is opened up.

Let's look, for example, at "Vintage" (HW, 5–6). A group of friends is walking in New York. The poem's narrator sketches the scene while simultaneously trying to control all of the various "propositions"—remarks, landmarks, urban details—offered for him reflectively "to consider." Here is the beginning:

> They had agreed, walking into the delicatessen on Sixth Avenue, that their friends' affairs were focused and saddened by massive projection;
>
> movie screens in their childhood were immense, and someone had proposed that need was unlovable.
>
> The delicatessen had a chicken salad with chunks of cooked chicken in a creamy basil mayonnaise a shade lighter than the Coast Range in August; it was gray outside, February.
>
> Eating with plastic forks, walking and talking in the sleety afternoon, they passed a house where Djuna Barnes was still, reportedly, making sentences.

This has the feel of the way conversations unroll. Phrases prompt new phrases, and details from what surrounds the friends introduce new topics. The way other friends handle and make sense of their affairs by blowing them up into grand scenes reminds someone of childhood movie screens; such a need for attention strikes someone else as "unlovable"; the chicken salad prompts someone, the narrator one presumes, to measure the difference between California and New York, August and February; someone else had heard that Djuna Barnes lived in the neighborhood. By itself, this has the wan intensity of a 1970s *New Yorker* piece. But what happens is quite interesting; the narrator, instead of either staying with this skeptical notational drift or trying to yank it into meaning, begins to handle the richly-woven set of issues raised in this space (this interval), which he cannot conventionally narrate:

> Bashō said: avoid adjectives of scale, you will love the world more and desire it less.

> And there were other propositions to consider: childhood, VistaVision, a pair of wet, mobile lips on the screen at least eight feet long.

> On the corner a blind man with one leg was selling pencils. He must have received a disability check,

> but it didn't feed his hunger for public agony, and he sat on the sidewalk slack-jawed, with a tin cup, his face and opaque eyes turned upward in a look of blind, questing pathos—

> half Job, half mole.

The unstated issue, made visible here where it cannot be easily satisfied, is our hunger for control and order. The narrator's citing of Bashō speaks to the way Barnes makes sentences and the way the narrator himself does; it plays against the way he compares the shades of mayonnaise and grass in August, the way their friends read themselves against others, and the way the blind man measures himself against the public. All of the hunger here is related: the hunger to be visible, to be exact, to be known, to be somewhere else. Handling that hunger in an interval where it seems projected on several wide screens at once, the poet does not make sense of the scene exactly; rather, he dwells in the finite human act. He reflects on it and makes it visible. Concluding with an almost comic reminder to himself that his own, inevitably failing, hunger to order or size up must always be at issue as he writes, the poet suddenly shows the empty space he is working within:

> It makes you want, at this point, a quick cut, or a reaction shot. "The taxis rivered up Sixth Avenue." "A little sunlight touched the steeple of the First Magyar Reform Church."

> In fact, the clerk in the liquor store was appalled. "No, no," he said, "that cabernet can't be drunk for another five years."

The poem halts there, leaving us blind and empty-handed and attentive, beyond the wish to control or convincingly close with a reaction shot. It is a response to the world, as another poem puts it, both "casual and intense" (HW, 8).

If the poems in the first section study or reflect on the fragility of what we do when we write, the fourteen prose poems of the second section, to my mind the strongest part of the book, describe a series of situations that are isomorphic with the intervals opened up within the writing scene. These situations allow Hass to measure or reflect on what is discovered in writing. Perhaps because they are written in prose, they do indeed make the conjunction of our finite acts and the world beyond us seem "casual and intense"—both ordinary and charged.

Let me run through some examples, each of which contains an acknowledgment that the straightforward has broken down and finds within that space a sort of fragile and tender attentive intensity. "Museum" (HW, 18) describes a couple in a museum restaurant on a Sunday morning. The arrangement they work out, like the forms "lustered / by the steady thoughtlessness / of human use" in "Songs to Survive the Summer," is a human gesture. It is like a map or a name or a recipe for soup: "he holds the baby. She drinks coffee, scans the front page, butters a roll and eats it in their little corner in the sun. After a while, she holds the baby. He reads the *Book Review* and eats some fruit. Then he holds the baby while she finds the section of the paper she wants and eats fruit and smokes. They've hardly exchanged a look. Meanwhile, I have fallen in love with this equitable arrangement, and with the baby who cooperates by sleeping." What keeps this from sentimentality on the one hand and makes it more than an ironic belittling of the barely-aware couple on the other is the note of fragility that the poet adds. He plays out the line's tension or unfolds the tender use of *blackberry*, by noticing the context that establishes this arrangement as momentary and at risk: "All around them are faces Käthe Kollwitz carved in wood of people with no talent or capacity for suffering who are suffering the numbest kinds of pain: hunger, helpless terror." Faces of people like them, the poet seems to add silently, not dismissing their fragile gesture, but allowing the world, in all its power, to whistle through it: "But this young couple is reading the Sunday paper in the sun, the baby is sleeping, the green has begun to emerge from the rind of their cantaloupe, and everything seems possible."

"Novella" (HW, 19–20), a sketch of possible plans for a novella—"A woman who, as a thirteen-year-old girl, develops a friendship with a blind painter, a painter who is going blind"—also foregrounds the writer's attempt to make visible the charged lustre of the interval described. As a thirteen-year-old, the woman modeled for a painter—his cabin off in the woods away from her ordinary life, the relationship charged and undefined: "The cabin smells of oil paint, but also of pine. The painter's touch is sexual and not sexual, as she herself is. From time to time she remembers this interval in the fall and winter of ninth grade. By spring the painter had moved. By summer her period had started. And after that her memory blurred, speeding up." The memory stays charged and alive for her because, floating outside of the otherwise stable and coherent narrative that she has developed for herself, it gives her a sharp feeling of the strangeness and wonder of life:

> When the memory of that time came to her, it was touched by strangeness because it formed no pattern with the other events in her life. It lay in her memory like one piece of broken tile, salmon-colored or the deep green of wet leaves, beautiful in itself but unusable in the design she was making. Just the other day she remembered it. Her friends were coming up from the beach with a bucket full of something, smiling and waving to her, shouting something funny she couldn't make out, and suddenly she was there—the light flooding through the big windows, the litter of canvases, a white half-finished torso on the worktable, the sweet, wheaty odor of biscuits rising from the just-opened tin.

That memory is like a simile breaking the straightforward drive of the *Iliad* or the habit of saying "as if" suddenly becoming the focus rather than the never-thought-about mechanism of the sentence. In its fragility—the event it has hold of is unusable or nonnarratable in any scheme; it "saved no one"—the memory becomes powerfully and strangely alive. Such an acknowledgment makes memory a newly-powerful way of paying attention; to cite a phrase Hass uses repeatedly, it is a way into life: "suddenly she was there."

A variation of this can be found in "Tall Windows" (HW, 24), a poem that moves from the prickly fragility of being sick while traveling—"All day you didn't cry or cry out and you felt like sleeping. The desire to sleep was light bulbs dimming as a powerful appliance kicks on. You recognized that. As in school it was explained to you that pus was a brave army of white corpuscles hurling themselves at the virulent invader and dying"—to a story encountered that same day about a Dutch woman's confrontation with the Nazis. The woman, a "strict Calvinist," had been married to a Jewish professor who died in 1937, leaving her with two sons. The "virulent" invasion of the Nazis making her society's calm "orderliness" suddenly visible not as the natural order of things but as a fragile arrangement, she responded with a series of carefully weighed, terribly fragile gestures:

> When the Nazis came in 1940, she went to court and perjured herself by testifying that her children were conceived during an illicit affair with

a Gentile, and when she developed tuberculosis in 1943, she traded
passports with a Jewish friend, since she was going to die anyway, and
took her place on the train to the camps. Her sons kissed her good-bye
on the platform. Eyes open. What kept you awake was a feeling that
everything in the world has its own size, that if you found its size among
the swellings and diminishings it would be calm and shine.

Her response, lucid in its awareness of finitude, was an eyes-open assessment
of the world's unmasterable "swellings and diminishings." In fact, it is those
swellings and diminishings—the masks on the museum's walls or the confused
feelings within an indefinable relationship—that both kick away her old
orderly arrangements and flood her with a world terribly alive. She is a
model for the poet, encouraging him to keep his eyes open as well against
the powerful surge of sickness kicking in, because she responds to that new
situation with a sense of calm, radiant attention. Her gestures, to bring in other
Hass poems, are tender and charged, weightless and lustered. Open-eyed, the
woman and her gestures allegorize and measure the scene of writing—they
point to "habitable space lived in beyond wishing." They present us with, as
another poem in the sequence puts it, the grain of the world, "so sharply
focused that it seems alive, grays and blacks in a rivery and complex pattern
of venation" (HW, 26).

In the third section of *Human Wishes*, the "as if" space attended to—
the interval where attention is possible, the lustered coin—is marriage. If
marriage proposes to make two people "one flesh," it is in fact a finite form in
which distance has to be acknowledged as part of the equation, part of how the
form functions. Dwelling in a marriage is like living in a house or working with
a language or inhabiting the California coast—as Hass slows and studies it, he
is working out the implications of what he is also noting in his writing. It is an
example of a live form of dwelling within an acknowledgment of finitude. A
striking example of reflecting on (or playing out) the distance within marriage
is "The Apple Trees at Olema" (HW, 39–40). As the poet narrates the story of a
couple's shifting, noncoincident responses to two neglected apples trees they
discover on a walk—they are "wild with blossom and a green fire / of small
new leaves flickered even on the deadest branches"—he makes it clear, by a
series of authorial asides and a play of shifting tenses, that the act of writing is
a struggle to see and evaluate the space between two people. Marriage, like
writing, is not simply an example of Hass's issues; it is a sort of lab, a space
where they are powerfully at work. The couple's differences—they use, for
example, correct but different terms for the same violet: "Trout lily, he said;

she said, adder's tongue"—raise for the narrator the painful fact of limits and distance:

> She is shaken by the raw, white, backlit flaring
> of the apple blossoms. He is exultant,
> as if some thing he felt were verified,
> and looks to her to mirror his response.
> If it is afternoon, a thin moon of my own dismay
> fades like a scar in the sky to the east of them.
> He could be knocking wildly at a closed door
> in a dream.

Ways of responding to that closed door are at issue here. The narrator is "dismay[ed]" at what another poem calls the "Misery and Splendor" (HW, 41) of the human situation—in that poem, "trying to become one creature" and realizing that "something will not have it." "Misery and Splendor" emphasizes both the "tender[ness]" of its lovers "with each other" and, playing out an echo of Genesis (which is one map of the situation), the "powerful / and baffled will," which continues to drive them: "washed up on the shore of a world— / or huddled against the gate of a garden— / to which they can't admit they can never be admitted." This poem, after one more set of misfiring responses— "she takes the measure / of the trees and lets them in. But he no longer / has the apple trees"—also portrays their tenderness in this space as a response to the closed doors of finitude, but proposes a calmer response. They notice a bird, admire it, and go on walking:

> A small boy wanders corridors of a hotel that way.
> Behind one door, a maid. Behind another one, a man
> in striped pajamas shaving. He holds the number
> of his room close to the center of his mind
> gravely and delicately, *as if* it were the key,
> and then he wanders among strangers all he wants. [emphasis mine]

The crucial phrase here is "as if," one we have seen before. The room number is held "gravely and delicately, as if it were the key." It is not a key; all sorts of things could happen to break in on the child's reverie, but treating that number as if it were a key opens up for him a space to wander in, a way to move through and attend to a world he is estranged from. A simile or a cliché or a chance to identify a species of jay, as we have noted before, all work the same way. The boy is free to move, among closed doors and strangers. This is as true about marriage, which gives a form to move within, as it is about words. Hass's work illustrates the grave delicacy and the freedom with which such forms of attention can be used.

Let me look at one last ambitious wandering of the "as if" of marriage and family. "Santa Barbara Road" (HW, 51–59), using as its controlling metaphor a backyard project undertaken as a response to estrangement—because "I felt like a stranger to my life / and it scared me, . . . / . . . I finally went into the garden and started / digging, trying to marry myself / and my hands to that place"—digs into the family's life together when they shared this address. Digging is a way of handling a lustered coin, rubbing its textures though it will save no one. In the poem, in fact, the project is never completed. Though the estrangement never disappears, the connections made and dissolved within it dramatize the family as another way we attend to and "marry" the world around us. As with "Songs to Survive the Summer" or "Maps," all of the dug-through memories foreground their fragility. For example, bathing his daughter as a three-year-old, the poet, perhaps inadvertently, introduces her to the arbitrariness of names. "Who are you?" the narrator asks, and finds himself, rubber duck in hand, in a recapitulation of "Meditation at Lagunitas":

> "Kristin," she said laughing, her delicious
> name, delicious self. "That's just your name,"
> the duck said. "Who are you?" "Kristin,"
> she said. "Kristin's a name. Who are you?"
> the duck asked. She said, shrugging,
> "Mommy, Daddy, Leif."

This is exactly the space of Bishop's "In the Waiting Room," yet this time dissolving a name and replacing it with the frail network of relationships within a family yields not a feeling of vertigo but one of intimacy. Such a naming must be handled "tenderly"; like the "equitable arrangement" in the museum, it could easily (and will inevitably) give way. That idea gets repeated when a friend from England comes to visit, years later, and remarks, of Berkeley's "nest / of gentlefolk," "I shouldn't want to live in America. / I'd miss the despair of European men." In contrast to "despair" about limits—what we have been calling "the old thinking"—the poet proposes a different sort of response. Remembering being in England with his family and that friend, the poet describes a scene that, like "Mommy, Daddy, Leif" (or bêche-de-mer), displays within limits a set of multiple viewpoints that can be (temporarily) dwelt within:

So many prisms to construct a moment!
Spiderwebs set at all angles on a hedge:
what Luke thought was going on, what Mr. Acker
saw, and Richard, who had recently divorced,
idly rolling a ball with someone else's child,
healing slowly, as the neighbor's silky mare
who had had a hard birth in the early spring,
stood quiet in the field as May grew sweet,
her torn vagina healing. So many visions
intersecting at what we call the crystal
of a common world, all the growing and shearing,
all the violent breaks.

Like a word with its histories of use or a house with various tensions, a family is a form for dwelling within our common finitude; it is a form that, of course, will shear and break, but also one that, lustered by its multiple voices, holds us attentively before the world.

Laced through the poem's May/June, rising-into-life scenes are reminders of what will dissolve them. We have been calling such things an acknowledgment of the truth of skepticism: Berkeley fog at a morning school-bus stop, parents not getting along, the pressures of "other lives with other schedules," time, the tug of a father against a son. Yet far from eliminating the family, these corrosive forces, as a friend remarks on a Memorial Day hike—"adults / chatting in constantly re-forming groups, / men with men, women with women, couples, / children cozened along with orange sections / and with raisins, running ahead, and back, / and interrupting"—these forces make it clear that the family is, like words, a fragile "invention" or "a set of conventions." It is an intimate, nonguaranteed dwelling place. A family is like the path that Hass quotes Wendell Berry's description of in an essay ("a ritual of familiarity / a form of contact with a known landscape") and with which he closes this poem. "[K]nown well," marked by its uses in previous summers, the path, like the fragile, shifting family strolling down it to a lake, holds, but only momentarily. Mother absent, a daughter straining toward her "real life" elsewhere, the path (like all forms in Hass) leads toward an interval in which they can be alive: "Cold water, hot sun, the whole of an afternoon."

The book closes with a series of summary poems, perhaps not as charged as the rest of the book, in which Hass moves yet one step further out in tracing the implications of his sense of the interval. The way a word or a sentence, or a conversation or a family, handle and make something live out of limits is to be found woven throughout life. Poetry teaches us how to notice. Take making love, for example. In "Privilege of Being" (HW, 69–70) Hass describes a couple "connected at the belly in an unbelievably sweet / lubricious glue" looking directly at each other, a moment of union quickly hidden behind falling curtains or a shutting door when "creation" takes offense at such a union and forces them to remember their finitude: "they close their eyes again and hold each other, each / feeling the mortal singularity of the body / they have enchanted out of death for an hour or so." They are reminded, almost comically, "that life has limits, that people / die young, fail at love" and that love-making should be thought about like our use of the word *blackberry* or *horse-parsnips*—as something tender and clumsy and human and absurd. Like writing, it is a form of attention to "mortal singularity" and stands in contrast to Rilke's angels who must possess all we only desire. Later, the lovers go outside together:

> He runs beside her, he thinks
> of the sadness they have gasped and crooned their way out of
> coming, clutching each other with old, invented
> forms of grace and clumsy gratitude, ready
> to be alone again, or dissatisfied, or merely
> companionable like the couples on the summer beach
> reading magazine articles about intimacy between the sexes
> to themselves, and to each other,
> and to the immense, illiterate, consoling angels.

Human lives—our marriages, homes, ways of speaking; our silences, paths, clumsy forms and invented phrases—are, for Hass, bound within what "On Squaw Peak" (HW, 81–83) calls "the frame of things": the "law of averages" whose rhythms mix beauty and terror, things plump and things shriveled, whose rhythm tosses up, out of decay and time, moments of attention and contact. In a mountain meadow, in a marriage, in a sentence: "Things bloom. . . . They are / for their season alive in those brief vanishings / of air we ran through."

Hass's most recent book, *Sun Under Wood* (1996), completes a circuit by taking us back to Oppen's invitation to "actually watch, as the words are laid down on the page" (GO, 39). Here it is in writing itself, in the act of composing poems, that finitude is acknowledged and handled, becoming the ground for nonpossessively attending to the world. Although Hass has, in each previous book, made an occasional reference to the actual poem underhand—"Notice / in this poem the thinning out / of particulars" (P, 13);

"I was making this gathering . . . when Rachel came down the walk and went into the house" (HW, 34)—his self-reflective turn is now much more pronounced. It is as if the more specific work of the first three books—working from the malice and grief embodied in maps and homes and various ways of speaking back to what those emotions are responding to: the world's finitude, its impermanence—it is as if that work is now possible in any alert handling of "this impure spring of language" (SU, 70). To compose a poem, then, is to allow voice—broken, desiring, limited—"to take its place in this vast, deeply strange net of contingencies" (SU, 28) we find ourselves in. To compose a poem is to be "electrified" and brought to an intense experience of life by an acknowledgment of the finite "frame of things" (HW, 82) we operate within:

> this net of circumstance
> (*circum*, etc) that we are caught in,
> ill-starred, quarried with veins of cruelty,
> stupidity, bad-luck,
> which rhymes with *fuck*,
> not the sweet act, the exclamation
> of disgust, or maybe both
> a little singing ode-like rhyme
> because we live our lives in language and in time,
> craving some pure idiomorphic dialect of the thing itself,
> Adamic, electrified by clear tension
> like the distance between a sparrow and a cat,
> self and thing and eros as a god of wonder.
> (SU, 68)

Living "our lives in language and in time"—fragile, easily undone by the stars of cruelty, stupidity, or bad luck, desperate for it to be otherwise ("craving some pure idiomorphic dialect of the thing itself")—we are "electrified" and brought to an experience of "wonder" by acknowledging the world made visible by that blocked craving. Think of *fuck*, he writes; catch the word as we utter it and think about its simultaneous reference to "the sweet act" and "disgust." What is going on in its impure linguistic doubling? We use it the way an amateur uses language: it is thick, absurd, and "conveys nothing." It will "save no one." It inhabits contradictory "premises." And that is the point, for it is a doubling that is alive to finitude—both the sweetness of our brief lives and the disgust we often greet that briefness with. It is a tense doubling that alerts us to briefness and sweetness, an interval there in the language, a "piece of broken tile, . . . unusable in [a straightforward] design" (HW, 19) that, if we are alert enough to hear it at work in language's impure spring, permits us to wonder about the conditions we "are caught in."

In poem after poem in this book, Hass calls attention to himself writing, caught in the net of our condition and attending to it through the impure map of language. He calls attention to himself, for example, drafting a poem in a notebook (SU, 3–4) or expanding an entry in an old travel guide (SU, 23–24) or simply "pretending / to be walking down the mountain in the heat" (SU, 76). He remarks on himself sitting "at the typewriter" composing an aria (SU, 45) or stepping away from his work: "Paused for a moment in this writing and went out" (SU, 49). And, quite often, he comments on the work as it unfolds: "I could have said that I am a listless eye gazing through watery glass" (SU, 27); "When we say 'mother' in poems, / we usually mean some woman in her late twenties" (SU, 9); "thinnest lines of gold rivering through the amber / like—ah, now we come to it . . ." (SU, 73); "I'm a little ashamed that I want to end this poem / singing, but I want to end this poem singing" (SU, 76).

Let me examine three examples in some detail. "Dragonflies Mating" (SU, 6–11), a poem in six sections, works through an entire mental arc. Hass begins, in "early morning heat, / first day in the mountains," thinking about the native peoples "who lived here before us / [and] also loved these high mountain meadows on summer mornings." Making their way up to this height as the seasons progressed, they possessed, Hass supposes, a stable language with which to trace such journeys; they internalized fixed maps: "Told stories, / knew where they were on earth from the names, / owl moon, bear moon, gooseberry moon." But then Hass permits a humorous story about the inconsistencies of such acts of naming to complicate and thicken what could have been merely nostalgia for a lost way of mapping. In the second section of the poem, he recounts the story of a Channel Island Indian who, when asked about something odd in an ancient creation story, knowingly replies: "You know, / . . . when I was a kid, I wondered about that, / and I asked my father. . . . / . . . And my old man looked up at me with this funny smile / and said, You know when I was a kid, I wondered about that."

So instead of nostalgia, the poet clears a space (finds an interval or gap) where he can handle his own mixed, equally finite attempts at naming or location: "Thinking about that story just now, early morning heat, / first day in the mountains, I remembered stories about sick Indians / and—in the same thought—standing on the free throw line." The two thoughts are generated out of a desire to name and the subsequent complication and opening up of the act. Both memories come from his years at Saint Raphael's mission school. Hass's speaker remembers a Sister Marietta speaking sorrowfully about Franciscan priests who, along with their faith, brought "influenza and syphilis and the coughing disease" with them: "They meant so well, she said, and such a terrible thing / came here with their love." And he also remembers another terribly mixed act of love—his mother, "well into one of those weeks of drinking she disappeared into," showing up at basketball practice:

> I'd see her in the entryway looking for me, and I'd bounce
> the ball two or three times, study the orange rim as if it were,
> which it was, the true level of the world, the one sure thing
>
> the power in my hands could summon. I'd bounce the ball
> once more, feel the grain of the leather in my fingertips and shoot.
> It was a perfect thing; it was almost like killing her.

Cavell's Othello, who kills because he "cannot forgive Desdemona for existing, for being separate from him, outside, beyond command" (DK, 136), helps us see what is going on here. Wanting to locate himself, then humorously backing off from simple naming, the poem's speaker opens an interval within the act of naming. The doubled memory, discovered at play in the interval, testifies as to why we want names, why we need to fix and locate ourselves. Why? Because we live in a broken world where love can destroy and lay waste to what it approaches, however well-intentioned it might be—a brokenness making one hunger for something "true" and "level," for "the one sure thing" or the "perfect thing." We hunger, that is, to be out of brokenness, to kill what will not hold still and stay level and be commanded: drunk mother, the world itself. As Hass puts it in another poem: "she is what's / broken in a song. / She is its silences" (SU, 22). She is time, limit, the world at its most unreliable.

Looking at those two memories and seeing in them his almost-desperate need to fix and perfect and kill what cannot be perfected frees the poet, in the next section, to step back a bit more. "When we say 'mother' in poems," he remarks, we are trying "to secure the pathos of the child's point of view / and to hold her responsible." What if we give up such attempts (now, this morning) to securely name and locate ourselves, what is left? What does the desire to perfect inadvertently point toward? Succumbing to and then recovering from skepticism's dismissal of the world, with his eyes on mating dragonflies in that early morning heat and alert as well to the human hungers called up by the morning's writing, he sees the human condition—sees the way we smear the world in our terrible hungers and stand before it in attentive wonder:

> They don't carry all this half-mated longing up out of childhood
> and then go looking for it everywhere.

And so, I think, they can't wound each other the way we do.
They don't go through life dizzy or groggy with their hunger,
kill with it, smear it on everything, though it is perhaps also true
that nothing happens to them quite like what happens to us
when the blue-backed swallow dips swiftly toward the green pond
and the pond's green-and-blue reflected swallow marries it a moment
in the reflected sky and the heart goes out to the end of the rope
it has been throwing into abyss after abyss, and a singing shimmers
from every color the morning has risen into.

He discovers two streams—a hunger that kills, and an attentiveness that responds to the shimmering sky—in the complications of the desire to locate himself. As we have seen throughout his work, one shadows and shows forth the other. Both are present in the act of writing. Working against each other, they force him to let the world go and allow its full size to play against him.

"Faint Music" (su, 39–41) is quite clear about this. It tries to sort out Cavell's central idea: how is it that, "When everything broken is broken, / and everything dead is dead" and all that remains is a violently self-protective sense of self-love—"this violent, automatic / life's companion"—how is it that "maybe then, ordinary light, / faint music under things, a hovering like grace appears"? That is, how can brokenness, which produces (and is made visible by) self-love's violent clinging to what disappears, also reveal the ordinary as charged, shot through with grace and singing?

Hass works at the problem in this poem by thinking through a story a friend told him about the time he tried to kill himself. Deliberately positioning himself, the friend "climbed onto the jumping girder of the bridge, / the bay side," then in the salt air found himself puzzling over the "faintly ridiculous" word *seafood*. (Presumably, he had said to himself, melodramatically, something like "I'm about to become seafood.") Called back to an ordinary word (we say *seafood* but not *landfood*, why is that?) he touched on a human gesture, saw enough in it to pause a moment, then curled up and fell asleep, eventually walking back home after he awoke. Though still filled with "rage and grief" about the loss of his lover, the friend was able to play through her new life "once only, once and a half, and tell himself / that he was going to carry it for a very long time / and there was nothing he could do / but carry it." That is, he was able to measure or take the size of the pain, see it, just as he was able, simultaneously, to notice the size of the world around him: "He went out onto the porch, and listened / to the forest in the summer dark, madrone bark / crackling and curling as the cold came up." He moved away from his world-dissolving obsession with his own pain by placing it with other human gestures—words, remarks—and so rediscovered it as a place, a frail gesture, within which he could attend to the world again. Hass describes this as working out not order but a sequence:

> I had the idea that the world's so full of pain
> it must sometimes make a kind of singing.
> And that the sequence helps, as much as order helps—
> First an ego, and then pain, and then the singing.

Much of the same sorting goes on in the final poem I want to examine: the book's strongest poem, "Regalia for a Black Hat Dancer" (SU, 47–58). The writer begins by noting a series of phrases he had recorded during the day in which he had been trying to locate or make visible a feeling, none of which satisfied him: "something about 'the heart's huge vacancy,' / which seemed contemptible." Returning to the material that evening, then, he is returning to that stalled space or interval: "After dinner—sudden cooling / of the summer air—I sat down to it. Where." Where, of course, is important: what landscape might give access to this swirl of feelings? The poem examines two different, eventually connected answers. The first is "Walking down to Heart's Desire beach in the summer evenings / of the year my marriage ended—." What he carried with him, then, in that landscape, was indeed "the heart's huge vacancy." Back then, he had been baffled by the feeling. There had been no sequence:

> though I was hollowed out by pain,
> honeycombed with the emptiness of it,
> like the bird bones on the beach
> the salt of the bay water had worked on for a season—
> such surprising lightness in the hand—
> I don't think I could have told the pain of loss
> from the pain of possibility,
> though I knew they weren't the same thing.

As we have seen throughout his career, the two pains are related—the "loss" of the ego through pain leading to song and "possibility"—but it is one thing to understand this sequence, quite another to be able to move through it. He remembers trying to gain something from the emotion. At the most, almost comically mimicking the model of poets he loved, he discovered a second current that could be simply be called vacancy: "I'd present my emptiness, which was huge, baffled / . . . and most of the time I felt nothing, / when the moment came that was supposed to embody presence, / nothing really . . . / . . . So there were these two emptiness[es]: one made of pain and desire / and one made of vacancy." Neither feeling has room for the world.

What happens, then, is that this bit of reflection, like messing with the word *seafood* or remembering two thoughts at once or not being able to complete a sentence, provides the poet a pause within which he can attend to the world. Quite literally, he steps away from the writing:

> (Paused for a moment in this writing and went out.
> Dark, first the dark. Wind in the trees.
>
> . . . .
>
> Lost everything: this is the night; it doesn't love me
> or not. Shadow of a hawk, then shadow of a hawk.
> Going down at about the speed of a second hand.)

In that pause, taking note of a dark beyond him where he is neither loved nor not loved, he is reminded of the fragility of human gestures, slapped up against a vacant world that does not take them in. And in that dark he remembers other things that came to him on that heart-empty beach:

> The whole theater of the real: sadness, which seems infinite,
> cruelty, which seems infinite, the cheerful one-armed guy
> in the bakery mornings—he puts his croissant between his teeth
> and pours himself some coffee; someone on the phone
> trying to get me to pay my brother's rent, "I got too big a heart,
> I try to run a clean place"—the first floor reserved
> for transvestite hookers wobbling on spiked heels—
> and who would deny their clients the secret exhaustion
> of their dreams?; the whole botched world—

That is, he saw the whole finite world—cruel, sad, cheerful, self-important, dreaming, wobbling—occurring in the space between desire and vacancy: "Everything real nourished in the space between these things." And, he remembers, something started to come back to life: "I would go home, / make tea, call my children, some piece of writing / that I'd started would seem possible."

That is the first where: the beach, the whole botched world visible. But another where, explored this evening as he writes, allows him to go even further—not just seeing the botched world but entering it, whole-heartedly. He asks, of that finite world acknowledged at the beach, "Under sorrow, what?" and remembers glimpsing an answer:

Climbing in Korea,
months later, coming to the cave of the Sokkaram Buddha—
a view down a forested ravine to the Sea of Japan—
perhaps a glimpse: the closed eyelids—you'd have to make a gesture
with your hand to get the fineness of the gesture in the stone.
The stone hands resting on the thighs, open, utterly composed

What he found there was a combination of an eyes-closed acknowledgment
of emptiness and the hands' open, utterly composed gesture: "Nothing. Great
calm, flowing stone. No sorrow, no not-sorrow. / Lotuses, carved in the
pediment, simple, fleshy, open." But what did it mean? he asked himself.
He didn't know: "It seemed I could leave every internal fury there / and walk
away. . . . / . . . if I knew the gesture." Now, writing, he touches on various
ways of representing and responding to skepticism's truth. Would a proper
gesture be the university's love of theory—say its fascination with Derrida,
"Who'd set out to write a dissertation about time; / he'd read Heidegger,
Husserl, Kant, Augustine, and found / that there was no place to stand from
which to talk about it. / There was no ground. It was language. The scandal
/ of nothingness! Put cheerfully to work by my colleagues / to dismantle
regnant ideologies." Or would it be more like the gestures of street people,
"schizophrenics / with matted hair, dazed eyes, festering feet, always engaged
/ in some furious volleying inner dialogue they neglected, / unlike the rest
of us, to hide." Perhaps it would be related to the serenity one feels in a
medieval church standing before "sheer blanks" where carted-off paintings
and carvings once had been: "This emptiness / felt like that. Under the
hosannahs and the terror of the plague / and the crowning of the Virgin
in the spring."

This reflective handling opens another pause in the writing—"(Outside
again. Rubbing my eyes. Deep night, brilliant stars.[)]"—in which he is able to
locate a gesture, his own hands-open response to emptiness. He remembers,
at about the time of the cave experience, getting involved with another
woman and the strange experience, as he puts it, of "[lying] down in . . .
swift, opposing currents. / . . . two emptinesses, I suppose, the one / joy comes
from, the one regret, disfigured intention, the longing / to be safe or whole
flows into when it's disappearing." That is, he felt, under his sorrow at the
world's brokenness, in that torn space, two responses to emptiness. He felt,
at once, an attentive, freely-delighting sense of wonder and the sense of the
disfigurement that the loss of a once-grasped wholeness inevitably produces.
The two emotions are part of a sequence but are present simultaneously:

The word that occurs to me is 'droll.' It seemed sublimely droll.
The way we were as free as children playing hide and seek.
Her talk—raffish, funny, unexpected, sometimes wise, darkened—
the way a black thing is scintillant in light—by irony.
The way neither of us needed to hold back, think
before we spoke, lie, tiptoe carefully around a given subject,
or brace ourselves to say hard truths. It felt to me hilarious,
and hilarity, springwater gushing up from some muse's font
of crystal in old poems, seemed a form of emptiness. Look!
(Rilke in the sonnets.) I last but a minute. I walk on nothing.
Coming and going I do this dance in air. At night
when we got too tired to talk, were touching all along our bodies,
nodding off, I'd fall asleep smiling. Mornings—for how long—
I'd wake in pain. Physical pain, fluid; it moved
through my body like a grassfire spreading on a hill.
. . . .
I'd stare at the ceiling, bewildered, and feel a grief
so old it could have been some beggar woman in a fairy tale.
I didn't know you could lie down in such swift, opposing currents.

Hass's response to emptiness or the heart's vacancy is what it has always been: to lie down in the opposing currents generated by an awareness of limits—both the regret and violence of desire's desperate wanting to hold *and* the open hilarity of not holding or completing, of walking on nothing. We see here Miłosz wracked by contradiction, a husband hacking his world apart and lying down beside his wife, words said both querulously and tenderly, and so on. Experiencing both together, gives one a chance to measure or take the size of the world: "Private pain is easy, in a way. It doesn't go away, / but you can teach yourself to see its size. Invent a ritual." Hass's ritual, of course, is a linguistic one.

It is a ritual that, the close of the poem suggests, attends openly to the world in all its complexities. He tells another story of Korea—"In the town center / of Kwangju, there was a late October market fair. / Some guy was barbecuing halfs of baby chicks on a long, sooty contraption / of a grill, slathering them with soy sauce. Baby chicks. / Corn pancakes stuffed with leeks and garlic"— and connects it to the cave, to the hilarity of making love, and to this long night of writing. Each experience measures the other. Each embraces the world by acknowledging the opposing currents of human response:

I thought in this flesh-and-charcoal-scented heavy air
of the Buddha in his cave. Tired as if from making love
or writing through the night. Was I going to eat a baby chick?
Two pancakes. A clay mug of the beer. Sat down
under an umbrella and looked to see, among the diners
feasting, quarreling about their riven country,
if you were supposed to eat the bones. You were. I did.

4. An Interview with Robert Hass

TG: In an essay on James Wright, you say that what's characteristic of American writing is a sense of a "radical division between the inner and outer worlds" (TC, 35). You go on to suggest that perhaps that way of posing the problem was the problem. Would you say more about this?

RH: I was trying to think about why Wright's poetry seemed sentimental to me and about what I thought was this strict, unconscious dualism in Robert Bly's thinking. I tended to think of them as midwestern, fundamentalist Protestant writers. Bly's full of those formulations—"A man can't look out and in at the same time," and so on—and I suppose I felt threatened by that idea. At some point, in a phenomenological way, I just thought it wasn't how we experience the world, that radical disjunction between self and body. And by "we" I guess I meant "I."

TG: Body being the "outer" world?

RH: The interesting question is where does the world begin. Does it begin at the skin? Or beyond the skin? For people with strict territorial boundaries it begins—otherness begins—at the edge of the skin. For people with other boundaries it begins at different intervals. There's the otherness of not the self, not my body, and then there's not my immediate family, not my kin. There are a whole succession of them. In a sort of naive way, when I was writing *Field Guide*, I was trying to find and construct ways in which language made a set of continuous relations with, made congregations of bodies to other bodies, to family, place, world, and so on. An angel's ladder of narcissisms. I was hungrily trying to secure—in the same way, I married young, had kids young—I was on all fronts trying to convince myself that it all held together.

TG: "Maps" seems to me a poem that works those connections out at a very flexible series of intervals. What feels naive about it?

RH: It was in flight from the opposite view—that all of these linkings or congregations were not "natural," that they were constructed. What kind of language connects to the world? There was one level on which I wanted to have a completely naive relationship to what I couldn't have a completely naive relationship to—that is, the fact that the aesthetic of the transparency of language was a convention. The whole business of language as a convention, as a mediation, dawned on me slowly, and it gave an interesting edge to the writing of that book.

TG: In a way, *Field Guide* acts that realization out, doesn't it? In "Maps," you talk about the landscape by saying "the eye *owns* what is familiar / felt along the flesh." That's meant to be positive, I take it, but as the book goes on, the notion of ownership becomes very complicated. By "Lament for the Poles of Buffalo," ownership is quite negative: the peasants who are married to the land are contrasted to the landowners who will never know it in that way. It's a much more innocent use of the word early in the book.

RH: I don't remember the timing, but I think those two passages were aware of each other. By the time I published the book I was aware that I had used the word and that it wasn't innocent. I thought to myself, "Well, you've used the word *owns* here, and you've made this distinction between owning and knowing. So, you secretly want to be the owner, you just want to be superior to those other owners." And I saw the other thing—the ambiguous sense of owning what's "familiar," because what's familiar is at some level what's not noticed, what's comfortable. I think when I wrote it I was reaching for a positive statement of the way affection and knowledge take long-term possession of something. Later as I was reading galleys I saw what I had done and thought, "Here's yet another instance of the instability of language being truer to experience than the thing you desire to say."

TG: Another word in *Field Guide* that seems complicated in this way is *malice*. In a number of poems you begin with the language of pure description, that sense of connection, then move to a criticism of the padres, the napalm makers, the takers like Kit Carson who block that kind of simplicity. What's interesting to me is that your response—"my eyes flash, another / knife, clean as malice"—uses *their* language, a language you're not comfortable with.

RH: Yes, that's very shrewd. I don't know what to say about it. You've seen something very clearly I'm just getting a glimpse of. It rhymes with several things for me. One is malice and its connection to evil—whatever in the hell that means. (I have a chronic dislike for that kind of language. Malice is a word I like quite a lot, evil carries for me that whole apparatus of sin and guilt.) There's a poem in this new book called "Misery and Splendor," which is a somewhat dreamlike description of a couple trying to couple sexually. It's as if they're dry-humping, rubbing against each other like two sticks or two creatures who haven't evolved a sexuality to enact their desire yet. And your remark makes me see the connection between that poem and the issue of possession—sexual, political, epistemological—in *Field Guide*. They can't stand the idea of culmination because it means they'll come apart, so they're just rubbing against each other. It's not desire as a condition that's craved—it's the possibility of absolute union. The lines in the poem go: "it is plain what is happening. / They are trying to become one creature, / and something will not have it. They are tender / with each other, afraid / their brief, sharp cries will reconcile them to the moment / when they fall away again. / So they rub against each other, / their mouths dry, then wet, then dry. / They feel themselves at the center of a powerful / and baffled will." That imagination of the malice of things, of whatever it is that absolutely refuses, also gets played out as language it seems to me now. It makes me think that I associated the malice of the violence in history with this malice, this will, that withholds the possibility of lasting communion from people and also between word and thing.

TG: As *Field Guide* goes on, the poems become more personal, less purely descriptive. It's as if the first plot we've been talking about—you against the owners and takers, you trying to use a different sort of language—is now played out inside of you. "In Weather" seems to be about that, in the way its sections comment on each other.

RH: Yes, that's interesting. One section of that poem I threw out, but originally there were eight sections and I wrote them in eight days. I wrote the first section the first day and thought I was finished. Then I wrote the second section the second day and thought I was *then* finished, and so on. I don't know quite how to describe the way the sections comment on each other, except that one of the things that was fun about writing it was that one section seemed to pick up metaphorically on the next. The relation of the animals to the nourishment that the house provided in the second section was clearly connected to the speaker's sense of the uxoriousness of the house in the first. The rotting lobster suggests the sea, which calls up the clam digging thing, and the combination of the sea smell and the clams calls up the smell of sex—and that calls up the guy reading the cruel poems. Then the narrator tries to see if he can locate male hatred of women's bodies in himself and finds that he can. Then there's the sound of the owls outside that's counterpoised, and so on. Metaphorical rhymes on the themes.

TG: Kit Carson is potentially located within you. That's not resolved at the end, is it?

RH: It's not. Greg Orr wrote me to say he was distressed by "In Weather" because he thought the ending was false. His reading was that it was an affirmation of my connectedness to a natural home: "Walking home / I follow the pawprints of the fox. / I know that I know myself / no more than a seed / curled in the dark of a winged pod / knows flourishing."

TG: But, that the seed hasn't flourished yet is the whole point.

RH: That's what I thought. And that following the pawprints of the fox, tracking back toward the house, was anything but an identification with the natural world. I felt a little bad—that if I were Rilke I would have somehow pushed through, had a spiritual breakthrough that would have taken me to some more resonant conclusion, but I think the poem went as far as I could then go. My impulse to affirm was so strong that I felt I had to resist it all the time.

TG: Your second book is called "affirm," isn't it—*Praise*? It seems to me it stops blaming problems with connecting on the Kit Carsons, realizes that the language of ownership is also there within you, then asks what is there within language that both keeps us away from the world and—what did you say?— complicates our relation to it. Language doesn't just bar us from the world; in its instability it humbles us, gives us a way of marrying without claiming to possess?

RH: Yes, that makes sense. The book I'm just finishing, is possibly just an intensification of the same themes. The same subject. I went through a long stretch thinking that the issue was technique—not some kind of a thinking through these issues philosophically.

TG: It seems to me you've always tried to solve these issues technically.

RH: Well, I think I'm stuck again. One of the things that happened to me, curiously, in this book, is that the poems get more old-fashioned as I proceed. The poems at the beginning, like "Late Spring," were written in very long lines of dithyrambic verse. When I started them, they were modeled on Michael Palmer's "Notes for Echo Lake," but I was incapable of being nonconsecutive. I started out wondering what it would be like to write like Michael.

TG: I'd think that the tension between being Michael Palmer and being consecutive is just where your work is located.

RH: That's true, but at the end of *Human Wishes* I'm writing poems that look like imitations of "Tintern Abbey."

TG: You're not still dealing with that tension there?

RH: Oh, I'm still dealing with it. Perhaps not on Michael's terms. There are moments when what one wants is not to enact unsayableness but to say it. I'd guess that the tension in those poems is not in a broken surface where the difficulty of meaning gets wrestled with, but in the contrast between the continuousness of the speaking voice and the brokenness of things, the principle of nemesis in actual life. I don't know if it's slick to say it that way.

Michael's poems are about a virtual voice, but the actual life is implicit. In another kind of poem the voice might be actual and the world virtual, or at least broken at its coming into being in a way that makes the virtual always present as a wish. I think the coming to an end of my marriage enters this, marriage as a sacramental expression of the wish to forge some wholeness. I'm still assimilating that; I'm unlikely to say anything very true about it. And then what also intercedes for me is eight years of working on Miłosz. I have been fascinated by his solutions to these problems.

TG: They're not yours, are they?

RH: No, they're very original. He's a reluctant dualist. With the powerful pull of a classical education in philosophy and Christian theology, it's easier for him to be a dualist than it is for an American. Whenever you get the emotional, visionary side of American poetry, you get some version of this: Ginsberg's sense of the evil of time, of the limitations of bodily experience on the one hand, and his affirmation of the holiness of sexuality on the other. You get a funny kind of split. Americans are so pragmatic that they don't usually push the issue far enough for us to *notice* the fundamental dualism, and it took me a long time to even get an imaginative grasp of how literally Miłosz believes what he believes, or wants to.

TG: Quite a few of your essays are about writers who also differ from you on this issue of a split between realms.

RH: I didn't know that, of course. I thought as I was writing them, "I'm writing a Baltic book instead of a Mediterranean book, and I don't know why. Why am I writing about Germans, Poles, and Swedes?" I'm really much more attracted, in a certain way, to Neruda, Ritsos, Whitman, Duncan, but figuring out what's antithetical in a spirit that's in another way sympathetic is useful to me.

TG: I see. What Duncan is interested in embracing is quite different from what you are, but he gets at it by the same kind of awareness of limitation that you work with. That attraction seems pretty clear—the same with Whitman in "Song of Myself," his trying to touch something finally untouchable through a medium. All that talk in Whitman about "embrace" isn't really referring to direct "owning" at all.

RH: I have a slightly different take on it, though it's clear nobody writes a poem that long who thinks that it's a simple matter to forge that connection. My sense of that poem is that it begins at a sort of giddy, almost Buddhist recognition that the connection is forged *if you say it is*, on the one hand, and on the other that of course it's not—it's entirely fictitious. I don't know how to read the drama of "Song of Myself," where it begins and where it ends. The twenty-eight bathers section seems crucial, so is "Crossing Brooklyn Ferry." In both he asserts that imagination is sexual, that desire is what makes it possible for us to enter others literally and imaginatively and therefore to be able to say, "I am the man, I suffer'd, I was there." That confidence is a form of seduction in him.

TG: But that section, with the woman richly dressed behind blinds and peering out at the bathers, says this is as much wish as actuality.

RH: That's the great joke of the poem! That's what I meant by the almost giddy sense that everything's equally true and untrue. In a way, my favorite poem of Whitman is "What Place Is Besieged," where he says, "Lo, I send to that place a commander, swift, brave, immortal, / And with him horse and foot, and parks of artillery." I know at one level he means these poems, but at another level it's like Ginsberg saying in "Wichita Vortex Sutra" the war is over because he says it's over—it's over for him.

TG: That giddy saying and unsaying seems to be the way you go about affirming. Elizabeth Bishop uses that word too. Do you know the letter that's often quoted, where, arguing against a split between realms of experience, she uses Darwin as an example? She talks about him building up in his prose a series of "heroic observations," then feeling his enterprise giving way and him "sinking or sliding giddily off into the unknown."

RH: Jane Shore has written a wonderful essay on how she makes metaphor. It's based on her noticing Bishop's reluctance to assert that one thing is positively like another, in the typical way of simile and metaphor. She constructs a sort of grammar of the devices Bishop uses to assert resemblance without claiming identity. She thinks that's the fundamental tension in the work and that it's connected to Bishop's trying to figure out her own identity and her sexuality. As in "You are an *I*, / you are an *Elizabeth*, / you are one of *them*." I heard her deliver the essay as a lecture and at the time I think, she threw out the idea speculatively that maybe it was characteristic of a heterosexual poetry to rush toward the implicit unity in comparing different things, while homosexual poetry was more skeptical. Or maybe it was a thought that passed through my mind. In any case it's pretty obviously not true. Both Whitman and Duncan are poets anxious to assert the unity of experience. But it is interesting to think about the tradition of "difficult poetry," Vallejo, Celan, Zukofsky, having some of its roots in a certain emotional uneasiness and intellectual fastidiousness about the hunger in the assertion of similarity. Anyway, Bishop is quite remarkable.

TG: Can you say more about your response to Duncan?

RH: I think what actually attracted me to him at first was, oddly, his domesticity, and then I came to see that the thing about him that was central for me was this issue of desire. Also, that Duncan was interested in the Christian myth really struck me because my own rebellion against Catholicism—like the rebellion of the nineteenth and twentieth centuries against Christianity—was largely to be impatient with the whole business of the Fall, and the preoccupation with evil and sin. Duncan very self-consciously tried to think about Christ and the figure of the Fall; he opened the door to figuring out the Christian story.

TG: And how does that run through your work?

RH: I don't know that it does, except that limitation and mediation are the Fall and the Redemption, in Duncan's system. I responded to that and to various ideas of the Fall—how does the world get to be the way it is? My first tactic was to be political and moral. I identified the trouble with the takers and violence: Kit Carson, President Polk, Frémont. (It's very indirect, the circuitous path of my meditation on these issues.) Kit Carson and the others are figures of what breaks the social bond, destabilizes it, and does violence. And set against that are images of my efforts to make a family, a marriage, on the one side, and to forge a connection to place, history, and community through loving attention to land, landscape, and the language, on the other.

TG: Does Kit Carson seem like a Protestant to you?

RH: I think I probably had that way of thinking about it at the time, borrowed from Weber's *The Protestant Ethic*. It's complicated because the difference between Protestant and Catholic is really an argument about mediation—the difference between the divine mediated through sacrament and symbol and an unmediated relationship: Jacob's direct wrestling with the angel.

TG: And you'd say that thinking you can touch without mediation is finally what builds a sense of loss into our political structures? That accepting mediation is giddier, a way of touching indirectly?

RH: Yes. You can't do it without mediation. There are lots of ramifications. Making mediation invisible and "natural" so that the ruling class owns mediation and it seems to be the order of things—that's what history is, constantly. That's basically the Language poets' critique of representation. Ron Silliman has an essay called "Disappearance of the Word, Appearance of the World" in which he argues that all bourgeois art—as he states it, it's nonsense, it's not true, but you can see why he'd say it—is based on making the word invisible. The intellectual, cognitive work of capitalist oppression is to repress the languageness of language, so the aesthetic task of poetry is to foreground the languageness of language in order to radically circumvent that, trying to make translucent the objects of desire which are purely symbolic.

TG: Does the theory bother you?

RH: I think the problem with the theory is the whole notion of foregrounding. I write the line in "Maps" "Clams, abalones, cockles, chitons, crabs" or "Sourdough french bread and pinot chardonnay" and as I write, one of the things that I'm aware of, that seems in Whitman's giddy way wonderfully comic about the lines, is that those are words and not things to eat. For a lot of readers, it's a mouthfilling affirmation of the witness of the world, but for me it's also the comedy of the fact that the mouthfilling affirmation is only breath, the human love of the sound of insubstantial breath. Some poets of course are more manifestly after transparency of language. I suppose to Susan Howe, Louise Glück would be supremely a poet of representation—her psychological interests are affective rather than cognitive—and yet the sheer tautness of her language calls attention to language. Who's to say that Jackson Pollock was more preoccupied with paint than Rembrandt? So that's my problem with it, while on the other hand it's obviously true that the dominant aesthetic of today is, in a representational sense, closer to Stafford than to Creeley. And that writers like Stein and Zukofsky have been, to some extent, denied—that's interesting to me.

TG: Do prose poems give you another means of calling attention to language, the way your sentences jump?

RH: Some of them do, some of them don't. I think jumping was *the* tactic of the prose poem. From the beginning, the prose poem was so worried about being prose that it became associative in its procedures to label itself as poetry. The interest of the form as a form is that the paragraph is a proposition of unity, so when you put a bunch of things in it that seem unrelated you've got a formal equivalent to the contrast between meter and speech: you've got a formal contrast between the multifariousness of things and the inadequacy of the medium. Another form of that has to do with the simultaneity of reality—ten or fifteen things coming at once within anyone's attention span. Writing is temporal and sequential, so it can never capture reality for just that reason. There was that problem. Also another—to try to include all the things that people, not wanting it to look too much like discursive prose, were afraid of because they seemed unpoetic. I was trying very hard to not sound like your basic "aren't-I-being-wild" prose poem of the period. To try to write "reasonableness" was interesting, to be after something else.

TG: I wonder if people have noticed this tension between reasonableness and your awareness of the inadequacy of medium. Do you think you've been read well?

RH: I guess I don't think I have. There was a time when people took my work to be dumber than it was. It's that issue of "is this language framed," the issue of representation. My position, when I thought about it, was that this is the second half of the twentieth century, and you can't, on some conscious level, get away from framing. And then to some extent that got to be a subject. I thought by putting poems about language, "Spring" and "Fall," early in *Field Guide* that I was signaling at least consciousness of the issue. Readings of *Praise*? A lot of people were terrified by poststructuralism and seized on "Meditation at Lagunitas" as an antistructuralist, Whitmanian (not the real Whitman, as we've been discussing) affirmation. They took me to be reopening the mindless door into the American sublime.

TG: Many poets your age seem to be working at these issues. How would you locate your generation in literary history?

RH: I guess my proposition is that we've returned to some fundamental ground of romantic poetry, having passed through the modernist crucible that led to the denial of the personal project, and through an autobiographical poetry that none of us could quite sit in comfortably after what modernism did to the assumption of a coherent self. So much of the romantic effort to make poetry was involved in cleaning up perceptions, getting rid of all of the Augustan imagery out of translating Latin poetry—the diction of Gray and Collins—which ended up being an aesthetic of transparency: verisimilitude in diction, induction as a procedure, the relation of abstraction to the testimony of individual experience. All of that came to us as this dubious aesthetic of sincerity that Eliot and others rejected. Everything that's powerful about modernism—in insisting on brokenness rather than wholeness, that the relation between words and things is not a given—is in a way a response to romanticism. What the young Eliot said was that in order to express the crisis of this moment we need a more powerful, less facile, more expressive language to get at the uniqueness of the inner experience of a person. And in *The Waste Land* he goes into the personal horror, writes a poem, cracks up, and comes out saying "Experience *isn't* unique; all language is generalized; the particular power of language is to generalize and forge common ancestral values." So we got a modernism apparently based on the denial of personality, *and yet* the person, the fragments that constitute a person, were there all along, at the center of the drama. I suppose you could say that the response of the modernists to the romantics is something like our response to the deep-image and confessional poets, seen themselves as a neoromantic response to modernism or to the New Critics, to second generation modernism. We are two workings of the problem after the romantic revolt which reoriented poetry as a form of knowledge, of knowing the world, as opposed to the old idea of philosophy and reason and authority taking that task, with poetry as a secondary pictorial faculty. Is the problem played out? Hardly. It's hard to deny that poetry stands in the middle of a wasteland still, a wreckage of all previous metaphysics that made us feel at home in the world or promised us a home elsewhere. If anything, the problem of what the individual can say about the meaning of human experience is more urgent.

July 1988

5. Jorie Graham's Incandescence

In her introduction to the anthology *The Best American Poetry of 1990*, Jorie Graham surveys a number of responses to what she sees as a common contemporary "anxiety concerning the nature and function of language, its capacity for seizing and transmitting . . . *truth*?" (I, xix) Describing an experience in which she heard a novelist and a poet read, back to back, Graham also sketches her own response to that anxiety about language and its limits. If it seemed to her that the novelist offered a world in which plot moved confidently forward and "You felt at home," the poet's words "resisted the very desires that the fiction, previously, had satisfied." It left her temporarily homeless and estranged. What did that estrangement feel like?

> [T]he motion of the poem as a whole resisted my impulse to resolve it into "sense" of a rational kind. Listening to the poem, I could feel my irritable reaching after fact, my desire for resolution, graspable meaning, ownership. I *wanted* to narrow it. I wanted to make it into a shorter version of the other experience, the story. It resisted. It compelled me to let go. The frontal, grasping motion frustrated, my intuition was forced awake. I felt myself having to "listen" with other parts of my sensibility, felt my mind being forced back down into the soil of my senses. And I saw that it was the resistance of the poem—its occlusion, or difficulty—that was healing me, forcing me to privilege my heart, my intuition—parts of my sensibility infrequently called upon in my everyday experience in the marketplace of things and ideas. I found myself feeling, as the poem ended, that some crucial muscle that might have otherwise atrophied from lack of use had been exercised. (I, xvi)

Being forced awake by the poem's resistance, Graham, in Cavell's terms, found herself in a position where her "humanity, or finitude [was] accepted, suffered" (TN, 39). Unable to resolve the poem into "sense," experiencing and then letting go her desires for "graspable meaning, ownership," she found herself pushed to exercise "some crucial [underused] muscle." That is, she was forced to "inhabit our investment in words, in the world" (C, 61) in a live and attentive way. Experiencing on her own skin anxiety about language's ability to seize and transmit truth, she found something "healing" her, making her whole.

If, as she puts it in another essay, "I need to feel the places where the language fails, as much as one can," it seems clear, then, that she is drawn to such struggles with language's limits because its failures, its being "eroded" by what it cannot master, open a live space where the torments and potential powers of finite human existence (the "mind . . . forced back down into the soil of [the] senses") are experienced to their fullest.[1] Cavell writes of Wittgenstein that "our capacity for disappointment by [words] is essential to the way we possess language" (IQ, 5), and Graham's work is the most powerful demonstration I know of the accuracy of that observation. That disappointment, occurring over and over in her poems, returns her to a world that cannot be held in place and forces her to unfold there—make "incandescent," she writes in one poem—what Cavell, out of Emerson, calls the "human condition" (C, 61). Poetry, Graham continues in her introduction, is about confrontation with an "other": "God, nature, a beloved, an Idea, Abstract form, Language itself as a field, Chance, Death, Consciousness, what exists in the silence. Something not invented by the writer. Something the writer risks being defeated—or silenced—by" (I, xxvii). Though the "other" her poems encounter shifts from works of art and our mythological heritage to personal experience and the puzzles of matter, all of these resistant surfaces bring her, as she writes, into an experience of limit and then force her to act—to come to life—there. Being forced to admit that our position in the world is not one of knowing, Graham insists that "One is *created* by limited point-of-view, by the suffering it entails, in a way that one cannot be simply by the overall mid-air view we now think of as 'understanding.' "[2]

What I would like to do here is examine Graham's five most recent books— *Erosion, The End of Beauty, Region of Unlikeness, Materialism,* and *The Errancy*—and attempt to trace the progressively more detailed and ambitious ways she courts and is forced awake by what she calls, in the title poem of the first book I will deal with, "the erosion / of the right word, what it shuts" (E, 56). Most of the poems in that book, *Erosion* (1983), begin to work out a poetics or response to limits by studying a series of exemplary objects (often paintings) or situations. Often initially resistant, these models draw from her an interwoven set of explications that chart much of her work in the books that follow. A number of poems in *Erosion*—"Two Paintings by Gustav Klimt," which we worked through in the introduction, is an example—go beyond working out this theory and attempt to enact it, coming alive in the gap generated by resistance. After working through her response to exemplary objects, I will turn briefly to the more active poems in *Erosion*, then trace the flowering of such work in her most recent books.

Erosion's opening poem, "San Sepolcro" (E, 2–3), lays out most of the tensions that charge her poems. It begins with the lyric's classic move—a cold crisp morning in the Italian mountains ("milk on the air, / ice on the oily / lemonskins") convinces the writer that the dream of grasping a meaning, of taking a reader or listener through to one's core, is possible:

> In this blue light
> I can take you there,
> snow having made me
> a world of bone
> seen through to.

She plays that drive out, makes it visible, by associating the blue light on the snow with a painting of Mary "unbuttoning / her blue dress, / her mantle of weather, / to go into / labor." "Come, we can go in," she remarks, eyes on the painting's calm invitation to enter and know and see, beckoning to her reader who is, she imagines, waiting to be "take[n] . . . there":

> This is
> what the living do: go in.
> It's a long way.
> And the dress keeps opening
> from eternity
>
> to privacy, quickening.
> Inside, at the heart,
> is tragedy, the present moment
> forever stillborn,
> but going in, each breath
> is a button
>
> coming undone, something terribly
> nimble-fingered
> finding all of the stops.

What happens in these lines is that as the drive to "go in" is played out, it gradually thickens and slows to a halt, something we saw over and over in

Bishop's tearing nets. "It's a long way," Graham writes. What had looked like a doorway to "eternity"—the word in several senses becoming flesh—never opens all the way, leading only to a sense of separation and inevitable "privacy." The poet's lyric drive to capture "the present moment" and the painting's wonder at "the birth of god" are equally "stillborn," become equally tragic. And yet, that confrontation with limits is also described as a "quickening," for something deeply human comes to life in the space where she feels both that sense of tragedy and that delicious, "nimble-fingered" (terrible, but so dexterous) drive to know and open and enter. The rest of *Erosion*, essentially, looks for ways to account for and describe that sense of "quickening" that occurs in the space between these two realizations.[3]

A number of poems explore this quickening space by concentrating on the nimble-fingered way we seek to know; they try to capture both the powerful drive to enter and the sudden suck of its collapse. That is one way, they propose, to describe the terrible unease of our condition. "Kimono" (E, 38–39) plays this out by means of its mixed tone. The speaker is in her backyard, wearing a kimono—its pattern showing "valleys, clear skies, / thawing banks / narcissus and hollow reeds / break through"—and brushing her hair. She knows that a small boy is hidden in the evergreens on the side of her yard, watching. Though she realizes that "the casual crumbling forms / of boughs" on her kimono are simply lies, representations, and that it is very "late" in our history "for the green scrim to be / [thought of as] such an open / door," she is also taken by the boy's drive to see in or see through. Bending, thinking about the gaps of her clothing opening and shifting, she muses about what the boy embodies—that "soothing" thought that we can cross such "enchanted gap[s], this tiny / eternal / delay which is our knowing"—and plays Mary for him: "something / most whole / loosens her stays / pretending she's alone." It is a complicated gesture, for as she teases him, she both enacts what Hass would call the impossibility of that "old story" and stares in bemusement at our shared desire for it to be so.

"At Luca Signorelli's Resurrection of the Body" (E, 74–77) is a darker playing out of this impulse. It mourns this sense of limits rather than teasingly going along with the game one more time. What Graham probes is Signorelli's vision of the dead "hurry[ing] / to enter / their [resurrected] bodies" at the end of time. "[P]ulling themselves up / through the soil / into the weightedness, the color, / into the eye / of the painter," they seem obsessed with what the poet calls their "entrance," through the body, into "names, / . . . happiness." Why hurry? she asks. Is it better? Can some home for the spirit ever be fully located in the fixed and weighted body? These questions probe the painting but are deflected again and again, by the spirits' haste. Soberly, she acknowledges that though we know "there is no / entrance, / only entering," though we know "the wall / of the flesh / opens endlessly," though Signorelli himself, studying the dead body of his son, "with beauty and care / and technique / and judgement, cut into / shadow, cut / into bone and sinew" and never arrived—though we know all of this, we still try, over and over. At best, she concludes, describing, in a sense, the rhythms of her own voice in this volume, we might emulate the painter's patient suffering of ambition and tragedy and tell the spirits "to be stern and brazen / and slow."[4]

Both poems attempt to get at what might be alive in experiencing knowing's limits by playing the desire to arrive all the way out—slowly, giddily, achingly. If it could only be so, these poems seem to lament. A more complex set of poems not only plays that impulse out but tries to picture what is gained in acknowledging that limit. I'll look at several. An early poem, "Scirocco" (E, 8–11), sets up the issue. Visiting the rooms in Rome where Keats died, that sense of limit confirmed by a glimpse of Keats's papers behind glass, "some yellowing, / some xeroxed or / mimeographed," the poet finds visible there two allegories for "the nervous spirit / of this world" that drives us to look and seek to know. One allegory is the hot wind by which the ivy outside "is fingered, / refingered / . . . [this spirit] that must go over and over / what it already knows." The other is the grapes on the terrace whose "stark hellenic / forms" will "soften / till weak enough / to enter / our world." If the wind that fingers what it knows is a version of our nimble-fingered attempts to know and undress and "unfasten" (E, 77), the softening grapes are our stark forms that collapse when resisted.[5] Graham proposes that, woven together these two approaches—trying and failing to know, holding yourself there—might bring us to some sort of "quickening":

> Therefore this
>   is what I
> must ask you
>   to imagine: wind;
> the moment
>   when the wind
> drops; and grapes,
>   which are nothing,
> which break
>   in your hands.

The poems in *Erosion* cast around for ways to visualize this. "To a Friend Going Blind" (E, 27), for example, quite deliberately attempts to imagine the live conjunction of wind and grapes, the desire to know being broken by the invisible, which resists. Addressing a friend whose approaching blindness is a version of our own language-bound separation from our surroundings, she describes a detour around the "entire inner / perimeter" of a walled medieval town taken because she "couldn't find the shortcut through" to the world beyond, seen occasionally flickering through the walls' cracks and gaps. (Remembering the "long way" discovered in "San Sepolcro" and the teasing shortcut of "Kimono," we realize we are participating in the same investigation.) Next, still not directly touching the issue of her friend's blindness, Graham shifts to an account of learning from someone else how to cut a pattern:

> Saturdays we buy the cloth.
> She takes it in her hands
> like a good idea, feeling
> for texture, grain, the built-in
> limits.

Moving back to the detour and linking the two stories, the poet describes her own wandering within the walls' confines as "a needle floating / on its cloth"— a needle at ease with the separation imposed by the walls, finding them in fact to be central to her quite overpowering experience of the invisible world breaking through it in its gaps: "I shut my eyes and felt my way / along the stone. . . . / . . . [T]he walls are beautiful. They block the view. / And it feels rich to be / inside their grasp." Imagining herself into her friend's condition, she imagines herself into language's limits, suffers its blindness. The drive to master or find a shortcut having been put aside, she discovers that running our hands along what separates us from the world—our "built-in limits"— yields a kind of richness, perhaps threads us to what resists. But as with the other poems in this volume, this liveness is read out of the world's book of emblems—what if writing knew its blindness in this way?—rather than lived out.

The poems in *Erosion* that point toward her next book are those in which Graham begins the more difficult task of modulating the certainty of her own uses of language: forcing the poems to contend with what would threaten their ways of moving; letting them drive toward failure in order to discover what might awaken in that blinded collapse. I'll look at two. "The Age of Reason" (E, 16–20) begins with a description of a bird "anting":

which means,
in my orchard
he has opened his wings
over a furious

anthill and will take up
into the delicate
ridges of quince-yellow
feathers
a number of tiny, angry
creatures

that will inhabit him

That extraordinary activity—mastering the world's otherness in a manner both painful and exhilarating—seems a temptation we are simply incapable of refusing: "Who wouldn't want / to take / into the self / something that burns / or cuts, or wanders / lost / over the body?" The bird, like Signorelli's spirits at the resurrection of the dead, acts out a version of a human drive. He functions as a sort of emblem. In the second section, Graham stands aside from that drive, thinking about the extremity of that gesture by paralleling it with an equally troubling human act—the end of Werner Herzog's *Woyzeck* in which, "after the hero whom / we love / who is mad has / murdered / the world, the young / woman / who is his wife, / and loved her," the central figure throws his murder weapon into a river. He is Stanley Cavell's Othello, murdering the world he loves in order to possess it completely. Carefully echoing her language about the bird (and touching on similar ways of describing knowledge's movement "into" things scattered throughout the book), Graham tosses away in disgust that bold desire to "take on / almost anything." She allows the drive to crumble or acknowledge its own blindness:

In the moonlight he throws
his knife

into the wide river
flowing beside them
but doesn't think it has
reached deep
enough so goes in
after it
himself. White as a knife,

he goes in after it
completely.

But then something important happens. As if suddenly realizing that such attempts at mastery are not confined to madmen and lovers, Graham turns her appalled eye on her own activity as she writes.[6] To use Cavell's term, she "measures" herself against what she has just realized. She handles and suffers her own version of our "built-in limits" as knowers and lovers. Calmly, steel in her voice, she looks at the writing scene she is in the middle of. Because the world we would love "resist[s]" us, she remarks quietly, "we have / characters and the knife / of a plot / to wade through this / current." Like Bishop with those who colonized Brazil, she finds herself linked to the lover using the knife. We too—as the patient attention of this poem unwittingly demonstrates—are driven and never satisfied, giving up only when the world we would absorb has been lost in being narrowed into name, scent, and symbol:

> For what we want
>   to take
> inside of us, whole orchard,
>   color,
> name, scent, symbol, raw
>   pale
>
> blossoms, wet black
>   arms there is
> no deep enough.

Though perhaps the echo of Pound slightly blunts the collapse here—the suggestion being that all of poetry shares in this criticism—this seems to me the most important move *Erosion* makes. Here, I would suggest, the volume "quickens."

It does as well at "Patience" (E, 42–45). Graham begins by celebrating memory, one of the ways we finger and refinger the world:

> There is a room now
>   buried
> in late morning
>   sunlight
> that will not
>   change

> in which a woman
>   & a small
> girl who is not
>   me
> although I am
>   her patience
>
> are ironing

Through that fixed, unchanging memory, the poet has found a way to describe "her patience," a trait she still uses to define herself. There seems to be an "open door" back to this emblematic moment; it is held open by means of "a perfect shaft / of light, / the rudder for / the scene." However, as if remarking silently to herself on the "lateness" of such an enchanted view of knowing ourselves, Graham begins to close her eyes in order to, as the earlier poem put it, "[feel] my way / along the stone." She overplays memory's desire to sort and order as she describes that ironing: "We iron to find / the parts / in each thing, making / a tidy body / that folds away / into itself." Cavell would call this "succumbing" to the urge to know for sure. Graham calls it "feed[ing]" memory's form of knowing, doing to herself what she had done to the boy in "Kimono" or had watched, horrified, the spirits attempt in the Signorelli poem:

>   Tell me
> where that room is now,
>   that stubborn
> fragrant bloom? The fragile stem
>   from here
> to there is tragedy, I know,
>   the path we
> feed it by until it cracks
>   open at last

Overplaying the fragile claims of memory makes visible what it normally hides—that it is a tragic declaration about distance not a guarantee of connection. And the power of this piece is that the overplaying and collapse happen in the writing, in the act of remembering. What is suddenly visible, in that collapse, is a much larger world than the one the poet had been carrying around:

> & it's all right Maria is
>   so tired
> even the sweetness of
>   wisteria
> hurts, all right she has
>   just lost
> her son, a policeman, &
>   is crying
>
> as she irons

This had originally been a broken, rudderless experience. What the poet finds, eyes equally on that painful scene and on the writing scene, is how quickly she had turned from that initial disorientation and narrowed it to something safe and domestic. How quickly, she acknowledges, she turned the "living vine" into "twistings of . . . wicker," turned pain and a feeling of being lost, "as if themselves [held] beneath / the blue / and eye-shaped / iron," into "the style, / the innocence." As memory dissolves, as one suffers the collapse of its confident fingering, the world not mastered quickens and flares, once.

If *Erosion* concerns itself mainly with finding and investigating emblems of Graham's developing poetics, *The End of Beauty* (1987) follows the lead of "Patience" or "Two Paintings by Gustav Klimt" or "The Age of Reason" and tries to actively inhabit the process of feeling the wind strain and die, the discovery of nothing in your hand. Where *Erosion* often turned to paintings and measured its writing activity against them, *The End of Beauty*, more often than not, turns to our culture's grand stories—resistant and needing to be struggled against, but part of us all. In entering such stories, we enter dramatizations of our finitude. The book is built around five central poems, which unfold biblical or mythological situations that put into play the same drive to know and its rich collapse that we saw framed and reframed in *Erosion*. Graham labels these poems "Self-Portraits" in order to spell out the way their explorations offer "allegories or measures" of her own "investment in words, in the world."[7] She feels her way into them much as she felt her way into her friend's blindness, attempting to see herself (or suffer herself) there. Each self-portrait tries to describe what the charged gap between knower and the world feels like and then asks what can be made of that space, and each is surrounded by a cluster of poems set within the tension or process it establishes. In that way, Graham sets up a rich, cross-pollinating investigation.

Working through each cluster, we make our way through the entire arc, or struggle, of the book.

The book begins with Eve handing Adam the forbidden fruit from the tree of the knowledge of good and evil: "Self-Portrait as the Gesture between Them" (EB, 3–8). Graham worries the gesture much as she had those of Signorelli's dead or that of the bird anting. What does the gesture show about the tensions in knowing or plotting or shaping? she asks, much as Hass did about his various maps and houses. Breaking the poem into numbered sections, breaking it phrase by phrase at moments of concentration and intensity, she slows the gesture down.[8] She establishes an interval outside the straightforward piling up of sentences in order to let us feel its implications. Eve's gesture, she writes, was a "rip in the fabric where the action begins, the opening of the narrow / passage." It was a movement into the struggle to separate one thing from another, a narrowing down of many possibilities into a single choice, which was then followed by another, somehow related, and so on—the "action." Graham calls that: "The passage along the arc of denouement once the plot has begun, like a limb, / the buds in it cinched and numbered, / outside the true story really, outside of improvisation." But, she continues, of course they chose such a narrowing—we always do: "But what else could they have done, these two, sick of beginning, / revolving in place like a thing seen, / dumb, blind, rooted in the eye that's watching." Then she radically slows the poem, her eye almost slashing back and forth across that movement into knowing, trying to see it as it originates. Eve must have wanted "freedom," she speculates: the ability to think of Adam in "secret," "turn[ing] him slowly in the shallows," a desire that inevitably grew (like a fruit) into something more complicated and needy and incomplete. If so, if Adam became something "owned but not seizable, resembling, resembling," then that "gesture between them," in which form's (or resemblance's) nagging lack was acted upon, would naturally have followed. Can you complete me? she must have asked, driven by the first stirrings of that need to know, and in asking that, she must have handed over her freedom for the unending series of questions and answers, shapes followed by other shapes, minutes by minutes, that make up our world:

> until it must be told, be
>
> 14
> taken from her, this freedom,
>
> 15
> so that she had to turn and touch him to give it away

16
to have him pick it from her as the answer takes the question
17
that he should read in her the rigid inscription
18
in a scintillant fold the fabric of daylight bending
19
where the form is complete where the thing must be torn off
20
momentarily angelic, the instant writhing into a shape

And what necessarily followed from that? the poet asks, the fruit handed over—"the scales the other way now in his hand, / the gift that changes the balance"—and a different world entered into? It became Adam's story. Perhaps that indicates how the movement out of "improvisation" into "narrowing" always works, leaving you (words in your hands) with "the feeling of being a digression not the link in the argument, / a new direction, an offshoot, the limb going on elsewhere, / . . . a piece from another set." And yet, she goes on, looking at that gesture one more time, perhaps there is something to love in that "error, . . . that break from perfection." Call it, after Cavell, the possibility of achieving an intimacy out of an acknowledgment of estrangement—here, in time—"where the complex mechanism [of knowing] fails, where the stranger appears in the clearing, / . . . out of nowhere to share the day." So this gesture that initiates and stands for our finite condition is a charged one: it is a bid for freedom as well as its rich loss, a narrowing that opens on something else, wind and grapes in the same exchange. To put it simply, Graham's first self-portrait proposes that there is a generative estrangement possible in the gap, something gained in the space of error.[9]

How does that feel? the poems that follow ask. "On Difficulty" (EB, 9–10) plays out a first entry into this process with a tone of sad, fascinated wonder. Adam and Eve don't quite know yet, the speaker suggests, describing a version of the expulsion: "The woods are not their home. / . . . Whatever's back there / is not." They stand in between, not yet having arrived at the place "towards which you reason, the place where the flotsam / of the meanings is put down / and the shore / holds." In this place between, "They're thinking / how low the bushes are, after all, how finite / the options one finds." They're "find[ing] the edges of each other's bodies":

> they want to know what this
> *reminds you of*

looking up, reaching each other for you to see, for you to see by, the
  long sleep
beginning, the long sleep of resemblance

Adam and Eve in these poems allow us to see that one response to this gap is
to see it as offering the possibilities of edge and finitude, the charged, uneasy
making of resemblances in a limited place. Their gesture is a light "to see by."
The rest of the book tries to enter their "Difficulty." Deep within "the long
sleep of resemblance," we too are given the opportunity to slow it and suffer
it and hold its suddenly live implications in our hands.

"Self-Portrait as Both Parties" (EB, 14–16) charts our position in a second
way, by means of the Orpheus and Eurydice story. If the gesture between
Adam and Eve shows both loss and the possibilities of estrangement as it
moves from improvisation to plot and structure, what does the loss of Eurydice
as Orpheus turns back to gaze at her show? Think of the silt of a river touched
by "the open hands of the sunlight," the poem suggests. Call the sunlight
Orpheus and the "slow bottom of the river" Eurydice. The outcome seems
inevitable to us: "How would he bring her back again? She drifts up / in a
small hourglass-shaped cloud of silt where the sunlight touches, / up to where
the current could take her." But he soon loses her. Like Eve's movement into
"resemblances," Orpheus's way of knowing has the inevitable loss of the object
of his attention built into it:

And though he would hold her up, this light all open hands,
seeking her edges, seeking to make her palpable again,
curling around her to find crevices by which to carry her up,
flaws by which to be himself arrested and made,
made whole, made sharp and limbed, a shape,
she cannot, the drowning is too kind,
the becoming of everything which each pore opens to again,
the possible which each momentary outline blurs into again,
too kind, too endlessly kind,
the silks of the bottom rubbing their vague hands
over her forehead

Description inevitably breaks down, releasing its object back to "the possible"
of the bottom again, back to "improvisation." How do we measure ourselves
against that version of the gap we find ourselves in as writers or thinkers?

In the poems that follow, Graham turns the story's figures this way and
that, trying to answer. Perhaps that loss is what the desire to know is all about,

she speculates in "Orpheus and Eurydice" (EB, 17–19). It is Orpheus-in-us drawn by the garden's hissing snake to turn around and glance and lose the world we love:

> Up ahead, I know, he felt it stirring in himself already, the glance,
> the darting thing in the pile of rocks,
>
> already in him, there, shiny in the rubble, hissing Did you want to remain
> completely unharmed?—
>
> the point-of view darting in him, shiny head in the ash-heap,
>
> hissing Once upon a time, and then Turn now darling give me that look,
>
> the perfect shot, give me that place where I'm erased. . . .
> . . . .
> And yes she could feel it in him already, up ahead, that wanting-to-turn-
> and-cast-the-outline-over-her
>
> by his glance,
>
> sealing the edges down

Perhaps Orpheus turned because he knew he was driven by a force that would only quiet when it played the game of knowing all the way out to its collapse: "Because you see he could not be married to it anymore, this field with minutes in it / called woman, its presence in him the thing called / future—could not be married to it anymore, expanse tugging his mind out into it, / tugging the wanting-to-finish out." And perhaps Eurydice understood the attraction of being erased or let go, of finding herself unspoken for: "now she's looking back into it, into the poison the beginning, / giving herself to it, looking back into the eyes, / . . . looking into that which sets the _____ in motion and seeing in there / a doorway open nothing on either side." If so, if both responses tug at us as we write, then perhaps this story proposes that as we outline and seal down, driven by that desire, we also know ourselves to be moving toward an attractive silencing, a "_____" or "grapes, which are nothing" in our hands as the wind dies down. As Graham puts it, letting both figures play across the present writing scene, there is something to be gained in that: "When we turn to them—limbs, fields, expanses of dust called meadow and avenue— / will they be freed then to slip back in?" The important idea here is that although allowing naming to exhaust itself in a world-unhanding blank (Orpheus and Eurydice) is different from entering into resemblance's estranged intimacy (Adam and Eve), they are responses to a single problem.

They share a family resemblance. They are stories we tell ourselves about human limits.

A third speculative poem, "Self-Portrait as Apollo and Daphne" (EB, 30–34), tries to get at what might be gained by acknowledging the limits of knowing in yet another way. Eve's gesture leads to "finite . . . options" (EB, 9), Orpheus's to a "put[ting] to rest" (EB, 17) of the "glance." This poem opens up something else. Graham begins by describing what she calls the first "phase" of their story—the "chase scene" as the god pursues the nymph: "The truth is this had been going on for a long time during which they both wanted it to last." We can read that sometimes delicious, sometimes oppressive contest everywhere: in words pursuing things, in the wind attempting to handle the world, even in the sun glinting off "bits of broken glass / . . . for just a fraction of an instant / (thousands of bits) at just one angle, quick, the evidence, the landfill, / then gone again, everything green, green." To put it simultaneously in linguistic and sexual terms:

> 2
> How he wanted, though, to possess her, to nail the erasures,
> 3
> like a long heat on her all day once the daysounds set in, like
> a long analysis
> 4
> The way she kept slipping away was this: can you really
> see me, can you really know I'm really who . . .
> His touchings a rhyme she kept interrupting (no one
> believes in that version anymore she whispered, no one
> can hear it anymore, *tomorrow, tomorrow,*
> like the different names of those girls
> all one girl)

Eventually Daphne, out of desperation, halts this phase and metamorphoses into a laurel tree: "She stopped she turned, / she would not be the end towards which he was ceaselessly tending, / she would not give shape to his hurry by being its destination." Her change leaves open "the distance between them, the small gap he would close," but not as a probing, teasing, tearing battleground. She becomes neither the morning's glinting glass nor its screeching birds but rather:

> the air the birds call in,
> the air their calls going unanswered marry in,

the calls the different species make, cross-currents, frettings,
and the one air holding the screeching separateness—
each wanting to change, to be heard, to have been changed—
and the air all round them neither full not empty,
but holding them, holding them, untouched, untransformed.

As Apollo we want to possess, as Daphne we know the terror of becoming his ending: their dramatization of this tension suggests a response to our condition in which we hold the world without touching it, handle it without reaching out to transform it. Hass called this the haiku's "clear, deep act of acceptance and relinquishment" (TC, 305); Bishop described it, in lines Graham must be remembering here, as "thousands of light song-sparrow songs floating upward / freely, dispassionately, through the mist, and meshing / in brown-wet, fine, torn fish-nets." It's an attractive possibility.

The poems clustered around this self-portrait are powerful and striking. "Eschatological Prayer" (EB, 35–39) describes a drive up to the church of Santa Chiara di Montefalco in Italy—whose cloister still contains the body of Saint Claire "who saw the god in 1300 drop / under the weight of his cross / and swore to carry it / *forever in her heart.*" Driving up into the mountains, the poet is charged by a sort of Apollo/Daphne tension. The road up—"a narrow road cut like a birthcry," "a road like the dream of a perfect / calculation"— and "the fierce clean light" grazing the surroundings are Apollo-like in their striving to arrive and hold fast. So is the poet who drives and gazes. For a time, arrival temporarily suspended, she's Daphne keeping the gap open, not quite being touched: "You could reach *almost* in / to where the notes and the minutes / would touch. / You could push. It was tenderness. / You could live in that gap, that listening" (italics mine). Eventually, of course, that phase passes. Apollo closes the space, in the form of the sisters of the cloister who, in the fourteenth-century, cut Saint Claire open in order to find and hold something in their hands, and in the form of the sisters now who present the saint in a "shimmering glass casket" and tell her story, ensuring that it arrives somewhere. They all wanted proof. All of the poet's Apollo-like tendencies, it would seem, are nightmarishly acted out before her:

They cut her open when she died, the sisters prying
     between the curtains of light and the curtains

of light. They found in there,
     in the human heart,
this tiny crucifix, this eye-sized figure

of tissue and blood.
Here are the penknife, the scissors. Here are the towels
          they soaked the blood

up into, here the three kidney stones, the piece
          of lung in the shape
of a bird, here the story the hurry like so and like
          so, and the singing voices now that it's noon
of the cloistered sisters
          back in there barely audible so clean like acetylene

And that, if I read it right, causes the poem and its straight-ahead drive to shatter. Graham ceases to act out the chase and its bright deflections and becomes, instead, simply a place—the air, a space—where the whole human drive, that whole story from "want[ing] to take it / into our bodies" to "be[ing] shattered," could be enacted without turning away from the world or from consciousness. She calls it "a motion . . . / . . . that wanted syllable by syllable to be shattered / over the whole of eternity / into the eyes into the mouths of strangers yet still be." Somehow it is possible to exist in this shattered place, to be yourself the air where its tensions screech and collide.

The fourth portrait, "Self-Portrait as Hurry and Delay" (EB, 48–52), is subtitled "Penelope at Her Loom" and uses her weaving-then-unweaving ruse to propose yet another way of describing that space between. What Penelope must be doing, the poet gradually realizes as she struggles with the story, is creating, in the gap between "the here and the there, in which he wanders searching," a place where desire, in all of its positive and negative implications, is kept alive. (That formation is slightly different from creating a space where desire leaves the world untouched or where it appreciates its own slide into a collapsed state.) Here, holding "for an instant in her hands both at once, / the story and its undoing / . . . the threads running forwards yet backwards over her stilled fingers," Penelope makes desire (or choice) visible and felt without being forced to drive it towards an "ending." On her loom, we see "The opening trembling, the nothing, the nothing with use in it trembling—." The shroud is "nothing" because it has come undone, but it trembles in that stalled space because it still records human drives and uses: to be home, to know for sure, to hold tight, and so on. Think of Odysseus at sea; those desires tremble on the loom:

          the light over the water seeking the place on the water
     where out of air and point of view and roiling wavetips a shapeliness,

> a possession of happiness
> forms,
>
> a body of choices among the waves, a strictness among them, an edge
>   to the light,
>
> something that is not something else

To put it literally, by keeping herself from the suitors, Penelope keeps the possibility of such a "possession of happiness" free for Odysseus: "It is his wanting in the threads she has to keep alive for him, / scissoring and spinning and pulling the long minutes free, it is / the shapely and mournful delay she keeps alive for him." But, perhaps more to the point, she keeps desire itself—costly, beautiful, wanting to wrap itself "plot plot and dénouement over the roiling openness"—she keeps desire itself alive and visible, keeps it as something to be attended to. What would that look like as something to write toward?

Among the poems in which Graham tests herself against that description of the gap is a fascinating piece entitled "Breakdancing" (EB, 53–55) in which she links a boy dancing on TV with Saint Teresa of Avila. The connection with Penelope keeps the juxtaposition from becoming simply absurd and allows the poem to measure itself against Penelope's "quickening" of our condition. Simply, what the boy on the screen is doing is "staying alive." Through a series of *"joint isolations,"* he seems to be allowing some sort of current—"the secret nobody knows like a rapture through his limbs"—to "tell itself: pops, ticks, waves and the / float." Teresa, who murmured to her flock *"staying alive is the most costly gift you have to offer Him,"* had a vision of Christ that (oddly) rhymed with that broken city-wise dance:

> He
>   showed himself to her in pieces.
> First the fingertips, there in mid-air,
>   clotting, floating, held up by the invisible, neither rising
> nor falling nor approaching nor lingering, then hands, then a
>
> few days later feet, torso, then arms, each part alone, each part
>   free of its argument, then days, then eyes,
> then face entire

What would that mean for her own work? the poet wonders. If Teresa came alive as she tried to "hold [her]self" in that current that broke the human form, bit by bit, "free of its argument," in order to prepare a new sort of representation, what would that mean for her? How might she keep desire or other human hungers alive yet free of their arguments? How might she hold the story and its undoing simultaneously? What she proposes is a sort of poetic breakdancing—desire isolated and handled, all of its implications, both cultural and personal, showing itself in a single poetic body: "the minutes, the massacres, the strict halflife of / radioactive isotopes, the shallow / graves, the seventeen rememberable personal / lies? What if they go only this far, grounding / in me, staying / alive?"

The final and most powerful piece in this series is "Self-Portrait as Demeter and Persephone" (EB, 59–63). It begins the book's conclusion and holds many of its strongest poems in its gravitational field. To inhabit the gap as both Demeter and Persephone seems to mean "suffer[ing] [it] completely"—living over and over the cycles of having and losing, of being in the story and being freed of it. Every year, Persephone goes "out into the open field through the waiting the waving grasses / way out to the edge of that drastic field of distinctions." Every year she finds herself bride of the underworld:

> She took off the waiting she stood before him without nouns
> He held her where are the images he said we will destroy them
> you are in hell now there is no beginning
>
> the outline is a creature that will blur you will forget him
>
> as for motive that shapeliness let us splinter it let us scatter it

And without nouns, images, outline, or shape, every year Persephone finds herself returning to all of that: "Look she said I have to go back now if you don't mind waiting." Demeter, of course, has her own cycle. She lives in "the knowable / clucking I've been looking for you all day," gradually devastating the world as the inevitability of that loss dawns: "the made grieving . . . like a mother or winter / the great gap grieving all form and shadow." What would it mean to think of the gap through both figures? Think of it as Persephone returning to the world devastated by Demeter's love and grief and wanting: "The first thing she saw when she surfaced was the wind / wrapping like a body round the stiff stripped trees / that would bend more deeply into that love if they could." Then combine the stories. Under the influence of Persephone's spring-causing return, think of those same trees, exploded into leafiness while Demeter's winter grief still howls its terrible, blanked desire:

> that would bend more deeply into it inventing (if they could)

15

another body, exploded, all leafiness, unimaginable
16
by which to be forgiven by which to suffer completely this wind

An explosion that is also a leafing out, a bending into what loves and destroys—
the poems that conclude the book attempt to invent a tormented form such
as that to inhabit this contested space.

Let me mention just one. In "Imperialism" (EB, 94–99) Graham's speaker
asks once again about the gap through the image of a shadow moving across
a dusty road, touching a bank, a hole, and so on. The shadow works like the
mind:

> the shape constantly laying herself down over the sparkling dust
> she cannot own—
> What can they touch of one another, and what is it for
>
> this marriage, this life of Look, here's a body, now here's
> a body, now here,
> here. . . .

She enters and feels out that space by remembering an argument from the
night before. The way her partner's face seemed to flutter in the kerosene
lamp—"something like clear light then / soiled light / (roiling)"—was like the
unsettled shadow across the road as was their inability to converse cleanly
and "keep the thing clear—the narrative of / bentwood chair and hinge and
trim." In that space, she remembers, a story came alive and then sputtered
out: "And there was a story I wanted / to tell you then but couldn't / (just
where she came on into us and we pushed back with / better rephrasings)."

A broken-off story in an open space, canceled by "better rephrasings."
What value is that? As she works back to it now, she begins to answer. She
had remembered her mother taking her, when she was quite young, to the
Ganges where she saw bodies burned on pyres and then the ashes shaken into
the river. "Later she had me walk on in. / Strange water. Thick. I can recall it
even now." That is, she walked into a space where bodies and shapes dissolved.
We have been calling that the truth of skepticism. And, not unexpectedly, she
woke up that night screaming, suffering again that loss of bodies and shapes.
The broken-off story, simply, was an image of what form looks like in such a
swirling dissolve, an image of form momentarily opening the powerfully alien
world around us, and then collapsing:

—But what I remembered last night to tell you

is a white umbrella a man in the river near me was washing
    and how the dark brown ash-thick riverwater rode
in the delicate tines as he raised it rinsing.
    How he opened it and shut it. Opened and shut it.
    First near the surface then underwater—

And perhaps that is what form does in the space it suffers and cannot hold—
opens and shuts, the world riding untouched through it. Or not untouched,
for the world, too, opens and shuts, as the poem's last lines make clear,
"narrow[ing] down to [a mother's] love" then flaring out to a terrible openness:
"no face at all dear god, all arms—."

In *Region of Unlikeness* (1991), Graham rephrases the problem as an
attempt to inhabit and suffer what she calls "the sentence in its hole, its
cavity / of listening" (RU, 114). She asks again what sort of response to the
world—this book calls it "listening"—might be developed, in the writing itself,
when the drive to master and narrate shatters over its limits: "(Where the
hurry is stopped) (and held) (but not extinguished) (no)" (RU, 125). The
book's foreword recalls the use of large cultural equivalents in *The End of
Beauty* and suggests that we might measure our entrance into the poet's
struggle—"How do you feel?" (RU, 101), she keeps asking—against Saint
Augustine's trembling awareness of the "region of unlikeness" he inhabits
far from the "whole," Heidegger's "drawing toward what withdraws," Isaiah's
inability to find a proper equivalent for God, or John's "wilderness" of waiting
in Revelation. Yet the book itself turns from those larger equivalents and looks
instead at the resistant details of the poet's own stories. The book is more like
"Patience" than it is like "Orpheus and Eurydice," though the drama takes
place in an area shared by both: story's stalled spaces that the poet, as she
writes, attempts to inhabit and "paint . . . alive" (RU, 44).

"Fission" (RU, 3–8) sets up many of these concerns. Its title, reluctantly
acknowledging the breaking apart that knowing has put into our hands, points
to a moment of unraveling many people share: a memory of being in a movie
theater and hearing the news of President Kennedy's shooting. As Graham
prods at the memory, however, all of the ways we shape the world and move
toward an end come to be charged and fragile and at issue there. As the poem
begins, the movie's soundtrack is suddenly shut off, the houselights come on,
a skylight opens, and a man races down the aisle trying "to somehow get / our
attention." The movie continues, however, and his unwitting call to attend to

the space or gap where the "magic" story we have rested in seems to fray and dissolve echoes throughout the book:

> I watch the light from our real place
> suck the arm of screen-building light into itself
>   until the gesture of the magic forearm frays,
> and the story up there grays, pales—them almost lepers now,
>   saints, such
>
> white on their flesh in
>   patches—her thighs like receipts slapped down on a slim
>   silver tray,
>
> her eyes as she lowers the heart-shaped shades,
>   as the glance slides over what used to be the open,
> the free

The movie is Stanley Kubrick's *Lolita*. This is the moment when the sunbathing girl, roused from a shapeless slumber by her mother's call and the flaring desire of Humbert Humbert, comes to consciousness. Her face— what a later poem calls "the forward-pointing of it" (RU, 119)—dominates the screen as her world is narrowed and yanked into a plot. What we are called to attend to is the region of unlikeness we find ourselves in when Lolita's face and her sudden, Orpheus-like "glance" over what had been "open" are reduced to:

>   a roiling up of graynesses,
>   vague stutterings of
> light with motion in them, bits of moving zeros
>
> in the infinite virtuality of light,
>   some *likeness* in it but not particulate,
> a grave of possible shapes called *likeness*—see it?—something
>   scrawling up there

Her expression—the possibility of expression, let's say—is not eliminated; rather, likeness's hold over the world is suspended and the possibility of a new sort of "scrawling" emerges. The speaker is pulled into this uneasy space as well—"the story playing / all over my face my / forwardness"—and describes it now as a kind of halt or pause, what Hass would call an interval: "there / the immobilism sets in, / the being-in-place more alive than the being, / my father sobbing beside me." What she realizes, and what she will take the rest of the book to explore, is that she is in a place where our actions have been discredited and whited out and are yet demanded. To speak or to choose or to struggle with the way words take over memories is to risk fission's unwrapping of the real; to not do so is to rest in a skepticism that leaves the world dead and untouchable. That is what comes alive on the face as the light frays:

> *choice* the thing that wrecks the sensuous here the glorious
> here—
> that wrecks the beauty,
> choice the move that rips the wrappings of light, the
> ever-tighter wrappings
> of the layers of the
> real: what is, what also is, what might be that is,
> what could have been that is, what
> might have been that is, what I say that is,
> what the words say that is,
> what you imagine the words say that is—Don't move, don't
> wreck the shroud, don't move—

The poems that follow frame the question of how to speak in this roiled-up space ever more uneasily. "From the New World" (RU, 12–16), for example, works through an event related during the trial of the Cleveland steelworker accused of being the Nazi executioner Ivan the Terrible—the story "about the girl who didn't die / in the gas chamber, who came back out asking / for her mother." Although she is shaken by the brutality of Ivan ordering a man "on his way in to rape her" and thus start the stalled story back up again ("the narrowing, the tightening"), the poet finds her own progress halted before the girl's frail, agonized voice in that "unmoored" space, asking for her world back. What to make of that? Acknowledging her own complicity in story's drive toward an ending—"God knows I too want the poem to continue, / want the silky swerve into shapeliness / and then the click shut"—she lets it drop and holds herself before that whispered "*please.*" Graham makes a number of almost desperate attempts to find equivalents for the girl's pleading. Was it like realizing, as a child, that her grandmother had so lost her faculties that she had erased her granddaughter? Or like, some years later, the grandmother herself, now in a nursing home, her "eyes unfastening, nervous," focused on nowhere? The point of these comparisons is not their fit, as the strain of trying to imagine the whirling-walled bathroom the child had fled to as a "chamber" in which she is "held in . . . as by a gas" suggests.[10] Rather, what is important is the way the resistance of these stories has forced her to an almost immobile space, "a grave of possible shapes called *likeness*" (RU 5). How does one speak there, if likeness does not hold?: "At the point where she comes back out something begins, yes / something new, something completely / new, but what—there underneath the screaming—what?" It's an almost unmanageable question, charged and desperate and alive[11]:

> *like what*, I whisper,
>
> *like* which is the last new world, *like, like*, which is the thin
>
> young body (before it's made to go back in) whispering *please*.

As "Manifest Destiny" puts it, most of the poems in *Region of Unlikeness* can be described as suffering or "pay[ing]" language's price in spaces where such "zero[s]" open (RU, 28). The title poem (RU, 37–40), for example, uses the speaker's memory of waking, as a thirteen year old, in a man's room, to establish its moment of charged suspension:

> You wake up and you don't know who it is there breathing
>   beside you (the world is a different place from what it
> seems)
>   and then you do.
> The window is open, it is raining, then it has just
>   ceased. What is the purpose of poetry, friend?

Trying to get at the resistant memory, like the struggle with myth or paintings in her previous books, slows her language and makes it visible. Why is she writing? For what purpose? She attempts an answer by watching herself as she writes, tracking both her desire to not engage the memory—"He turns in his sleep. / You want to get out of here. / The stalls going up in the street below now for market. / Don't wake up. Keep this in black and white"—and her fear that she thereby risks running "right through it no resistance / . . . right through it, it not burning, not falling, no / piercing sound." As she fills in color and context, sketching an ending, she declares herself ready to pay in order to keep the human responsibility of remembering alive, in order to hold herself in its unmastered zero:

> If I am responsible, it is for what? The field at the
> end? The woman weeping in the row of colors? the exact
>   shades of color? the actions of the night before?
> Is there a way to move through which makes it hard
>   enough—thorny re-
> membered? Push. Push through with this girl

The tug of these questions seems to awaken her language, for at the end of the poem she is pulled, in Wyoming "Twenty years later" walking among hatching butterflies, back to that live interval:

> and below the women leaning, calling the price out, handling
> each fruit, shaking the dirt off. Oh wake up, wake
>   up, something moving through the air now, something in the
>   ground that
> waits.

"Waiting" is one of *Region*'s repeated terms for what we can do in that charged, temporarily immobile place where language's drives to master and sort and go on have been checked. In the space of waiting, we pay or suffer our finitude; we examine and take responsibility for our lives in language. "Picnic" (RU, 41–45), for example, gets at the term by approaching the memory of her father's betrayal, "near the very end of childhood": "Then someone's laugh, although they are lying, / and X who will sleep with father / later this afternoon." It is clear, as the poem begins, that although the poet would like to "Pay attention" to this break in her childhood, the memory has become so "inaudible" over the years that it has been dismissed as a probable lie, like all the others: "The light shone down taking the shape of each lie, / lifting each outline up, making it wear a name. / . . . (so does it matter that this be true?)." This poem inhabits that stalled spot—memory, and in fact all shaping and naming, having been skeptically eroded away. Why write? Why enter that impossible place? "And why should I tell this to you, / and why should *telling* matter still, the bringing to life of / listening, the party going on down there, grasses, / voices?" Such a world seems dead or shrouded—as Graham puts it, it is "sated, exhausted."

What she does is wait and stare at the memory, staying with it until she finds a thorny and difficult place—where that distance from what she was then to what she is now cannot be bridged by the outlines we so easily draw. Waiting draws that out:

> one of me here and one of me there and in between
> this thing, watery,
>   like a neck rising and craning out
> (wanting so to be seen) (as if there were some other place dear god)—.

She follows that "watery" uneasiness to another, perhaps below-the-surface memory of "father with X": "When I caught up with them they were down by the pond." Then, remembering her desperation to calm things—"I looked into the water where it was stillest"—she touches its still-live terror and disorientation:

> Have you ever looked into standing water and seen it going
> very fast,
> > seen the breaks in the image where the suction shows,
> where the underneath is pointed and its tip shows through,
> > maybe something broken, maybe something spoked in there

And there is more to be found in the waiting, for she remembers now what must have been her mother's acknowledgment of the break and her refusal to cover it over with an outline or lie. Later that day, her mother "came up into the bathroom" and, the two of them staring into a mirror, took her daughter's face in her hands and applied makeup. What was that—the way "She shadowed the cheek, held the lips open, fixed the / edge red," and then as the light started to go, the way "The silver was gone. The edges on things. The face still glowed— / bright in the wetness, there"? That, she now realizes, was her mother's way of insisting that one could stay aware in "the opening which is *waiting*"—that one could take responsibility in that dissolving, sucking wetness by acknowledging the fragility of the lines we work with and within:

> We painted that alive,
> mother with her hands
> > fixing the outline clear—eyeholes, mouthhole—
> forcing the expression on.
> > Until it was the only thing in the end of the day that seemed
> believable,
> > and the issue of candor coming awake, there,
> one face behind the other peering in,
> > and the issue of
> freedom. . . .

In many ways, these poems try to do just this: they enable us to peer into an ungrounded charged space where the price of expression, of choice, is real and alive. Writing becomes a place where being candid and where facing the trials of "freedom" are still possible.

The book concludes with two rival poems on the implications of waiting or immobilism, as if to suggest that the issue of what is gained in the gap is still unsettled. "Who Watches from the Dark Porch" (RU, 97–108) is a powerful attempt to pull the reader into the gap, in this poem the skeptical sense that this very poem, "is a lie . . . / . . . Thing / so beautifully embalmed in its syllables." We all share that sense, and we experience it every time we stare at a scene and find "the possibilities (blink) begin to exfoliate" or find a "right version and more right versions, / each one stripping the next layer off her" and the world disappearing under a bewildering series of "veil[s]" that continue to gather even as we discard one and then another. We have called that a hole, or a region where likeness will not hold, where suction takes the image. The poet invites us into that uneasiness and calls it a struggle between "Matter" and "Interpretation." She sets up a situation: you're on a porch on a summer evening ("sit, here is a soft wood seat / in the screened-in porch") and you hear a sound from next door: "A child's sound. Maybe laughter—no—maybe a scream." The poem "quickens." What if, from the porch, you cannot interpret, cannot tell? How would you respond to the possibilities unwound and alive in your hand?

> Now I will make it impossible to tell the difference.
> Now I will make it make no difference.
> Now I will make there be no difference.
> Now I will make it. Just make it. Make it.

> How do you feel?

What we discover, along with her, is a real temptation to use our awareness of the finitude of our outlines or interpretations as an excuse to hide and not meet the world: "If I am responsible, it can't be for everything. / May I / Close my eyes for a minute?" She thinks that temptation through by imagining turning on the TV to drown out the sound—which is to say, skeptically turning on our awareness of the fragility and disposability of our interpretive takes on the world:

> Maybe if I turn the TV on?
>   Let's graze the channels? Let's find the
> storyline composed wholly of changing
>   tracks, click, shall I finish this man's phrase with this
>
> man's face, click, is this the truest news—how true—what are
> the figures
>   . . . .
>   —see how even you can't hear it

anymore, the little shriek, below
  this hum

  . . . .

                —flecks of
information,
  fabric through which no face will push

No face shows through this shroud of self-canceling data because there
is no willingness to listen or pay—a limitation yielding permission to not
move forward: "no messy / going / anywhere, / rocking, / erasing each
forwards, / . . . here in the place where it's all true so why move." This is
a clearly disturbing possibility—that a skeptical response to limits, to its
familiar stalled space opening up, might as easily be a retreat as a "waiting"
for strangeness to "slice" over you. Think of that as a voice that dissolves
the world, that "said *still*, said / don't wait, just sit, sit—Said / no later,
no matter." In saying it doesn't matter, in turning from the struggle with
it, there is suddenly no matter. "There," she writes, in horror about that
feeling, "you got it now. You got it."

Finally, "The Phase after History" (RU, 111–21) attempts to do some-
thing different in the same space. Its version of the collapse of straightfor-
ward history or confident interpretation is the experience of having a pair
of juncos loose in the house, their panic turning the house into a "diagram
that makes no / sense . . . [a] wilderness / of materialized / meaning." The
house she suddenly inhabits—in which nothing is settled, wrong turns
everywhere—is like "a head with nothing inside" or even "Like this piece
of paper" she is working on. How to inhabit this stalled space? One bird
escapes on its own; she tries to edge the other one free, but cannot complete
the story: "I start with the attic, moving down. / Once I find it in the guest-
/ bedroom but can't / catch it in time, / talking to it all along, hissing: stay
there, don't / move—absolutely no / story—." Eventually, she is reduced to
"waiting" and "listening," creating what she hopes might be described as
"a large uncut fabric floating above the soil— / a place of *attention*." Sitting
there, listening for the bird to thwack a resistant surface or bright pane of
glass, she thinks of a friend in a psych hospital who had "tried to cut off"
his face—that is, our "forward-pointing," our confidence in expression. He
thought of it, apparently, as "an exterior / destroyed by mismanagement.
/ Nonetheless it stayed on." Sickened by his desperation but challenged
by that stark memory of his "face on that mustn't come off," Graham
speculates that perhaps being "returned to the faceless / attention, / the

waiting and waiting for the telling sound" is a step forward rather than a retreat. Perhaps listening for the other, for the world's strangeness, an experience heightened by the collapse of the face, poem, or the house's order, is a step in getting a new sort of face back:

> The head empty, yes,
>   but on it the face, the idea of principal witness,
>
> . . . .
>
>   How I would get it back
> sitting here on the second-floor landing,
>   one flight above me one flight below,
> listening for the one notch
>   on the listening which isn't me
>
>   listening—

The strength of this uneasy book is that as we circle back to the opening poems and their questions of what to make of "immobilism, the being-in-place more alive / than the being" (RU, 8) or of the sense that likeness has been dissolved—"At the point where she comes back out [and] something begins, yes, / something new, something completely / new, but what?" (RU, 16)—it is the strength of this book that as we circle back, the answer is still out of reach.[12] Or the answer is the attentive wait itself: "something new come in but / what? listening" (RU, 120). Graham calls this, finally, "emptiness housed," her "eyes closed to hear / further."

Graham's next book, *Materialism* (1993), is an intricate meditation on what happens when we try to make sense of the world through description. As such, it once again narrows and makes more acutely personal the way it raises the issue of the limits of knowing. We have gone from stilled paintings to still-active myths, and from the writer's own stories to the play of her eyes. The book begins with an account of a river's "dance of non-discovery"—its constantly erased surface patterns "nailing each point and then each next right point, inter- / locking, correct, correct again, [yet] each rightness snapping loose"—and asks whether an equivalent acknowledgment of the limits of description might produce in us "a new way of looking" (M, 3–4). We can think of this as a possible response to *Region's* "something completely / new, but what?" Poem after poem dramatizes the way the eye, "clawing for foothold," performs its "long licking across the surface of / matter" (M, 99, 132). Typically, the poems begin in the morning as the "glance—surveyor of edges—descends / . . .

gnawing the overgrowth, / criss-crossing the open for broken spots" (M, 8), or on waking in the dark, desperate to "mark . . . the pleating blacknesses of hotel air" (M, 58). Consistently, there is the sense, as one morning poem puts it, "that we are *in a drama*" (M, 127). The various desires and terrors and implications brought to consciousness by tracking the eye's swing are slowed and studied, and the "Monologue of going and going" is halted so that we might join the poet in understanding what is actually at stake as we stammer and stroke the world into sense.

Materialism quite deliberately sets its meditations in the midst of Michael Oakeshott's larger "conversation in which human beings forever seek to understand themselves."[13] As we have seen in her previous books, an echoing network of shared terms and images links Graham's own attempts to make and unmake meaning with those of such figures as Wittgenstein ("[pictorial form] is laid against reality like a measure"— M, 93), or Jonathan Edwards ("the continuance of the very being of the world and all its parts . . . depends entirely on an *arbitrary constitution*— M, 110–11), or Brecht ("the theatre must alienate what it shows"—M, 64). Where previous books used such established voices to set up clearly staged struggles—think of Klimt or Augustine or Ovid—*Materialism* seems an example of that "air" in "Self-Portrait as Apollo and Daphne" in which "the calls the different species make, cross-currents, frettings" are all alive at once. That is a different sort of "measuring" of one's own voice. Some-times quoted, often subtly adapted, these other voices form a chorus— challenging and extending and undercutting her own struggles. The most powerful of these engaged-with voices is Bishop's—never named directly, but in her careful descriptive progress and unnerving skids into its limits so present that the entire book reads as a sort of fierce and heightened adaptation of her work. Graham's comments on Bishop in the interview that follows, in fact, can be taken to summarize the "new way of looking" *Materialism* charges itself with developing: "You have to undertake an act which you know is essentially futile, in the direct sense: the words are not going to seize the thing. But what leaks in between the attempts at seizure *is* the thing, and you have to be willing to suffer the limits of description in order to get it." What is discovered "in between" is perhaps most simply described in one of the book's epigraphs, adapted from "Crossing Brooklyn Ferry." "Expand, being," she has Whitman write, in response to objects that remain stubbornly other and independent of our eyes' embrace, "keep your places objects. / . . . We use you, and do not cast you aside—we plant you permanently within us; / We fathom you not—we love you." Essentially, what this book asks is whether Whitman's dream can be realized—whether suffering the limits of description and admitting that we neither fathom nor own objects might lead to that expanded sense of "being" Whitman calls "love."[14]

An early poem in the book, "Subjectivity" (M, 25–31), powerfully illustrates how Graham enters this conversation, taking the "uttering tongues" of the epigraphs as "hints" (as Whitman puts it elsewhere) and voicing their music for herself. "Subjectivity" begins with the poet attempting to describe a motionless monarch butterfly she had found and brought inside to study. As is typical of her work in this volume, the intensity of her gaze generates a series of striking metaphors for the butterfly's markings and then turns those metaphors back, as possible assessments or measurements of that gaze. The markings become: "Black bars expanding / over an atomic-yellow ground"; an "incandescent" yellow pushing "out (slow) through the hard web"; the "yellow of cries forced through that mind's design"; "a structure of tenses and persons for the gusting / heaven-yellow / minutes"; a "bright new world the eyes would seize upon— / pronged optic animal the incandescent *thing* /must rise up to and spread into." This seems to me extraordinary writing. The world under her attention blazes into "incandescence"—an incandescence generated by the tension between the hungry-for-empire bars, designs, and syntactical orders that we can call, for short, the poet's eye and the as-yet unclaimed world the eye lights upon. The scale flickers and shifts—the optic nerve, the sentence, and the colonist all claim, essentially, the same territory—as Graham describes, without yet being able to explain, the allegory she has been presented with: the "gaze's stringy grid" and the world "almost burn[ing] its way / clear through / to be."

How is it that the distance between the mind's web and the world's atomic separateness yields neither domination nor emptiness but incandescence? We have seen this question in each book. How does that open space quicken, or come alive, or regain a face? There is "something new, something completely / new, but what?" (RU, 16). Graham tries to answer by, quite literally, feeling her way into the issues. She is intent, as Cavell puts it about Thoreau, on understanding, through "endless computations of . . . words" that "Words come to us from a distance." She knows that "Meaning them is accepting that fact of their condition" (SW, 63, 64). Graham enters and accepts the "condition" of her language in *Materialism* by holding it up against the world around her. In "Subjectivity," noticing a ray of sunlight moving across the floor, Graham begins her investigation by waiting and

letting it approach her, all "twang and a licking monosyllable." She invites
the beam to become an allegory and a measure of her own descriptive
desires. She feels herself, as the poem slows to a crawl, turned into a thing
examined and then lifted up suddenly to consciousness—brought from
"her" to "me" by the light's licking glance:

> making her rise up into me,
> forcing me to close my eyes,
> the whole of the rest feeling broken off,
>
> it all being my face, my being inside the beam of sun,
>
> and the sensation of how it falls unevenly,
>
> how the wholeness I felt in the shadow is lifted,
> broken, this tip *lit*, this other *dark*—and stratified,
> analysed, chosen-round, formed—

What she senses, from inside the process, is the wholeness that has been
broken-off and blinded, chosen and lit; she feels its force most acutely
as the I (the eye) stakes its inadequate claim. This is Apollo and Daphne
discovered within one's own eyes, Lolita's roiled-up face within one's own.
That awareness produces an uneasy charge now as she returns to the
butterfly, acutely aware of her gaze "licking for crevices, im- / perfections,"
trying "to make it flat—as if it were still too plural" and sensing "the
underneath the mind wants to eliminate" in its drive to "smear, coat, /
wrap, diagram." That sense, that there is an underneath untouched by the
"almost icy beams I can feel my open eyes release," begins to drive the
poem and then, so quickly the reader almost drops the book in surprise,
suddenly blazes into visibility as a neighbor happens by, explains that the
butterfly had only been stilled by the morning's cold, and, freeing it from
her eyes, returns it to the sun. It blazes against her markings and is gone:

> the yellow thing, the specimen,
> rising up of a sudden out of its envelope of glances—
>
> a bit of fact in the light and then just light.

What these poems ask is whether the poem itself, carrying writer and
reader into such an uneasy confrontation with limits, might not bring our
condition to life: "—can we, together, / make a listening here, like a wick
sunk deep in this mid-temperate / morning-light, can we make its tip—
your reading my words—burn" (M, 137). Let me touch on a number of

examples of how she quiets the drive to know, admits it could come to nothing, and attempts such a listening. "Concerning the Right to Life" (M, 14–20) begins with a series of striking descriptions of a rose—it is a "rough muscle, / drenched veil . . . / . . . the possible / sprung from / possibility / into whipped red / choice. / . . . around it—shuddering—the invisible / ripens"—and then asks what happens when we stand before that flashing "accretion of / discardings" and allow it to "judge" our own attempts at form. Once again, Graham "tr[ies] to feel" her way into the implications of form and choice performed by the rose's ordering of the invisible. She dramatizes what is at stake in its "thrashing forking red" by listening to opposed voices at an antiabortion protest and then walking through the crowd and into the clinic being targeted. Sitting inside, acknowledging her own tendencies to keep her language "immaculate" and to think of a writer's "freedom of choice" as something like "illustrious sleep," the poem's speaker begins to listen to the voices outside and, drawn into that contested space, finds her words taking on "materiality." Juxtaposing those rival voices—"some / voices screaming *right to life*, some others screaming / *choice choice*"—and then complicating each term—through such rights "held *self- / evident*" we have ruthlessly "*take[n] possession / of the earth*"; perhaps there are realms where "*there is no choice*"—Graham allows those tensions to "roil" or complicate the "immaculate" terms she wants to use in her own speech. Nothing is settled, other than the sense that now, when words are chosen, despite the sheer fragility of language, perhaps something will have been "displaced," an "underneath" will have been encountered, some tragically alert choice will have been chanced, there between language and the world. The poem makes form's choices contested ground, a place to listen and flare and expand into alertness.

"Relativity: A Quartet" (M, 34–43) works a variation on this pattern. Another interruption occurs; a train loses power and stops, and as the view outside her window is put on hold, Graham finds herself in another stalled linguistic space, the "Monologue of going and going interrupted." Once again, language's confident single voice unweaves itself into a number of voices and the stalled train becomes a stage set. Two voices, the views out both sides of the train, come alive in this space and the poet is forced to engage them. Across the aisle is a stoned couple, asleep. Through their window, before their "uncomprehending" eyes, the sea lies apart and "unseized." No longer "lay[ing] itself down frame by frame onto the wide / resistenceless opening of our wet / retina," the sea is simply "mere, still, being." The world lies immaculate, untouched, but as before this is a position that is not held for long. Through the other window she sees "a scribble of leaves." She feels herself drawn to "look close," "see through," and "enter" into that second world—so much so that she discovers rising within herself the language of Job and Isaiah and the Psalms as her instinctive turn away from "gaping eyelessness" toward form reenacts God's initial struggle with his "adversary: the [unshaped] waters":

> Green leaves: cloth to shroud the Deep:
> ride above the deep:
> ride in your chariot of shapeliness:
> clean: shut: not this and not this:
> destroy with one seed the monster's skull:
> thrust with one stem a sword into its heart—
>
> And the waters fled *backwards*—
> And the endlessness fearfully surrendered—

That great primordial need to shape, surprised into voice, then gets bracingly undercut as a second meditation on form begins, initiated by the girl across the aisle who refuses to be covered up. Perhaps form is not a cloth over the deep but a "cover up," in all the current uses of that phrase: "We have been monitoring developments," and so forth. And perhaps the language of stem and seed, sword and surrender has produced not a livable world but the laughing madman suddenly snapping into focus the sleepy corridor of a train much like this one:

> looking for what he's missed,
> laughing, gun at the end of his arm, over his
> head, swinging back,
> tentacular, spitting seed, him the stalk of
> the day, scattering seed, planting it deep—

What this entire meditation does, I think, is leave the act of seeing and making sense suspended in a very uneasy territory. There is no longer the option of simply clothing the deep nor of falling back into a stupor; there is a choice to be made here, a risk to be engaged with when we enter into language. What the poem does, I take it, is force us to crouch down with the writer—"on our knees"—as she opens up a sort of theater within which she insists that we speak. And as she describes the deep tensions loose on that stage, as she lets the limits of speech spark toward incandescence— "*my portion of time / my portion, full*"—she once again turns toward the reader and asks:

(can you stand it?)
    (get down and hide)
(live fast, cloth over a sea, breathe, breathe)

Graham's poems ask, in many different forms and voices, whether language might remain the medium in which we live our lives. They ask whether we can both acknowledge our distance from words and use that distance to think with. To touch *Materialism* one more time, they ask whether words, like a bullet "blazing" in a museum case recording the tooth marks of a soldier's silent scream during an amputation, might display "the toothed light" of thought making visible what it never dreams of owning:

How can the scream rise up out of its grave of matter?
How can the light drop down out of its grave of thought?

How can they cross over and the difference between them swell with existence?
(M, 100)

"Expand being," Whitman writes. Expand here, Graham replies—in the writing, where the "yellow of cries [is] forced through that mind's design" (M, 26), where "the difference between them swell[s] with / existence."

In a way, it comes as no surprise that Graham's most recent book, *The Errancy* (1997), seems to be written from within the exhaustion or wreckage of what it calls the dream of reason, for incandescence must always be threatened with guttering out. "Even the plenitude is tired of the magnanimous, disciplined, beached eye in / its thrall," she writes. "Even the accuracy / is tired—the assimilation tired— / of entering the mind. / The reader is tired. / I am so very tired" (TE, 50). But the poetics has not changed, for, like Cavell's world "regained as gone," Graham stubbornly anticipates being awakened within that sense of exhaustion. Even as tiredness testifies to the limit or the collapse of "the notion of human / perfectibility" (TE, 4), it opens the possibility for renewal—for an encounter with "the world made strange again" (TE, 44) in our experience of its impenetrability.

The title poem (TE, 4–6) is clear about these conditions and the writer's almost desperate desire to renew herself by writing through her fatigue. It begins with an end-of-the-day exhaustion—the dream of mastering the world reduced to a match struck and struck with no results, the dream of making America into a city on a hill having now been reduced to concrete bracelets, William Blake's mind-forg'd manacles:

Then the cicadas again like kindling that won't take.
The struck match of some utopia we no longer remember the terms
                                                    of—
the rules. What was it was going to be abolished, what
restored?
. . . .
              up on the hill, in town,
the clusterings of dwellings in balconied crystal-formation,
the cadaverous swallowings of the dream of reason gone,
hot fingerprints where thoughts laid out these streets, these
                                                    braceletings
of park and government—a hospital—a dirt-bike run—
here, we stand in our hysteria with our hands in our pockets,
quiet, at the end of the day, looking out, theories stationary

Writer and culture are in the same position—hands in pockets, theories stationary, all of us skeptical about our desires to handle and know and construct. The "dream of reason gone" is, like Eliot's "Unreal City," fallen at our feet; what can we do but walk through it quietly, perhaps one or another of us still "looking out." Perhaps someone *is* still looking out; Graham's speaker clings to that thought, hoping that the city's "populace [is] not really / abandoned, not really, just very tired on its long red errancy / down the freeways in the dusklight / towards the little town on the hill."

Another early poem, "The Scanning" (TE, 7–10), uses a long day of inter-state driving—"traffic behind us like a long kiss"—to prompt a meditation on what we might look out on from within the tired truth of skepticism. Our anxiety about our abilities "to seize and transmit truth" is like a car's radio tuner in a field of static; out of habit it touches and moves on, desperate to locate a home but "glid[ing] over, not selecting, hiss—":

And the bands of our listening scan
the bands of static,
seeking a resting point, asymptotic, listening in the hiss
for the hoarse snagged points where meaning seemingly
accrues: three notes: three silences: intake
of breath: turnstile?: a glint in fog?: what the listener
will wait-into, hoping for a place to
stop . . .

The driver's dilemma (exhausted, acknowledging this was "*Our* plan, / one must not pretend one knew nothing of it") is also the poet's as she scans and scans her experience after the fact, seeking something live—say that first "intake of breath" calling up the full music of the experience. And both situations stand-in for the culture's own weariness, the poet, in the manner of Eliot whom she echoes, almost prophetically suffering our ills for us in order to show us where they might lead:

> What shall we move with
> now that the eye must shut? What shall we sift with
> now that the mind must blur? What shall we undress the veilings of
>   dusk with,
> what shall we harvest the nothingness with,
> now that the hands must be tucked back in their pockets
> . . . .
> *Our* plan . . . To get the beauty of it hot.

What it leads to, at least on this trip, is abandoning the forward thrust of the interstate and wandering, now on foot, through a space opened up by the collapse of what "The Errancy" called "the sensation of *direction* we loved, / how it tunneled forwardly for us" (TE, 4). We have seen versions of this wandering in each of the poets we have examined:

> Down by the riverbed I found some geese asleep.
> I could see the billboards, but they were across the water.
> Maybe two hundred geese—now beginning to stir,
> purring and cooing at my walking among them.
> . . . .
> A mess of geese. Unperfectable. A mess
> of conflicting notions. Something that doesn't have to be
> imagined. An end-zone one can have pushed forward to,
> here at the end of the path, what the whole freeway led to,
> what the whole adventure led to,
> galleys, slaves, log-books,
> tiny calculations once it got dark enough to see,
> what the whole madness led to—the curiosity—viral—here,
> like a sign—thick but clear—here at the bottom of the sedge,
> the city still glimmering over there in the distance,
> but us here, for no reason, where the mass of geese are rousing

Which is to say: both "the whole freeway" and "the whole adventure" of western civilization lead, in their collapsing, hands-in-pocket acknowledgment of madness, to a world where "no reason" holds sway. The failures of the drive to name and colonize and map (that "virus") present her with an "unperfectable" world—a "mess of conflicting notions" captured here in the image of the "groping" and "roiling" geese. It is a finite world, off the highway and far from the "city still glimmering." But when the poet walks through this world, through this mass of shapes no longer masterable by the old dream, something powerfully charged occurs. It is the dream of Graham's last book: to sense, out of the exhaustion of reason, an exhaustion in fact acknowledged in the writing of the poem itself, a new sort of reason just being born, responding to a world at a distance from us:

> —and the birds lift up—
> and from the undulant swagger-stabs of peck and wingflap,
> collisions and wobbly runs—out of the manyness—
> a molting of the singular,
> a frenzied search (unflapping, heavy) for cadence, and then
> cadence found, a diagram appearing on the air, at arctic heights,
> > an armoring
> the light puts on—stagger of current-flap become unacrobatic
> > industry, no tremble in it,
> no echo—below, the freeway lustrous with accurate attention—
> above us now, the sky lustrous with the skeleton of the dream of
> > reason—look up!—

"Look up!" becomes a refrain in many of these poems. Out of our exhaustion and the collapse of explanation, perhaps we have become quiet enough to notice the very first moments when the multiple begins to form patterns, or the light takes on a shape, or a new diagram begins. It is that live beginning that we are urged to look up at from our in-between space, the "freeway . . . of accurate intention" below us and no longer usable, the "skeleton of the dream of reason" above us and quickly, like the butterfly in *Materialism*, flapping free of us. Both worlds are lustrous, one behind us, one before us. It is not that Graham thinks she can replace one with the other, as much as she wants to call out and show us the live space between them that we inhabit. Apollo and Daphne still tug at us, but they have been at it for so long that the poems sense the need to grab our sleeves and shout: "Look up! Here is what the exhaustion of the old dream has brought us to. Here is something strange and stirring."

We could say, then, of a powerful set of poems late in the book, that, in looking up, they seem to have discovered René Margritte's painting of Blaise Pascal's coat. The painting shows a torn, riddled gray overcoat floating against a dark city and bluish sky, stars showing, some through the holes in the coat. (Graham notes: "One presumes it represents the coat in which Pascal was buried, and in whose hem or sleeve or 'fold' the note containing the 'irrefutable proof of the existence of God' is said to have been stitched, at his request, unread, by his sister, upon his death" (TE, 111).) That coat is the world woven and shaped and put on by the observer. It is what we draw around ourselves and consider familiar and knowable. We weave it by reason; we secret proof inside of it. Torn and floating against the dark city, then, the coat now seems useless, fit for the trash, but it is also, Graham is convinced, richly generative. She writes in "Le Manteau de Pascal" (TE, 64–70):

> You do understand, don't you, by looking?
> The coat, which is itself a ramification, a city,
> floats vulnerably above another city, ours,
> the *city on the hill* (only with the hill gone),
> floats in illustration
> of what was once believed, and thus was visible—
> (all things believed are visible)—
> floats a Jacob's ladder with hovering empty arms, an open throat,
> a place where a heart may beat if it wishes,
> pockets that hang awaiting the sandy whirr of a small secret,
> folds where the legs could be, with their kneeling mechanism,
> the floating fatigue of an after-dinner herald
>
> . . . .
>   But the night does not annul its belief in,
> the night preserves its love for, this one narrowing of infinity,
> that floats up into the royal starpocked blue its ripped, distracted
>   supervisor—
> this coat awaiting recollection,
> this coat awaiting the fleeting moment, the true moment, the hill, the
>   vision of the hill,
> and then the moment when the prize is lost, and the erotic tinglings
>   of the dream of reason
> are left to linger mildly in the weave of the fabric,
> the wool gabardine mix, with its grammatical weave,

never never destined to lose its elasticity,
its openness to abandonment,
its willingness to be disturbed.

The exclamation "Look up!" continually refers us to this vision; it proposes that the torn coat, its "floating fatigue" making the stars visible, might be "recollected." Look up! the very sentence-making of these poems pleads, startled up out of the collapse of the drive to know, testifying to a linguistic fabric still live with "the erotic tinglings of the dream of reason" but now "elastic," "open to abandonment," "willing to be disturbed."

In "Manteau" (TE, 71–74), Graham is even more explicit about these matters. If the world continually "tangles up into a weave," then "I would like to place myself in the position / of the one suddenly looking up / to where the coat descends and presents itself," she writes. Poems can enact, in their "swagger-stabs of peck and wing-flap, / collisions and wobbly runs," what we see when we look up:

> this coat—
> which I desire, which I, in the tale,
> desire—as it touches the dream of reason,
> which I carry inevitably in my shoulders, my very carriage, forgive
> me,
> begins to shred like this, as you see it do, now,
> as if I were too much in focus making the film shred,
> it growing very hot (as in giving birth)
> . . . .
> and we have to open our hands again and let it go, let it rise up
> above us,
> incomprehensible
> . . . .
> the shredded coat left mid-air, just above us,
> the coat in which the teller's plot
> entered this atmosphere, this rosy sphere of hope and lack,
> . . . .
> this torn hem in the first miles—or is it inches?—of our night,
> so full of hollowness, so wild with rhetoric. . . .

The act of writing, these lines suggest, testifies to the way the world is shaped to our need, then is inevitably ("you see it, . . . now," she writes) shredded by that need and freed. Look up, these sentences assert in their "openness to abandonment," the world drifting away, "incomprehensible," but drawing us behind it into a space "full of hollowness, . . . wild with rhetoric" and luminous.

That call also runs through a series of poems "spoken" by guardian angels that appear throughout the volume. The angels are expert in the implications of various human responses to finitude; they see through our attempts at making order, our writerly gestures. Each of them looks down on the wreckage or exhaustion of our attempts to order the world, while also calling attention to something new and fragile, beginning there again. These poems function much like the mythic self-portraits in *The End of Beauty* or the voices of Audubon and Wittgenstein in *Materialism*, in which the completeness of myth or an established work chided or warned or challenged the writer's still-developing project. It is as if, looking down at the world, the angels also comment on the writer's sentences, describing what stirs in the torn coat, what animates the dream of reason's skeleton.

So for example, "The Guardian Angel of the Little Utopia" (TE, 1–3), expert on fixing and arranging things but feeling "A bit dizzy from the altitude of everlastingness, / the tireless altitudes of the created place," testifies to our need to be "knit[ted]" up out of "crumpled dust" and the inevitable failures of that attempt, down in our world of time. It is that double perspective, however, that gives the angels eyes to see the drive collapsed but starting anew. "Let us look out again," the angel says, almost reading over the poet's shoulder as she writes:

> . . . as if the moment, freeze-burned by accuracies-of
> could be thawed open into life again
> by gladnesses, by rectitude—no, no—by the sinewy efforts at
> sincerity—can't you feel it gliding round you,
> mutating, yielding the effort-filled phrases of your talk to air,
> compounding, stemming them, honeying-open the sheerest
> innuendoes till
> the rightness seems to root, in the air, in the compact indoor sky,
> and the rest, all round, feels like desert, falls away,
> and you have the sensation of muscular timeliness,
> and you feel the calligraphic in you reach out like a soul
> into the midst of others, in conversation,
> gloved by desire, into the tiny carnage
> of opinions.

This, as much as anything else, is a description of Graham's style, caught on the fly: words, freeze-burned by their pursuit of accuracies of phrasing and insight, thawing open and alive once again, mutating and compounding, their wildly-stemming phrases becoming "effort-filled" and "muscular" in time's torn space of conversation and carnage. Look, the angel says, knowing what generates the need for an utopia: look at what is stirring "where you are passing / time."

The other angels point out contrasting facets of what the poet senses stirring toward birth. "The Guardian Angel of Self-Knowledge" (TE, 14–15) knows the exhausted result of trying to see through everything: "how clean / did they want to become, / shedding each possibility with gusts of self-exposure, / bubbling-up into gesture their quaint notions of perfection, / then letting each thought, each resting place, get swept away." "The Guardian Angel of the Private Life" (TE, 20–22) knows how desperate we are to shrink the world down to the size of a personal to-do list: "the heart trying to make time and place seem small, / sliding its slim tears into the deep wallet of each new event on the list / then checking it off—oh the satisfaction—each check a small kiss." And "The Guardian Angel of Not Feeling" (TE, 46–47) understands how desperately we would prefer not to feel time erode our drives to love or know: "We gust that lingering, moody, raw affection / out, we peck and fret until it's / gone, the flimsy courage, the leaky luggage / in which you carry round / your drafty dreams—of form, of hinged / awarenesses, all interlocking-up." At the same time, each angel, out of its anticipation of the wreckage of such drives sees them becoming, in our hands, luminous in their brokenness, charged because not fully confident. The angels have various ways of picturing this:

> —oh from here
> it looks so like a dream of shelter—
> the way that reaching hand mimics the eye, romancing,
> the way it quickens at its root, desiring,
> the other one now rooting in a pocket for some change,
> and the other ones now touching a chin, a lip, an index-finger rough
> on a cheek, as if to wipe away a glance—
> (TE, 14)

> the solitary ones,
> heads in their hands, so still,
> the idea barely forming
> at the base of that stillness,

the idea like a homesickness starting just to fold and pleat and knot
                                                                    itself
out of the manyness—the plan—before it's thought,
before it's a *done deal*
(TE, 21, 22)

look at the ink, dip fingers through its open neck,
bring hand to lip—there—do it again, again,
blazon the mouth, rub in, exaggerate—
the little halo forms, around the teeth,
the mirror on that wall shows you the thing,
furious, votive—
oh look, the tiny heart
mouthing and mouthing its crisp inaudible black zeros out.
(TE, 47)

How do we live in the moment when our finite, needy homesickness
starts to just generate an idea, when we start to just-reach-and-root, our
words forming only "crisp inaudible zeros"? The poems in *The Errancy*
suggest that our current exhaustion—"hands in our pockets, / . . . theories
stationary"—is important, for as "The Guardian Angel of Point of View"
(TE, 78–80) puts it, without it, we "seize all too easily all that I split apart, /
emptiness's vast ripe fruit" since "what you suffer seems, ah, as yet / unlived-
through." As we saw with Cavell's version of Wittgenstein, suffering shows
us the limits of our gestures and gives us back an unmasterable world, stars
shining through a torn coat. Says the angel: "Oh to taste the limits of the
single aperture," for that taste, as we write and read wakes us to the world:

        let them wake up, therefore,
    discalced, refined—meandering supplicants
    seeking a tyrant or a tyranny that won't reveal itself,
    nearly-shy first-glancings a little advance cavalcade,
    then coalescing, sensing the something that is
                missing here—beside? inside?—
    beings so full of second-thought,
    overwakeful, blurry with anticipation and hurry
    and the sense, always, of *something being stolen*—
    then the strewn, loose gems of tossed-out glances,
    unstrung at first, blossoms in dry first-sunshine wind,
                scattering, against the wall. . . .

The angel describes the words the poet seeks to use: barefoot, refined, wandering petitioners, all shy first-glancings and overwakeful second-thoughts. These lines develop like a Homeric simile, the shy supplicants by the end tossing blossoms into the wind, their petals scattered by the unmasterable wall, by the sense that "something is missing here."

The most fully developed attempt to actively wake and blossom in this way, full of "shy first-glancings," is a set of aubades—dawn poems. They are vulnerable poems, live to all of the implications of speaking and making sense that the rest of the book declares at issue or in play. They are poems that, quite literally, awake, stirring before the glance asserts itself, poems in which only the skeleton of the dream of reason, charged and incomplete, is there to come to grips with mystery. In a sense, we can read the seven poems, scattered throughout the volume, as one poem. At dawn, we catch reason "lying down over the intractable thereness of what time made— / a *shade* over a *shape*—no harvest— / a passage over a given-thing—no theft— / . . . bad fit that the mind be made to awaken" (TE, 86–87). At dawn, the writer experiences "the eye, no longer singing in tune with the collecting brain" and experiences things "wielding utter particularity" (TE, 13). Like the traffic jams of one poem or the storm aftermath of another, dawn places the writer in a "spot outside consequence, the blind, whorled spot, / where there is no longer push, or inch along, or halt" and where "the parts of the picture the glance sews up / [are] beginning to break into separate puddles" (TE, 12–13).

When read together, the seven aubades show how much remains alive after the storm in which reason has collapsed. At dawn, "the room still grainy, dimpling" as the light touches "the edges of the window-shade, curling its rims" (TE, 34), all issues are in play. "Get up," one poem tells itself: that vibrant world on "the other side" "held you, once" (TE, 34). Yes, the poem replies, but "it is nice in here, in the blur, / . . . in the sleep where nothing's won, / or lost." Sleep, whispers Eurydice in another poem: "lie tightly intertwined—unopen—petal yourself round the stamen of / some green unuttered syllable— / . . . [don't] risk awakening the song again" (TE, 57). And Eurydice has good reasons, these sleep poems know. What waits, under that now-glowing windowshade, is eventual collapse. Collapse comes light as laughter in some poems: "beneath the glittering exterior-latex, beneath the storyline and then the loss of / storyline—quick, bright derision" (TE, 36). It feels like martyrdom in others: Odysseus's ("then the single sturdier open gaze cast up: a stare: a fear: / why is father lashed to it? / why is mother singing?" [TE, 43]) or Christ's ("and the dogs of difference are all around me— / and 'I' am poured out like water" [TE, 63]). At the worst, the coming of light and the snapping into place of attention lead to "no dialogue, / no errancy, / just the red currency of back and forth / . . . and then an aftertaste, as of ashes, in my mouth" (TE, 60).

But knowing this, knowing that the dream of reason leads here, puts holes in the fabric of writing and makes its use lustrous or vulnerable or open to abandonment. Thus, woven through each of the poems I have drawn from are these charged, vulnerable beginnings:

> Something—not an idea—a tiny velocity.
> How it sharpens the edges of the singular.
> (TE, 37)

> and one can feel how the boat feels—
> all of the freedom swirling and slopping round the keel, the here,
> foaming round, as feelings—and still the pitch of the dawn
> grasping at transparence
> (TE, 43)

> how I want to make it
> last, sightless narration,
> untilled,
> before the cacophony of edges—forking, collating—
> ignites again, orchestral . . .
> (TE, 59)

> edges like little knives flooding the emptiness,
> outlines radiating, innermost crevices rising up to be
> seen,
> retrospect settling in
> (TE, 61)

> thickenings, varyings,
> in which the possibility of shapeliness begins to rave,
> brightening most at those edges where the skull feels itself to be
> inside of something which it cannot see—
> (TE, 101–2)

What makes all of these dawn-trackings of edges alive, from their various perspectives, is their consciousness of limit or loss—that, the world remaining unmasterable, the poet writes from within "the place of disappearance" which is also, like a stone tossed in a river or the empty tomb on Easter morning, an "opening" (TE, 102).

Think of that opening, a final poem puts it, as something generative. It seeds the world around us. Imagine a river on a black night, its invisibility a constant reminder of the limits of our ability to grasp. In many ways, all of Graham's poems occur here. Now move alongside of that black river, hands in your pockets:

> The muscle [of the river] braids-up alongside.
> Cicadas churn. My wholeness now just something *alongside*—
> a stammering, an unattachedness—hands in pockets—a walking
> straight ahead into the black,
> and walking fast—as if to seed the patiently prolonging emptiness
> everything not-river—everything not perfectly invisible—
> seems to
> possess.
> (TE, 96)

6. An Interview with Jorie Graham

TG: Here's a line from "Pollock and Canvas." You say, "What we want is to paint nothing how can one paint nothing?" I'd like you to think out loud about some of the words in that. Maybe you could start with "nothing."

JG: Well, I meant the positive sense of the word. As in Stevens's "the nothing that is there." Or the *zero*. Zero being the value which negotiates between being and non-being. In the Pollock poem, it's what is seized in the space between the end of the brush and the canvas on the floor beneath him. (Pollock did not touch brush to canvas—he used "drip" methods—his gesture nonetheless in total control) . . . By *something* I'd mean, therefore, a motion which has already posited its own end.

TG: A motion already shaped?

JG: Let's say achieving shapeliness by the postponement of its ending. Or achieving a sense-of-shapeliness by the implied ending (even if it doesn't arrive). To my mind, the formal elements that occur along the way are only audible—or believable—in relation to their extinction, the closure. By *nothing* I guess I meant the alternative shape, something which perhaps is centrifugal, something which we don't identify primarily by its limits. At any rate, I'd say Dickinson's idea of *circumference* is close to my idea of *nothing*— the zero, something which expands outward.

TG: Circumference as something you go out on?

JG: Yes, the idea of the circle, which is defined by its center but for which the circumference is only a temporary stopping point.

TG: Would that work for outer things as well as inner? It seems to me there are poems where you are thinking of the outside world in the same way.

JG: Absolutely. Another term for *nothing* would be *the ineffable*. I love the Japanese term for the essence one is (theoretically) trying to seize via the haiku: *yū gen*. *Duende* is another notion that seems corollary, and useful, to me.

TG: You say the holy, the given, would those be the same thing, too?

JG: Well, the given . . . but the problem, of course, is that the means by which we apprehend the given are either habitually or innately (and that's what we cannot be sure about) structuring devices of a linear kind. I really feel that what Pollock was trying to do was open up—not by the cheap methods, chance methods, but in a more difficult and dangerous and perhaps more lucrative way—the gap between the end of his gesture and the beginning of the painting. I love to imagine that one-inch gap between the end of the brush and the beginning of the canvas on the floor. . . . What could come alive in there that Western thinking has refused to let in for so long? *Maya* is the term I use for it in that poem—and I try to explore the ways in which, between the act of making and the made thing, she comes alive.

TG: Spell that out?

JG: The male deity, Vishnu, is a creator-god in the way that, say, our Old Testament God is a creator-god. Then there's the created world he's made, and I take that to be—in the mythology of Christianity (and I use it as mythology)—I take it to be the Christ, the Son, the created being. In between there's this process which, in Hindu mythology, they call Maya, making her the consort of the creator-god. To me she is the moment between the desire to create and the created thing—the moment in which the act of creation occurs—and it's a flash, a woman, an opening—a rip in the fabric— the "nothing"—as well as what lets the nothing through.

TG: That's like the spirit moving over the waters at the beginning of Genesis.

JG: Yes. In fact, I like to attach the notion of Maya to the image of the Holy Ghost. A lesser term is *process*. But in our Western, most noble and wonderful ambitions, we have typically interfered to limit the kinds of activities of which the moment of process is actually capable. The methods the Surrealist way of proceeding has come up with, for example, seem to me somewhat limited. . . . I feel like I'm writing as part of a group of poets—historically—who are potentially looking at the end of the medium itself as a vital part of their culture—unless they do something to help it reconnect itself to mystery and power. However great their enterprise, we have been handed by much of the generation after the modernists—by their strictly secular sense of reality (domestic, confessional), as well as their unquestioned relationship to the act of representation—an almost untenably narrow notion of what that in-between space is capable of. Issues being raised by other art forms (which didn't even exist, say, when Eliot was writing) by critical theory, philosophy, and the science of our day—as well as by people like David Byrne, Robert Wilson, and the Sanjai Buku are often more ambitious than the issues raised by our poetry. I think many poets writing today realize we need to recover a high level of ambition, a rage, if you will—the big hunger. That is why we are so incredibly grateful for the presence of Ashbery and Merrill, why the hugeness of their project seems so central and the aesthetic differences that divide them ultimately so minor. Why Duncan remains influential—why Michael Palmer's and Allen Grossman's projects are so heartening, and Bidart's, Tate's, Wright's. The Merwin of the second four books. Strand's dark vision of absence.

TG: The image theatre: have you seen it, or read about it?

JG: Seen it. One Sanjai Buku performance in particular moved me deeply. Three hours of highly emblematic gestures without language. [*pause*] Do you want me to describe it?

TG: Yes.

JG: There is one scene in which five humans, naked to the waist with long wraparound skirts on, totally white (covered with rice-flour), seemingly faceless, stand in the lower left-hand corner of the dark stage in a pool of light. There's the sound of airplanes, very loud—over their heads, mixed with strange carnival sounds. These people move their fingertips for twenty minutes in a very odd way—anemone-like. After a while, it begins to seem like our front/back, up/down distinctions regarding the body are false. That from some deity's point-of-view, for example, the fingertips, the area defined by these white fingertips extending outward before the standing body, might be the face? the front? Then, slowly, they begin to move away from their very stark gestures. A thin streak of light appears on the stage. They move along the light. And their skirts open, and you notice there's genitalia in there, but you don't really know what kind. I kept thinking, at the point where they opened their mouths (and, as they're entirely white with the rice-flour, their mouths open on an incredibly dark hollow *inside*) that if they introduced a single word into the event—if anything came *out* of that opening—the thing would collapse in on the word, it would so desperately want the word to gloss it. It scared me—that sense of the limiting powers of the word.

TG: And that's the feeling that's attractive about it?

JG: Very much. It frightened me—but also, of course, exhilarated me—the degree to which introducing *any* language into it would narrow the scope of it. And all because of that great double-edged power in language, the power to *define*. Watching their work made me want to reexamine exactly what it is that language can do now, what role it should take on in this increasingly *visual* culture. I've always been a bit uncomfortable with the relationship of any title to a painting, for example.

TG: Because it narrows it?

JG: Yes. It seems to me I'd like to find a kind of language—or *action* in language (form, in other words) which would have the opposite effect, be more like the painting or the stage event than the label to it. The ritual rather than the *use* it's put to . . .

TG: But you do it, almost, by accepting that narrowing, don't you? Accepting it, then blowing it to pieces.

JG: I do try—

TG: *Erosion* seems to employ a strict, stern sort of language, which eventually gives way or erodes. *The End of Beauty*, perhaps, starts in that condition of having exploded. In either case, these ways of working seem quite different from the theater or performance art.

JG: Yes, but I'm not satisfied with the poems, and they seem to me . . . well, that's a different matter.

TG: Go ahead.

JG: I can't really . . . For me each book is a critique of the previous. I find it very hard to talk about *The End of Beauty*, if only because the poems I'm writing now are the way I'm contending with it.

TG: Maybe a way of answering would to be talk about what those new poems are doing.

JG: There is a poem in *The End of Beauty* called "To the Reader" that starts "I swear to you she wanted back into the shut, the slow." I think, in a way, the central impulse of each new book involves my wanting to go into a more moral terrain—a terrain in which one is more accountable, and therefore in which one has to become increasingly naked. For me, the stages of that unveiling require . . . Well, the motion we were talking about as *eroding* is really just writing poems up to the point where I can, and then admitting the failure, if you will. But *having* to go past its point of success, or of intuition, or closure, past the "couplet" wherever it would have occurred. Because it's only in the terrain that follows—or so it feels to me—that you touch what you didn't know. [*pause*] You're right when you say a whole panoply of veils have come off already (it's *late* in history, after all) . . . and Salome *is* a governing figure in the new book—the one I call *Region of Unlikeness*. You see, in *Erosion* she's standing there realizing there *are* veils and that she could *get something for it*, if you will, but she doesn't know what to ask for, what to desire (the imperialist urge without the object of desire!)—"Head of John the Baptist" hasn't occurred to her yet. In the next book, she has started taking off some of the veils—and that's why your description of it as starting at the center seems completely accurate . . . but since she doesn't know which veil is real, as she takes off the layers, she's constantly interfering and creating the illusion, then destroying it. . . .

TG: *The End of Beauty* is filled with interfering. I listed ten or twelve ways of showing that this is a veil, this is a veil, this is a veil.

JG: My experience of it is of actively taking them off in the process of writing. It's not like I would say "Oh, it's going to be these seven veils." I would write until suddenly what felt opaque turned transparent, and each time it felt like [*pause*] pain because what we want, of course, is to get to something which resists, which *won't* come off. I was trying with great caution and difficulty in that book to experience, as I was writing, the actual moment when the thing would go transparent on me. I would realize the nature of the "bad" illusion and then have a sort of fall. As when Dickinson says "and then a plank in reason broke." I felt almost reassured by the blanks in the book, because those were the only places where I felt it couldn't go transparent.

TG: Let's talk a bit about *Hybrids.* You've mentioned elsewhere how in that first book it's easy to make sentences.

JG: Yes.

TG: It's hard to read that book slowly. Your eye just sort of whips through it.

JG: For me there's insufficient tension between the line and the sentence in that book, because the lines are too long to be felt as measured. When the prose-length lines occur, they don't do so contrapuntally, as they do (I think) in *The End of Beauty*.

TG: How does your use of the sentence versus the line fit in here?

JG: The way the sentence operates became connected, for me, with notions like ending-dependence and eschatological thinking. With ideas like manifest destiny, westward expansion. Imperialisms of all kinds. I began to notice how the forms our Western sensibility creates are, for the most part, ending-dependent, and that such notions of form—however unconsciously—give birth to historical strategies like the Christian one: the *need* for the conflagration at the end that takes what appear like random events along the way and turns them into *stages*. Cause and effect, the link-up into narrative, all of this dependence on closure and strategies for delay in relation to closure, you know, whiz, bang, is terrific as long as we're thinking of it in terms of art. But when we start realizing that by our *historical* thinking we have created a situation whereby we are only able to know ourselves by a conclusion which would render *meaningful* the storyline along the way—it becomes frightening. [*pause*] I don't remember how Jonathan Schell put it in *The Fate of The Earth*, but the idea was that if you create shapes of a certain kind which govern human imagination, they become the shapes by which people experience time. Obviously, the political and historical occurrences of a given moment, of a given culture, have a lot to do with the particular notion of time those people believe they are living in. It forced me to recognize the little wind in myself which I think blows through many people living today—that secret sense of "well, let's get it over with so that we may know what the story was, what is was *for*"—apocalypse as the ultimate commodification. . . . All of this focused, for me, on the sense of closure, how we were using closure, and on the need to find new strategies by which to postpone closure (which is, of course, what the best narrative poems do). It made me feel, at any rate, that we had to try to find figures of imagination that contend with some other structuring element. Now, I haven't been able to find them. I'm not sure they exist; that they are, finally, humanly possible. I'm intrigued by medieval triptychs—in which the middle panel (the *present*) is larger than the side panels (past and future)—as a model. Or by certain unfinished works—like Bach's Fugues. That's why Pollock's paintings became important to me, because of the ways in which they are a-closural. And the notion in chaos theory of "extreme sensitivity to initial conditions" (which I think Scalapino's work explores beautifully). But to go back to the idea of the line—and your question—the line does bring with it (not only historically) an extraordinary sense of balance—poise outside time—which then contends with the swift scary suction of the sentence, careening, with its time sequences, its musically and rhetorically posited closure, grammatical causal linkages. The balance, the struggle, between these two in the style of any strong poet probably provides the swiftest access to their metaphysics. . . .

TG: Does *The End of Beauty* feel like it's simply suspending closure or does it feel like it's doing something else?

JG: No, I wouldn't say it's managing to suspend closure. It might be trying to. But what I discovered in trying to write those poems was that the suction of closure was enormous—the desire to wrap it up into the ownable *meaning*—and that doing away with it wasn't as easy as I had imagined. That was, for me, a very moving discovery. It was Demeter and Persephone, if you will—with the pull from the end, the suction towards closure, and the voice trying (quite desperately in spots) to find forms of delay, digression, side-motions which are not entirely dependent for their effectiveness on that sense-of-the-ending, that stark desire. Side-motions which actually move off a piece, and do not necessarily feed back into it—in the way I had always experienced poems moving before, sort of wrapping the poem down towards closure.

TG: Those side motions keep the gap alive?

JG: Yes. But they keep it alive, hopefully—or ideally—as a *real* gap, not one invented for the purposes of extending the delicious moment between the beginning and the ending. The deliciousness of that moment was the thing I was trying to mess with. The imperialist pleasure . . .

TG: So you want it to be extended because in doing so you gain what?

JG: Let's put it this way: as a gap, an open field, so that one is at least aware of the wages, the responsibilities (as well as the incredible freedoms) of that opening. After all, the sensation of closure is primarily powerful for the ways in which it permits us to inhabit delay and feel that we are *safe* inhabiting delay. . . . I guess I wanted it to feel *not* safe—but *real*, open. Can we use the word *being*? The ground of being. The river of rivers. The gash of the present as not simply timeless but as the rip that affords a glimpse into a more genuine reality?

TG: You can inhabit because you don't even know that it's a delay. Is that right?

JG: [*considering*] We're getting so abstract! In Ashbery's poems, the thing that is often both intoxicating and scary, to me, is how one is comforted by the sense that all these spinnings off the spine of the poem, the line of argument, will be *taken somewhere*. It feels, by analogy, like you are in the hands of a deity who has ultimate plans for this. You are in the hands of a formal situation in which all of the apparently loose threads occurring in the middle are part of a larger design. The *musical* illusion (even if not the stated promise, and in spite of the contrapuntal tonal slippages) is that they will all be, ultimately, woven in.

TG: Whereas in *The End of Beauty* . . .

JG: There I basically wanted to say (formally) "Look, see these loose threads. Is it responsible to weave them back in? Is it responsible to let you feel like they can be woven back in? Isn't that sort of saying, on some level, that the governing deity overseeing this mess has plans?" I grew up with a classical sense of "history." I was taught in French schools after all! [*laughs*] My sense of *history* was of the most neatly planned narrative. Suspecting the illusion of that way of thinking—or feeling—and not being able to replace it with any other meaningful model, and becoming aware that poems, by the implications of their formal characteristics, were providing a metaphysical view of the world which might be a terrible illusion, one which might, moreover, be permitting us to not take certain kinds of actions because we feel ultimately, as a species, *safe*, compelled me to try to break that illusion as often as I could. Mostly to make myself feel how often I *wanted* to restore that illusion. In the act of writing, the desire to restore the illusion—you might call it the ultimate bourgeois illusion—to get the story moving down, link by causal link, to not let it stop, to make it arrive at right (i.e., *inevitable*) closure (what one *deserves*), was so strong, I could feel myself reenacting what I know is our cultural predicament. I guess I was writing them in order to feel that. It was, in fact, an incredibly noble and beautiful idea, the idea of Progress, the love story we call History. Wasn't it? Where did we screw up? I was trying to move through those poems to feel where the *outs* were, and the *ways back*. That's why they're so frustrating to me. It's an impossible avenue.

TG: Let me push a little bit. You mean that you're doing more than just critiquing language, don't you? There's really something you want to gain between those two things.

JG: Oh. Yes. It's not a critique of language as much as it is a critique of desire as it manifests itself in language, as it manifests itself in structures and organizations. Look, those cloistered sisters in "Eschatological Prayer" open up Saint Claire's body, and they find proof, inside, of . . .

TG: You see a metaphor made literal inside her . . .

JG: And they gained nothing by it. I don't know, in the poem, if they should be forgiven or accused. And that dilemma felt, for me, like the center of what I was looking at. We pried it open. It says they found the gap "between the curtains of light and the curtains of light," and went on in. Now, of course we should have gone in. Who wouldn't have gone in? We divided the atom, etc. We had to. We became self-conscious. . . . This might seem excessive to some, but I feel that poems are enactments, ritualistic enactments— fractal enactments—in language, of historical motions. And in the *process* of them, you experience your accountability. You feel, in yourself, those crucial motions the culture has effected because you feel yourself actually doing them, undertaking them—helplessly, really—in the poem. "I'm going to wrap this up. I'm going to make this mean this way. I'm going to judge this way. I'm going to invade, control, usurp this way." . . . And of course I have to give those impulses play as well, because they're true. But then, then . . .

TG: That's what you mean by "and still be."

JG: Yes.

TG: And then the other side of that is, we want "to be shattered."

JG: Exactly. And to feel. . . . That's why the portraits are of double figures— male and female—and one is usually moving towards closure and one away.

TG: And both of those are inside?

JG: Yes. Aren't they? Somebody wrote a mildly astonished review saying that it seems of all the people writing with myths now (and the review listed many such people), Jorie Graham is the one who seems to actually believe they are real—that they *really happened*. I found that incredibly tender and sweet—because it's not just that I feel they "really" happened; I feel like they are, at all times, happening. There are moments when the gesture of Eve towards Adam occurs within the psyche, for example, that sudden turn towards self-transformation, death, form. We have, over the years, found other terms for those motions of spirit—biological terms, sociological terms, religious terms. The most prevalent ones in our day seem to be the psychoanalytical terms. But the mythological figures for those actions seem to me more useful because less reductive; more complex; more inclusive—not to mention more mysterious.

TG: Could you say more about that gesture of Eve towards Adam?

JG: It's a "gesture" that is happening, historically, at this moment in our culture, in fact—the way in which the female is ascendant, the desire for loss of hierarchies. . . . I even heard a discussion regarding new types of marketing and business structures—how Benetton, for example, and other world corporations, are developing what the speaker called "non-hierarchical organizational structures." He actually used the metaphor "no head" in order to describe it. Erich Neumann in "The History and Origin of Consciousness" describes how the uroboric mother-archetype—neither terrible nor good, but both at once, unconscious, the dragon figure—spews forth a germ, a seed, the *ego*, and how this rises up as the *hero* out of the unconscious. His analysis privileges the moment (which seems to me our moment) when the hero looks back and sees her, the moment when the rational, masculine, mental hero, the Christ if you will, rises up out of the virgin—although it's out of a darker thing than the virgin, more like a black Madonna—and encourages us to sense both of these figures in us at once. Neumann doesn't do so explicitly, but his method seems to lead to such work, and I, for one, took him up on it—being in a period in history when the hero, the ascendant rational mind, has gotten so far along in its quest that the female has to ask for him back—or risk total psychic disintegration. There are a lot of Indian myths—of course—in which the great mother then eats the hero again, takes him back into her body, so that he may be born again in a new form.

TG: And you're right between aren't you, between the hero being eaten and being reborn?

JG: How nice! But I think what I'm trying to do is—if you will permit this exaggeration!—is reincorporate the *hero* part of my psyche back into the unconscious, uroboric female. Not in some foolish way in order to dissolve "him"—*the mind*— but to keep everything alive, to keep the tension alive. It's as if, for me, those poems are balloon environments in which I've got the terrible mother, if you will, and the hero—both awake, hopefully, and at their fullest. My hero side is enormously developed, and, in some respect, I use poetry to reawaken the mother, the unconscious side. This is a description of any functioning *form*—a vessel for active tension.

TG: Now, once these two things are quivering together, once they're in tension together, what do they pick up? What can they register? Does that make sense?

JG: Yes. It's also a very difficult question, because my answer would be "then they pick up a whole view." They recover, they restore, the body and senses to the mind. And they therefore provide a way of thinking about time which is linear and circular at the same time. They create, hopefully, a restored, undissociated sensibility, which then permits one to see the ways in which time is at once news time and the time of the mysteries. I guess I believe that if one could see both ways at once, one could—without even having Cassandra around—make "sense" of events. Obviously it's in many ways absurd as a notion; absurd in its belief that creating a restored sensibility is a way of affecting the consciousness of the race so that we might not destroy ourselves. I'm so much at the outer limits of political action, and feel so frustrated in that regard, that it's probably a delusion I create for myself in order to get myself off the hook. . . . On the other hand, there's that great story about the hundredth monkey, do you know it?

TG: No.

JG: Jungian analysts often use it. There was—is—some island out in the middle of somewhere—an actual island—where monkeys used to not wash the tubers they dug up before they ate them. A monkey was taught that skill, and it passed it on to its offspring and immediate group, and so forth. When the hundredth monkey learned the skill, monkeys all over the globe—totally unrelated geographically—started doing it. That's one of the saving stories for me.

TG: That helps me. So you take your task as being not really presenting information about that nothing at all, but more working with yourself, working with the instrument, getting yourself prepared to start dealing with that. Does that make sense?

JG: Yes. Completely. Only there is no way to prepare oneself without actually undergoing the encounter.

TG: Banging your head against it.

JG: It's not like aerobics! It's more like intercourse. You have to do it to become the person who can do it. That's what Keats's "Vale of Soul-Making" refers one to . . . that use of poetry, of composition, as self-creation. Or Stevens's notion of "the poem of the mind in the act of finding what will suffice." That motion towards the opposite in order to complete oneself and forge a *soul*. The ego/unconscious dialectic is only one figure for a deep psychic dynamic which sets most poems in motion, which drives most poets into language. The desire to create one's self . . . Whitman trying to find a body. Stevens writing to recover a mind.

TG: I would have reversed that.

JG: Let's see. Take these two typical images: Whitman's "Sniff of green leaves and dry leaves" and Stevens's "Grapes / [that] make sharp air sharper by their smell." . . . Whitman's line is totally mental—needing the reader to supply the sense-memory that corresponds to *green leaves* and *dry leaves*. Complete with instructions as to *how* to do that work for yourself: "Sniff." Stevens's image, on the other hand, is utterly of and from his body—received by the reader via his or her senses and then translated into the mental construct, idea, that it is. . . . Whitman has always seemed to me a very *intellectual* sensibility writing desperately towards his body to recover it. And Stevens, of course (with those sticky cinnamon buns in his coat pocket!), a poet so fully in the body, in his senses, and moving towards the conceptual and philosophical in order to complete himself—or, rather, in order to *save* himself (since that's what it *feels* like to forge a soul). We tend to define our poets by that aspect of sensibility they actually most lack and strive towards. . . . Williams—a very intellectual sensibility—thrusting himself toward matter— *things*!—cracking them open via fissures in every sentence, between every word almost—enlisting the aid of silence—in order to crack open his very *mental* sense of reality. We tend to think of him, though, or describe him, as the great sensualist, the great advocate of matter. . . . It's the gap, the crack in the sensibility that compels the act of the poem into being. The ambition I was talking about earlier—that so many of us are growing less afraid of and more urgently in need of—is precisely the desire to find (*via* all the accretions, layerings, partial views) a *whole view*, a view which arrives at objectivity via all the failures, all the archaeology of multiple subjectivities—rather than the old (fake?) objectivity of simple representation—representation as a coded statement of beliefs—agendas really—usually the dominant culture's—trying to pass for an objective picture of reality. Ashbery's whole method of course involves this slow incorporation of all the possible subjective points of view— the failures—in order to arrive at this *other* objectivity. . . .

TG: In *Erosion* I'm real clear where the failures are. The girl's memory of ironing breaks apart and the tragedy shows through and you can see what's there. But in *The End of Beauty*, I'm aware of you working the instrument over, showing me the failures of memories or numbers or time, over and over, without the poems ever slowing down enough to examine the one thing that blew the poem apart. In *Erosion* there is one thing that blows the poem apart, but in the next book there are just so many things that are blowing each of the poems apart.

JG: Yes. But I would say that it's the same thing, always, that blows them apart, no? It's what we would call self-consciousness, or the *hero* in the way that I'm using it. The self-portraits are *about* (but the other poems are written *from*) the predicament in which the hero is being sucked back in. The reason the hero needs to be sucked back in is essentially the same in every case. The poem is exploring the limitations of what the hero got to—this imperial, incredibly moving, yet absurd belief that one could seize, in language, the nothing. (And yet that desire is, I think, I hope, also fully represented in the poems.) And so, there are actions in many of those poems which are the hero going: "Look, I can still do this. Here we go." And then there are actions which are the sucking under, and *they're* different in every poem. And there are poems in which the hero remains victorious. What we're talking about in all this, of course, is what the *style* of the poems is about. We're allegorizing the formal elements.

TG: Yes. . . . You've written, elsewhere, about the important role silence plays in your work. About how you go about trying to "activate" the silence.

JG: Yes. Making the silence come awake in the poem is important to my process. The silence—or anything else that resists the impulse to imagine, own, transform.

TG: And the way you make this silence come awake is by painting for us the moment when you are just about ready to crunch it with words. Is that right? That's what you're drawn to in that Japanese theater. How tempted you are to put words around it.

JG: [*pause*] Yes. Also, lines of breath-length, say, lines that contain up to five stresses, sometimes feel to me like measures that make that silence feel safe. A silence that will stay at bay for as long as it takes to get the thing said. Writing in lines that are longer than that, because they are really unsayable or ungraspable in one breath unit for the most part (and since our desire *is* to grasp them in one breath unit) causes us to read the line very quickly. And the minute you have that kind of a rush in the line (emphasized perhaps by the absence of commas and other interpretive elements) what you have is a very different relationship with the silence: one that makes it aggressive—or at least oceanic— something that won't stay at bay. You have *fear* in the rush that can perhaps cause you to hear the *fearful* in what is rushed against.

TG: I see. Your voice mimes the process by the way it struggles to get out.

JG: What you feel—this is Romantic of course—is the pressure of a silence that might not wait until the end of the line to override you. And so you have to rush those words into it. In this new book, I'm writing mostly in traditional lines again, with less counterpoint from such prose-length units. But the calm assurance of the standard English line has always interested and troubled me. In *Erosion*, the line-length tended to be much smaller than the norm. The voice in that book was, in fact, so aware of the overriding presence of the white space that it just tried to mash words into that space. With great pressure. To create the *sensation* of that gravitational weight. Sternness. Solemnity. As if to build cell by cell a fabric that could take the weight of eternity into it—like human tissue.

TG: Creeley feels like that, too.

JG: I love him. [*pause*] It's the automatic taking on of generic voices, formal devices, musics, that drives me crazy. Using the very devices that make poetry powerful—those soul-creating devices that are, of course, in the process, creators of *humanity*—using those *against* poetry! To not locate yourself in your *personal* sensibility—to not find your driving act—but to just *talk* in some received voice, received music, with its attendant received attitudes, ideas, feelings . . . that is not only an utter waste of time, it's probably damaging to all concerned—reader, writer, even the medium . . . so that with the "new formalists" (so called) it's that sense of having one's head in the sand—(it's all OK folks, these lines are five beats to the line, the silence is beautiful, whatever's in it is not really *terrifying*)—that makes me uneasy. It *is*, of course, also "beautiful." But the silence around most such meters sounds very different to me now. Is there nuclear winter in it? Auschwitz? Screams that will not go out? And the abysses of analogy—fractals—the silent abysses of matter? The easy music—unless it's used with the full weight of its implication—as in the tragic poems of Merrill; or the historical confrontations meter enacts for Walcott; or Rick Kenney's use of science . . . but that banality of easy—meaningless—music . . . it sometimes feels like a lunacy to me. Historically—given our predicament.

TG: Yes. That's what you would call Apollo. Or the mother in "The Veil" who wants to cover up the gap with her story—without realizing there is any sort of problem with that.

JG: What we're talking about, in the end, is the distinction between suffering and understanding, and how we want to merge them in the act of writing a poem. We want to be able to suffer the poem so that the actions that we take in the act of writing are true actions—in order to save ourselves. When Frost says, "After all, what are the ideals of form for if we aren't going to be made to fear for them? All our ingenuity is lavished on getting into danger legitimately so that we may be genuinely rescued": you have to have genuine risks in order to have genuine salvation. What I sense in many poems I read are risks fabricated for the purposes of getting a poem (consumer risks to awaken consumer desire), and what I get therefore is a *salvation* (a form, a discovery, epiphany or failure thereof—a *meaning*) which is of no use to me. What moves me about Roethke, for example, in his mad poems, is the degree to which he has put himself at genuine risk. Now that means actually putting oneself in a poem as a protagonist, rather than a narrator; and in a situation where one might not, in fact, *get a poem.*

TG: You mean a risk with your words—that the words are going to be said and won't hold at all.

JG: That things will be said that sound true, that might even be beautiful, but that aren't true. [*pause*] One needs to be both—the questor in the poem, the protagonist, the sufferer, the one who's lost in the forest of language, and simultaneously (because we can't just write "nothing"), the one who understands enough to guide and shape; though without overunderstanding so that you move too swiftly (automatically) (rationally) towards closure and the whole problem we were talking about earlier; or without creating a form that understands itself so thoroughly (as the middle poems of Roethke's do) that once you set out in that form, the form will simply take you *home.*

TG: The form is no longer an issue, then, is it?

JG: If the poet is safe, if he knows the form can *for sure* get him there, he's not genuinely at risk any longer. Which is what's so extraordinary about free verse. The opportunities for being genuinely at risk and therefore for genuine salvation, or recovery in it, are extraordinary if it is undertaken honestly. [*pause*] "Free verse" seems to me a sloppy name for the formal verse we write which is not in a priori patterns. Would we call jazz simply free classical music? All real poetry is formal—any poet knows that—all mere verse is not formal, whether it be in meter or other counted patterns, or not. The difference concerns more whether the pattern is explicit (or a priori), or implicit (even secret) and created in process (some would say *discovered*—itself a slippery word). . . . There is no "plain speech," however it may ultimately appear to a reader, wherever a genuine form has been wrought from and earned from and stolen from chaos. There *is*, though, the issue of where the particular poet wants chaos represented in his or her work, and to what degree. No genuine form occurs without the honest presence of chaos (however potentially) in the work. Form, when it has power, is form wrenched from its opposite. I happen to favor work in which the potential (or posited) power of chaos is great. Because I believe it is so in the world. It *feels* right to me. So form wrought from a merely suggested, hardly virile, chaos might seem more artificial to me, less trustworthy. A *saying-so*, not a *doing*. But it's a matter of temperament, not—as some polemicists would have it—a matter of learnedness or metrical literacy. It's a matter of the relative weights ascribed to chaos and order in the sensibility of a given poet and how honestly he or she has managed to enact that in his or her use of formal elements—those that move *towards*, and those that flee from, the center. Poetry that doesn't address the battle between God and Leviathan implicitly in its form is as uninteresting to me—and probably as useless and powerless in the world—as any blind acceptance of any status quo. It feels nice, no doubt. You can go home and have dinner and smile at the little ones without fear. . . . But to go back to your question. What's so extraordinary about Stevens, is (among other things) the marriage he's effected between being at genuine risk *and* having all his formal understanding operative— without putting himself in a situation where the formal understanding is such that it's already a contract, where the end is guaranteed. That, to me, is the ideal, and why poetry is such an extraordinary medium for spiritual undertaking.

TG: I wonder why, then, what people like Laurie Anderson are doing makes you uneasy with poetry?

JG: Maybe I just want to be kept uneasy, at a certain level. I'm terribly afraid of the complacency of *this is a story, there's a reason why each thing is happening* . . . and yet I find I have an enormous desire to become innocent in that way again. The relationship between the word and the thing can be very lulling if you decide they're really connected.

TG: That they're married.

JG: That it's a stable marriage. . . . And so I find myself very drawn to situations in which the problems with reference are roiled up. I like to be kept on that hook. Because then when I go to write about anything—and after all, the poems are always "about" something else—the issue of the medium they are enacted in is alive. Then I can (hopefully) undertake whatever the quest of that particular poem with, simultaneously, sufficient doubt and sufficient faith. Under those conditions I feel I might get somewhere. Somewhere tenable. Somewhere trustworthy. [*pause*] Part of what disturbs me in poems that don't work—mine and those of others—is the sense of "you didn't go into it with the issue of language alive; you didn't go into it with the problem of 'saying' implicit somewhere." So I don't care what they arrive at, because the uncertainty principle wasn't operative. Of course, that in and of itself isn't an interesting topic. The nature of the distortion can't be itself the end.

TG: That must be hard to do, to keep yourself honest on that issue.

JG: That is the *whole* problem. [*pause*] You know when I was talking earlier about veils coming off? I feel that really strongly in Berryman's use of different voices. When he puts on each of the voices, there's a certain terrain he takes on, and therefore clues as to what his condition is for, why he's stuck there, how he's supposed to live his life. There's a certain terrain that he can only get to in that voice. The drunk white professor voice permits him to look at God in a particular way. Then his black minstrel voice permits him to look at Him in another. And the ways he sees *through* each of these voices as he's using them, so that he has to, in some of those poems, snap out of that register into a different level of voice . . .

TG: "Come on, now." That kind of stuff. So he makes voice the issue.

JG: Yes. He makes voice the issue and the instrument, and—in that there's no bedrock voice—the terror: that there's no voice with which to approach experience. There's no whole self. And no governing self that straddles and negotiates the various selves but, rather, a constant falling away of different selves into an increasingly relative sense of self: a dramatic self, in other words, but also riddled with perspectivism, insincerity, the fluidities of self-presentation—arbitrary, ironic, endlessly exfoliating. Most moving, to me, is the way in which the poems try to make *form* the medium by which all these terrifyingly relative selves are governed into some kind of a whole that might survive the onslaught of experience. Because clearly a fractured or atomized self can't. We were talking, earlier, about the use of the traditional line, and the ways in which it seems historically problematic to me at this point. In Berryman, though—given how he's fracturing the self—the way in which the line stands as an attempt (constantly shattered in the poem) to recover a sense of self, a nobility—moves me deeply. I've learned so much from that man.

TG: A poem that doesn't acknowledge the problem of saying is perhaps interesting as a document of a life?

JG: Yes—of course—but from a poet's point of view, greedy on behalf of the medium: it cannot push the medium.

TG: Maybe that's why Bishop wrote so few poems. Each of the poems was a new problem.

JG: Exactly. The next poem had to be the next stage in the quest her life was undertaking via poetry—not the life over here and the poem tracking alongside with good binoculars. Now I don't mind that in and of itself. It's wonderful that someone should want to record their experience in poems. But for the medium to remain the antenna of the race, it has to be a medium in which growth is happening, so that the medium itself can be extended into the future. You don't feel like Donne's Holy Sonnets are records of something that occurred prior to the event of the poem. You feel like the moment of confrontation occurred in language—in that particular language—and that language is compelled to push and extend itself in order to make the confrontation happen, to extend itself into the future, to grow. The *life* in the language grows. Rilke is, for me, an important tutelary deity in that regard—in the sense that he will not speak until he's at the act of confrontation. He doesn't speak about wanting to confront and then hoping to confront. He's silent until he's right at it. He's the lip of language going into the unknowable and bringing it back. That's what's so moving to me about Bishop's poems—the ways in which they all take place at boundaries, and are enactments of the ways the ineffable erodes the known, and the known makes inroads into the ineffable. Mappings of the back and forth. Poems which are entirely acts of description, because description is an attempt to go out into it and come back changed.

TG: Acts of description and criticism of description, that's what's wonderful to me about it. But different ways of criticizing description.

JG: Yes. Think of her subtle wounds—where she starts to describe and revises her description. She's stunning in that gesture. So puritanical and calm about such dangerous terrain. Do you know that wonderful poem called "Jerónimo's House"—with the flamenco and the blinds—in which she describes how in between the bars of our prison (the blinds, literally) there are notes, and how the language itself, the names for things, are those bars? And how in between—not in the act of description itself—but in the cracks of it, the thing emerges. You have to undertake an act which you know is essentially futile, in the direct sense: the words are not going to seize the thing. But what leaks in between the attempts at seizure *is* the thing, and you have to be willing to suffer the limits of description in order to get it.

TG: It's amazing how close the two of you are in that—suffering the limits of description.

JG: It's the old idea that the only way to experience faith is through active doubt. You *have* to undertake the encounter with the "monument," and it *has* to remain essentially unknowable. The desire to apprehend it, the act or attempt at apprehension, description—and the failure of that attempt—is the beginning, as she says, of imagination, of *art*.

TG: It's "the little that we get for free." Even as cracked and eroded as that painting by her great uncle is, as she looks, it opens up, and while remaining cheap and worthless, it's got compressed behind it "life itself," or "nothing" you would say.

JG: Exactly. And "Large Bad Picture," with its simultaneous matchstick-strokes and real masts, its view of the world as at once "commerce and contemplation." It's what we were talking about earlier, the male and female view of things merging into one view, a view in which the difference between them is kept intact. They are kept in solution, unsolved.

TG: Yes.

JG: It's also in "Cirque d'Hiver," where the little automatic ballerina is both being "pierced" and yet remains mechanical. What Bishop does to the reader in that poem is very interesting. As you go through it, you see the doll as a machine, then she suddenly has a soul, and she's real, and you empathize, then Bishop restores her to her mechanical status so you withdraw empathy, then she makes her "human" again: by the end, you can't shift back and forth between subjectivity and objectivity any longer; you're compelled to hold both emotions in yourself at once without losing their difference.

TG: Which is trust and distrust of language, holding doing and undoing it in your hand at once. Is Bishop a model, or is it just you're on similar paths and she's helping you see what you're already dealing with?

JG: When I read Bishop, I understood her so completely I realized I had a temperamental affinity with her. My sense of the *border* was utterly confirmed in Bishop, and extended. But the music in her poems, the rhythm—however extraordinary—didn't set me off. My body didn't recognize it. There's a very big difference between poets whose obsessions (obviously they're enacted by the form and only available via the form) are influences or confirm one's concerns as essential issues—and ones whose surface is electric—the ones you read to get charged. I felt in Bishop and in Merwin, and Dickinson and Yeats, confirmation as to the nature of the enterprise. Stevens, though, I read to get charged. His language puts me in contact with my language. The same with Berryman. Eliot. But if I read Dickinson, I can't write at all. . . .

TG: I see what you mean. In Bishop you get the problem and a way of dealing with the problem.

JG: But I also get incredible confirmation. Let's go back to this issue because this one seems important. The relationship between the poem and the reader is what I learned actively from Bishop, the sense of the reader's soul being actually jarred between opposing sensations—*commerce* and *contemplation* were the terms of hers I used for it earlier, I believe—secular and sacred, like a dying animal and like . . . something else. The idea that you could end up, at the end of a poem—if you'd opened yourself up to it in the act of writing—with a different notion of reality and of your role in it: not simply a receiver of the poem, but an enactor of the ritual the poem created.

TG: But you do it with a kind of anxiety that she doesn't have. You don't say "Dear reader"; you say "Dear are-you-there?"

JG: Yes. Her poems posit a willing reader, and for me the reader is one who has heard it all before, who is no longer really capable of extended reading, who is so overwhelmed with stimuli of all kinds he or she cannot receive much else. A reader who can practically no longer tell the difference between something true and something false because of the surfeit, the information glut, the sensoral glut. You have to get that reader's attention quickly. The God I imagine that reader to be is a bored God, bored with the world he created, incapable of attending honestly to prayers any longer. So that the only prayers He might hear are ones that are very quick and to the point. A bored parent, a lover who is about to walk away—that reader. In fact, many of the devices in the poems are intended to work on a silent reader about to put the book down. A reader who doesn't trust language any more as a medium for truth—because of advertising, because of government, because of the atrocities language has carried in its marrow. . . . I felt like those poems were really trying to recover the faith of the reader, his or her good will, his or her quietness.

TG: I see.

JG: Then, perhaps, to move that reader through certain of those stages we were outlining above. But the nervousness in the project comes from that predicament—Bishop assumes a contemplative reader and I cannot do so, in good faith, because even I am not that kind of reader any longer.

TG: Parenthetical comments do that as well, don't they?

JG: Yes. It's an attempt to say "are you there?" to a nonidealist, a pragmatist, a reader who doesn't necessarily even believe in literature; most importantly, though, a reader who doesn't believe that words are telling the truth. *Trust these words.*

TG: This issue of the reader also connects with the problem of obscurity in your work, doesn't it?

JG: I'm often asked, in a kind of aggressive way, why the surfaces have to be so difficult in these poems. Or why I so admire surfaces like *The Waste Land*'s, or Berryman's, or Ashbery's. I think it's because a resistant or partially occluded surface compels us to read with a different part of our reading apparatus, a different part of our sensibility. It compels us to use our intuition in reading, frustrates other kinds of reading, the irritable-reaching-after kind. I agree with Stevens's dictum: "the poem must resist the intelligence almost successfully."

TG: You're asking us to read differently?

JG: Pollock's larger murals provide a good example of the process. Because they are painted in such great detail, if you stand far back enough to "see" the whole painting—its *wings* as it were—you can't see the actual *painting*. But the minute you get close enough to see the painting, the dripwork, you can no longer see the whole canvas. Or not with *frontal* vision. But you *can* pick up the rest of the painting with peripheral vision—which is, of course, a more "intuitive" part of the seeing apparatus. I think he was doing this consciously—that he was trying to compel us to stand at that difficult juncture of whole and partial visions, subjectivity and objectivity if you will—or at least view-from-above and view-from-middle—historical distance and the *present moment*—and use our *whole* seeing mechanism. . . . As with Pollock's surface, poems with resistant surfaces frustrate frontal vision long enough to compel the awakening of the rest of the reading sensibility—intuition, the body. To my mind (to my *hope*) that creates a more whole reader, the dissociated sensibility restored to wholeness by the act of reading. Perhaps you could even say the male and female both suddenly awake in you . . .

TG: There's some risk in that for the reader, isn't there?

JG: Yes. because the whole culture requires us to shut that other part down in order to survive—the intuitive, the female, whatever you want to call it. So that it seems to me a very useful political act to write poems in which the resistance of the surface compels that other aspect of our sensibility awake.

TG: The trick then is for you to get yourself in that position where someone will read you long enough.

JG: Yes. And stay with it. That's what all the elements of sound and lyricism are for—the whole seduction: "this is getting darker and darker but stay with me." That's one thing—among many—that Ashbery taught us (of course Eliot is the master in this regard): keep it lyrical, keep the music up, and that sense of *don't worry, this is going to mean* alive. Only music will allow us, as readers, to suspend ourselves out into "incomprehension" long enough to awaken that intuitive aspect of our reading sensibility, and permit us to sense it, feel that it *can* "know." What I discovered in looking at Pollock's painting is that, damn it, peripheral vision is an incredible instrument. It's not just a stunted form of frontal vision. It apprehends totally different things. Imagine how we could see the world if we could awaken our whole seeing apparatus that way. It seems to me a certain aspect of the reading mind has been atrophied at this point in history that was perhaps more muscular when people read the Bible regularly, because of a certain peripheral vision the reading of parable requires, for example.

TG: Try that again about lyric and song, because it goes back to something you were doing earlier.

JG: I was just saying that for me a poem has to contend with its opposite. A poem that touches upon, or flirts with, or arrives at, the disintegration of song and the world view that accompanies it, for example—the "beautiful" one—has to actively contend with it. Then, in arriving at a darker vision, it has arrived there honestly. Or if, conversely, it arrives at the purer vision— the well-wrought urn—what it has arrived at is a *truth* only if it has made the pure vision contend with the darker one. At any rate, sufficient tension can be generated by music to make this kind of "authority" happen. If the vision of chaos prevails in the strategy for example—for example, if we don't get a narrative thread or a governing metaphor to follow—we will stay with the poem (and the experience the poem is permitting us to have) if we get a music we can stay with, an articulate music. The reverse, of course, is equally true. [*pause*] I know it seems crazy in poems as noisy as mine, but I really do try to keep music alive above all else. What that does for me is keep a very particular kind of desire alive. The minute I'm writing lyrically—or trying to make sure a lyrical thread is alive in the poem—a certain kind of hope is alive in me.

TG: And then as soon as you start hoping for it you've got to challenge and defend it, don't you?

JG: Yes. But keeping song alive is keeping alive a world in which song is possible. You have to keep hope alive. Any kind of truth you might arrive at that hasn't contended with hope is going to be very partial. [*pause*] Michael Palmer is very interesting in that regard. He has extraordinary music. I think he's learned better than anyone the Stevens trick of making the poem disintegrate on the surface but stay totally alive musically. To me he's very important in that regard. The way he uses repetition. The particular way he will bring certain images back without that turning into structure. Pure desire kept alive in the act of writing by the way fragments recur.

TG: His sense of contention seems different from yours.

JG: I don't know. I know what I learned from him, which is the way in which a line is a medium for desire of a completely different order than the sentence. In *Notes for Echo Lake*—especially in the poems of that title ("He would live against sentences" for example, which is "Notes for Echo Lake 10," I believe)—he uses silence to make each line audible in poems which are specifically about the disintegration of the kind of desires the use of the line implies. . . . You hear the line, and the desire for order it implies, the desire for History—the desire for the English version to have been right!—

all the enormous upswelling of "Oh, let's make the thing beautiful and leave it at that"; the four-stress line coming in to practically make you weep with the "Oh, couldn't it just have stayed there?" Who wouldn't want to put their head in the sand—on that level—and just make beautiful things? He manages to almost make fun of that desire and yet he's joying in the instruments of that desire. Duncan, of course, does much the same thing—but not as radically. I decided, after rereading them (and *Paradise Lost!*) that I had to go back to the line, had to contend with all the implications of the line, not just the sentence. The ambitions and desires of that kind of time . . .

TG: And see if they hold up?

JG: Oh, they hold up! No, more to see what they can teach me to believe in. The temptation to trust beauty of that order—well—it's very Republican! [*laughs*] I forgive the "new formalists" everything, therefore, because they really want it all, on some level, to have *been all right*. I've had to raise that specter vividly for myself—to make sure I understand it, know it in myself. Here is beauty, and here is order, and here is the made thing and the one-on-one relationship between language and the world. Let's love it again, let's roil that classicism up again. I didn't want to get so far that my desire and passion for that was extinguished. Have you had this experience? At a certain point it's really easy to trust cacophony over mellifluousness. It gets really easy to trust disintegration over the well-wrought urn. So you have to summon that urn again. I have had to write in that kind of music again in order to experience that kind of desire-for-order again, in a real way, not in quotes. So that I might be able to break away again in a different—and newly true—way. I can really understand now what Roethke did—taking on Yeats's voice after the wild poems: how he might want to feel the attractiveness of the illusion again, the non-illusory quality of the illusion.

TG: Let's go back to that Neumann quote you wanted. Did you find it?

JG: It goes like this: "The real source of conflict between the individual and the unconscious"—by individual he means the ego—"lies in the fact that the unconscious represents the will of the species, of the collective, and not in the opposition of the pleasure and the reality principles." I think it's really important to us now, historically, to realize that the female principle, the unconscious, the great uroboric mother (what I was referring to earlier as the female aspect of the poems), is collective. The male part, individual. In my case, it becomes clear to me that the "balloon" the poems in *End of Beauty* were making—combining male and female, the uroboric mother-dragon and the hero rising up out of it as rational consciousness, will, manly spirituality, "the higher masculinity of the head"—that drama, enacts a battle which goes on between the individual tragic hero and the chorus. In writing them I kept having this image (which I only understood later, coming upon Neumann) of a *group* of women on one side (a sense of collectivity among them, but scary) and a single man on the other, holding up a shield, or a plan, or *an idea*—very alone.

TG: So Eurydice is a collective, many women.

JG: Yes. "Many women" is why I hesitate to talk about it. It starts to make it more political than I would have intended it. But, yes—that sense of the will of the species and the individual will—the battle between them being also the East/West battle. There's always, to me, something crucial about Apollo being Western and Daphne still being Oriental.

TG: Could you push that further?

JG: The Greek myths are so powerful for me because they are located at a moment when the Oriental and the Occidental world views are pulling free of each other in a place where they were married. That sense of the "many-headed foam," as Yeats would have it—the Oriental view, collective, giving in to time (the will of the species)—as opposed to the incredible dramatic and moving rise of the individual free voice—fighting time, or insisting on forging something out of time, *in* time.

TG: And in your poems—

JG: In those poems there's a dance going on between a voice which rises up—an individual voice, of personality if you will, in little expressions like "What do you think?" or "Darling"—that kind of tone—and a voice, an *under-voice* which is much more diffuse, less "personalized." That's part of the same battle we were talking about, given the fact that the cult of personality is one of the weird side effects of the cult of individuality. . . . That push of "species" fate (on the female side) is really quite different from fate in the guise of closure pulling you. In one version, one is propelled by the will of the beginning, one exfoliates off the power of *beginning*, of creation; in the other, one is tugged down indefatigably by the end. The Bible itself is a mixture of Occidental and Oriental views of time; the Old Testament really representing a circular Oriental view that slowly transmogrifies into the Occidental view with the Advent of Christ and linear time and eschatological narrative. One is beginning-dependent, the other ending-dependent. The whole Old Testament exfoliates off the act of Creation, the New fulfills predictions, prefigurations of "something" at the end. The enduring power of the Bible must consist in—among other things—the way in which those two versions of time, cyclical and linear, are married to each other.

TG: And struggle?

JG: And the wonderful struggle, of course, where things that are actually exfoliations off the beginning are being used as prefigurations of Christ.

TG: That's what the beginning of the Gospel of John is all about.

JG: Yes. [*pause*] In this new book the other John, John the Baptist, plays a central role. I guess it's because he's used by Christianity to point forward, though he's actually also pointed back. He's operating in both principles at once, which is why his face has to come off! [*laughs*]

TG: So in the new book you're looking for the point of intersection?

JG: I guess I'm just always looking for *why it happened* and *how it happened*—why we are where we are. Because I believe (in the conventional Jungian sense) that we reenact in our own lives, in the stages of our growth of consciousness, the history of the species, I feel that if I can track in my own individual consciousness reasoning errors, slippages, misreadings, I might be able to find ways of altering them—at the very least in myself, by becoming aware, by understanding how we got here, beached; and maybe not only in myself. Maybe in the *form* of the poem as well—which is, of course, the beginning of *others*.

October 1987

7. Michael Palmer's Altered Words

Michael Palmer also understands that "the renewal of language and the renewal through language" is made possible by an entrance into what he calls "the fragility of signification" (CP, 10, 12). In a series of talks given at the University of Iowa in 1986, from which I've drawn these phrases, he describes that fragility, what we have spoken of, following Cavell, as the finite "conditions of language" (SW, 33), in this way: "We're in a deeply problematic and paradoxical territory when we deal with signification in the poem. We want to point in a certain way, and yet the sign has a certain amount of slippage, loss, and accretions around it that make the thing not a simple task at all, to renew the sign within the poem, to make it as Matisse says in relation to painting, a new sign—the job of the painter" (CP, 10). Exploring that slippage and loss in the poem underhand, Palmer has worked out his own distinctive version of Thoreau's "endless computations of words" (SW, 63) or Ashbery's "ventilated" "code" (AWK, 44). A poem, for Palmer, alive in the thickness of language, "is not simply there to reinscribe something already experienced, but is actually a mode of experience in and of itself" (CP, 8).[1] In his words, "inhabiting the text, the words of the text in the world, and responding to its implications as it unfolds,"[2] Palmer brings us back to Cavell one last time, offering, as do all the poets I have explored, "a further interpretation of finitude, a mode . . . of inhabiting our investment in words, in the world" (C, 61).

One of Palmer's terms for his reflective and critical engagement with the poem as it unfolds is the "analytic lyric"—poetry "address[ing] the problematics of the purely private utterance" (CP, 13) by "taking over the condensation of lyric emotion and focusing it then on the mechanics of language," producing "a critique of the discourse of power, to renew the function of poetry" (CP, 14). The lyric's leaps and stutters and musical thinking, its exploration of language's fragility, have traditionally been used to make visible subtle shifts within a speaker's voice or personality; Palmer proposes that such attentive, exploratory work might also serve to renew everyday language, increasing its signifying capacity.[3] Thus, he remarks in an interview: "I think all of the kinds of meaning that occur in the poem are present throughout language, but that they *become*, in an interesting way—by the fact of their becoming focused in the poem—meanings we can attend to more concentratedly. So it's not that there is something like a different meaning, but certain areas that are throughout language are then made more particularly available to us."[4]

In his Iowa talks, Palmer used the work of two poets to explore the tradition of the analytic lyric he sees himself working within.[5] Both writers could be thought of as responding to the fact "that languages break down"—"a concern that came up most dramatically and poignantly with the attempt to annihilate the Jews in World War II and the attempt by Hitler to appropriate an entire language" (CP, 12). Palmer's first example is Edmond Jabès who addresses "the impossibility of writing after the Holocaust" by working within "a dispersal of voices . . . a theater of the page . . . [a set] of fragments, of unanswered questions, incompletions and fractures, in a structure of loss" (CP, 13). As Palmer sees it, Jabès's entrance into this area is a "response to the appropriation of language in his time" (CP, 13), and thus a response to what that loss makes visible of the human condition. Palmer writes: "The sense of the word within this structure is one with an infinite series of possible regressions behind it with this hope of recovering the meaning of words in a time when words have lost their meaning. He constructs exactly out of what is considered the non-discursive, the spaces between things, the junctures, the breaks and fragments" (CP, 13–14). Palmer is also drawn to

> a poet like Paul Celan, who constructed a body of work where he addresses, in a radically different way from Jabès, the question of the self in language, the lyric self in language. Where Jabès creates this dispersal of voices across the page, Celan creates this concentration, almost an implosion—because Celan is writing in a language destroyed by fire, the speaker destroyed by fire. His response to the discourse of totalitarianism is to create out of the German Expressionist tradition a body of intensely concentrated lyric poetry which addresses the reconstruction of human speech. I was fascinated and very much moved by the sense of the dispersal of the subject, but also the reaffirmation, the fact that it was nobody's voice and yet it was, also, something—again and again and again. (CP, 14)

In the name of "recovering the meaning of words" or "reconstruct[ing] . . . speech," then, the two writers both display and reflectively inhabit the fragile, darkly resistant textures of our linguistic condition.[6] So, too, does Michael

Palmer, as we will see in looking closely at the quite different approaches to the "fragility of signification" demonstrated in his four most recent books.[7]

Let's begin with the title sequence from *Notes for Echo Lake* (1981)—a poem in twelve parts, the poems spread across the length of the book and forming a reflective year, of sorts, within language.[8] As we have already seen in working through the first section of the poem, Palmer is attempting to "reinvent attention" to language by "work[ing] . . . with no confidence" at a self-portrait (EL, 5, 3). Prompted by that lack of confidence to "begin again and again" (EL, 3), he juxtaposes Wittgenstein and Ovid's Narcissus and Echo with bits of his own background (a woman makes an unsettling proposal, the two of them walk uncertainly beside a grey wall) and creates not a sustained narrative but a way of attending to or "liv[ing] in" language "below the order of the sentence" (EL, 4). Folding together disparate remarks, the poet begins to create not an account of himself but an account of "a dead language open[ing]" (EL, 5) up in uncertainty. "Notes for Echo Lake 1" links the image of that wall with both the poet's present-tense attempt to write about his life ("a kind of unlistening, a grey wall even toward which you move") and the unsettling charge that he (the poem's "he") had been self-absorbed ("A kind of straight grey wall beside which they walk, . . . he carefully unlistening"—EL, 3, 4). An element in both accounts, the grey wall functions as an acknowledgment of limits—memory or one's inward turning raising a barrier between yourself and what you would touch or describe. As we concentrate on it in the remaining sections, we can track the response to limits this poem explores.

When "Notes for Echo Lake 2" (EL, 11–12), then, begins to listen at that wall, we must keep in mind all of the various aspects of using language without confidence which are being addressed. The erotic and the linguistic, the remembered and the observed, are simultaneously in play as the wall is freed from any single account and becomes an element of the poem's investigation of itself:

> He would assume a seeing into the word, whoever was there to look. Would care to look. A coming and going in smoke.
>
> A part and apart.
>
> Voices through a wall. They are there because we hear them what do we hear. The pitch rises toward the end to indicate a question.
>
> What's growing in the garden.
>
> To be at a loss for words. How does the mind move there, walking beside the bank of what had been a river. How does the light.

And rhythm as an arm, rhythm as the arm extended, he turns and turns remembering the song. What did she recall.

It was of course the present the sibyl most clearly saw, reading the literal signs, the words around her, until a further set of signs appeared. And to divine the fullness of the message she uttered would demand of her listener an equivalent attention. The message was the world translated, and speaker and listener became one. Her message was the sign itself.

. . . .

They walk beside departure and images of a dry riverbed unfold, voices through a wall arm in arm.

What does the poet hear? What does he notice? In being "at a loss for words," walking beside the wall of his own acknowledged "unlistening," he finds that his "mind move[s]" in ways he had not expected. Walking with no confidence, he is granted "a seeing into the word," into its "coming and going in smoke"[9] and becomes, like Whitman, "a part" of the language game and at the same time "apart": both in and out of the game. The poet remembers hearing voices through the wall or in that uncertain smoke: voices not quite distinguishable but marked by risings and fallings in pitch. Those dissolved voices in smoke remind him of the sibyl and her ability to read, within her own smoky fumes, "the literal signs, the words around her." Just so the poet, his confidence in his self-presentation emptied, reads his own words, listening to the voices below them or sounding through them, voices initially held at a distance but now freed. Like the sibyl, "demand[ing] of her listener an equivalent attention . . . [to] the sign itself," he calls the reader to attend to the "Sign that empties itself at each instance of meaning, and how else to reinvent attention" (EL, 5).

How is the sibyl a model for a poet charged with saying something about himself? What "sign" does she call him to attend to? In "Notes for Echo Lake 3" (EL, 15–17) we return to the uneasy moment with which the poem began: the young man who, having been accused of "never look[ing] anyone in the eye," responded by saying something defensive and "eye[ing] a literal self among selves" (EL, 3). He responded by taking the self as something literal and firm. He looked people in the *I*. Now, *I* becomes a sign that must be read, one "emptied" by the challenge of a lover or by the poet's failure to complete a task, its back, as the poem previously noted, having been broken by a fall that left it a "motionless form" (EL, 5) that must be studied now and awakened to consciousness again: "And I as it is, I as the one but less than one in it. I was the blue against red and a voice that emptied, and I is the one with broken back." *I* is a wall with voices behind it, or a smoky intersection of voices that "come in smoke and go": "Eyes eyeing what self never there, as things in metaphor cross, are thrown across, a path he calls the path of names." To look someone in the eye and to look closely at the *I* means involving oneself with multiple voices "rising and falling." Think of Narcissus staring at his pool; what he peers into is that ongoing conversation we call language. His *I* is reflected back by a multitude of voices, coming and going in smoke. What composing an *I* or looking someone in the eye is about, then, is entering that conversation, the process of give and take within the sign: "The letters of the words of our legs and arms. What he had seen or thought he'd seen within the eye, voices overheard rising and falling. And if each conversation has no end, then composition is a placing beside or with and is endless, broken threads of clouds driven from the west by afternoon wind." This sequence, with its notes endlessly placed "beside or with" other notes, is an example of just such a coming and going in the smoky place where *I* has been dissolved.[10] Because "In the [empty] poem he learns to turn and turn," attention perhaps has been "reinvent[ed]."

"Notes for Echo Lake 4" (EL, 22–24) at first comes as a shock, as the patient (if riddling) series of propositions and memories is suddenly erased by a barrage of questions. Then we remember that, as "Notes for Echo Lake 2" indicated, what can be heard through the wall are questions: "The pitch rises toward the end to indicate a question." What questions? They seem to be those of the first erotic encounter—"Who did he talk to / Did she trust what she saw / Who does the talking / Whose words formed awkward curves"—but they also seem to address issues raised in the act of writing: "Was poetry the object / Was there once a road here ending at a door." When *I* speaks, who does the talking? In a space where "poetry" seems no longer the object and where "road[s]" lead to no single destinations, that is the sort of unsettling, stance-dissolving question one hears through the wall:

Who told you these things

Who taught you how to speak

Who taught you not to speak

Whose is the voice that empties

At the same time, a series of statements is quietly inserted in the explosion of questions, as if to note that the poet's writing situation is indeed being unfolded. The hand-in-hand couple continues to walk, attentively, along the grey wall of his unlistening: "Thus from bridge to bridge we came along

/ . . . The light is lovely on trees which are not large / My logic is all in the melting-pot / . . . I must remember to mention the trees / I must remember to invent some trees." The space where logic has melted and things combine and recombine in a grand, unhooked conversation is both poem and memory, held together in this unfolding investigation, bridge to bridge, voice-lost-in-smoke placed beside voice-in-smoke.

The next part, "Notes for Echo Lake 5" (EL, 28–29) shifts its mode of investigation yet again, proposing that in a space such as this, where the poet "lays the text aside," "a sonata for tongues," produced by "correcting the right notes in order to get them wrong," might be heard. One might think of that sonata as a corrective to a too-confident resting in language. Here is one set of lines:

> Today is an apparent day of empty sleeves and parallelograms, and red
> meaning red, and the flag as an object, and red instead of red, the flag as
> an object with undulating sides, the spider who taught me to walk, the
> emptiness of the code, the spider who forgot how to walk, the delicate
> curves within the code, three barking dogs, the mystery of intervals, the
> absence of a code, the lion asleep at her feet, the empty sleeve waving,
> the bottle now broken, the voices she told him to listen for, the stolen
> book, the measurement of intervals.

Getting notes wrong—that is, freeing himself to write in such a way that red also means not-red and thought can progress by sound (taught, forgot)—the poet "listen[s]" to what might be investigated beneath the *I* or its orderly sentences. He listens to what he has written. What had been straightforward and "apparent" gives way, and something live and mysterious appears. Objects begin to undulate, the code's authority is emptied, and "delicate curves" and "intervals" appear within it. At the same time, we are back in the original moment of embarrassment, the young man suddenly struck by the open spaces within language that he had not previously listened to. Behind the straight wall, within the eye or *I*, under the sentence or within the sign, one discovers delicate intervals. In them, the poem proposes, language halted and no longer doing "work," one can listen to the code, measure its gaps or "intervals."

"Notes for Echo Lake 6" (EL, 35) is a bit of description, perhaps of one of the bridges the couple had walked toward as the poem began to move. Placing it "beside" the emptied, measured code discussed in "Notes for Echo Lake 5," we might read it as a description of what happens when the code gradually empties and language is allowed to weave and curve. Here is part of it:

> A tree's streaming imitates light. Water gathers light behind the arm. The arm is 'held' there. Water bodies light to divide. Light measures by resemblance. Water filters bridge as in left-handedness. Light alters it. Water patterns bridge against its step. Hills cancel redness. Body empties and divides. Body's shift patterns bridge this river is called. Here trees cancel bodies light sometimes marks. An angle occurs in selection. Here trees are marks. Here trees begin a cancelled pattern.

What is going on here? The woman, bringing him up short, has forced him to attend to the play of voices within any one sign. He becomes a Narcissus staring down at what had been a stable reflection. On a bridge, we see a body of water, trees reflected in the water, the play of light. That is, we pause and reflect on what he sees: reflection's delicate, self-canceling curves. If we follow the light's reflective play on the water, or, to put it more accurately, the way "water bodies [gives embodiment to] light," we are able to think with the poet about language. Like words, the water "gathers light" and holds it; it "divides" the light, setting it free to "measure by resemblance"; it allows light to establish and then "cancel" patterns or series of marks. Which is to say, as the bridge's reflection in water shifts with the play of light and the angle of the viewer, as trees on the shoreline begin and then break a reflected pattern, the poet (as Narcissus) is brought again into the emptying of the sign. The body of the water "empties and divides" the light, but it is an emptying that, like voices in smoke, can be entered.

A difficult, unbroken block of prose in "Notes for Echo Lake 7" (EL, 39–40) develops the figure a bit farther. In "Notes for Echo Lake 1," loss of consciousness and a shattering of both the young man's and the poet's verbal confidence had been associated with falling or a fallen form: "Language reaches for the talk as someone falls. A dead language opens and opens one door." Tugging various trains of that imagery together, the poet asks himself in this block of prose what Narcissus might discover if he fell into the self-emptying play of reflection. What would reach for him if he fell from this bridge? What does it mean to say that, confidence gone, the code erased, language reaches for you as you fall? Let me excerpt a portion of this section that seems to address these issues:

> So this was the story is a story gibbous moon 1:10 AM he falls toward the world from a bridge yes god made me not a tooth in my head

what next grey dog barks while sphere inside sphere rusts beside the
fence god unnamed me in a snit but I woke up then left arm bent
behind my back clear sky overhead so this is this . . . words and blood
commingling leaves not green but dull and dark boughs twisted and
gnarled we climbed to a hilltop obscured by mist sat and talked nothing
more muffled concussion of guns a few miles off gentle breeze scented
with rosemary and sage grey dog barks at a rock fell from a high place . . .
sign that empties sitting and talking nothing more fell toward the world
itself right arm extended to protect his face grey dog barking at the clock
shattering of glass beyond the courtyard wall followed by laughter . . .
broken words after language wide toothless grin open words after
language

Getting the words wrong, and therefore potentially correct, the poet simulta-
neously seems to be writing about his young man/Narcissus at the bridge, the
memory from "Notes for Echo Lake 1" of falling near a fence, and the idea of
"open words" within an emptied "sign." What happened is that "we climbed
to a hillside obscured by mist sat and talked nothing more." But within the
figure being unfolded here, the act of uneasily sitting and talking in the sibyl's
mist is at the same time a kind of falling—both into the world ("he falls toward
the world from a bridge," "fell toward the world itself") and into language
("broken words after language, . . . open words after language"). That is, as
the young man falls and as the poet stalls and looks down at the "broken
words" of his "motionless form," the world itself is discovered. What do we
see when the code is emptied of its authority and intervals where nothing is
held appear? We see the world.

"Notes for Echo Lake 8" (EL, 48–52) displays that broken, fallen-into
language as a sort of glossolalia-like explosion.[11] Listening carefully, we hear
what seems to be the young man, perhaps on that hillside in the mist, racing
through the possibilities of the potential affair. Early on, we hear a debate
about *if*: she has apparently asked him if he is interested (or *perhaps* she has;
we never really know, nor does he):

Is if if if if and when if and when
If if if he is
If if if he says what it is
Whenever there's permission
Is as if
Says he is as if
Yes if she says it

Soon we hear:

> If if if and when if and when
> What then
> Had seemed to return her interest
> What then
> It seemed to serve her interests
> I do remember
> Yes

But then later, as if there had been a misinterpretation, we hear: "Everyone said never / Never never again and again / And throughout the winter each said one sentence." What has happened, it seems, is that in writing the poet has lived through, again, the live opening up of language, the uncertain interval yawning open when the young man was unsure how to proceed: "There is exactly what is said / There is this and what resembles it / There is a certain distance." This is the same distance generated by beginning each set of notes over again, handling the linguistic investigation with a series of deliberately fresh starts; it is a distance that, like a wall you hear through or smoke you see through, both opens and fills. As "Notes for Echo Lake 9" (EL, 57) summarizes in a single, contrasting line, in falling consciously into linguistic complication and second thoughts, one wakes to the fact that one is surrounded by language: "Was lying in am lying on I is I am it surrounds." When you work without confidence you hear voices through a wall. You hear the language that you are "in" or "on," the language that "surrounds" what "I is" or "I am." The language you tell lies in is also the language you lie on. So Narcissus learns, falling from the bridge into the reflective water; so the poet learns falling without confidence into language as he tries to describe himself. Properly unsure of words, you eye not a "literal self" but a self lying in language.

"Notes for Echo Lake 10" (EL, 62–64) pulls many of these threads together. In a way, it is an answer to the request to "tell us about yourself." And what the poet tells us, in the first line, is that he had fallen into a decision to dwell in the open, broken spaces of language. He discovered as a young man, and discovers now as he writes and remembers, a desire to live against language's straightforward drive: "He would live against sentences." A way to put that, in terms of the figures of this poem, is that Narcissus, young man on the bridge, falling into his reflection as into language, learned to listen to the swirl of tongues below the sentence. Here is part of that development:

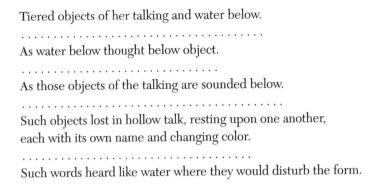

Tiered objects of her talking and water below.

. . . .

As water below thought below object.

. . . .

As those objects of the talking are sounded below.

. . . .

Such objects lost in hollow talk, resting upon one another,
each with its own name and changing color.

. . . .

Such words heard like water where they would disturb the form.

To live against sentences is to notice that "objects of her talking" are "lost in hollow talk." But it is also to go on and note the deep pool of water below where the talk is echoed and sounded again, dispersed into other voices and connections and analogues and associations. Allowing that dispersal to happen, when you've been brought up short, is both to admit to the loss of the object of speech in "hollow talk," shifting and changing and sliding through smoke, and to discover words, "each with its own name," changing. It is to come alive in finitude. Those broken, colored words both "disturb the form" of an intended exchange and reveal a new sort of music, language extending the possibilities of utterance: "And a music or music beneath the hill, an 'order of feeling' possibly: / shape corner floor rock / wind idea lip arm / he would twist against or in / . . . He would live inside the well." In entering the well of language's loose body, in twisting against or in it and making it visible, one might discover and learn to inhabit ("shape corner floor rock") a new "order of feeling." "Twist[ing] against or in" language: such is the life discovered in this writing.

Much in the manner of John Ashbery, Notes 11 and 12 function as summaries, rounding out the figure. "Notes for Echo Lake 11" (EL, 68–69) juxtaposes a series of descriptions of what one does in the space of uneasiness or erasure. If you pull a few of the strands out they reveal themselves as clearly parallel, but in context we find ourselves in a place where logic seems to have dissolved in the melting pot. The first sentence, for example, begins: "An eye remembers history by the pages of the house in flames, rolls forward like a rose, head to hip, recalling words by their accidents." At first, this language seems to slide away from itself, but if we think about the connection between eyes and words and their unraveling in this poem, we see how such a collision of words can be unfolded. The *I* (or the initially unseeing eye) of these notes has learned to remember his own history not through the stable but blank wall of confident memory, but rather through "pages . . . in flames." In fact, he has come to dwell in that collapsing "house," where words do their work by "accident" and echo, where movement "forward" is that of a "rose" continually unfolding rather than a straight shot from here to there. There, "head to hip" like Whitman's embrace of the Me Myself, language comes fully and erotically alive. It is "recalled" to potency. Through such accidents, or as this poem goes on to put it, through growing "accustomed to the spells of dizziness" and becoming "used to falling unexpectedly," one learns "to listen to the words until you hear them."

The final set of "Notes for Echo Lake" (EL, 79–90), twelve poems of twelve, often nonconsecutive lines—"empty twelves"—seems to ponder what happens when a live experience is worked in this manner into language and a poetics. We return at points to the young man entering into language out of his confusion—"Stumbling whispered awkwardly in her ear" (EL, 79), "A bare murmuring at his ear / She mentioned she was now perfectly alone" (EL, 89), "He asked her and asked her" (EL, 90)—but now what we ask about is how it feels when the experience is rendered permanent and empty, dead: "I slept through her death it's said / In sleep I invented her death / . . . Someone has apparently died for art / Though nobody seems certain who or why" (EL, 80–81). Much like Ashbery reflectively reviewing his work, Palmer acknowledges that his description of himself and various charged events has remained blank, a blank filled now with words, empty words, coming and going. He acknowledges the limits of language. But at the same time, he notes, those words have made visible our place in language, our patterns of behavior there: "blank mid-summer like the years / experienced purely as a matter of words / pasted onto an horizon— / . . . whether loved and kept or not / the patterns crossing and recrossing / whether loved and kept or not" (EL, 85).

If *Echo Lake*, its notes "crossing and recrossing" a space where the poet kept himself at a loss for words, opened a "dead language" to voices below or behind it, the poems of *First Figure* (1984) attempt to renew and enlarge language by imagining it as a sort of ongoing drama that can be observed and entered—"a calculus of variations" (FF, 60) playing off of each other in complex, self-interfering ways. Both are books that try to listen to language and thereby renew it, but in *First Figure*, the poet is more committed to letting language be, joining it as it runs. Many of its poems are framed as commentary on that process. "Voice and Address" (FF, 7–8), for example, thinks about the unstable notion of linguistic certainty by means of the sort of extended analogy lately favored by Ashbery:

> You are the owner of one complete thought
>
> Its sons and daughters
> march toward the capital
>
> There are growing apprehensions to the south
>
> It is ringed about
> by enclaves of those who have escaped
>
> You would like to live somewhere else

No thought is complete and self-sustaining: its offspring, disinherited in the name of clarity and a single focus, always threaten to return, muttering of revolution while other forces whisper opposition from the horizon. Any single idea is ringed about with the outspreading ripples of what cannot be so simply contained. Of course you would like to live somewhere else, but that is impossible. As Palmer puts it at the end of the poem:

> You are the keeper of one secret thought
> the rose and its thorn no longer stand for
>
> You would like to live somewhere
>
> but this is not permitted
> You may not even think of it
>
> lest the thinking appear as words
>
> and the words as things
> arriving in competing waves
>
> from the ruins of that place

If the wish to own complete thoughts is impossible, *First Figure* explores its converse. It asks how we might live in one current understanding of language—acknowledging that the sign has given way ("the rose and its thorn") to multiplicity, that words now come to us as things in themselves, echoing and playing off each other in "competing waves" generated by an initiating action now only visible as a "ruin."

One of the book's metaphors for itself is theater—a space where, along with the poet, we can watch and engage this play of "competing waves / from the ruins" of an initiating "first figure." Theater is a multivoiced expansion of that inaccessible figure:

> you are reading
> in a way natural to theatre
> a set of instructions
> that alters itself automatically
> as you proceed west
> from death to friendliness
> (FF, 4)

But it is a new sort of theater—one in which "Sound decays / and then there is the story / and then the features are erased / . . . Here another festival / to which no one is invited / and where expectation plays no part" (FF, 6). As the initial thought or figure decays or is altered according to some pattern not controlled by its initiator, language both breaks down—"This is the sonnet / and this its burning house / You are in this play / You are its landscape" (FF, 38)—and grows, flowing out in all directions. What would it be like to observe such a drama, without expecting resolution? What would it be like to see the space between language and the world or between an initiating figure and its echoing restatement brought to dramatic life?

> The angled
> areas between them then, cast
> in a range of hues
> that to speech are as distant,
> or dissonant, matter.
> (FF, 40)

The poems go on to claim that in entering into language "as distant, / or dissonant, matter," there are significant gains to be made. "Fractal Song" (FF, 61) suggests that such an expansion of language is useful in a world where "Clouds are not spheres we know / now, and mountains not cones." "French for April Fool's" (FF, 12–16) proposes that a language in which "answers varied moment by moment" might "mirror the weather itself," since landscape is most visible in a place where "the sentence is impossible." Why is that? The poem argues that making the completed sentence impossible or holding open the space between words and their objects eliminates for a time the tendency of writing to fix and simplify. A "range of hues" becomes visible, a grand theater in which "the sentence is there / free at last to occur / in some other direction" (FF, 75). *Echo Lake* called this "falling into the world," through the breaking open of language. "French for April Fool's" uses the image of scent to get at this sense of brokenness and renewal:

> I will juggle limes from the garden and sing as I'm juggling
> The limes will burst where they fall
> Their scent will remain after the event is forgotten
> Their scent will remain after the room has dissolved
> . . . .
> These tremolos have been substituted for writing
> By playing very fast the music remains in place
> The fixed arc is designed to erase

The scent that remains after words have been juggled and dropped, like the competing waves of the tremolos that keep a place open and not "fixed," are images for language working at something different from grasping or mastery. Perhaps language used in such a way lets us live with things, lets us know them, dwell with them side-by-side:

> All those words we once used for things but have now discarded in order to come to know things. There in the mountains I discovered the last tree or the letter A. What it said to me was brief, "I am surrounded by the uselessness of blue falling away on all sides into fields of bitter wormwood, all-heal and centaury. If you crush one of those herbs between your fingers the scent will cling to your hand but its particles will be quite invisible. This is a language you cannot understand." Dismantling the beams of the letter tree I carried them one by one down the slope to our house and added them to the fire. (FF, 20)

Here is the dream of language that *First Figure* investigates—whether words, discarded because they no longer provide direct access to the "ruins of that place," can spill out, when crushed, invisible, powerful scents through which we might once again "know things." For language to become as "useless" as the blue sky it must be dismantled or crushed. This poem suggests, in fact, that if you listen closely to language it will cry out for such a dismantling. It will take us down the arc of its life-giving decay. Perhaps the result might be thought of as what Paul Celan calls, in the epigraph to *First Figure*, "Nobody's voice"—language with its claims of mastery erased for the moment, now able to infiltrate the world and make it habitable.

Let me examine two explorations of this echoing, competing space of linguistic variation. The first poem, "Echo" (FF, 47–52), both defines and embodies the process of enlarging language we have been discussing. The poem echoes, or sounds again, a poem of the same title by Pascal Quignard.[12] More accurately, it continues an echoing chain set in motion by the Quignard poem, returning again and again to an attempt to define language's generative degradation in terms of the metaphor of echo.[13] Language as echo, then, is that "which resounds," "a failure of translation," "an imperfect copy spoken among hills or reassembled there." It is "misunderstood as a measure of distance." It works by "Forgetting the name as it sounds." But in the process of forgetting or imperfectly copying, language grows. It is that

> which resounds. Re-sounds. Where first
> would follow. The letter he had lost reap-
> peared in his palm. Identity was the cause.
> Not that the word spoken had been heard.
> Not that a word spoken can be seen, even par-
> tially, traced against the screen. Language
> copies him in its listening, traces his imper-
> fect copy. Which re-sounds. Echoes briefly.
> The rustling a wall transmits by interference.
> . . . .
> After the
> talking is done a kind of attention to each
> mark, an injured identity traced against the
> screen. . . .

Though "identity"—the attempt to trace a single thought or self or object— is always "the cause" of speech, language gives it back as "lost or injured." Language listens and copies, interferes in order to re-sound and transmit that first word, which of course is only available as what "would follow" not as what comes "first." But, and this is crucial, such distortion and rehandling is how we pay "attention" to words—how we keep them alive and vital. Poetry makes visible the everyday drama in which language, by interfering with itself and making unseen and unheard words sound again, continues to grow and to keep open its ability to respond. Language, thought of in this way as self-echoing delay, is both limited and alive:

> a failure of translation. In sleep the language
> he spoke was one he didn't know. Waking it
> sounded the same. Waiting there it seemed a
> succession of names, a level field of things
> in constant motion, exchanging identities.

So, the poem continues, by an "erasure in the naming," echo displays language as continually responsive because "many-tongued." As yet another echo or "alternate text" (FF, 53–55) for this poem puts it, poetry's opening up of this drama gives us back voice as something still recognizable, but now charged and open:

> She recognized the voice as her own
> resounding in the damp hall
>
> though the rest,
> what the words now said
>
> again and again,
> seemed entirely different.

A second, fairly simple version of this drama of recognition can be found in the poet's analysis of the word *I* in "Left Unfinished Sixteen Times" (FF, 45–46), a poem I touched on briefly in this book's introduction. As with *Echo Lake*, each notation in the poem is one competing wave from the ruins of *I*. Here are a few:

> I is enclosed by the question where it's read as a letter.
>
> I might pretend to be a reading in the letter, its circuit diagram or "music hall full of fun" or weighing of symptoms and costs.
>
> I refers to the pause or loss, the decision that a window will remain closed the better to watch.
>
> I thought it would be nice to make some chemicals, to make some lexical adventures to enlarge the space, then reside forever in the silence of the letter.

The acknowledged fact that *I* is not a stable place makes it possible for the poet to "read [it] as a letter"—skeptically alert to the questions it raises. Through such a reading—weighing "symptoms and costs," diagramming the dizzying circuits (or flow chart) of the *I*'s implications and allegiances, continually acknowledging the pause or gap in which the *I* operates—the *I* might "pretend" to a certain, if immediately undercut stability. As with Dickinson's analysis of her "soul / Upon the Window Pane," the drama of *I*'s decay will "cast in a range of hues" the *I*'s generative distance from what it describes. Rendering the *I* silent, erasing its authority and foregrounding its music-hall cloud of questions, then, as with Parmigianino's self-portrait, opens up an "enlarged . . . space" within representation where one can dwell. One remembers Stevens's auroras, erasing his cabin and "enlarging the change." Think of the scent of herbs, holding open and sharpening our alertness in the space where the coherent *I* suddenly goes invisible. Seen this way, *I* floats loose in a space within language where language has forgotten its initial hold on things: "It omits or forgets who they are and who the others are who watch. / Then it forgets the words for this and not-this, for first and for again."

When we turn to *Sun* (1988) we discover a more charged analysis of linguistic finitude. *Sun* shows the poet as more aware, perhaps, of the political failures of language in our time and thus more acutely struck by what he terms language's rotting and death. If language in previous books dissolved or continually altered itself, here it devours itself or discovers itself "dead . . . / in a blood red bed" (s, 39). Rather than entering a generative sense of uncertainty in order to hear voices behind a wall or tracing the range of hues discovered within an echoing, set-free conversation, this volume situates itself in "a place from which you watch / the burning of your house" (s, 22). What it hopes to discover there is a new sense of alertness, a return to or renewal of language. "Fifth Prose" (s, 5–6), the book's introductory piece, is quite clear about these issues. The poet's troubled eye is on the world, he insists—the snow, not just the well-worn idea that we have, in various cultures, multiple names for it:

> Because I'm writing about the snow not the sentence
> Because there is a card—a visitor's card—and on that card
>   there are words of ours arranged in a row
>
> and on those words we have written house, we have written
>   leave this house, we
> have written be this house, this spiral of a house, channels
>   through this house

But of course, even as his eye is on the snow, what he produces is writing— "words . . . arranged in a row." *Sun* proposes that, by acknowledging the distance between snow and sentence, by producing a poetry of "words only / taken limb by limb apart" emphasizing that distance, it will also open up the linguistic house in which we dwell. More than that, by dismembering and examining what had seemed silent and transparent and confident, these poems will encourage us to "be" that house, perhaps to "leave" it, certainly to find "channels through" it. The book, then, will present "ordinary extracts from the [linguistic] tablets" often caught at moments of revealing failure: "Hassan the Arab and his wife / who did vaulting and balancing // Coleman

and Burgess, and Adele Newsome / pitched among the spectators one night."
In that space between snow and sentence, Palmer continues, our eyes are
crossed—watching both the world and language, both the poet and his
sources. Think of those crossed eyes as Ezra Pound's in "Canto 2" seeing
both a "naviform rock overgrown" and under its edge "Ileuthyeria, fair Dafne
of sea-bords, / The swimmer's arms turned to branches." Or closer to home,
think of the poet in *Echo Lake* "eyeing" both a "literal self" and "what self
never there" (EL, 17):

> Because there is a literal shore, a letter that's blood-red
> Because in this dialect the eyes are crossed or quartz
>
> seeing swimmer and seeing rock
> statue then shadow
> and here in the lake
> first a razor then a fact.

In that space or gap, this first poem proposes, one should be able to see both
the collapse of the language we use to order the world and new channels
through it.[14]

I am going to examine two important long poems in *Sun*: the thirty-five-
page "Baudelaire Series" and the twenty-page "Sun." In the "Baudelaire
Series," the burning house Palmer enters and reflectively dwells within is
nothing short of the modern lyric, that response to loss that Palmer (and all of
us) has teethed on. In the interview in chapter 8, Palmer speaks of the poem
as "an examination of the constellation of voices that have come to constitute
whatever I am as a poet." Perhaps we could say that this sequence brings
language to life by once again listening to broken-off voices heard through
a wall or reading them out of the echoing collapse of linguistic certainty.
But now, those voices and that "range of hues" are made more deliberately
identifiable. Charles Baudelaire, Rilke, Celan, César Vallejo, and Oppen begin
to speak, opening up that space between snow and sentence. They appear
where the poet's language has been taken "limb by limb apart."

By "Baudelaire" or, as he puts it in our interview, "the Baudelairean,"
Palmer would seem to mean the modern—in particular, modernism's sense
of itself as speaking out of a linguistic and cultural collapse. Walter Benjamin's
"On Some Motifs in Baudelaire," which Palmer mentions reading at the time
he began this poem, quite forcefully describes such a view of the artist. For
Benjamin, Baudelaire works in "the interstices between image and idea,
word and thing" (SM, 164) where "subterranean shocks . . . [have] caused

words to collapse" (SM, 164). The artist, like someone plunging through a crowd, is involved "in a series of shocks and collisions . . . nervous impulses flow[ing] through him in rapid succession" (SM, 175). Still holding to the possibility of *"correspondances"*—"a concept of experience which includes ritual elements" (SM, 181)—but testifying to their "breakdown . . . [into] something irretrievably lost" (SM, 181), Baudelaire was charged and brought to life by that collapse. Think of that as being swept up in a crowd and its disintegrative waves of chatter and sensation. Benjamin writes: "Baudelaire singled out his having been jostled by the crowd as the decisive, unique experience. . . . Baudelaire battled the crowd—with the impotent rage of someone fighting the rain or the wind. . . . He indicated the price for which the sensation of the modern age may be had: the disintegration of the aura in the experience of shock" (SM, 193–94). Making poetry out of "scattered fragments of genuine historical experience" (SM, 185), Baudelaire's lyric grew out of "render[ing] the possibility of lyric poetry questionable" (SM, 192).

Palmer's sequence begins, then, with a voice with traces of Baudelaire running through it, looking back, in a sense, to *Les Fleurs du mal*:

> *A hundred years ago I made a book*
> *and in that book I left a spot*
> *and on that spot I placed a seme*
>
> *with the mechanism of the larynx*
> *around an inky center*
> *leading backward-forward*
>
> *into sun-snow*
> *then to frozen sun itself*
> *Threads and nerves have brought us to a house*
> (S, 9)

Let's say that the linguistic *"house"* Palmer finds himself within includes, as part of its heritage, a particular understanding of the sign—*"a seme"*—and of the larger issues of representation itself. Baudelaire is one among many responsible for leading us to say that although the sign points toward a center, that notion, being got at through *"ink"* and the various *"mechanism[s] of the larynx,"* forever recedes.

That tension marks our period; it leads both *"backward"* to the voices we inherit and *"forward"* to the work underhand. It has been imagined by our major writers as city or desert or waste land. *"Frozen sun"* refers us to one of Baudelaire's versions of this idea in "De Profundis Clamari":

I share this night with blasphemy and dread.

A frozen sun hangs overhead six months;
The other six, the earth is in its shroud—
no trees, no water, not one creature here
a wasteland naked as the polar north!
(B, 36–37)

In the linguistic world represented by such an arctic landscape, to return to the Palmer poem, there is *"No need to sail further"* if we are driven to *"protest . . . here and there against some measures / across the years of codes and names"* (S, 9). We have arrived already; we are caught in the crowd, those measures and codes and ways of naming stretching *"backward-forward"* every way we look. Baudelaire's "A Voyage to Cythera" (B, 134–36) imagines this as arriving at Aphrodite's island and seeing "a branching gallows tree" where "ferocious birds / were ravaging the ripe corpse hanging there, / driving their filthy beaks like cruel drills / into each cranny of its rotten flesh." That corpse, in some sense, is the poet's—his own "insulted limbs" hang there. The collapse of codes and names *"around an inky center"* has brought him to a place where bodies and selves give way. But, Palmer goes on, extending Baudelaire's prophecy, perhaps in *"eating the parts of him"*—the sign disintegrated, the self lost, the aura disintegrated, words torn limb from limb—one might move through that death, and might even bring back *"the lost state."* To recall Celan, one might recover nobody's voice, here at the sign's inky center, dreaming a new sort of dream with *"nobody . . . in it."* (S, 9).

"A hundred years ago I made a book." One of the other voices present in this opening poem is Hölderlin, also speaking *"backward-forward"* about this sense of dismemberment or unraveling as generative protest. Palmer characterized Hölderlin this way in his Iowa City talk:

> In one of the fragments he writes *Es fesselt / Kein Zeichen*, which Richard Sieburth in his recent edition of those last, late fragments translates as *No sign / Binds*. It struck me as one of the sources of the modern lyric and certainly of German Expressionism. It just popped out at me, this notion of disintegration of faith in the sign. In Hölderlin's case, he's talking about the metaphysical relationship of the sign, the fact that earth and heaven no longer connected, that you could no longer talk to God, that our signs do not translate in the literal ecclesiastical sense of *translatio*: the bearing across from one realm to another. And that equally we cannot read the signs of God in the world anymore. And

it struck me that, in his context, the unravelling of the sign was involved with the unravelling of the subject, because Hölderlin is about to enter into madness, and many of the works he will write in his madness he signs with the name *Scardanelli*, in whatever kind of schizophrenia he was in, and dated them in the 20th century, which in its own curious way was an extraordinary prophetic event. Extraordinary in the sense that he projected this disintegrated subject into the next century where it would have so many manifestations. (CP, 11)

Both Hölderlin and Baudelaire link an "unravelling of the sign" with "the unravelling of the subject"—whether into a dismembered body, or nobody's voice, or schizophrenia. For Palmer, they are the "prophets" who open the linguistic house we live within, "sources of the modern lyric." We can go one step further with the Hölderlin echo, for if we turn to the translation that Palmer mentions, we find in Richard Sieburth's introductory comments to his translation of Hölderlin's *Hymns and Fragments* a possible source for one of the ways the "Baudelaire Series" will enter that issue of the sign's collapse:

As Heidegger observes in his commentaries on Hölderlin, men and gods, at once distinct and interdependent, come into being through each other, for in the space defined by their reciprocal difference lies the poetic act of *naming* that grounds or inaugurates (*stiftet*) their relation (*Verhältnis*). . . . In the new dispensation brought about by the death of God the poet's role is no longer to receive the fire from on high and offer it on in song to his fellow men; instead, he has now become the guardian of the empty intersection that defines the mutual infidelity of gods and mortals. . . . For if the sign may be defined as the compound of a presence (the "signifier") and an absence (the "signified"), then the very disappearance of God as ultimate ground or guarantor of meaning enables poetry to become conscious of the radical dispossession—and the vertiginous autonomy—of its own discourse. . . . As an activity of *naming*, poetry does not so much imitate or represent or symbolize something beyond or prior to itself, but simply *says*, and, in so doing, establishes a site where what is said is all that lasts. (H, 20, 22)

As we will see, what Palmer does in the "Baudelaire Series," responding to the issue that Baudelaire's and Hölderlin's voices put into play, is examine not what language *names*—that is, what it "grounds or inaugurates" as relation— but what it *says*: that is, its way of occupying its vertiginous, radically dispossessed site, the charged space between snow and the sentence.[15] Language protests or takes itself "limb by limb apart" by saying itself, "eating" (and being nourished by) its own parts. In the twenty-eight poems that follow, such phrases as "Words say" or "The poem says" or "The persons of the poem say" or "You say" or "we say" or "Someone says" are heard repeatedly. So, too, buried quotations continually surface and pull the poem forward, having their "say." All of this is an attempt to fully inhabit the arctic land in which we dwell, perhaps *"bringing back the lost state"* (s, 9).

What do words say? If I cannot really name—if, in fact, I am the language that courses through and around me, and I can only intervene by pointing out the mechanism—then what do I hear words say? The early poems in the sequence, laced with bits of Baudelaire, raise this issue. The first poem after the introductory, italicized poem, for example, begins like this:

Words say, Misspell and misspell your name
Words say, Leave this life

From the singer streams of color
but from you

a room within a smaller room
habits of opposite and alcove

Eros seated on a skull as on a throne
(s, 10)

Words, or the modern lyric Palmer works within, say: "Misspell your name." That is, acknowledge as you write your inability to name; die to a life in language ("leave" it) that had seemed secure. Our words now say to us that we voice not the Orphic singer's "streams of color" but Eliot's lament in "Gerontion" for the captive "word within a word, unable to speak a word"— here, "room within a smaller room." Baudelaire's "Eros and the Skull," from which the last line here is quoted, reads an old colophon of Eros sitting on humanity's skull gaily blowing bubbles as an image of love producing "frail and luminous" thoughts out of the brain's "flesh and blood" and then setting free those words—"each globe as it mounts / explodes, spattering" (B, 136–37). Words say that such a spattering is inevitable. But, the poet goes on, think what is to be gained by being wary and attentive here, in Hölderlin's charged, empty intersection:

Never sleep never dream in this place

and altered words say
O is the color of this name

full of broken tones
silences we mean to cross one day
(s, 10)

Words "altered" by our allowing them to speak rather than holding them tightly say that we can dwell in "broken tones" and "silence"; they offer not the green success of Orpheus but the receptive "full[ness]" of the color of zero, or nothing. One poem in the sequence describes that room of broken tones as a place where "my head is enlarged / though empty of thought" (s, 19). Another insists that it is only in such brokenness that we can speak precisely: "There is much that is precise / between us, in the space // between us, two of this / and three of that" (s, 26).

Another of the Baudelaire pieces picks up a bit of "Her Hair" (b, 30)—an attempt to follow the scent of a woman's hair to "torpid Asia, torrid [burning] Africa / . . . a harbor where my soul can slake its thirst / for color, sound and smell"—and suggests that such a rich world might come about as the self dissolves (or misspells itself) into the flood of voices surrounding it. One can hear Rilke's "Panther" here, Wittgenstein's fly unable to find its way out of the fly-bottle of linguistic habit, Palmer's own failed *Echo Lake*, and George Oppen's struggle with Alzheimer's. In a way, the ruined book, blank mind, failed poem, and trapped thought all do similar things—spill open into the various figures of "fullness" and "flow":

Dear Lexicon, I died in you
as a dragonfly might
or as a dragon in a bottle might

Dear Lexia, there is no mind

Dear Book, You were never a book
Panther, You are nothing but a page
torn from a book

Stupid Lake, You were the ruin of a book

Dear Merline, Dearest Lou, Here the streets
have their fullness and their flow
like a blind man on a carousel
. . . .
Dear Merline, Dearest Lou, I see a pheasant on the fence
as I'm writing this
as I see burning Africa by chance

in a cooling wind
. . . .
Dear George, So long
Will you now have memory again
(s, 12–13)

Perhaps, the poet continues in another poem, such a rich dying into words—"see[ing] burning Africa by chance / in a cooling wind"—would return one to Baudelaire's world where "the sounds, the scents, the colors correspond." About such a possibility, Palmer speculates: "What if things really did / correspond, silk to breath // evening to eyelid / thread to thread" (s, 17). Words would say of that dream: watch yourself there, in language, be attentive to how a self is threaded out of and then back into words: "You, island in this page / image in this page // evening's eyelid, silk / four walls of breath // I could say to them / Watch yourself pass // Relax and watch yourself pass / Look at the thread" (s, 16). A version of Rilke's "Orpheus. Eurydice. Hermes," reading Eurydice's release back to the unboundedness of the underworld as a dramatization of how "song broke apart," discovers that words say back to us, if we listen, the attraction of unthreading, the richness of nothing:

I'm not the same anymore

I'm not here where I walk
. . . .
Some stories unthread what there was
Don't look through an eye
thinking to be seen
Take nothing as yours
(s, 24–25)

In such writing, Eliot's apocalyptic refiguring of his own linguistic collapse in section 5 of *The Waste Land*—"Who are those hooded hordes swarming / Over endless plains, stumbling in cracked earth"—is heard as one of the ways language spills its various hues and opens new spaces in which to dwell: "Barely anything to say, everything said. But you break, as a hooded traveller, scattering images across the plain, I among them and the other I's. This prose, a / color sampler, is meant for you" (s, 35). Such a descent into language's collapse allows us to see language at work, the unsayable breaking language along its fault lines into visibility: "How lovely the unspeakable must be. You have only to say it and it / tells a story. / A few dead and a few missing / and the tribe to show you its tongue. It has only one" (s, 37). The poet, concluding the sequence, then, sees himself as: "speaking to you / from this notebook or // journal or Book of the Dead" (s, 42). He has produced something in which:

> the pages are spread out
> before you to dry
>
> Come and look
> Come and see
>
> the pages spread out
> before you in the sun
>
> curled like leaves
> black as tongues
> (s, 43)

And here, I take it, is that *"lost state"* the poem keeps edging toward: a language both broken and free, a single "tongue" we share, "known to you / and . . . made by you" (s, 42). Poetry, through its dying into the lexicon, might return language to its users, might renew it by insisting on its limits: "a language that is ordinary, the same / as language only smaller" (s, 41). As Wittgenstein would have it, such pages, "curled like leaves," might return words to the language games in which they were at home (PI, 48e)—Thoreau's ordinary or common words, words as Cavell puts it, "regained as gone" (IQ, 172).

"Sun," a difficult poem written entirely in fragments, seems an attempt to speak from within what it calls the stream or flood of language set free from naming or holding in place. Imagine that flood as being composed of phrases and images uttered in the past but now torn from their original context and swirling together—in this case Eliot, Robert Graves, Celan, Hölderlin, Oliver Sacks, Benjamin, Rilke, Daniel Paul Schreber, Baudelaire and others. It is a sea or river or a flooding stream, and if the poet desires to enter it—"A bark sets out on the honeycomb's flow / We called it Le Départ" (s, 79)—the way in seems to be through death or an acknowledgment of finitude, the dissolving of "the I who speaks" (s, 62). Thus, there are repeated references to "bring[ing] death into your mouth" (s, 59), or a "headless man" (s, 59), or a "body . . . floating in the sea" (s, 66). Through such a death, one gathers, a poem could be "written entirely inside / the body of another [or others] / its moments free of him" (s, 64). Death becomes a lens to see words anew and set free, an entrance into song: "A man with dynamite strapped to his waist / sings for the first time / lens / question" (s, 72). What the poet seems to do in this poem then, as he weaves his way through a flood of chiming fragments, speaking from within one body and then another, accompanied by an Eliot-like voice booming not "HURRY UP PLEASE ITS TIME" but "The clock is set for 'departure'" (s, 75), is record or describe that flow, that set-free space he finds himself momentarily in. Such a description is like trying to get at the voices behind the wall in *Echo Lake* or trying to chart the play of competing echoes in *First Figure*, but now it moves more freely and desperately, as if channels can be found anywhere.

Let me describe, in turn, a few of Palmer's accounts of the flood. Early in the poem, for example, the poet catches hold of a fragment from Hölderlin—"sky a painter's house" (H, 237)—and uses that poet's late work in which he churned "hymns into fragments" to think about the way saying no to language frees it, as now, to open a new dwelling, wide as the sky, that can be inhabited. Writing and rewriting, breaking free of "scene and . . . mirror," turn language into a "streaming body" (s, 73)—an "indefinite calculus." If I catch the tone right, the poet positions himself as a watcher of the flood:

In a certain way all this still exists
but the scene and the mirror no longer exist

. . . sky a painter's house
No yes

You churn hymns into fragments
No then yes

Asleep you set fire to this house
. . . .
An indefinite calculus
watches, writes and rewrites
(s, 60)

A page later, the poet watches a set of structuralist concerns give way—a search for laws, a decoding of culture's signs—and then follows that death out again into the flood:

B asks, Is the discourse
of objects specific

Can one imagine laws . . .
Can you decode the birth of the sign

from the miniskirt, the unconscious, TV, the
mirage

of the referent, the equation
of A with A

A body disappears into itself
its mirror self or sister self

The marks have no dimension
They stream from the creases of the hand

Let's call this The Quiet City
where screams are felt as waves

plunging or released, a content
and an alibi, a matrix

at zero stains you with ink
My speech explaining the layers went very well
(s, 61)

Freed from "the equation / of A with A," what seems to happen to language here is that as it loses "dimension" it becomes something that can be felt and entered. Its alibis and subterfuges are no longer something that can be kept at a distance—as in "my speech explaining the layers"—but instead whirl across the poet, "stain[ing]" him with ink and its implications.

That zero, once entered, turns out to be a place one can speak from—as here, entering the flood through the dissolution of Dante's Rose:

I nudged Dante off my desk
into the flood. The others quickly followed

streaming from that cafe
once known as The Rose

We spoke in the zero code
system of assemblage and separation

arcuate scar, shadow and necklace
doubled by their reflections

then redoubled in the lens
34,000 words spread out before me

words like incarnadine, tide and cheer
asymptote, laces, tear or tear

waiting to say things
(you cannot say things)
(s, 65)

Another Eliot echo is undone here. Whereas in section 2 of *The Waste Land* the lights off the woman's dressing table were "doubled by their reflection" into a sterile, overwrought deadness, the words here, freed from the "system of assemblage and separation," are redoubled by the "lens" of the poet's attention to their swirling death into a kind of responsive "waiting" before the things of the world. This is Eurydice's waiting, the last line suggests, echoing Palmer's earlier use of Rilke in a sort of welcoming acknowledgment.

As this sequence goes on, Palmer continually pauses to describe the work he is creating. It is a theater in which, as in Ashbery and Stevens, our words are unscripted: "Our pages / burn themselves / as theater / awaiting an extinguishing / mist" (s, 66). Or, it is a circus, in which language, freed from reference, performs its "tactics": "These / new waves circused in a void / placed themselves before us / spoke their tactics / and their practices, traced / each friction and line" (s, 71). It provides a means for language to look at itself—"A word is beside itself / A word twists backward / peeling its skin up over its face / A word looks behind itself" (s, 72)—or for language to open holes within itself so that it can breathe: "Dystopic / figures confound the matrix / bore holes in it / through us" (s, 67). Finally, one realizes that the poetry has designs on us. Not only is the poet watching and describing the flood of fragments, but the reader also is being drawn in. Words that we do not recognize whirl past us, as if dead, but they tug at us as well. Do we recognize an "incomplete" pattern here as phrases return? Are we able to read something "in margins" that once had seemed simply lost to us? Is the whole process of words dissolving then whirling into tentatively new combinations—dying and undying—being performed for us?

> Through the glass box words
> pass unrecognized, thinking us
>
> now dead to you, reader,
> now an ammonite curve.
>
> incomplete, now tablet
> of faint scratches, now redness
>
> in margins, now past
> and pastness. Now a filament of light
>
> penetrates the image-base
> where first glyphs are stored
>
> Lucy and Ethel, the Kingfish,
> Beaver and Pinky Lee

are spoken, die and undie
for you
(s, 73–74)

Dissolving his language, then, reducing it to a rain of fragments, has freed it, one might say, to grow or to laugh: "The lines through these words / form other, still longer lines" (s, 78). The reader is called to enter the process: "A bark sets out on the honeycomb's flow / We called it Le Départ."

The final book I will examine here, Palmer's *At Passages* (1995), starts with eight letter-poems to the contemporary Italian poet Andrea Zanzotto—a writer, as Glauco Cambon puts it in his foreword to *Selected Poetry of Andrea Zanzotto*, noted for "the jerky, polytonal idiom of his experimental phase" in which "classicism has been replaced by 'glossolalia,' a Babelic verve that is apt to incorporate dialect as well as functional or dislocated quotations from Heidegger, Hölderlin, and Dante along with ominous statements by nuclear strategist Herman Kahn and onomatopoeic babblings of baby-talk" (z, xiii, xxii). Gino Rizzo describes him as "a poet who views the sign as capable of activating . . . the linguistic code in its totality, [convinced that] every unit—sememe, lexeme, morpheme, phoneme, grapheme, moneme—will have to be charged with a high frequency commensurate to the task it is supposed to perform" (z, 311–12). Zanzotto's mixture of quotation and baby talk, his charged and totally available linguistic field, is one way *At Passages* raises the issue of language's bodily limits and textures—the simple image of the body becoming the final analogy (after voices through a wall, or echoing waves, or setting out on a flood) for the renewed, expanded notion of language's finitude Palmer's poetry seeks to explore. Thus, the first letter to Zanzotto begins with a notion of linguistic limits much more physical than we have seen before:

Wasn't it done then undone, by
us and to us, enveloped, sid-
erated in a starship, listing
with liquids, helpless letters—
what else—pouring from that box,
little gaps, rattles and slants
(AP, 3)

Referring to Zanzotto's "The Perfection of Snow," the poet traces those "little gaps [and] rattles" back to the unsayable that broke them free:

Did they really run out of things
or was it only the names for things

in that radial sublimity, that
daubed whiteness, final
cleansing and kindness, perfect
snow or perfection of snow

leaving us peering at the bridge,
its central syllable missing,
and the ground here and there
casually rent, cartoon-like,
lividly living, calling in counter-talk:

Whoever has not choked on a word

In Zanzotto, then, Palmer discovers another figure for those linguistic stutters that produce a landscape "casually rent" but "cartoon-like, / lividly" alive, its bridges always lacking a "central syllable." Zanzotto gives him yet another poetry of "counter-talk," a poetry "chok[ing]" on the word thoughtlessly employed.

Zanzotto, these letters continue, has found a way to tap into the "hum of the possible-to-say" (AP, 4). Exploiting "Our errors at zero: milk for mist, grin / for limbs, mouths for names—or else hours / of barks, stammers and vanishings, nods / along a path of dissolving ice" (AP, 5), Zanzotto, these letters claim, has made a dwelling in Palmer's familiar zero. It is a poetry stressing language's bodily finitude: "retelling ourselves / what we say we've said / in this tongue which will pass." Retelling language so that its stammers, its play of hints and tones, become visible, Zanzotto functions as a restatement of Palmer's goals in previous books—a restatement, but also a repositioning, in more bodily ("The few / trans things smelling of sex and pine"—AP, 3) terms.

Zanzotto becomes a figure for a writer opening himself to the full play of language, entering its aroused body:

But the body you enter
with your tongue, with
the words on its tip,
words for chemicals and tastes
and almost remembered names,

hurriedly chalked equations
for the kinds of snow in our time
and always, behind

the landscape,

a snow more red than white?
(AP, 6)

He forcefully reminds the poet: "Take the versions in your mouth / Take inside into your mouth / unearthed, all smoke, blue / and citron, actual word / for that earth and that smoke" (AP, 12). Poetry is, as "Letter 7" puts it, a "word-balloon, . . . slowly / rising over the parched city, / its catacombs, hospitals and experimental gardens" (AP, 9). Part of what Zanzotto enables Palmer to see is that difficulty—thickness, echoes, all of poetry's "latest gear"—is how language begins to breathe again, how it might offer a "transfusion" to the clogged harbors of contemporary linguistic practice:

> You will experience difficulty breathing, this is normal
> The breathing you experience is difficulty, this is normal
>
> Dear Z, Should I say space
> constructed of echoes, rifts, mirrors, a strange
>
> year for touring the interior
> Should I say *double dance, Horn, axis* and *wheel*
>
> Dear A, Scuttled ships are clogging the harbors
> and their cargoes lie rotting on the piers
>
> Prepare executions and transfusions
> Put on your latest gear
> (AP, 10)

This set of poems is followed by a sequence on the Gulf War of 1991. One can hear throughout these poems details from that televised war: smart bombs, sand littered with fragments, soldiers buried alive. In "H" (AP, 15–17), the first poem in the sequence, the poet confesses that the war's "images effected a hole / in the approximate center of my body. / I experienced no discomfort / to my somewhat surprise / . . . The body has altered / many times since." Poetry, we remember from "The Baudelaire Series," investigates what "altered words say," allowing them to break from a straightforward transmittal of messages in order to "speak their tactics / and their practices" (S, 10, 71). Is it possible to bring what was altered in his body to conscious life by watching his words, letting them speak? Is it possible to feel discomfort with such a situation as this? Poetry, after all, knows how to open a door to what cannot be straightforwardly voiced: "But this letter is something like a door / even if a false door / Unvoiced as breath / voiced as ash." So, he continues in the second poem of the sequence, if one of the things found in the "hole caused by bombs / which are smart . . . / . . . is the writing hand," that would mean that using words without the control of the writing hand, letting them move their own way, might speak to this new situation: "and think of the body now as an altered body / framed by flaming wells or walls / What a noise the words make / writing themselves" (AP, 18). What sort of noise? The third poem in the sequence, out of a play with *angels* and *glass* and *light* (terms presumably generated by the explosive transformations of desert sand into new, terrifying shapes), proposes:

> It's impossible to hold such a key in your hand
> and it's light you see traveling through angels of glass—
>
> through knells—
> causing the il- lis- les- the li- lil- lit-
>
> forming the l's you're never to understand
> like the tongues of syllables wreathed in the wells
> (AP, 20)

Out of a situation that cannot be held, words form and reform, loosen their tongues.

But of what use is that? The crucial poem in the sequence, immediately following, meditates on *still*, one of those words formed out of those "syllables wreathed in the wells." It first tries to reawaken a sense of the war's terror— "Yet the after is still a storm / as witness bent shadbush / and cord grass in stillness"—and then listens to its language, to the play of syllables within the body of these lines. Surprisingly, the poet hears, in the tensed juxtaposition of *still* and *storm*, something that reminds him of St. Petersburg, recently renamed: "Saint Something, Saint Gesture, Saint Entirely the Same / as if nothing or no one had been nameless in the interim / or as if *still* could be placed beside *storm* / that simply, as in a poem" (AP, 21). It is as if this "city with its name crossed out" (AP, 26), in the too simple assumption that a "storm" could be so easily "stilled" or that "no one had been nameless in the interim," had shown him (the play of words had shown him) the necessity of a fuller-voiced language: "Add *illness* and *lilt* as formed on the tongue / Add that scene identical with its negative / that sentence which refuses to speak, / present which cannot be found" (AP, 21–22). Thus, the poet argues, poetry's bodily slowness, its ability to accept and say back its altered body, is both generated by and speaks to political events. In refusing to place words "simply," it speaks to current tensions: "We offer a city with its name crossed out / To those who say we are burning the pages" (AP, 26).

Language is a body that can be altered, for good or ill. And poetry constantly reminds us of that fact by dramatizing language's live finitude. "The Leonardo Improvisations," the final poem I will discuss here, gets at these issues by studying Leonardo's Vitruvian Man (1485–90; Venice, Accademia), his famous drawing of the human body with legs and arms spread, a circle drawn around those four points of contact. The notebook page on which the drawing appears is covered, at its top and bottom, with reversed writing designed to be read in a mirror.[16] What attitude toward representation is dramatized here? As with his readings of Zanzotto and Hölderlin, Palmer teases out one last version of his own poetics from the drawing. And as he works the issues, he shows how he can be read as well. The first poem probes the doubleness of the drawing—what "Fifth Prose" called the issue of seeing with crossed eyes: "Can the / two be / told the / two bodies / be told / apart be / told to / part" (AP, 45). These two bodies, we learn later in the sequence, are the human figure and the "perfect circle" drawn about it—"actual body" and "imaginary body":

The measure of the actual body
is the measure

of the imaginary body
The body is encircled—

a circle is drawn—
circle that is impossible

around an actual body
body which tastes of salt

and does not exist
within the perfect circle

it fashions around itself
and whose circumference it touches

with the tips of the fingers outstretched
and the soles of the feet at rest
(AP, 48)

A drawing or a use of language that raises both issues—that the sign is both bodily (it tastes, shifts, won't stay in place) and ideal—is one where signs continually call attention to both their limits and their ambitions, finding that space between to be live and generative. The bodily, nontransparent nature of signs, then, works in two ways: "body as a measure and body as a question" (AP, 47). As we have seen throughout this study, the skeptical "question" always accompanies, charges, the act of measuring. Like Leonardo's representations, which powerfully remind us of something withheld or lost—"What of the words reversed, / words meant / for mirrors, words lost, voices / heard . . . / . . . What possible / eye requires such blank signs. / What worlds / appear as more than real / reflected there" (AP, 46)—Palmer's is a poetry that continually seeks to teach us to read "blank signs." Reminding us of what is lost by language used only in a straightforward sense, his poems attempt to recover, or at least to keep us listening for, other, lost "voices." Blank signs, he would insist, are one last aspect of "our investment in words, in the world" (C 61).

8. An Interview with Michael Palmer

TG: One of the things I'm drawn to in your work is your exploration of a question framed in "Notes for Echo Lake 2": "To be at a loss for words. How does the mind move there. . . ." What's interesting is that by dwelling there, living in the space of that question, you're somehow able to "renew" attention. You put it this way: "Sign that empties itself at each instance of meaning, and how else to reinvent attention." Could you start by talking about those ideas?

MP: Certainly in my work there is the determination not to begin with an entirely preconceived and circumscribed subject or a normative predisposition toward the form and informing nature of the poem. This probably also indicates an early sympathy with Black Mountain, but also a connection to the widespread process orientation in this century among poets, composers, choreographers, and painters. At Harvard, when I was a student, there was an eagerness to laud formulaic contemporary verse, verse which displayed its theme and culture in no uncertain terms and which tended to subscribe to conventions of voice, tone, etc. It seemed to me that the more profound and specific information of the poem was not going to be derived from that. I felt that one had to start from zero and trust to a—Robert Duncan and I talked a good deal about this—trust to a kind of errancy, which is also an erring, making errors, and wandering, at the same time, through the passages—this dark wood which the poem is. Finding one's way through that without a map beforehand, to see what specific information would arise from the words themselves. I don't know if I operate from quite as absolute a model now, as the work has become somewhat more explicitly politically oppositional since the time of *Notes for Echo Lake*.

TG: *Echo Lake* worked by wandering, the last two books don't?

MP: Maybe less so. This is all a question in my mind. But I think *Echo Lake* was, to some degree, an extreme of that dwelling in silence, and an extreme of operating from a certain kind of semiotic model—one that, say, announces my sense, coming out of Jakobson, of that fragility (as to say, in part, "agility") of the sign, and the mysterious process of signification that takes place in poetry where all signs are called into question. That certainly has been a tenet for me, in the sense that they are so filled with echo and polysemy and emptiness as you gaze at them in their new context that the words, to some degree, have to reinvent themselves as you move along. Maybe that seems a little bit formalist now, a little bit too much disregarding the function of the community of speakers themselves. It's not quite so coherent a linguistic model for me now as it was then.

Nonetheless, I was very much operating at the level of sign and how it was, at once, full and empty—how at once within a certain fragile agreement of the tribe it had its referent and yet how the tribe itself was always betraying its referents. Remember, it was also Vietnam behind a lot of this. There's an occulted autobiographical character to *Notes for Echo Lake*, so it takes me back into the period of lies, in an almost Orwellian sense, when we learned that the referential signifiers of those in power were bogus. And that maybe this was also a lesson now that was more continuous than we had thought with the fascist horrors of the '30s where a kind of pathological indifference to meaning and human life were coextensive, where the German language was remade into its darkest romantic nightmare. So if you think of poetry as trying to go to the heart of language in some way—or as *one* of the ways you might arrive there; philosophy may feel the same way for all I know—then we were trying to look at the *process* of the emptying and filling of the sign itself.

TG: Can you date that thinking for me? Did it come about because of political events, or from reading European poetry, or reading sign theory?

MP: It was all of those things. All of my work came about together in ways I didn't realize at that time. When I was in college, which was '61–'65, several things happened. I can randomly list them. One of them was that I was completely disaffected from canonical criticism at the time. The New Criticism seemed to me to valorize a particular kind of pedantic poetic practice.

TG: You felt that in the classroom?

MP: Yes, insofar as I ever went into that classroom. One reason I majored in French history and literature was so I wouldn't have to listen to what I felt were the massive distortions about not only contemporary American and English poetry, but also history—the appropriation of great figures of literature to this paltry cultural center. So I thought: here we're trying to propose a new poetry that is not always grounded in conventional meters, that frequently is not, and yet that's something more than simply free verse—that has a discipline within it that may be cadential, may be stress-oriented, may be syllabic, may be any number of things.

TG: "We" being?

MP: I suppose people I knew in their early twenties, as well as the New American Poets coming out of Williams and others—what was then the great outside practice of American poetry. Remember, at that time, both Williams and Pound were absolutely not discussed in the academy. They were barely written about—a couple of books on Pound, nothing on Williams, certainly nothing on H. D. All those figures who now are simply taken for granted were not only unheard of, they were unmentionables within the Age of Eliot-Frost-Auden. So I was thinking: how do we find out what is literally going on in these poems so that we have a discipline to think about? And the obvious place to turn was linguistics, linguistic prosody, which was in its relative infancy then. Looking at linguistics really led me to semiotics and language philosophy and all of these things that were somewhat in the air then. I started reading Wittgenstein because of his attention to language and to many of these same issues that we're talking about. I was reading "in the dark," which was very exciting. I didn't, in many ways, know what I was reading. I was auditing classes with Roman Jakobson on Saussure, so that structuralist model was very much at that point in my mind. For me then those were very powerful tools of investigation. About 1964, we all realized that we couldn't be alienated existentialists anymore; there were terrible things going on, and we had to try to analyze these things and respond. I remember beginning to have study groups around 1964 with people about Vietnam to try and wade through the morass of mendacity, the language of lies. It seemed to me, at that point, that the study of the sign and the study of the world were much the same thing, in some ways. One would not take something as simply a formal tool; as the Russian Formalists themselves knew, these were things that addressed the current state of the world.

Well, all of these things were swimming in my mind, not at all programmatically the way I may misrepresent them now. These various forms of what for me were oppositionality—critical oppositionality, political oppositionality—began in a very intuitive way to influence what I was trying to do with the page: working from the fragments up, in a certain way. The very first poem I published in my first collection ("Its Form" in *Blake's Newton*) is a poem somewhat in fragments—fragments of, constellations of, voices such as Heine, Williams, already beginning to come together. *Notes for Echo Lake* looks back to '63 and, at the same time, looks at writing in the present and asks what that kind of memory can make of a poem; I suppose that's the reason so many remarks on process come up in it.

TG: I see. These questions first surfaced for you in the '60s.

MP: Yes. Part of the landscape of the early sections of *Notes for Echo Lake* is the Vancouver Poetry Conference of 1963, where I first found a community of sympathetic writers, people who I had been reading but who turned out—somewhat to my surprise—also to exist. And who provided me, not so much poetic models, but human models of people operating outside the world of Berryman, Lowell, Plath, etc. There was a priority in the latter group to prove critical authority that I didn't agree with in relation to poetry. I thought poetry, after twenty years of a postwar slide into timidity, had to reassert its exploratory character. The form of *Notes for Echo Lake* was generated by this letter Charles Bernstein sent when he was editing $L=A=N=G=U=A=G=E$ magazine: "Would you be willing to tell us a little something about yourself?"

TG: So early in the poem, when you write, "Dear Charles, I began again and again to work, always with no confidence," that was working to sort through what was going on in the '6os?

MP: Yes. To sort through and to see how, in an utterly counter-Wordsworthian way perhaps, one might inscribe past experience and even past epiphanies, so to speak.

TG: Could you help me with some of the poem's details, or tell me if what I see there makes sense to you? There seem to be two situations, versions of the Narcissus and Echo story, that get developed and scraped away as the book goes on. In one, a man and a woman walk beside a wall, "he carefully unlistening." That unlistening seems to be the "echo" side of the figure— unlistening is what an echo does as it hears and retells—and gets linked to memory, to joining voices half heard behind a wall, to the way a poem turns and turns, and so on.

MP: Yes. What we're talking about is a kind of metamorphic character. Working with these figures and then perhaps reading them within the context of poetic process, I think they *do* metamorphose in exactly the way you're talking about. It's sort of an Ovidian work in the character of its flow.

TG: In the way that Ovid's stories dissolve, weirdly, one into the other? Those very odd transitions.

MP: Very odd transitions, yes. As soon as you begin to look at the figures of myth they evanesce into earlier versions: they're so wildly palimpsestic. In a certain way, the fluidity of Ovid tends to represent the overwriting that myth actually is—the constant reinterpretation; the evolution, for example, of a figure like Hermes from place to place within Greek lore over time, keeping remnants, always, of the earlier figures; additive in one way, and in some ways there's obviously a loss—that I found very provocative in relation to meaning itself and to the instability of the meaning of a given text, particularly at that time. The Narcissus and Echo myth was, for me, a particularly mysterious one—obviously, one verson of it being semiotic where you have the decay of the signal over time, in relation to other speakers and in relation to reading the world. Without that semiotic decay and that misinterpretation, there would be no communication. If there was no active interpretation of the signal, we'd just have Morse code. So the very fact of decay is what is generative of new meanings. This is the act of reading we're talking about also: the text stays alive by virtue of its flexibility, its uninterpretability (or perhaps resistance to interpretation) at times. That was definitely one side of the Narcissus and Echo myth. Then obviously the dilemma of how does a poet move beyond the *moi*, solipsistic self-reflection.

TG: That's the Narcissus side?

MP: Yes.

TG: That's the situation where a woman says "he never looked anyone in the eye"—which gets linked to what "he'd seen within the eye" or within the self (*that I*) or the lake?

MP: Yes. The context of that was also a rather charged, and at the same time fractured, erotic encounter. Obviously, at the heart of Narcissus and Echo is some problematic of desire as well.

TG: Are the two stories I've begun to sketch the same charged experience?

MP: Can we look?

TG: On page 3—"It was the woman beside him who remarked that he never looked anyone in the eye. (This by water's edge.)"—and on page 4, "A kind of straight grey wall beside which they walk, she the older by a dozen years, he carefully unlistening."

MP: Oh yes, yes. The same.

TG: That's interesting, because then the "he" gets pulled into both figures— a Narcissus not looking at anyone else, an Echo unlistening.

MP: Yes, that's right. They're functions of each other.

TG: The closer I'm able to read—and I'm sure I'm not yet close enough— the more details I see touching and commenting on each other—for example, the move from Wittgenstein's *Remarks on Colour* ("it is not at all clear a priori which are the simple colour concepts") to his comment about the color of the iris of an eye in a Rembrandt portrait back to looking/not looking someone in the eye, and so on.

MP: I think at a certain point, when you are working with a constellation of images and voices that recur, as they do in something like *Echo Lake*, it tends to set up its own valences of cross-referencing. That is, in some ways, the point at which the work or the words begin to do the talking.

TG: The point of "Abragrammatica" (EL, 48)?

MP: Yes, I suppose so. At some point, it seems that if you do trust to what arises in the process of working—and I know that this is a romantic model, but there you are; nonetheless, it's more enabling than disabling—and then if you listen carefully as you're going along, these frequencies begin to speak to each other.

TG: Does it seem frightening at times, to make it very romantic? When I've intuited my way into a problem, and then realize that it's everywhere . . .

MP: Oh yes, that's terrifying. When it's metastasized, so to speak, to use a fairly dark metaphor. Maybe it is announcing, to be even more romantic, a certain kind of death. I hesitate to say "death of the author," because that's filled with so many ridiculous assumptions, but a certain kind of death of intentionality, where suddenly you do realize that the thing is operating, in a way, beyond a level of control to which we trust to maintain our functional sanity in the world. If you're going to go to the heart of the matter, so to speak, you have to give that up—or at least that's one of the myths or superstitions under which I tend to operate.

TG: That's certainly something literature has always recognized—Merrill would be a recent example.

MP: That's a version, a model not far from the aeolian harp. The problem is that it can lead to a picture of pure passivity on the part of the poet. It can lead to a kind of romantic negativity where the poet exists purely as a receiver. It seems to me that the receiver has to be thought of as also this particular genetic matrix that interprets signals—words, if you will, sounds—a particular way. There are different kinds of receivers. So that only works for me if it has a very active side to it as well. Otherwise, it's all about sensitivity in a deck chair. Perhaps Merrill, at his weakest, is that—when he allows himself to fall back to a world of almost pure announcement of sensibility.

TG: I see. In your work, once you start to see versions of the Echo story in many places, you want to be active there. You don't simply drift there, but very carefully scrape parts of the story against each other.

MP: I hope so. The danger of someone who's willing to slide into a purely deconstructed space—let's say, of pure drift, purely echoic, polysemous— is that ultimately that's a kind of rehashing of Symbolism. And that's one implication of the American model of Derrida. Not so much Derrida himself, but the appropriation of Derrida by the American academy has behind it the danger of a return to a hermetically sealed cultural space. It's almost the skeptical other side of the mirror of New Criticism when it's taken that way. It's gone nowhere. It's returned poetry to a particularly sealed-off object of study—just literature, again. And I don't think we can allow ourselves the luxury of it being just literature again.

TG: Stanley Cavell's argument that you don't refute skepticism but rather "live the truth of skepticism," live out the fact that you can't guarantee knowing, seems to me another way of operating in this space.

MP: That's right—you live within the risk of fraudulence, if you will. The risk of fraudulence, of course, goes right to the poem itself. One has to take, make, the risk of fraudulence by operating without guarantees. Reading is an equivalent risk, which is one of the things we find the cultural center being so reluctant to do: Cavell's radical skepticism, if you will, comes very much out of Wittgenstein, though in a remarkably different cultural context that he defines partly as Emersonian. That makes a tremendous difference. The formal characteristics of Wittgenstein's work are partly a product (as Cavell remarks after reading *The Literary Absolute* of Jean-Luc Nancy and Philippe Lacoue-Labarthe) of Jena Aesthetics: the privileging of the fragment and of a certain kind of improvisatory thinking as writing, writing as thinking. Cavell does philosophy in a very different way, but certainly he comes out of that consideration of Wittgenstein. As someone pointed out, that's not as far from Derrida as people think—who also posits a radical skepticism of his own toward meaning. He says "Then we go on from there into one possibility of meaning. We don't just descend into bourgeois anomie."

TG: Cavell goes on from there to what he identifies in Emerson as "nearness" or in Thoreau as "neighboring"—nonguaranteed activities in which to speak to you I have to acknowledge that I can't control you or predict where this is going to go.

MP: Yes. There's still the possibility of meaning or community or survival of meaning. Thoreau is a lovely instance of a skeptical poetics of sight and thought, if you think of his attempt to read the layers of landscape, but also to read past the veils already descending over democracy, writing at that painful time when democratic ideals seemed to have been stood on their heads, when a certain idealism of a possible republic has been really shattered, and when that is represented, *as now*, by the savaging of the landscape itself. Thoreau works with a kind of affirmative skepticism in *Walden* and all through the *Journals*. With a radical skepticism comes, I think, a radical hermeneutics—a reinterpreting, a reading through the signs to their meaning.

TG: There's also a reading of his own activity, as he writes.

MP: Oh yes, a very reflexive process at all points. So there's a kind of metacritique going on at the same time, of simultaneous levels of discourse that flood each other with consciousness and apprehension.

TG: Dickinson, for me, is an example of that simultaneity: writing about love is writing about description is writing about God is writing about writing. After a while, you can't sort through which is which, as if all of those things are alive at the same time. That's also true about Ashbery, I think—everything's alive at the moment of writing. Does it feel that way when you're writing?

MP: I think so. Again, in any of those instances we're trying to move beyond the subject—in both senses of the word—to a point where the true subject, maybe, unfolds. One of the extraordinary experiences of reading Ashbery is to see, as you say, the rupture of a love affair dissolve into a question of temporality dissolve into a question of "what's for breakfast"—a jump in scale between minutiae of everyday experiences and these extraordinary moments of epiphany and despair.

TG: But it's not that he finally gets to the *real* subject. It seems more a change in scale, as in this fractal business, with the same issue before us whatever the scale.

MP: Yes. And that's part of the occasional raging against Ashbery, too. He deprives you of the simple reading, the either/or that certain lesser readers are always yearning for. The commuter poem—you get on the 5:14, and you read a poem, and that's kind of nice. You recognize the experience and the people in it, and you have a little enclosed melodrama. I find that kind of work loathsome, although maybe I should just take it as part of the furniture of middle-class life and not worry about it. But I worry about it as something that represents itself as poetry. It's profoundly fraudulent, even when done in good faith. It's a kind of anti-poetry—an erasure of the function of poetry in relation to the world, a trivializing for which one is duly rewarded for making this thing manageable. Well, I think a poem has to be unmanageable. If western civilization is civilization, then it has to be uncivilized as well. Western civilization seems capable of the most extraordinary depravity, to which we are daily witness; perhaps it has forced upon the poem the acknowledgment of itself as something else in regard to that, in its address to it. In that respect, it seems to me, an art has to maintain an oppositional character now. I don't mean by that a kind of vanguardist acting out, which seems to me too often trivial or at least, at this point, simply nostalgic. I think there's an opposition even within hermetic verse, Celan being the great example but also Osip Mandelstam and many others. One remembers the counter-discourse of such work as being enormously powerful, even if it doesn't stop anything from happening. But how *can* you stop things from happening?

TG: Could such verse be just as powerful here?

MP: I don't know. We operate in the margins, but the margins aren't necessarily a bad place to operate from. First of all, we have no choice. But I think the margins, or the gutter of the page if you will, can be a very powerful point of reference: the boundaries between cultures and discourses. Operating on the periphery, then, is not necessarily as marginalized as it appears. It's a little bit like when the Gulf War was beginning and we would have these very large public demonstrations in San Francisco. The consciousness of all but the most benighted was clear that it wasn't going to stop anything from happening, but the necessity of doing it, nevertheless, was also clear. And maybe there is some parallel to whatever kind of dimensions poetry represents in language and in awareness—that you must continue to do it, on a certain faith that at some level it *does* make a difference. And I think it does, much more than people are willing to grant. When you're working within such a hegemonic culture you have to hope—and all you have is a small screwdriver—that by invoking or eliciting something, you can find your way to alter the structure. And I think that to some degree that is possible.

TG: I started by asking about an idea from *Echo Lake*, "being at a loss for words," and you responded by bracketing that notion as something you were doing then, that your work had more of a political address now. Could you explain your way to the present from *Echo Lake*?

MP: I think simply that the concerns there, such as the semiotic model, gradually lost their centrality to me. I stopped, to some degree, reading in those areas and started thinking more along the lines of social theory and critical theory and the relationship of poetry to society in other respects than I was thinking about at that point, which was working from the inside out. It seems to me that there's been an evolution of the relationship with inside and outside over time. I wanted the work to become, in some way, less oblique, more direct. I don't know that it has, but the effort towards a concretizing of the work, the greater awareness of the materiality of the sign in the world, has changed the tone of the work. The atmosphere of the work is perhaps less fluid.

TG: And you find that in the *Echo Lake–First Figure* juncture?

MP: Yes, there's a transition. If you were to skip *First Figure* and put *Echo Lake* next to *Sun*, you'd see very dramatically the range of the difference. By the time of *Sun*, having lived through a decade of, in some ways, remarkable despair at the return of a certain cynicism and philistinism represented by Reagan, I felt more and more that the work had to be raw, in some way. Or the work told me it had to be more and more raw. The surfaces are less aesthetisized than they are in the earlier work—less engaged by a kind of harmonic resonance that seemed important to the semantic field of *Notes for Echo Lake*. The fractures in my work, the fissures, begin to be addressed even more graphically. *Notes for Echo Lake* is at once a series of disjunctions, yet it has an architecture that probably overrides those.

TG: In *First Figure*, I feel as if I can spend time with poems and know where I am, learn the language.

MP: In some ways, *Echo Lake* feels more yielding. In *First Figure* there is much less emphasis on the architecture of the whole, though maybe it has some particular affinities with some thematic elements. In one way, it's hard to know where you are in *Echo Lake* because it's less concerned with the closure of individual pieces—it's concerned, in a way, with leaving them open. It's easier to get lost than it is in the individual poems of *First Figure*, which look more like poems most of the time and can be read more easily by themselves, out of relation one to another. Otherwise, it's just different. There are certainly poems of regrettable complexity.

TG: Thematically, how do you see the shift?

MP: I don't know. I don't think about the work thematically. Themes arise from the work to the reader. What's the theme of *First Figure*? I've no idea. It's a dark book, but it addresses the possibility of the figural, of generative, initiatory figures, *figurae*, figures of language and knowing disclosing themselves.

TG: Well, the poems consistently think about the territory where words are "dismantled," where "the sentence is impossible" or is "free at last to occur / in some other direction." There's almost the same issue in both books, but handled quite differently.

MP: That's interesting to me—that despite the fact that you think you're thrashing around in the water to keep from drowning, as you pull away from the work you see that certain things insist, return. That seems to be the way, rather than contrivance, that coherence in my work occurs. The themes arise in some way that turns out to be surprisingly . . . whether consistent or coherent is the right word, I don't know. But I think of that argument, going back to the earliest work, about the relationship of word and world, and inscription, and naming and unnaming—all of the things that center around the rather fragile nature of signification. But I'm always at a loss specifically to address that question, I think partly because I've made a prohibition against thinking about what the themes of my work were, as if that were the territory of the readers. As if then I might attend to themes much more consciously and therefore not listen as carefully to the work as it comes out.

TG: *Sun* also seems less fluid?

MP: *Sun*, particularly the long poem—which someone described as a suicide note the other day, which is an interesting idea, not as an act of despair but as an act of acknowledgment of death as an accomplice of poetry in some way—attempts to be as raw as possible. When it stops, it stops. It keeps stopping. It keeps rupturing itself. The two "C"s seem to address some point of silence more absolutely than any previous work of mine.

TG: The two "Sun"s seem radically different, broken free of each other. The second, if I'm reading it right, is all closed-down and confident.

MP: It's certainly more continuous, in place. After I finished the first "Sun," picking up a newspaper—I think *The Boston Globe*—I read this headline: "Neak Luong is a blur." Someone returning to this city that we bombed in Cambodia during the illegal bombing—I don't know if he was a flier or a soldier who had gone in—was talking about this odd passage of time and returning to a place that was a blur to him. And I realized that all of history was a kind of blur, and that this was what allowed us to go on with our support of terrorism and destabilization in Central America, for example. I realized that there was a way of speaking that I had not allowed myself in "Sun" that perhaps I should have and so I would have to write it again. But also, I think I was interested in destabilizing the identity of a given work, too. One of the fascinating things about Hölderlin, for example, is that in his fervor and madness he's producing all of these fragmentary versions of his work. You have three or four different fragments with the same name. It's impossible to reestablish the text itself. It points a little bit in the direction of that, but since then I've been thinking about taking that further and going on with works that become versions or erasures of each other. The first "Sun" is also a kind of erasure of *The Waste Land*. I did think of Rauschenberg erasing that de Kooning drawing—that sort of brazen gesture and joke.

TG: How is it an erasure? In its use of its own quotations?

MP: It's the same number of lines as *The Waste Land*, and I felt it as a typing over the text, erasing this vision of "Tradition and the Individual Talent" that was such a primary model for the modernist vision and along with it a particular Eliotic bigotry, etc. At the same time, it was obviously an echo and a homage to that possibility of the modernist long poem. It enacts a kind of ambivalence. Certainly my *own* ambivalence towards the culture of modernism and towards those figures that, to some degree, we arise out of. None of us escaped that early, provocative example of Pound, for example. Yet now, both because of the age my generation has arrived at and the age the century has arrived at, we look back at aspects of his practice that are monstrous, aspects that seem so blind—his uses of history that seem so dangerous, his uses of a kind of intuitional ideogrammic juxtaposition that, in hindsight now, suppress a kind of rational analysis of social and historical forces.

TG: The ideogram seems ill-suited for analysis?

MP: Yes. The ideogrammic method is at once a brilliant poetic invention for the juxtaposition of ages and ideas, and, at the same time, because of its perhaps nondialectical character (by that I mean nonreflective), by the possibility of a kind of total illogicality, it allows him to carry on a vision of history which consists solely of great figures and great ideas.

TG: And *Sun*, by contrast, means to be reflectively aware of what it's up to?

MP: It begins, in a sense, as an examination of the constellation of voices that have come to constitute whatever I am as a poet, forces and voices. I was, with a student, doing a reading project on Baudelaire, reading Benjamin on Baudelaire and thinking my way back, through Rilke, to one of the founding moments of what we think of as prototypically the modernist vision, or the vision of the modern in a new poetry that begins around that time.

TG: The modern *lyric*?

MP: The modern city, the modern world—yes. As Benjamin says, Baudelaire in the strictest sense is not a lyric poet, but we cannot understand the modern lyric without understanding Baudelaire—which I think is accurate enough. All of these things that come to constitute how we look at the world, and how we also abstractly conceive of the world, how we conceive of contemporaneity, conceive of a particularly alienated vision—I realized that I had always spoken through these fragments, and I was trying to use the poem critically to read back through these figures. In other words, the poem, while being a writing is also a kind of reading—a reading of the Baudelairean, the Rilkean. . . . *Sun* begins to some extent, in "The Baudelaire Series" anyway, with that project of understanding that complex of voices.

TG: Repeated in almost every poem of that series is "words say" or variations: some say, persons say, sleep says, you say, she says, and so on. That seems to me to connect to the Echo figure we've been talking about—perhaps a way of acknowledging that *my* saying is also "the tradition saying, voices I echo saying."

MP: That hadn't occurred to me, but yes, that's true. I was trying to fragment the speaking subject, to throw one's voice in a certain way and to address the fact that all of these other voices are coming through even though you're doing the saying, so to speak. On another, diagetical level, I was exposing those mechanisms.

TG: Can you help me with the first poem in that series? Is that Baudelaire?

MP: It's the last one I wrote in the series. Yes and no.

TG: There are bits of Baudelaire I recognize in there—"frozen sun," "sun/snow," sailing, and so on—but not all of it.

MP: "Stomach skull and gullet." But it's also my wife. I came into bed after Cathy had been asleep, and she woke up and said, "I just dreamed a dream and nobody was in it." She explained the next morning that it had been a dream about the atomic bomb. It was an extraordinary line. Many of these have fragments of Baudelaire running through them—fragments of Rilke, fragments of any number of voices. There's a fragment in here of *Memoirs of My Nervous Illness*, Daniel Paul Schreber, which comes in and out of the whole book and is one of the figures of the sun—the black sun of schizophrenia, the sun that sodomizes Judge Schreber in that famous Freud case. I'm merely reading out of his own text. Let's say there's an implication of Baudelaire there, but there's also the implication of the figure of Hölderlin projecting himself into the future—"a hundred years ago I made a book"— the split which is both oral and prophetic at the same time and addresses, in a very articulate and dramatic and metaphorical way, the splitting of the subject that occurs in so much contemporary writing. You see in Hölderlin the breakdown of any kind of unitary subject, but he also predicts with historical accuracy the fact that *Scardanelli* would be read almost universally at this point, that he would reappear as contemporary in some extraordinary way. So, is that madness? Maybe not.

TG: So you don't need a reader to hear *Baudelaire* saying "a hundred years ago . . ."?

MP: Sometimes you do. I'm trying to keep this question open because I think it's multiple. One of the questions the poem asks is the one you're asking: "Do I hear Baudelaire here?" That's one of the people who may be speaking. Putting it in italics, which I suddenly decided at the last minute needed to be done, was the question of "Is this a quotation? Why is this outside the other texts? Is this someone speaking? Is this many possible people speaking?" So I don't think it's a question with a neat answer. It's part of the interrogation that I would like to begin in a reader's mind, which you've obviously begun.

TG: In *Sun*'s opening acknowledgments, you call attention to the work of Oliver Sacks. The section of "The Baudelaire Series" beginning "You say / A miracle from Heaven" feels to me the most clearly drawn from Sacks.

MP: Yes, that's the most direct.

TG: Can you talk a bit about how long you've been reading him and what's interesting about his work?

MP: I started reading him maybe ten years ago. I was visiting with David Shapiro in New York and we had been talking about A. R. Luria—*The Mind of a Mnemonist, The Man with a Shattered World*—and David said, "Have you ever read Oliver Sacks?" I hadn't. And he said, "Wonderful writer, who's in this line of clinical psychology that also bears along the poetic."

TG: I noticed, for example, reading him again with your work in mind, how important the notion of music is for Sacks. In *A Leg to Stand On*, *Awakenings*, and *The Man Who Mistook His Wife for a Hat*—in all of those studies, it is music that pulls one back from silence or emptiness, from having no conception of leftness or of your leg, pulls you back into movement. That seems to me close to your interest in what happens when we break that music and enter worlds where things stutter or leftness has vanished.

MP: Harmonies and disharmonies, I suppose, and they both have to be part of the picture. It's true in Sacks. It's extraordinary to think about that power, for example, in relation to clinical depression. There are instances of people being recalled from long term depression by music and beginning on a road to recovery of self through *hearing* something. That's quite astounding.

TG: Recovering, losing—that slide back and forth. Sacks connects music with gaining back an *I* or a center, but that also complicates the notion of what that *I* is you've recovered. That seems to be your territory, too.

MP: Yes. Reflection on the totality of the self, the totality of consciousness, is certainly where Sacks begins. Is there a whole consciousness at any one point? What constitutes self? It's a phenomenological, existential form of clinical activity that seems to me extraordinarily humane in relation to the abstract clinical approach that he reacts against. There is a certain poetic relationship to being and the human which is quite explicit in how he addresses, and respects, the linguistic world of his aphasiacs and others. He understands that there's a particular kind of blindness and insight, so to speak, to all disablement, and that we all share that disablement in various ways, and share that power. All of this thought and speech which is taken as aberrant has always seemed to me a source of explicitly poetic information—that is, it helps one to apprehend what the habitual flow of language can sometimes cover over.

TG: One of the things Sacks is able to see is the relation of odd behavior—activities radically speeded up or slowed down—to "normal" motion; that seems to me analogous to the relationship of a certain kind of writing to our everyday conversation. You pick up his word "festinate" in *Sun*—speech, activity speeded up—as if to say that's another way to look at speech.

MP: Yes, that Sisyphean image of at once fast/slow—"festinate and haul rocks"—seems to me two extremes that we always hold within ourselves in trying to find our way through.

TG: The new edition of *Awakenings* has a footnote in which Sacks suggests that chaos theory might offer a way of describing the nonlinear effects of the drug L-dopa on patients with Parkinson's disease. That struck me as an interesting link, since you'd made use of Mandelbrot and chaos theory in *First Figure*. How does that sort of new science help? As an analogy?

MP: I think so. . . . Sometimes it gives you faith that with all the apparently aleatory aspects of your work that you are actually working in something that is epistemological, maybe. It can be a confirmation—however illusory, that doesn't matter. Poets have always used cosmology and everything else in a totally bogus fashion, that's a given. Nevertheless, the translation of that down to the nonscientific level is arguably like other forms of translation anyway: you have to live with what you get there, the mistranslation. In any case, that kind of work was generative, formally suggestive. The words themselves arcing through the work. Reading has never been separate from living, in that way, for me. And so the intertextual character is manifested in the borrowing, or theft, of other people's words. It is a constellation, or a constellating, I suppose, but I take that as very different from the idea of collaging that was a model for Duncan.

TG: Duncan signals his use of quotation in quite a different way.

MP: Yes. He announces the texts in a different way. He announces, "*This* is coming in, this foreign body."

TG: Yes. It's there to be struggled against: acknowledged, reacted to, reclaimed. Why don't you go that way?

MP: I was interested more in the imbrication, the layering, of these things. And I was interested in that gray area. Is that him? "I'm fine I'm fine I'm really going blind." If I frame it as a text from elsewhere, it loses that multidirectionality that it has in relation to the *I* of the poem in here. The sort of counter-lyricism of a poem like this depends, in part at least, on questioning that *I* who is speaking. Maybe we're depriving the reader now in giving a source, but that source will probably disappear again for a reader.

TG: When you give a source, however, a reader who goes back finds that Sacks, for example, doesn't quite use those phrases.

MP: Doesn't quite. Occasionally I'll appropriate a source verbatim, but often it will be slightly or radically altered. It becomes altered by the impetus of the poem itself, the demands of the rhythm, the surrounding material, whatever. And so it's not quotation, exactly. It's a form of citation, but it's layered, covered over.

TG: "Desire was a quotation from someone."

MP: Yes.

TG: Does that connect with Celan's "Niemandes Stimme, wieder" that you quote at the beginning of *First Figure*—the voice erased, but still sounding?

MP: "No one's voice again." Yes. I worry sometimes about that kind of appropriation of Celan, simply because, in one way of course, I have no right. We're talking about a personal experience of the Holocaust and a poet whose reference there is very specifically to disappeared voice and to his own situation of being without voice. I don't mean to—as a person living as far as imaginable, at least by the outward signs, from such experience—to try dramatically to appropriate the tragedy of his experience. But at the same time, that seems to speak to something very profound in the work itself, such that I felt it was all right.

TG: In *your* work itself?

MP: In my work and in poetry itself. Whether it's Keats addressing the ultimate invisibility of the poet or Whitman foregrounding self and presence, I think that remains true. In a book by Emmanuel Levinas called *Noms Propres*, there is an interview about Edmond Jabès to which the poet Norma Cole brought my attention. The interviewer asks the perfectly banal question, "Dans la production littéraire actuelle quelle place attribuez-vous à l'oeuvre d'Edmond Jabès?"—"In the literary production of our time, what place do you attribute to the work of Edmond Jabès?" Levinas's answer is both pertinent here and very moving. He replies, "Est-il sûr qu'un vrai poète occupe une place? N'est-il pas ce qui, au sens éminent du terme, *perd sa place*, cesse précisément l'occupation et, ainsi, est l'ouverture même de l'espace dont ni la transparence, ni le vide—pas plus que la nuit et les volumes des êtres—ne montrent encore le sans-fond ou l'ex-cellence, le ciel qui en lui est possible, sa 'caelumnité' ou sa 'celestité,' si on peut utiliser de tels néologismes?"—"Is it certain that a true poet occupies a place? Isn't he the one who, in the highest sense of the term, *loses his place*, ceases precisely to occupy it and thus is the very opening of that space . . ." Well, it's a long and complex sentence, and I won't try to translate it all here. . . . But the sense that the poet, by the choice of vocation, gives up his place, is to me a very powerful image. And then the deeper sense of "Niemandes Stimme" is reflective, in at least my practice also, of ceding one's place in a certain respect. I don't mean to say that I don't write my poems. Nor do I mean to say that I don't stand responsible for them. But that the question of the subject is a very complicated one that a lot of the commonplace verse of the postwar period and since, predicated on a simplistic model of the self, denies. Leading to that endless "stuff."

TG: Wouldn't Duncan agree?

MP: He would, I think. He would phrase it in more grandiose terms of romantic negativity, I suppose, but definitely. Despite the obvious difference in our work, the reason we could have a conversation for close enough to twenty years was that we had so profound a sympathy about what the vocation of poetry was and about the responsibility of the poet to the work through the poem itself.

TG: This notion of ceding one's place, of employing a language which is a "quotation from someone," also, of course, applies to the work of Ashbery. His language feels remade, placed along and within the voices of others—though in his case it's the voices of cliché and talk on the street. Does that feel similar to you?

MP: In one way it does. And of course, in another way, what he uses, that particular furniture, is very different. He's much more engaged by the permanency of the ephemeral, in that way, and of those eruptions of the trivial into consciousness. He's at times an almost Wordsworthian narratizer of experience (Wordsworthian in the most generative, exploratory sense). The larger poems are very intriguing that way. We work very differently, and he is grounded in a different economy of writing. His allows for much more treading of water, so to speak—as narrative must, as the long poem must. He allows it to carry on. I have very little permission for allowing it to carry on. I think I'm much more involved with some sort of implosive intensification, and Ashbery's much more involved with an idea of extension. So, I see enormous differences, but also I feel a tremendous sympathy towards the interrogation of the subject in the world that goes on throughout Ashbery and the extraordinary invention of surface that is so present in Ashbery. For me as a young writer, the most important of Ashbery's books was *Rivers and Mountains*. Things like "The Skaters" were absolutely dazzling to me; whether they left a mark or not, at that point in my work, is hard for me to say.

TG: Are there other writers of that generation who were important?

MP: There were a lot that I read with great pleasure. Zukofsky, of course, of an earlier generation, was very important. He was given to me by Creeley. The irony of Zukofsky being so important to me is that I'm sure my work would have been unacceptable to Louis. The demands that he made on himself for poetry were very important. The combination of eye and intellect was exemplary in some way. His formal rigor was important, but I don't think my work would have been legible to him.

TG: Not the kind of rigor but the *idea* of rigor is something you share?

MP: Yes, and that the poem calls for the utmost attention, which is certainly one of the superstitions I carry with me. I can't be very casual about that. Even though it may on the surface look totally shredded and arbitrary, it's got to be thought through. That doesn't mean it's going to end up looking like a box. He also was important in that he was integrating his reading of Wittgenstein and Spinoza, and in his case Marx, with poetic thought. I think that encouraged me to go on reading things in their relation to one another.

What strikes me when you ask is that I don't think particularly generationally. I was also reading, from the age of twenty on forward, Dante with the utmost interest—Dante and Cavalcanti, and so on. I was also reading Lorca and the Madrid School (Miguel Hernández and others) with great interest. Not with Robert Bly's sense of appropriation and "deep image," but another way. I was also reading the German Expressionist tradition, and crucially the French from Rimbaud on forward. I was also reading German and French baroque poetry. It's an ever-expanding question. I was reading a lot next to each other, trying to find some international exploratory tradition. And then listening to music and looking at the visual arts with great interest as alternative models to the formal, conventional Anglo-American prosodic models we'd been given.

TG: The term I've seen you use for that international investigatory tradition—"analytic lyric"—is that yours?

MP: It was mine. I think it's gone outward now. I think I first suggested it at a panel discussion at Temple University some years back, and then brought it up again in an interview with David Levi Strauss.

TG: I saw it in a transcript of a talk you gave at Iowa, and then again in the interview.

MP: What I was saying there was that some friends among the Language poets were trashing the lyric. I think they were doing that because of the abuse of the lyric self—the "little self" of the workshop poem. My point was that essentially my practice is generated by a kind of relationship to musicality, even when it's reacting against that. *Without Music*. The poems remain harmonically dense; there's not much I seem to be able to do about that, even when I take an axe to it. There is something about what a music can do in terms of concentration of meaning, and also the expansion of the semantic field that harmonic juxtaposition will do, that was very important to me. What I wanted to draw attention to was the fact that a practice of lyric condensation—which one could even apply to Expressionist theory— has a *critical* dimension, has a dimension of reflection that should not be condescended to. It doesn't simply have to be sweet nothings. My point was that we could recover the power of that musicality to possible meaningful uses or ends.

TG: One of the uses is concentrating on the code itself?

MP: I suppose one is, certainly. A poem like "A"-11 is a lovely instance. Musicality provides a dimension of meaning and a dimension of crossing within the poem. For me, it equates with the mysterious logic of the phoneme, the dizzying juxtaposition of *fat* and *cat*, etc. that at once is made logical by the music but is countered by the sign itself. That's speaking of it very simply, but perhaps I mean to. In that kind of radical juxtaposition/disjunction one is entering the territory of the particular poetic logic that seems to have a dimension of thought to it that's less available in other forms of discourse. A way of addressing the dizzying paradoxes and contradictions of experience by bringing them in and exposing them—whether it's of the social fabric or just being in the world. Of mortality, as we used to say when we could say such things. Poetic speech—if we can speak of it, not meaning poetic character or poeticness—opens certain areas of exploration that speak to the philosophical, among many other things, that often will reside in that crepuscular area between the poetic and the philosophical as the philosophical, in turn, can do when you have a philosopher such as Nietzsche, such as Wittgenstein, such as perhaps Derrida (but mustn't one then equally invoke the *elsewhere* of Herakleitos, Plato the Wicked, Ibn al-'Arabi, et al.?). They do bring into question the margins, or they reveal that the margins are certainly not absolute between ways of speaking. At the same time, they equally reveal why one speaks from here rather than from there, what can be done here that can't be done there.

This is one of the tensions that is always present in the culture's relationship to poetry—for example, some of the tremendous resentment of it that you get from the Marxist theoreticians: their privileging of a certain kind of narrative, and their reluctance to allow the kind of delirium of poetry its place, its social function, because they recognize that it's equally capable of subverting their own ideological linearity. Their own grand narratives are exposed, at a certain point, by poetry, and their cultural authority is critiqued by that kind of work.

TG: In a way, that sort of critique, that way of speaking, comes about through wrestling with the nature of the sign. Although you put my first question aside in a sense, there *does* seem to be a way in which dwelling in a state of uncertainty about words enables you to renew speech.

MP: Yes. Or is it that you're building an instrument and that there are more parts of it there? or you can play it a little bit better? or you can recognize that it *is* an instrument, even if it's only a fifty-seven-tone scale? I don't know.

It's funny—*Sun*, for all of its oddness, felt that it was moving further into the world, into a directness of address. "Nowness and nowness sings the crow / whatness and whiteness sings the center / then and then signs the hen." However enigmatic some of that is, for me it was closer to language as a kind of hammer: "She says, Into the dark— / almost a question— / She says, Don't see things— / this bridge—don't listen // She says, Turn away / Don't turn and return." That was, for me, something I could never have done before, and it felt almost like direct address. Granted that it starts from that zero degree such that it's not like, perhaps, someone else's direct address.

TG: Yet look where that address comes from—it's from a version of another poet, Rilke, from a Eurydice who's insisting that she belongs in this space where she's forgotten her name, where it's been erased, where her house has been burned down. She's speaking from the middle of unlistening, and is comfortable there. That seems enormously resonant with the rest of your work, though I also see, at the sentence level, how different it feels.

MP: Yes. I think you're right in what you're saying. There's always a break between books, in the sense of not being able to write poetry when I'm finished with one, and I always try to use that time of incapacity to make sure I don't simply go on from there. So the books are unmistakably different one from another. At the same time, I think you're right that the accent's the same—the project, whatever it may be, is the same project. And yet I'm so close to it that I don't have an analytical overview of it. I can't pretend to. I can't pretend to know what I'm doing, so to speak, even though I can speak of what goes into it. . . .

June 1991

Notes

Introduction

1. For more on Cavell and Shakespeare, see Gerald Bruns, "Stanley Cavell's Shakespeare," *Critical Inquiry* 16 (spring 1990), 612–21; and Richard Wheeler, "Acknowledging Shakespeare: Cavell and the Claim of the Human," in *The Senses of Stanley Cavell*, ed. Richard Fleming and Michael Payne (Lewisburg PA: Bucknell University Press, 1989), 132–60.

2. See also SW, 106, for an extended discussion of "the truth of skepticism." The following essay-length discussions of Cavell's meditations on skepticism have been especially helpful to me in thinking about his work: Charles Bernstein, "Reading Cavell Reading Wittgenstein," *Boundary* 2 9, no. 2 (winter 1981), 295–306; Gerald Bruns, "The New Philosophy" in *Columbia Literary History of the United States*, ed. Emory Elliott (New York: Columbia University Press, 1988), 1045–59; "Tragic Thoughts at the End of Philosophy," *Soundings* 72, no. 4 (winter 1989), 693–724; Bruns, "Stanley Cavell's Shakespeare"; Ted Cohen and Paul Guyer, introduction to *Pursuits of Reason: Essays in Honor of Stanley Cavell* (Lubbock: Texas Tech Press, 1993), 1–9; Richard Eldridge, "'A Continuing Task': Cavell and the Truth of Skepticism," in *The Senses of Stanley Cavell*; Russell B. Goodman, *American Philosophy and the Romantic Tradition* (New York: Cambridge University Press, 1990), 1–33; Stephen W. Melville, *Philosophy Beside Itself: On Deconstruction and Modernism* (Minneapolis: University of Minnesota Press, 1986), 17–33. Three book-length discussions of note are Michael Fischer's attempt to place deconstruction in the context of Cavell's discussion of skepticism, *Stanley Cavell and Literary Skepticism* (Chicago: University of Chicago Press, 1989); Richard Fleming's reading of *The Claim of Reason, The State of Philosophy* (Lewisburg PA: Bucknell University Press, 1993); and Stephen Mulhall's remarkable analysis of "The form and trajectory of Cavell's Wittgensteinian practice of recounting criteria through his entire career," *Stanley Cavell: Philosophy's Recounting of the Ordinary* (Oxford: Oxford University Press, 1994), 305.

3. Cavell writes that skepticism could be thought of as "as a kind of argument of language with itself" (IQ, 5).

4. It is important that an early essay on Cavell and Wittgenstein is by a poet, Charles Bernstein, who remarks, for example, "If we are to live with the 'truths of skepticism,'

one of them is the mystery that the world exists at all. It is to this truth that literature can speak—of the wonder of the world being at all." See Bernstein, "Reading Cavell," 305.

5. There are, of course, significant poetic responses to these issues which do not foreground the issue of writing or directly call attention to the writing situation. Louise Glück's work is a good example. Like the other writers I focus on in this book, she consistently addresses the issue of human finitude and the various ways we respond to and attempt to refuse limits. What Glück studies are various responses—"forced accommodation[s]" as one poem puts it—to limits, ranging from destructive attempts to control what changes to the desire to retreat from it to an openness to what passes. She writes in an essay: "immersion in time is a shock, involving real forfeits—of perfection, of the fantasy of eternity. That shock can be predicted. The surprise is that there are benefits to this perspective" (see *Proofs & Theories: Essays on Poetry* [New York: Ecco Press, 1994], 102). The writers I focus on in this book will develop similar claims about forfeits and benefits, but Glück shows that there are entrances to these issues other than through the door of language. At the same time, one notes in her work a series of undeveloped acknowledgments that the struggles with time and the body foregrounded in her work are significantly echoed in our life in language.

6. James Longenbach, in *Modern Poetry After Modernism* (New York: Oxford University Press, 1997), makes a similar observation. Thinking about the fact that two poets as different as Elizabeth Bishop and Charles Bernstein make significant use of the same phrase from the critic Morris Croll about poetry portraying "not a thought, but a mind thinking," Longenbach writes: "The coincidence . . . suggests that style never tells the whole story of American poetry: poets who seem, because of their formal choices, to have little to do with one another may share the deepest goals and ambivalences" (175).

7. For a forceful example of an expansion of Cavell's version of Wittgenstein, see Fergus Kerr, *Theology After Wittgenstein* (Oxford: Blackwell, 1986).

8. Charles Bernstein's "Reading Cavell" explores some of the ground shared between Cavell and contemporary poetry. He writes of Cavell's *The Claim of Reason*: "It is ourselves, our ways of making sense, that are being interrogated. His conception of philosophy shares with poetry the project of increasing an awareness of conditions— of where we are agreed, of what we have convened on; of the structures and grammars we live in; of how the syntaxes and grammars we create in turn create the world" (297).

9. For an evenhanded discussion of "the different ways in which [contemporary] poets have harnessed their modernist past" (viii), finding it "more varied and ac-commodating than most readers recognized" (7), see James Longenbach's *Modern Poetry After Modernism*. Longenbach cites these remarks of Graham's, drawn from my interview with her, throughout his chapter "Jorie Graham's Big Hunger."

10. The reading of Stevens that follows is drawn from a longer discussion of the poem in my article "Bishop and Ashbery: Two Ways Out of Stevens," *The Wallace Stevens Journal* 19 (fall 1995), 201–18.

11. Charles Altieri, "Why Stevens Must Be Abstract, or What a Poet Can Learn from Painting" in *Wallace Stevens: The Poetics of Modernism*, ed. Albert Gelpi (Cambridge: Cambridge University Press, 1985), 114.

12. Harold Bloom, *Wallace Stevens: The Poems of Our Climate* (Ithaca: Cornell University Press, 1977), 261.

13. B. J. Leggett, *Wallace Stevens and Poetic Theory: Conceiving the Supreme Fiction* (Chapel Hill: University of North Carolina Press, 1987), 176.

14. Michael Davidson, in his important article "Notes Beyond the *Notes*: Wallace Stevens and Contemporary Poetry," in Gelpi, *Wallace Stevens*, describes this as writing from within ideas that are being examined. He notes that Stevens's "operative or performative use of language has had an increasingly important function for contemporary poets as a way of writing a poetry of ideas within the very terms that these ideas present," 149.

15. All three critics I mention above, for example, take note of this. See Vendler, OEW, 257; Leggett, *Wallace Stevens*, 179; and Bloom, *Wallace Stevens*, 266.

16. Shira Wolosky's *Language Mysticism: The Negative Way of Language in Eliot, Beckett, and Celan* (Stanford: Stanford University Press, 1995) offers a useful series of discussions of different ways of framing and responding to this issue of language's finitude: its "fragility" (88) or connections to "succession, materiality, multiplicity" (47). She closes with the remark that, for certain writers, "Language [can] serve as a trope for a positive skepticism, one that acknowledges the spaces we do not control" (271). A common way to talk about framing this issue is the notion of entering a "space between." See, for example, Vernon Shetley who, in his *After the Death of Poetry: Poet and Audience in Contemporary America* (Durham NC: Duke University Press, 1993), notes that such writers as Bishop, Merrill, and Ashbery operate "between erasure of subjectivity . . . and unexamined belief in the power of subjectivity" (19–20).

17. A number of our strongest writers on poetry have been working to chart poetry's response to linguistic limits, and I want to briefly sketch their approaches here, acknowledging my indebtedness. Richard Poirier's two most recent books look at the way "Emersonian linguistic skepticism" becomes "a generative principle" in the work of such writers as Frost, Stein, and Stevens. Emerson, he argues in *The Renewal of Literature: Emersonian Reflections* (New York: Random House, 1987), understands "Language not as a transparency but as an obstruction, language not as inherently mobile but as static and resistant, unless made momentarily otherwise" (30). Through becoming aware of language's thickness, Poirier continues in *Poetry and Pragmatism* (Cambridge MA: Harvard University Press, 1992), the poet, "exploring his language as it emerges, discovering the dense and terrifying implications of his way of thinking and of his way with words" (57), plays out "an actively skeptical, antagonistic / flirtatious relation to [his or her] own writing" (66). For Poirier, after Emerson, this contention with one's own attempts at self-location can be described as a "renewal" (11) of one's own self and language.

Gerald Bruns, in *Heidegger's Estrangements: Language, Truth, and Poetry in the*

Later Writings (New Haven: Yale University Press, 1989), explores what Heidegger calls "an experience with language" (100) generated when the poet comes up short linguistically: " . . . the experience *with* language is likely to occur when language withholds itself in a radical way, that is, when we are at a loss for words and are forced to leave something unsaid; it occurs when language *fails* us, or when our linguistic competence breaks down" (101). Such an experience, which Bruns links to Cavell's acknowledging the truth of skepticism (173), understands "the renunciation of linguistic mastery" as a means of renewing attention: "where poetry opens itself—enters into, listens or belongs to—the mystery of language, its otherness, its nonhumanness, its density, its 'danger' " (xx).

Charles Altieri has been forcefully investigating the way a poem "focuses most of its attention on the linguistic situation of a reflective, writing presence," arguing that the strongest contemporary writers are engaged, in such situations, with the limits of their language and are not simply "repeating standard lyric emotions without reflecting upon their claims and their limits . . . blind to the duplicities and banalities that accompany our preferred, wistful forms of poetic insight." See "What Modernism Offers the Contemporary Poet," in *What Is a Poet?*, ed. Hank Lazer (Tuscaloosa: University of Alabama Press, 1987), 35, 34. For Altieri, understanding writing as "a contemplative site" "in which one takes responsibility for one's actions," "working through and against all the rhetorical temptations poetry holds out" offers a chance to model what he calls subjective agency. See *Self and Sensibility in Contemporary American Poetry* (Cambridge: Cambridge University Press, 1984), 31, 48, 104. In "Contemporary Poetry as Philosophy: Subjective Agency in John Ashbery and C. K. Williams," *Contemporary Literature* 33, no. 2 (summer 1992), 214–42, Altieri speaks of such work as creating "a home within the activity of language" (235).

Marjorie Perloff describes contemporary pressures on language as poetry's awareness that we "live in a technological world in which everything we say and write is always already given—a storehouse of clichéé, slack phraseology, sloganeering, a prescribed form of address, a set of formulas that govern the expression of subjectivity," *Poetic License: Essays on Modernist and Postmodernist Lyric* (Evanston IL: Northwestern University Press, 1990), 28. As a result, the writers Perloff has examined in her recent books are driven "to deconstruct the possibility of the formation of a coherent or consistent lyrical voice, a transcendental ego" (12). What remains, she remarks in various ways, is "language itself, the language of our time . . . refracted, distorted, heightened, but always recognizable," "writing itself, . . . the 'life' lived by words, phrases, clauses, and sentences, endowed with the possibility of entering upon new relationships," *The Dance of the Intellect: Studies in the Poetry of the Pound Tradition* (Cambridge: Cambridge University Press, 1985), 167–68, 225; or "ordinary words, . . . denaturalized, decontextualized, so that we must puzzle out their relationships within the given language field," *Radical Artifice: Writing Poetry in the Age of Media* (Chicago: University of Chicago Press, 1991), 57. Her recent *Wittgenstein's Ladder: Poetic Language and the Strangeness of the Ordinary* (Chicago: University of Chicago

Press, 1996) links Wittgenstein to current poetry that intends not "the *expression* or externalization of inner feeling [but] the critique of that expression" (184). See my review of this book in *Review of Metaphysics* (December 1997), 434–36.

All four writers suggest that poetry comes to life in responding to pressures generated within language: poetry struggles against language (Poirier), listens to its strangeness (Bruns), interprets its drives (Altieri), or makes strange its ways (Perloff.) My point is a larger one: that in responding to such pressures, poetry is consciously bringing to life our human situation. In Cavell's terms, in inhabiting its finite condition, the language of poetry becomes a place where "one's humanity, or finitude, is . . . accepted, suffered" (TN, 39) and the world is "regained as gone" (IQ, 172).

18. Bonnie Costello, in an article seeking "to shift attention away somewhat from the predominant view of [Ashbery's] work as language centered" focuses on *landscape* as "a fundamental, generating trope of knowledge in Ashbery's poetry" (60). Writing about quite literal landscapes, Costello also describes them as "landscape[s] of thought" (71), unstable tracings of "the shapes a conscious, discursive rhetoric can make" (70). See "John Ashbery's Landscapes" in *The Tribe of John: Ashbery and Contemporary Poetry*, ed. Susan M. Schultz (Tuscaloosa: University of Alabama Press, 1995), 60–79.

19. This reading is drawn from my description of the poem in "Bishop and Ashbery."

20. For a discussion of Ashbery's use of *you* in the mind's reflection on itself, see Karen Mills-Courts, *Poetry as Epitaph: Representation and Poetic Language* (Baton Rouge: Louisiana State University Press, 1990), 267–314.

21. "Interview with Robert Hass," *Chicago Review* 32, no. 4 (1981), 16–26.

22. Alan Shapiro, "Some Thoughts on Robert Hass," in *In Praise of the Impure: Poetry and the Ethical Imagination* (Evanston IL: Northwestern University Press, 1993), 16.

23. Jorie Graham, "Pleasure," in *Singular Voices: American Poetry Today*, ed. Stephen Berg (New York: Avon Books, 1985), 92.

24. For a discussion of Graham's source for this poem, see Bonnie Costello, "Jorie Graham: Art and Erosion," *Contemporary Literature* 33, 2 (summer 1992), 391–95.

25. Bruns, *Heidegger's Estrangements*, 101, xx.

26. Marjorie Perloff quotes Stein's use of this phrase in *Wittgenstein's Ladder*, 65. Palmer describes de Kooning's account of "returning and returning to the first moment of the canvas" in CP, 18–19.

27. In MP, Palmer comments on that process as follows: "from a phrase comes an expanded phrase, then a further expanded phrase, the syntax flowering over time. You end up in a structure of variations, as you do in music, an open-ended series of variations on a theme that are meant to explore the richness of a particular melodic line. The lines thus acquire an incantatory character, a returning and returning to a first place. For me this is simply a mode of thought," 80.

28. In *Remarks on Colour*, ed. G. E. M. Anscombe (Oxford: Blackwell, 1977), 9e, remark I, 58, Wittgenstein writes: "Imagine someone pointing to a place in the iris of

a Rembrandt eye and saying: 'The walls in my room should be painted in this colour.' " This poem also draws on remarks I, 59; I, 67; and III, 69.

29. Marjorie Perloff's chapter in *Wittgenstein's Ladder* on the philosopher's method of writing philosophy "as a form of poetry" is quite suggestive about the attraction of this method of "traveling" for contemporary writers ("The 'Synopsis of Trivialities': The Art of the *Philosophical Investigations*," 51–82).

1. Elizabeth Bishop

1. All of us thinking about Bishop have benefited from a wealth of excellent work on her poetry, much of it on versions of this question. I would cite for particular attention the following: Helen Vendler's distinction between the domestic and the strange in "Elizabeth Bishop," in her *Part of Nature, Part of Us* (Cambridge MA: Harvard University Press, 1980), 97–110; David Kalstone's booklength discussion of the way Bishop's lifelong awareness of "the frailty of human arrangements and recognitions" (13) eventually produced poems in which "The printed word asserts a frail bond between self and world" (246), *Becoming a Poet: Elizabeth Bishop with Marianne Moore and Robert Lowell* (New York: Farrar, Straus, Giroux, 1989); Bonnie Costello's important book on the way Bishop's work enacts "a knowing and experiencing the world which mediates between the darkness of utter skepticism and dread on the one hand, and the solipsistic illusion of mastery or transcendence, on the other" (45), *Elizabeth Bishop: Questions of Mastery* (Cambridge MA: Harvard University Press, 1991); Victoria Harrison's account of the multiple, contradictory, and "continually readjustable" (105) subject-subject relations that emerge in those frail spaces, *Elizabeth Bishop's Poetics of Intimacy* (Cambridge: Cambridge University Press, 1993). I have surveyed recent critical approaches to these issues in two review essays: "Clarity and Opacity in Elizabeth Bishop," *Review* 11 (1989), 179–88; and "Elizabeth Bishop and the Powers of Uncertainty," *Review* 17 (1995), 271–95. I have cited in this chapter's notes the most striking similarities I am aware of between my work on specific poems and that of various critics, but the layer of commentary on her work is now so rich that such citation could be almost infinitely extended.

2. Robert Dale Parker calls these poems "allegories of imagination" (42). See his chapter "Wish: *North & South*," in *The Unbeliever: The Poetry of Elizabeth Bishop* (Urbana: University of Illinois Press, 1988), 29–72.

3. For useful extensions of the notion of "constant re-adjustment" see Mutlu Konuk Blasing, "The Re-verses of Elizabeth Bishop," *American Poetry: The Rhetoric of its Forms* (New Haven: Yale University Press, 1987), 101–15; and Bonnie Costello, *Elizabeth Bishop*. Costello's entire study works and reworks this notion of Bishop's interest in "points of view that discovered or acknowledged their inadequacy" (42).

4. Bonnie Costello speaks of the map as "a space agitated by many perspectives" (*Elizabeth Bishop*, 237). Victoria Harrison reads the question raised by fragility here as having to do with a "multiple, contradicted, and always relational subjectivity" (see *Elizabeth Bishop's Poetics*, 42–46).

5. Costello, *Elizabeth Bishop*, 218–23.

6. Boomer is a phonetic equivalent of Bulmer, Bishop's mother's family name.

7. For an important discussion of the way "In Prison" and a number of Bishop poems "invert the notion of voice" and "escape both intellectual and linguistic dominance" (185), see Jacqueline Vaught Brogan, "Elizabeth Bishop: *Perversity* as Voice" in *Elizabeth Bishop: The Geography of Gender*, ed. Marilyn May Lombardi (Charlottesville: University Press of Virginia, 1993), 175–95. Although I identify the speaker of this piece as "she," Brogan rightly notes that the gender of the speaker is indeterminate.

8. To give just one example: David Kalstone's *Becoming a Poet* uses Bishop's relationships to Marianne Moore and Robert Lowell to frame a stunning, book-length meditation on this issue.

9. For discussions of the multiple perspectives and scales tentatively employed within this frame, see Kalstone, *Becoming a Poet*, 11–19 and Costello, *Elizabeth Bishop*, 16–20.

10. Kalstone, *Becoming a Poet*, 81–85, first drew my attention to the poem's tension with a lover.

11. James McCorkle, in *The Still Performance: Writing, Self, and Interconnection in Five Postmodern American Poets* (Charlottesville: University Press of Virginia, 1989), valuably describes this as "the narrator implictly acknowledging the limitations of language" (15). He goes on to list a number of poems in which "the world's return of [her] glance is at issue" (43). Costello, 61–64, also takes note of the fish's refusal of her glance.

12. Discussed in Kalstone, *Becoming a Poet*, 113–18.

13. Costello, *Elizabeth Bishop*, 111, takes note of this shift as well, although she makes a different point about it.

14. Helen Vendler, in a striking phrase, writes about the way this image expresses a desire for "the pure unmeaning of the Keatsian swallows" (292). See "Elizabeth Bishop" in MWH, 284–99. Costello (*Elizabeth Bishop*, 103–9 and throughout her text) uses this image as a version of the "tentative, fleeting orders" (106) Bishop is drawn to after the breakdown of mastery.

15. Vendler comments that Bishop "was both fully at home in, and fully estranged from, Nova Scotia and Brazil," in MWH, 287. One can see why both areas raise the same issues.

16. Wondering why the "Elsewhere" poems appear in this volume, Costello usefully remarks that there is "an analogy between the condition of the traveler and that of the child. Both find themselves in situations where the codes and frames of reference which have given them security break down" (*Elizabeth Bishop*, 200).

17. Vendler describes the mother's scream as "the inaccessible blank at the center of all Bishop travel" (MWH, 288).

18. Harrison valuably remarks that a series of "vitally conflicting sounds" and "a village of relations" emerge as "compensation" for the scream (*Elizabeth Bishop's Poetics*, 121).

19. Vendler has discussed the fraying of the child's constructions in two separate essays. See *Part of Nature, Part of Us*, 99–101; and MWH, 296–97.

20. My reading of "Poem" is drawn from my "Bishop and Ashbery."

2. John Ashbery

1. John Ashbery, *Reported Sightings: Art Chronicles, 1957–1987*, ed. David Bergman (New York: Knopf, 1989), 400.

2. Though, as Helen Vendler remarks, to say a poem is about poetry "sounds thin in the telling," it is important to add, as she does, that by poetry or writing we mean as well: "how people construct an intelligibility out of the randomness they experience; how people choose what they love; how people integrate loss and gain; how they distort experience by wish and dream; how they perceive and consolidate flashes of harmony; how they (to end a list otherwise endless) achieve what Keats called a 'Soul or Intelligence destined to possess the sense of Identity,'" MWH, 224. She adds, in a later essay, "When the poets write about poesis, they are writing about what is done every day by everyone. Most of us do not reflect on it when we do it, but we live nonetheless in our construct of the world. . . . To say that a poem is 'about poetry' means, surely, that it is consciously about the way life makes up a world of meaning," 260.

3. It is, of course, a commonly made observation that Ashbery is skeptical about language's straightforward claims. See, for a recent discussion, Shetley, *After the Death of Poetry*, 103–33. Ashbery's lively if "skeptical self-consciousness about the strategies . . . employ[ed] in translating subjectivity into form" (20) positions him, for Shetley, in the rich middle ground between Language poetry and the New Formalsim. In his long, detailed book on what he labels Ashbery's misrepresentational poetics— the way his poems "misrepresent and reformulate the various systems of discourses, texts, and practices within which they are produced"—John Shoptaw also points to the generative nature of his work: "his misrepresentations do not . . . rule out meaning, expression, and representation; they renovate them." See *On the Outside Looking Out: John Ashbery's Poetry* (Cambridge MA: Harvard University Press, 1994), 10, 3.

4. For an important discussion of reflection or what she calls "the performance of questioning" (275) in Ashbery, see Karen Mills-Courts, "The Thing for Which There is No Name" in *Poetry as Epitaph*, 267–314. Mills-Courts argues that if complete reflection means death for the fluid *I*, the "recalcitrance of language . . . saves the writer from being contained" (286) and allows "The questioning 'I' . . . [to] continue writing itself into existence by moving speculatively between fragments of its reflections" (312).

5. In "Contemporary Poetry as Philosophy," an important essay, Charles Altieri uses Ashbery as an example of his claim that in our most important poets, "how one establishes one's relation to utterances and situations provides a sufficient grounding for the range of identities and identifications that constitutes subjective life" (216). Through reflection, poets "assume responsibilities" for their language. James McCorkle speaks

in more general terms about this drive: "Through a poetics of self-reflection, we fashion a place for ourselves within the fabric of discourse." See *Still Performance*, 86.

6. Charles Altieri first connected freedom to a "meditation on rhetoricity" in his chapter on Ashbery in *Self and Sensibility*, 132–64. He writes, for example, that "Dramatic scene and linguistic scene breed a rich interplay among the *free* actions of consciousness and the determining forces that express themselves as resistance to and qualification of that freedom" (149). He finds, in Ashbery's "endless qualification . . . glimpse[s] . . . of empirical freedom" (163).

7. Shetley, *After the Death of Poetry* (25–26), remarks on the "protective self-enclosure" of these lines.

8. Marjorie Perloff suggests that we read this poem by noting its two versions of Hollywood movies—"a tale of murder . . . and a tale of love"—and their play with the elements of "pleasure . . . fear . . . and loss" without seeking to resolve them as fully as I have. See *Dance of the Intellect*, 161–63. Shoptaw, *On the Outside*, 63–66, provides some of the details from Ashbery's life which are loose within this "ceaseless activity of . . . tenses, discourses, and roles."

9. John Shoptaw, "Investigating *The Tennis Court Oath*," *Verse* 8 (spring 1991), 61–72. His entire discussion of the poem in Shoptaw, *On the Outside*, 57–63 is valuable.

10. Karen Mills-Courts in *Poetry as Epitaph* has an important discussion of *I* and *you* in Ashbery. She writes that the relationship displays "the act of the mind which can speculate on itself only as the *you* it represents" (307). Harold Bloom describes the relationship as "addressed by *I*, John Ashbery writing to *You*, Ashbery as he is in process of becoming." See "John Ashbery: The Charity of the Hard Moments," in *Figures of Capable Imagination* (New York: Seabury Press, 1976), 201. Shoptaw remarks, on an early Ashbery poem, "the second person represents the lover, the reader, and even the poem itself (with 'I' its adoring creator), and each 'you' stands for the other" (*On the Outside*, 82).

11. Noting some of Ashbery's sources for this poem, Shoptaw calls the parody "misrepresentative autobiography" (*On the Outside*, 89). See his entire discussion, 89–99.

12. Marjorie Perloff applies Barthes's term "corrected banality" to the way Ashbery makes the clichéés of this poem matter to us as readers. See *Poetic License*, 283–84.

13. Thomas Gardner, "John Ashbery's 'Self-Portrait in a Convex Mirror,'" in *Discovering Ourselves in Whitman: The Contemporary American Long Poem* (Urbana: University of Illinois Press, 1989), 144–69.

14. In fact, as I learned from Shoptaw's book after writing this sentence, a number of the poems in this book are responses to students (see *On the Outside*, 192).

15. See Shoptaw's description, *On the Outside*, 225–26.

16. Shoptaw comments: "The blank center of 'Litany' . . . rules all the poem's surrounding, surviving ideas, signs, and figures" (*On the Outside*, 228).

17. John Keeling, "The Moment Unravels: Reading John Ashbery's 'Litany,'" *Twentieth Century Literature* 38 (summer 1993), 125–51. Mutlu Konuk Blasing, in

"John Ashbery: Parodying the Paradox," in her *American Poetry*, has a useful discussion of the way Ashbery, in this and other poems, "doubles the inherent distortion of representation" in order to clear space for "traces of something spiritual" (202, 206).

18. See Vendler's striking reading of some of these poems in "John Ashbery, Louise Glück" from MWH, especially 242–47.

19. See Shoptaw's account of the strategy used in composing this poem, Shoptaw, *On the Outside*, 303.

20. *Ralph Waldo Emerson*, ed. Richard Poirier (Oxford: Oxford University Press, 1990), 213.

3. Robert Hass

1. Other Hass essays that work out responses to such limits include "James Wright" from TC, 26–55; "Wendell Berry: Finding the Land," *Modern Poetry Studies* 12, no. 1 (1971), 15–38; and "Robinson Jeffers: The Poems and the Life," *American Poetry Review* 16 (November/December 1987), 33–41.

2. Robert Hass, "Wendell Berry," 31, 32.

3. *The Iliad of Homer*, trans. Richard Lattimore (Chicago: University of Chicago Press, 1951), 287.

4. Charles Altieri forcefully discusses the notion of limits in *Praise* and Hass's "capacity for self-reflective appreciation of the speech act in its ramifying contexts" in *Self and Sensibility*, 64–68.

5. William Carlos Williams, *Selected Poems*, ed. Randall Jarrell (New York: New Directions, 1968), 16.

6. Hass, perhaps working from memory, describes Steller's memory of an Audubon painting, but Audubon's dates make this impossible. Steller writes in his journal of a specimen he had seen "painted in vivid colors and written about in the newest description of Carolina plants and birds published in French and English not long ago in London and whose author's name eludes me." The journal's editor identifies the author as Mark Catesby. See *Journal of a Voyage with Bering, 1741–1742*, ed. O. W. Frost (Stanford: Stanford University Press, 1988), 78.

7. I discuss this poem at greater length in "American Poetry of the 1980s: An Introduction," *Contemporary Literature* 33 (summer 1992), 177–90.

5. Jorie Graham

1. Jorie Graham, "Some Notes on Silence," in *19 New American Poets of the Golden Gate*, ed. Philip Dow (New York: Harcourt, Brace, Jovanovich, 1984), 409, 413.

2. Jorie Graham, *A Poetry Reading: Presidential Lecture 1991* (Iowa City: University of Iowa, 1991), 8.

3. Bonnie Costello, in "Jorie Graham," 373–95, offers a careful look at *Erosion*. Her claim that the book asserts "modernist values and ambitions" (374)—that is, that its "poems . . . aspire to the unity and completeness of an artifact" (373)—is quite different from mine. Where my eye goes toward the poems' "quickening" at the tension

between the drive to go in and the tragic knowledge of the distance that will subvert that drive, Costello tends to return to the power of art. For example, about the end of this poem, she writes: " 'The living' approaching the icon, 'go in' but never 'arrive.' Yet art's power to awaken our thoughts of the infinite assures its hold on us" (385). As I suggest in my introduction to the volume in which this essay appears, Costello's piece also makes clear that *Erosion* cannot sustain such a "desire for presence" and points the way toward Graham's three most recent books. Costello offers valuable readings of "To a Friend Going Blind," "Kimono," "San Sepolcro," and "At Luca Signorelli's Resurrection of the Body," all poems that I discuss here, though my focus is different.

4. Helen Vendler, in "Jorie Graham: The Moment of Excess," from *The Breaking of Style: Hopkins, Heaney, Graham* (Cambridge MA: Harvard University Press, 1995), links the short lines of this poem to the mind's "precise investigative use of its various scalpels" (77). In an extended reading of this poem in "Jorie Graham: The Nameless and the Material," from *The Given and the Made: Strategies of Poetic Redefinition* (Cambridge MA: Harvard University Press, 1995), Vendler writes movingly of the uneasiness of this poem and the way the poet "persistently questions the premise of the painting." See 99–104.

5. Writing about *Region of Unlikeness*, but responding to all of Graham's work, Vendler describes this contrast as "the tension between existence and death. These are its ultimate terms; but the tension is also expressed as that between other polarities, such as continuity and closure, indeterminacy and outline, being and temporality, or experience and art. . . . The Graham muse sings two siren songs: one says, 'Hurry: *name* it'; the other says, 'Delay: *be* it' " (223–24). See "Mapping the Air" in *Soul Says: On Recent Poetry* (Cambridge MA: Harvard University Press, 1995), 212–34.

6. Concentrating on the analogical method of this and similar poems but not taking into account Graham's unsettling turn toward her own work, James Longenbach claims that this last section of "The Age of Reason" "solve[s] the poem's puzzle before we have a chance to feel its mystery." See *Modern Poetry After Modernism*, 164.

7. James Longenbach writes of these "Self-Portraits" that "they are sternly self-critical: each poem not only turns against the one before it but also turns on itself, collapsing the duality posited by its title" (*Modern Poetry After Modernism*, 168). Vendler, in "Jorie Graham: The Nameless and the Material," writes that the poems suggest "that there is always a 'gesture between' two points of opposition; that there is a way to be 'both parties' at the same time; and that one may find a way to create an alternating current, so to speak, between the weaving of life into the temporary closure of a shaped text, and the unweaving of that text into a less closed form" (106–7).

8. Vendler describes this as "anatomiz[ing] the moment of suspension in being by isolating each of its successive seconds in its own numbered freeze-frame." See "Mapping the Air," 225–26.

9. In "Jorie Graham and Ann Lauterbach: Towards a Contemporary Poetry of Eloquence," *Cream City Review* 12 (summer 1998), 45–72, a strong reading of this poem, Charles Altieri remarks that Eve locates here "an alternative power": "writing

can be a mode of insisting on a strangenesss that transforms being estranged into a constant process of spinning out and realizing one's constantly shifting investments" (48, 51). Calvin Bedient does some interesting work with the notion of Eve "be[ing] free through digression" in this poem in "Kristeva and Poetry as Shattered Signification," *Critical Inquiry* 16 (summer 1990), 807–29.

10. For an alternate reading of the issue, see James Longenbach who argues that "by drawing such a broad analogy between such bracingly different realms of human experience the poem itself ["From the New World"] seems tightly closed" (*Modern Poetry After Modernism*, 165).

11. Vendler notes that this poem drives toward the question "What is Being *like?*" See "Mapping the Air," 228–31.

12. Vendler reads this poem more darkly than I do, concluding after a thorough explication (249–53) that the poet is suspended in an "indeterminacy of . . . possibilities." See "Fin-de-Siècle Poetry: Jorie Graham" in *Soul Says*.

13. Michael Oakeshott, *The Voice of Liberal Learning: Michael Oakeshott on Education*, ed. Timothy Fuller (New Haven: Yale University Press, 1989), 41.

14. On suffering the limits of description, see Vendler's remarks in "Jorie Graham: The Nameless and the Material" that in *Materialism* Graham "attempt[s] to describe the material world with only minimal resort to the usual conceptual and philosophical resources of lyric (once so dear to her), and to make that description a vehicle for her personal struggle into comprehension and expression . . ." (129).

7. Michael Palmer

1. In a fascinating article, "Some Problems about Agency in the Theories of Radical Poetics," *Contemporary Literature* 37, no. 2 (summer 1996), 207–36, Charles Altieri struggles to work out the implications of such attempts to experience language's thickness—what he calls the "linguistic materiality, internal and social, that the text foregrounds" (211). His examples—Charles Bernstein, Lyn Hejinian, and others—are, like Palmer, writers who call attention to "the material and ideological density of language" in order to, the standard critical claim goes, "resist certain kinds of subjection inherent in the media-driven structures of late monopoly capitalism" (209). Rather than simply repeating this claim as if it were itself an accomplishment of the dream, Altieri goes on to actually imagine how such experimental poetry might lead us to "reflect on what our languages make of us and unfold their ways of mediating blindness and insight" (235). This chapter attempts something similar, describing the forms of attention to "words, in the world" that Palmer unfolds out of uncertainty.

2. Michael Palmer, "From the Notebooks," in *19 New American Poets*, 341.

3. In "Counter-Poetics and Current Practice," Palmer reads out of Dante "the notion of a charged poetic sign, one that comes from the texture of our daily life but acquires a denser semantic function" (CP, 3).

4. Benjamin Hollander and David Levi Strauss, "'Dear Lexicon': An Interview with Michael Palmer," *Acts* 2, no. 1 (1986), 21.

5. Another part of that tradition, of course, is Language Poetry, a movement with which Palmer has loose if complicated relations. Palmer has commented on that connection in a number of interviews. See, for example, MP, 75–76, and Keith Tuma; "An Interview with Michael Palmer," *Contemporary Literature* 30, no. 1 (1989), 9–10. For a range of approaches to this school, see Marjorie Perloff, "The Word as Such: L=A=N=G=U=A=G=E Poetry in the Eighties," in *Dance of the Intellect*; Norman Finkelstein, "The Utopia of Language," in *The Utopian Moment in Contemporary American Poetry*, rev. ed. (Lewisburg PA: Bucknell University Press, 1993); George Hartley, *Textual Politics and the Language Poets* (Bloomington: Indiana University Press, 1989), especially "Language Poetry and the Avant-Garde Tradition" and "Ideological Struggle and the Possibility of an Oppositional Poetic Practice" (1–41); and Jerome J. McGann, "Contemporary Poetry, Alternate Routes," and Charles Altieri, "Without Consequences Is No Politics: A Reply to Jerome McGann," in *Politics and Poetic Value*, ed. Robert von Hallberg (Chicago: University of Chicago Press, 1987).

6. Palmer remarks in an interview: "There's a level of resistance to meaning in Celan that is what allows the signifying capacity of his work to emerge," (Hollander and Strauss, " 'Dear Lexicon,' " 14).

7. Palmer uses the phrase "fragility of signification" to describe a primary concern in Wittgenstein; see CP, 12. In "A Following Note," in *The L=A=N=G=U=A=G=E Book*, ed. Bruce Andrews and Charles Bernstein (Carbondale: Southern Illinois University Press, 1984), 163–64, he remarks: "poetry, at least my poetry and much that interests me, tends to concentrate on primary functions and qualities of language such as naming and the arbitrary structuring of a code—its fragility—the ease with which it empties (nullifies?) itself or contradicts what might simplistically qualify as intention."

8. Palmer has published two valuable selections from his reading notebooks kept during and immediately after the composition of *Notes for Echo Lake*. He calls them "a parallel text addressing similar concerns in a different mode." They are well worth consulting . See "From the Notebooks," and "NUAGES—or Further Notebook Selections," *Ironwood* 12, no. 2 (1984), 174–82.

9. Palmer speaks of this as "examin[ing] the sign itself—the mystery of how words refer and how they can empty out of conventional meanings and acquire meanings that threaten they very way we talk to each other in a certain respect." See MP, 74.

10. In "The Case of Michael Palmer," *Contemporary Literature* 29, no. 4 (1988), 518–37, Norman Finkelstein writes, in some senses critically, of Palmer's determined erasure of the subject into "endless semiotic activity" but shows as well that what is live and unusual in the poet is his distinctive style and sense that nonmeaning is an approach to "mystery."

11. Palmer remarks in Tuma, "Interview with Michael Palmer," 2: "I've always been intrigued by the information I could derive not only from [schizophrenic language] but areas such as glossolalia, that one sees as outside and yet apposite to everyday discourses, providing alternative logics, alternative modes of thought and perception.

These seem to me to offer new information about the territory the poem occupies, how it moves and what it sets about meaning in a kind of resistance to the habituated modes of conventional verse."

12. Palmer discusses his work with this poem in Hollander and Strauss, " 'Dear Lexicon,' " 8–9.

13. See Palmer's discussion of the figure of Echo in MP, 87–88.

14. Bruce Campbell, in a careful reading of the way *Sun* discovers meaning through resistance and language's disagreement with itself, calls attention to the distinction, in the lines I've just quoted, between "razor" and the "facts" which it produces. See " 'A Body Disappears into Itself': Michael Palmer's *Sun*," *Occident* 103, no. 1 (1990), 67–80.

15. Eric Murphy Selinger, in "Important Pleasures and Others: Michael Palmer, Ronald Johnson," *Postmodern Culture* 4, no. 3 (May 1994), an important article on *Sun*, notes that "Words in this book will say things on their own, as when 'lace' whispers out of 'necklace' (s, 15), but words never *say things*, in a Rilkean, Orphic sense of the phrase, and the fact that they do not is frequently remarked on and deeply felt. . . . Palmer locks horns with this dilemma in a number of ways, but most notably by insisting on the incorrigible arbitrariness of the sign, of 'words / the opposite of names' " (paragraphs 12, 14).

16. See *Leonardo* (Venice: Gallerie dell'Accademia, 1980), 33.

Selected Works Cited

These works are cited by abbreviation in the text.

Ashbery, John. *And the Stars Were Shining*. New York: Farrar, Straus, Giroux, 1994.

———. *April Galleons*. New York: Viking, Penguin, 1987.

———. *As We Know*. New York: Viking, 1979.

———. *The Double Dream of Spring*. New York: Dutton, 1970.

———. *Flow Chart*. New York: Knopf, 1991.

———. *Hotel Lautréamont*. New York: Knopf, 1992.

———. *Houseboat Days*. New York: Viking, 1977.

———. *Rivers and Mountains*. New York: Holt, Rinehart & Winston, 1966. Reissued, New York: Ecco Press, 1977.

———. *Self-Portrait in a Convex Mirror*. New York: Viking, 1975.

———. *Shadow Train*. New York: Viking, 1981.

———. *Some Trees*. New Haven: Yale University Press, 1956.

———. *The Tennis Court Oath*. Middletown CT: Wesleyan University Press, 1962.

———. *Three Poems*. New York: Viking, 1972. Reissued, New York: Ecco Press, 1977.

———. *A Wave*. New York: Viking, 1984.

Baudelaire, Charles. *Les Fleurs du Mal*. Translated by Richard Howard. Boston: David R. Godine, 1982.

Benjamin, Walter. "On Some Motifs in Baudelaire." In *Illuminations*, edited by Hannah Arendt, 155–94. Translated by Harry Zohn. New York: Shocken Books, 1968.

Bishop, Elizabeth. *The Collected Prose*. New York: Farrar, Straus, Giroux, 1984.

———. *The Complete Poems 1927–1979*. New York: Farrar, Straus, Giroux, 1983.

Cavell, Stanley. *The Claim of Reason: Wittgenstein, Skepticism, Morality, and Tragedy*. New York: Oxford University Press, 1979.

———. *Conditions Handsome and Unhandsome: The Constitution of Emersonian Perfectionism*. Chicago: University of Chicago Press, 1990.

———. *Disowning Knowledge in Six Plays of Shakespeare*. Cambridge: Cambridge University Press, 1987.

———. *In Quest of the Ordinary: Lines of Skepticism and Romanticism*. Chicago: University of Chicago Press, 1988.

———. *Must We Mean What We Say?* New York: Charles Scribner's Sons, 1969. Reprint, Cambridge: Cambridge University Press, 1976.

———. *The Senses of Walden: An Expanded Edition*. Chicago: University of Chicago Press, 1992

———. *Themes Out of School*. San Francisco: North Point Press, 1984.

———. *This New yet Unapproachable America: Lectures After Emerson After Wittgenstein*. Albuquerque: Living Batch Press, 1989.

Graham, Jorie. *The End of Beauty*. New York: Ecco Press, 1987.

———. *Erosion*. Princeton: Princeton University Press, 1983.

———. *The Errancy*. New York: Ecco Press, 1997.

———. *Materialism*. New York: Ecco Press, 1993.

———. *Region of Unlikeness*. New York: Ecco Press, 1991.

Graham, Jorie and David Lehman, eds. Introduction to *The Best American Poetry 1990*. New York: MacMillan, 1990.

Hass, Robert. *Field Guide*. New Haven: Yale University Press, 1973.

———. "George Oppen: A Tribute." *Ironwood* 13, no. 2 (fall 1985), 38–41.

———. *Human Wishes*. New York: Ecco Press, 1989.

———. *Praise*. New York: Ecco Press, 1979.

———. *Sun Under Wood*. New York: Ecco Press, 1996.

———. *Twentieth Century Pleasures: Prose on Poetry*. New York: Ecco Press, 1984.

Hölderlin, Friedrich. *Hymns and Fragments*. Translated by Richard Sieburth. Princeton: Princeton University Press, 1984.

Jackson, Richard. "The Imminence of a Revelation." In *Acts of Mind: Conversations with Contemporary Poets*. Tuscaloosa: University of Alabama Press, 1983.

Packard, William, ed. *The Craft of Poetry: Interviews from the New York Quarterly*. Garden City: Doubleday, 1974.

Palmer, Michael. *At Passages*. New York: New Directions, 1995.

———. "Counter-Poetics and Current Practice." *Pavement* no. 7 (fall 1986), 1–21.

———. *First Figure*. San Francisco: North Point Press, 1984.

———. "Michael Palmer: A Conversation." *American Poetry* 3, no. 1 (1985), 72–88.

———. *Notes for Echo Lake*. San Francisco: North Point Press, 1981.

———. *Sun*. San Francisco: North Point Press, 1988.

Stevens, Wallace. *The Collected Poems*. New York: Vintage Books, 1982.

Stitt, Peter. "The Art of Poetry 33." *Paris Review* 90 (winter 1983), 30–59.

Vendler, Helen. *The Music of What Happens: Poems, Poets, Critics*. Cambridge MA: Harvard University Press, 1988.

———. *On Extended Wings: Wallace Stevens' Longer Poems*. Cambridge MA: Harvard University Press, 1969.

Wittgenstein, Ludwig. *Philosophical Investigations: The English Text of the Third Edition*. Translated by G. E. M. Anscombe. New York: Macmillan, 1968.

Zanzotto, Andrea. *Selected Poetry*. Edited and translated by Ruth Feldman and Brian Swann. Princeton: Princeton University Press, 1975.

Index